Slavery and Serfdom in the Middle Ages

Published under the auspices of the
CENTER FOR MEDIEVAL AND RENAISSANCE STUDIES
University of California, Los Angeles

Publications of the
CENTER FOR MEDIEVAL AND RENAISSANCE STUDIES, UCLA
1. Jeffrey Burton Russell: Dissent and Reform in the Early Middle Ages
2. C. D. O'Malley: Leonardo's Legacy
3. Richard H. Rouse: Serial Bibliographies for Medieval Studies
4. Speros Vryonis, Jr.: The Decline of Medieval Hellenism in Asia Minor and the Process of Islamization from the Eleventh through the Fifteenth Century
5. Stanley Chodorow: Christian Political Theory and Church Politics in the Mid-Twelfth Century
6. Joseph J. Duggan: The Song of Roland
7. Ernest A. Moody: Studies in Medieval Philosophy, Science, and Logic
8. Marc Bloch: Slavery and Serfdom in the Middle Ages

SLAVERY AND SERFDOM IN THE MIDDLE AGES

Selected Essays by
MARC BLOCH

Translated by William R. Beer

Berkeley   Los Angeles   London
UNIVERSITY OF CALIFORNIA PRESS
1975

University of California Press
Berkeley and Los Angeles
University of California Press, Ltd.
London, England

Translated and extracted from
Mélanges Historiques
1966 by Ecole Pratique des Hautes Etudes
English translation copyright © 1975 by
The Regents of the University of California
ISBN 978-0-520-30727-8
Library of Congress Catalog Card Number: 79-123627

In Memory of Van Courtlandt Elliott

Contents

Translator's Preface	ix
1. How and Why Ancient Slavery Came to an End	1
2. Personal Liberty and Servitude in the Middle Ages, particularly in France. Contribution to a Class Study	33
3. The "Colliberti." A Study on the Formation of the Servile Class	93
4. The Transformation of Serfdom: Concerning Two Thirteenth-Century Documents Regarding the Parisian Region	151
5. Blanche de Castile and the Serfs of the Chapter of Paris	163
6. Serf de la Glèbe	179
Notes	203
Glossary	273

Translator's Preface

Scholarly essays are difficult to translate gracefully. Marc Bloch's style is full of explicit hesitations and doubts, and this is one of the qualities that have made his historiography great. In *How and Why Ancient Slavery Came to an End* and in *Personal Liberty and Servitude in the Middle Ages* he wrote primarily to be simultaneously exact and speculative, rather than to offer flowing prose. This is not to say that his writing is not readable and amusing. *Blanche de Castile and the Serfs of the Chapter of Paris* and *The Transformations of Serfdom* show his ability to pierce historical pretensions and ambiguities in a uniquely ironical fashion. Another complication stems from Bloch's frequent use of words themselves as historical data, for want of clearer records. Translating these words is always dangerous, as it can distort the logic of the argument. Thus, frequently, as in *The Colliberti* and *Serf de la Glèbe* some words have been left in French to preserve the clarity of the exposition. In addition, many technical terms were left in the original because there are no precise English equivalents for them. A glossary is provided to help the reader with these terms.

I wish to acknowledge with thanks the help of Professor Elizabeth Brown of the Brooklyn College Department of History.

William R. Beer

Department of Sociology
Brooklyn College
City University of New York

CHAPTER ONE

How and Why Ancient Slavery Came to an End*

In the Roman world of the first centuries A.D., the slave was everywhere: in the fields, in shops, in workshops, in offices. The rich kept hundreds or thousands, and one had to be quite poor not to own at least one. This is definitely not to say that servile labor had a monopoly on any activity, however humble. Many artisans were in a free condition, and innumerable fields were cultivated by peasants, small land-owners or tenant-farmers who had never been the property of a master. Vespasian reserved for the free workers of Rome those hard tasks that he refused to give to machines. Nonetheless, neither the material life of Greco-Roman societies, nor even their civilization at its most exquisite, could be conceived of without the existence of this forced labor. The Germans also had their slaves, either as servants or field hands. On the other hand, the Europe of modern times, with a few rare exceptions, has not known slavery on its own soil. For the most part, this transformation, one of the most profound that mankind has known, took place very slowly in the course of the high Middle Ages.

At the time of the barbarian invasions and in the early days of their kingdoms, there were still many slaves in all parts of Europe. There were more, it would appear, than during the early days of the Empire.

The great source of slavery had always been war. The victorious

* This essay was published as it was found among Bloch's papers by the editors of the *Annales d'Histoire Economique et Sociale*. It has a number of lacunae which the editors found it would be impossible to fill without an immense review of Bloch's work. Therefore, the lacunae in the data on the tenants of Saint-Germain and Saint-Rémi are merely noted.

1

expeditions of the legions during the Roman conquest populated the slave-pens of Italy. Similarly, beginning in the fourth century, the incessant struggles of Rome against her enemies, the battles that these enemies frequently waged between them and the brigandage of regular soldiers or of professional bandits (the distinction was not always easy to make, any more than it is in contemporary China), accumulated in the hands of one group or the other this booty of flesh and bone which was only rarely given back when the fortunes of war changed sides. "There is no house, however poor, where one does not find a Scythian slave"—that is, according to the usual vocabulary of the author, a Gothic slave—the African Synesius wrote, around the year 400. He was thinking of the eastern regions of the Empire, the only ones he knew from experience. But if we replace "Gothic" with a term more general, such as "barbarian," there is no doubt that in this form the observation retains its truth for all of the world that was still Roman. As for the invaders themselves, we know that a large number of the inhabitants of *Romania*, of all classes, had been reduced to servitude by them. In the biography of Saint Severin, which presents a day to day account of a sojourn in small towns on the Danube which were ceaselessly threatened by the German tribes around them, these raids for captives appear to be a common occurrence. Here and there in the texts we come across some tragic fates, which must have resembled many others: think of the great noblewoman of Cologne who, as a prisoner of the barbarians, served them as a slave for a long time. Or consider the other Gallo-Roman noblewoman whom brigands carried off: they displayed her for sale in the market of Clermont. The fate of runaways was not always better. Among the wanderers that the misfortune of the times cast upon the roadways of Romania, more than one fell into slavery, a victim of the same peoples among whom he had sought refuge.

The warrior who won his captives in great number with his sword did not keep them all among his followers. The principal profit that he expected was from selling them. Barbarians also came to offer slaves of Roman blood for sale in land that was still Roman. Such offers were so frequent that in 409 an imperial law could only recognize the validity of these sales, but on condition that the slave could always buy back his freedom, either by paying back to his new master the sum that he had paid, or by serving him for five years. The invasion of Illyria and Thrace, according to Saint Ambrose, had dispersed men for sale "throughout the world." Later, Gregory the Great saw Lombards leading prisoners "with ropes around their necks, like dogs," whom they had captured during an expedition to Rome, and for whom they thought they would find buyers in the Kingdom of the Franks. The great disturbances in Europe led to a recrudescence of the trade; the poverty of the people acted in the same way. In spite of Roman law, fathers sold their children; the fact was recorded in the sixth century in Corsica. Whereas during the first century, a time of peace and prosperity, Pliny the Younger complained that slave manpower was so rare, and while in the third century a slave was quite expensive, at the beginning of the Middle Ages, human merchandise had become abundant again at a reasonable price.

The trade continued to be very active throughout the era of the barbarian kingdoms and up to Carolingian times. As great businessmen before God, the Jews played an important part, but they were far from being the only ones to practice the trade. The biographies of saints, laws, and formulae mention it constantly. Great Britain furnished many slaves to the continent, as far away as Provence and Rome, torn as she was by frequent wars between the Anglo-Saxon kings or against the Celtic speaking peoples, who were themselves prey to internal strife. On the fields of the wealthy, slaves of every origin would rub shoulders, barbarians as well as Romans. As objects in ongoing exchanges, they served as a medium in transactions that at the time were very numerous, in which money did not appear, as a standard, and at times as small change. The texts show us a certain Gaul acquiring a field against payment of a sword, a horse, and a Saxon woman. In enumerating the principal "species" that merchants customarily sold, a capitulary cites gold, fabrics, and slaves. The traders' caravans were not just seen traveling from one country to another within Europe; in their commercial balance, servile livestock counted among the principal export products. The trade sent large numbers to Muslim Spain, and a lesser number, perhaps by way of Venice and the plains of the East, to the Greek and Arab Orient.

However, to look more closely, very clear signs indicate that after the ninth century slavery was far from holding a place in European society comparable to that which it previously had held. To understand and weigh these signs of decline, we must first trace the changes undergone by the economic implementation of servile manpower after the end of the Roman era.

Two methods were open to the master who wanted to make use of the living force that the law placed at his total direction.

The simplest consisted of supporting the person, as one would a domestic beast and, as with the animal, to use his labor in any way whatever. But the slave could also be set up on his own account. In this case the master exacted, in various forms, part of his time and the products of his toil, while leaving him the task of supporting himself. Now in the last centuries of the Empire, this second procedure was more and more widespread.

Even in industry the two procedures had been in competition. The wealthy, who owned great troops of slaves, had always recruited domestic workers from their ranks, thereby saving themselves, on many tasks and manufactures, from recourse to salaried labor or trading. This custom persisted until the ninth century. However, once the household needs were satisfied, was there a duly qualified surplus of manpower on hand? At all times one was forced to find a remunerative outlet for it in production for the market. This could be done by setting up vast workshops where the slaves were made to live laboring under the orders of and for the sole profit of the master of the plant. Here and there, in the first centuries of our era, we find actual factories, such as the famous workshops of Graufesenque and Lezoux in Gaul. Besides free workers they probably comprised unfree workers who either belonged to the employer or whom he rented from other masters. After the third century these establishments declined. Many manorial workshops did remain, but they hardly provided for more than the manor itself, and the imperial factories delivered their products to the state alone. Market demand had always been met by small-scale crafts, which thereafter encountered no competition. For want of work for laborers he could not afford to leave idle, the owner was forced to cut back. The slave exercised his trade for the public and after clothing and feeding himself on his revenue, turned over the rest to his master in various forms, which were frequently determined in advance. This practice, as old as craft production itself, became sufficiently widespread that it appeared necessary to rule on the judicial problem it raised. In the barbarian world itself, Burgundian law ruled.

It was in agriculture, however, that the transformation proved especially profound. Little farms had always occupied a large part of the soil of Romania—the greater part of it, probably, except in various regions of Italy. Their servile personnel were naturally very limited. Besides these, at the beginning of the Christian era, there were immense domains cultivated by veritable armies of slaves in bands, comparable to the Negroes of modern colonial plantations. Toward the end of the Empire, this system was generally abandoned. The large landowners, taking advantage of their possession of large expanses, parceled them into little farms whose occupants paid rent in a variety of forms. Among the beneficiaries of these distributions appeared a large number of slaves taken from the central work gangs, each one charged with the responsibility of his own fields. Some were enfranchised the moment they were settled. Many others, though they had become tenant farmers, remained legally in their previous condition. Of course, the slave-tenant was not entirely new. He had long been present, notably on small properties whose owners could scarcely run the risk of too-extensive enterprises. But his spread was a new thing.

The phenomena of parceling out *latifundia* and the decline of slave manufacturing, while of primary interest to the history of slavery, obviously go considerably beyond it. They amount to the triumph of small-scale over large-scale enterprise. They could not alone account for all the changes that thenceforth affected the employment of servile manpower, though. It would be very inexact to speak of a total disappearance of large-scale farming. The creation of little farms had considerably reduced the extent of the resources for direct exploitation, but it did not cause them to disappear. Around the end of the Empire, and until the ninth century, the majority of the great landlords still kept sizeable farms under their administration, though even then the methods of cultivation came to be modified.

Of course, the master did not cease to feed, house, and clothe the slaves under his control who helped him to cultivate his fields. They were, however, less and less suitable to the task. From then on, it was the tenant farmers, whose land had been placed under the tenure of the principal domain, who were called to do the greater part of the work required for its profitability. Doubtless some were peasants long used to living in dependency upon a powerful landowner or who gradually became so. Others had been settled only recently on their parcels of land. By giving up a part of his estate, the large landlord could thereby assure himself of the labor power demanded by the rest. As we have seen, there were many slaves among these newly established tenant farmers. They continued to toil for their master, but they were no longer supported by him, any more than a factory owner supports his workers today. The land that had been granted to them, aside from being subject to rents that do not concern us here, was like their salary, upon which they had to live.

What considerations, therefore, had induced slave owners, who also possessed vast plantations, to henceforth prefer the system of sharecropping to the seemingly more practical, direct utilization of human livestock?

In all societies that have used slave labor, from large-scale to the simplest form—those of Roman latifundia and those of the plantations of the East Indies—its use has been in response to conditions that are always the same, implacably required by its very nature. The slave is a bad worker; his output has always been recognized as fairly low. He represents, moreover, perishable capital. The present-day owner who loses a worker through death or sickness may have some trouble replacing him if the manpower market is unfavorable. But if he manages to replace him, he has suffered no loss since the wage remains the same no matter who the man. However, the master whose slave died or became ill or quite simply got old, had to purchase another. At one stroke he lost the amount of his initial investment.

Of course, to fill certain gaps, one could rely on certain slaves born into the household. They could not fill all the gaps, however; of all livestock breeding, that of man is the most delicate. These inconveniences were not very serious as long as the slave inventory remained abundant and hence of relatively low cost. To accomplish a small task, one had to waste a lot of slaves; if one of them turned up missing, it was neither a strain nor an expense to find a substitute for him. This was the state of affairs at the beginning of the Christian era, which had been created by so many victorious wars waged by Rome: it explains the existence of the great slave-gangs. But soon the recruitment of slaves became more difficult. Their value increased. *This was when people turned toward the land-tenure system.*

Let us imagine the slave established on a little farm on his own account. Living in better organized families, his kind perpetuate themselves more securely. On the fields that have been granted to him, his work is of better quality. Because the rent must willy-nilly be paid, the surplus of the produce on which his livelihood is based depends upon his own labor. There remain the obligatory services on the lands of the master. Doubtless their rendering was not the best, and this may have been one of the reasons that, much later, from the tenth century on, led in turn to their abandonment. At least one could expect that, in not wanting to see his holding taken away, a holding that was only granted to him in return for carrying out these tasks, the slave-tenant would acquit himself less badly than one who ate in the communal slave-stable. The renewal of the slave trade at the time of the invasions may have provoked a return to the old use of slave labor in vast rural work gangs. The documents are too imprecise to allow us positively to affirm or deny it. What is certain is that there was no revolution of any great scale. The change had been made.

Moreover, the Germanic chieftains, into whose hands so many great domains were falling at this time, were prepared to adopt the tenant-farming system. It was part of their peoples' traditions. In ancient Germany, general economic conditions were not favorable for any kind of large-scale enterprise. The noble and rich had many lands, many of which lay fallow, and had many slaves often captured in warfare. To make use of these vast reaches as well as they could, there was nothing for them to do but divide them up. To feed so many people, it was absolutely necessary to allot each one a plot of land, since it would not have been convenient to maintain them in the household of the master. At a time when the slave-tenant was still a rarity in Italy, Tacitus was noting its frequency on the other side of the Rhine.

Now this slave-tenant doubtless remained a slave in his personal status. Even in the Carolingian period, legislative precedents were forced to mention the distinction between *servus* and other dependants of the manor, such as the *coloni*. On many estates, while the duties owed by free men were generally fixed, the lord reserved the right to demand the labor of unfree tenants any time he deemed fit, "whensoever it should be commanded of them." It seems that their wives—and only their wives—were drafted into the manorial workshop to work there under the orders of the master, and they alone provided him with fabrics and linen. However, in practice, the destiny of the slave, established on a little plot of land whose cultivation was entrusted to him, was different from what the word "slavery" implies. He paid over to his master only a part of the fruits of his labor, and gave him only a part of his work-time, because even though his duties were theoretically limited, obviously the necessity that obliged the master to allow the villein enough free time to extract his livelihood from the holding and to pay his rents, also prevented those tasks from taking up all his time. He did not live out every moment under the orders of another man. He had his home and hearth, and he managed the cultivation of his fields himself. If he was particularly hard-working or particularly shrewd, he ate better than his neighbor; or insofar as there was a market, he could sell his surplus produce.

Juridical institutions were not at all slow to recognize the peculiarities of his condition. Since he was one of those tillers of the soil whose efforts were, above all, important to the prosperity of the Empire, the laws of the fourth century prohibited the master from depriving the slave-tenant of his land, as they also protected the free tenant. Doubtless this rule of "attachment to the glebe" was only observed for a little time and faded in the ruin of the imperial state that had proclaimed it.

But between the slaves who were *chasés*—that is, each provided with a house (*casa*) and adjoining lands—and those who were not, Carolingian law made a very important distinction: the former were considered as part of the real estate, the latter as part of the furniture. The laws governing their disposal were therefore entirely different. Above all, after the second half of the ninth century, the custom of the manor, which in the absence of a written law had long served to regulate the relations between the lord and his free tenants, extended its protection to the slave-tenant. Instead of the arbitrary power of the master, there was substituted the rule of a local tradition that was frequently quite harsh, but in applying to high and low alike prevented or was supposed to prevent new oppressions from being imposed. Even regarding strict law, the condition of *servus casatus* differed considerably from pure slavery. From an economic standpoint, the use that was made of his work did not correspond at all to the ordinary definition of slave labor.

Moreover, the way of life of many slaves soon changed from the classical mode; their very number rapidly diminished. To approach this phenomenon, let us put ourselves in the ninth century. Dappled with light, or to put it better, with half light, between two great darknesses, this century offers us, in its manorial rent rolls, the elements of statistics that are still very imperfect and quite fragmentary. But neither the preceding nor the following centuries can give us the slightest equivalent. We really have no enumeration of the number of slaves who were not chasés. Some texts—the accounts of the abbey of Corbie, or the abbey of Notre Dame de Soissons—enumerate the serfs who received the dayworkers' wage. But as they are preoccupied above all with the order of distributions, they neglected to make note of the differences in status of the people who took part. On the other hand, as far as the slaves who were chasés is concerned, the information is as clear as we could wish. On the lands of Saint-Germain-des-Prés, near the end of the reign of Charlemagne, lived (*here there is a lacuna in the text*) tenants of every sex and age, only (*here there is a lacuna in the text*) were of servile status. On the lands of St. Remi de Reims near the middle of the century, the proportion was (*here there is a lacuna in the text*). Doubtless these data are only valid for Gaul and Italy. Definite indicators permit us, however, to assert that in Germany the situation was analogous. As for England, if we want definite figures, we must look later, at the time of the Domesday Book, that is to say, the year 1078. Since the evolution of English society seems to have been substantially behind that of the Continent—where in 1078, as we will see, there were practically no more slaves to be found—this disparity in the dates of the documents is not terribly inconvenient. The Domesday Book only enumerates a total of ... (*here there is a lacuna in the text*).

Reduced to these data, there is nothing that would allow us to affirm that as time passed the classes of slave-tenants were thinned out. This leaves the door open, in fact, to another interpretation—that these classes might always have been scanty. But let us take our observations further. On the manors of Frankish Gaul and Italy, the greater part of the land given over to small farms, depending on the central domain, was cut up into indivisible tenures that were generally called *mansi*. These were not at all of the same sort: there were different categories alongside one another, each subject to its particular obligations. The most widespread classification took as its point of departure the personal status of the tenant. According to whether he was a slave or a free man, the *mansus*—to confine ourselves to this unit—was called servile or free, and taxed accordingly. At least that was the original principle. After a time that, for reasons discussed below, we can say coincided with the fall of the Roman Empire, this exact parallel between the condition of the man and that of the land ceased to be maintained. Whatever became of the legal situation of the tenant, the mansus henceforth kept its original status, free or servile according to the case, and remained bound by the obligations that this term expressed, with the result that the distribution of mansi of different types remained as a geological testimony to a long-vanished distribution of people.

Now, on the lands of Saint-Germain-des-Prés in the ninth

century only (*here there is a lacuna in the text*) servile mansi were really in the possession of slaves; on those of Saint Remi de Reims the figures are (*here there is a lacuna in the text*) on the one hand and (*here there is a lacuna in the text*) on the other. Does this raise the hypothesis of a simple coming and going of holdings among groups of people, each one of which remained of equal importance? In fact one does come across free mansi that have passed to slaves, but there are far fewer of these: (*here there is a lacuna in the text*) out of (*here there is a lacuna in the text*) at Saint Germain (*here there is a lacuna in the text*), at Saint Remi. Obviously, it was the number of slave-tenants, on the whole, which had diminished. At this time many portions of land that had been formerly assigned to them were now occupied by free men. What had happened? It would be absurd to think that among the tenants some mysterious psychological decay had set in among the slaves and the slaves alone. Certainly the free men who farmed the mansi originally created for the slaves were for the most part the direct inheritors of the original tenants. But at a given moment the family had received its freedom. Since no necessary relation existed any more between the status of the land and that of its possessor, doubtless among the tenants of mansi belonging to free men, there slipped in, besides slaves still attached to their servitude, the descendants of slaves who had been freed at some former time.

Also, the texts themselves, in spite of terrible gaps, remind us that there were a great many manumissions that were extended to very large groups of people during the epoch of the barbarian kingdoms. Not only is there scarcely any type of act of which the collections of formulae used by notaries offer us more examples. We also know of enough examples taken from real life so that we can be sure that they were frequent and widespread. How did it come about that so many slaves had thus received their freedom?

The necessity for answering this question leads us to introduce a factor whose influence on practices is always infinitely difficult to evaluate: representations of a religious order.

For once, a favorable circumstance is actually going to simplify our task. On the threshold of the Middle Ages, we are fortunate to find no longer before us a religious doctrine in the process of forming, with all the contradictory movements that this stage never fails to involve. From this time onward, Western Christianity had determined its positions on slavery. Just as they were at the time of the great councils of the Peace of the Church, or when Gregory the Great was writing (and in spite of the formal modifications introduced by the rebirth of the hard social philosophy of Aristotle), we find them inspiring the thought of Thomas Aquinas, of Luther, or of Bossuet. The problem had two aspects depending on whether one considered the sources of slavery or the institution as it was already formed. One could not avoid asking under what conditions, if ever, it was legitimate to reduce a human creature to servitude. Once this first difficulty was resolved, the existence in society of many slaves who for a long time and frequently by inheritance had been attached to their condition, remained an undeniable reality. In the face of this fact, what line of conduct ought to be adopted? Let us return to the first point later. Towards slaves subjugated from this moment onward, the attitude of the best authorized religious opinion can be summed up in several concise precepts that follow.

Nobody doubted that slavery in itself was against divine law. Were not all men equal in Christ? In this primordial thesis, pagans converted to Christianity could recognize an idea that their own philosophers and legalists had made familiar to them, and that, at any rate, had not been without influence on Christian thought itself—except that where the Church talked of "divine law," paganism had said "natural law." The parallel was so close that from the Carolingian era onwards theologians tended to identify the two notions with one another. We must avoid underestimating the practical value of the principle of equality thus proclaimed. But even if it could lead to the better treatment of individuals, even to their treatment in a fashion that contrasted with the classic use of slave labor, of course, it must not attack the institution itself at its foundations. Taken literally, the entire social edifice would have crumbled; all hierarchies and even private property were struck by the same theoretical condemnation. Doubtless before God, the slave was the equal of his master, just as in full conformity with the lessons of the Church, the Emperor Louis the Pious said in a capitulary that he was the equal of his subjects. However, no masters thought of abdicating their authority any more than the sovereign did and no one asked it of them. Natural law had always been conceived as subject to the correction of the particular laws of each state. As for the accommodations that divine law was obliged to bend itself to, theologians had learned to justify them by the myth of the Fall, from the first few centuries A.D. onward. Divine law had only reigned on earth before the great tragedy of the ancestral couple, and all the faults of society followed from the original sin. "It is not nature which has made slaves," wrote Abbot Smaragdus of Saint Mihiel under Louis the Pious, thus mixing the two vocabularies, pagan and Christian, "rather it is the Fall." And already in the sixth century, Isidore of Seville wrote, "Slavery is a chastisement inflicted on humanity by the sin of the first man." The thought of Saint Augustine, which was penetrated by dualist elements until after his conversion, dominated the Middle Ages, whose religion, even though maintained in the careful ways of orthodoxy, never repudiated some Manichean strain, notably in the conception of the Devil. Only the City of the Devil is of this world: the City of God is of the beyond. And actually, all ideology aside, that was the deep feeling that reigned in people's souls. Since this life is only a place of transition and by definition evil, and since the great task here below is to prepare for Eternal Life, attempting to reform the established social order from top to bottom in the hope of bringing about the triumph of a happiness that was in itself impossible could only be a vain undertaking. Even more, it would be a sacreligious waste of forces that ought to be reserved for a higher and more urgent task. Whether in thought or in action, one should not lose sight of this mystical background to whatever weighs on the medieval mind. Not all consciences were at all equally sensitive to it, nor did all perceive its presence with an equal intensity in all moments of life. But it nonetheless constantly gave the fantastic and fleeting characteristic of a stage set about to fall away to realities that seem to us essentially the concrete matter of our endeavors, such as society and nature.

Of course, this is not to say that in traditional instances the practice of Christian virtues was not strongly required. But each condition had its peculiarities and one's duty was to accept the particular case. The word of Saint Paul remained the law of the Church.

By the same token, the legitimacy of slavery was recognized. It seemed so evident to Saint Augustine that in encountering on his way the rule of Hebrew law according to which a slave of the Jewish religion had to be freed from his condition after six years of servitude, he had a great deal of difficulty in explaining how the new law prevented its application to the Christian slave. The councils of the Frankish era confined their ambitions to forbidding the export of slaves—especially their sale overseas, that is to say to Muslims or pagans—and to forbidding Jews to possess or trade in Christian slaves whose faith had to be protected against possible conversions. Also, individual members of the clergy, as well as the Church itself, which was a very large landlord as an institution, possessed a great many slaves. There is no doubt that in some isolated cases, the clergy drew the more difficult conclusions from the notion of original equality. Care was taken to condemn those who did so. In 324, in a canon that Western compilations would unfailingly reproduce, the Council of Granges proclaimed, "If anyone, under the pretext of pity, leads a slave to despise his master, to remove himself from slavery, to not serve with good will and respect, let him be anathematized." Practical life presented priests with affairs of conscience, and ecclesiastical authorities gave them solutions conforming simultaneously to Christian charity and to the established order. For instance, Raban Maur was asked if it was allowed to say masses for a fugitive slave who dies during his escape and hence in a state of sin. Of course, replied Raban, but one had to remember that as long as the slave lived, the preachers of Christ had an obligation to exhort him to return to his master. Finally, in 916, the Council of Altheim, in referring (inexactly) to a text of Gregory the Great, did not shrink from making a parallel between the slave who fled his master and the churchman who abandoned the Church, striking them both with equal anathema.

Moreover, the very existence of sizeable masses of slaves placed a delicate problem before the Church. Should one allow them into the priesthood? The question does not seem to have been raised before the fourth century. From the moment when it was, the response seems to have been what it was always to remain: uniformly negative. The principle of equality had bent before considerations of discipline, which the clergy could not defy without betraying its mission. How could a man whom the law placed under the aboslute domination of a master maintain the independence necessary to those who dispense the sacraments? The danger was all the more felt because despite repeated prescriptions of popes and councils, the ordination of slaves continued to take place in practice from time to time, and the troublesome consequences were thereby constantly obvious. This care for dignity, if not a horror of some original blemish attached to servitude, was so much the true motivation for the prohibition that we can see it equally applied in the Merovingian kingdom to coloni, who were juridically free men, but under the strict domination of a large landowner. Also, enfranchisement sufficed to remove the prohibition unless because of the very conditions of the act the slave remained in a state of too rigorous subjection to his former master. It was nonetheless true that in thus barring slaves from entering the orders, the Church once more strengthened slavery.

However, it was no small thing to have said to the "tool with a voice" (*instrumentum vocale*), as the old Roman agronomists called him: "you are a man" and "you are a Christian." This principle inspired the philanthropic legislation of the emperors during pagan times as well as after the triumph of the new faith. The Church did not forget this. After all, the maxim of Saint Paul was two-edged, and was directed at masters as well as at slaves. Of course, we do not know very well to what extent masters heeded the urging, and if we go by the texts of the councils and the penitentials, the churchmen's efforts to remind the forgetful of it do not seem to have been very well upheld. In the ninth century, Regino of Prum bade the bishops to pay attention, on their pastoral rounds, to the conduct of those who possessed slaves, but it was only to exhort them to deprive of communion, for two years, those who had killed slaves without a trial. Ordinary maltreatment evidently seemed to him unworthy of attention. Slightly earlier, in Great Britain, the so-called Penintential of Theodorus, renewing in a way the Roman legislation concerning savings, forbade the master to take away from the slave the money he had earned in payment for his work. This was a significant symptom of social evolution which tended to assure a feeling of economic independence to servile labor. But all that did not go very far.

A much more important fact was the recognized religious validity of marriage contracts made by slaves. By this, ecclesiastical legislation consolidated orderly households that multiplied the necessities of everyday life on the great estates. It thus gave its aid to the general movement that transformed slavery. Above all, manumission, which pagan morality of the previous few centuries had always considered a gesture of pity, passed the status of being an act of piety. Since God had originally created all men equal and since, in addition, Christ had suffered for all men equally and at the price of his blood had manumitted them from the servitude of Original Sin, to bestow liberty was for the master not a stern duty but at least an infinitely commendable act whereby the faithful, raising himself so far as to imitate the perfect life of the Savior, worked for his own salvation.

In fact, if we are to believe the preambles of the charters of "manumission" which the barbarian epoch has left us, no other motive had inspired their authors. Everyone knows that this phraseology must never be taken literally. The reasons that a man gives, publicly, for his acts are not always those he obeys in his innermost heart—far from it. Also, faced with a particular problem, the enfranchisement of its own slaves, the Church had to concern itself with putting an end to untimely acts of generosity. Its goods were in principle unalienable, and it was not the task of one of its temporal administrators to dispose of them even though this was to satisfy his concern, in the selfish sense, for his own salvation.

Two conciliar canons, cited by the Regino of Prum and thereafter ceaselessly repeated, forbade a bishop, unless he first recompensed the church for the loss, from his own personal goods, to free its slaves, and forbade an abbot to grant freedom to those slaves who had been given to his monks. But it would be childish to deny that the idea of the world to come, of its penalties and rewards, had contributed to the inspiration of more than one manumission. Among the manumissions we have record of, many are parts of the terms of wills.

The practice was already in favor during the Roman period, but there is no doubt that Christianity had greatly contributed to its spread. At the moment when anxiety about the world to come constrained with unusual force the soul about to depart, when a man also considered with more indifference than in the past those temporal goods that he would no longer enjoy, it was natural that even at the expense of his heirs, the rich slave owner thought about procuring for himself the benefit of a final act of charity. But would these considerations have been enough to overthrow the social order? This is the more difficult to believe because while to liberate slaves was indisputably a good act, to keep them under one's domination was not, after all, an evil one. Manumissions were a good deed; this is indisputably the truth, but in itself this cannot explain their frequency. If the frequency of manumissions at this point was considerable, it is because, as well as being a good act about whose nature slave owners were far from indifferent, the freeing of slaves constituted an operation from which economic conditions of the moment had removed all danger, revealing nothing but its advantages.

Apparently the right of manumission during the barbarian era was extremely complex. The forms of the act not only varied according to the countries, they presented a great diversity in their content. This is because the heritage of several juridical histories weighed upon the societies of these times. Sometimes people used procedures that came from the old customs of Germany. Sometimes, even though one might personally be from Germany and under German law, one had recourse to procedures of Roman law, which was always alive in the former Empire except in Great Britain, which unified the contributions of classical legislation and doctrine with new practices spread by Christianity. Each tradition offered its own procedures, which were more or less transformed over time. Moreover, the Latin tradition had a stereotyped phraseology that across the ages was to be applied, after the slaves of the high Middle Ages, to the serfs of the following centuries. But if we ignore the details of the juridical practices, we can attend to the concrete consequences of the act, and we see the different types grouped into two large categories. The collection of formulae distinguish them under the expressive names of manumissions with or without obedience, *manumissio cum* or *sine obsequio*, the only distinction which was really important from the point of view of the social structure.

It could happen that the master, in making a free man of his slave, discharged him forever from any obligation to him. He opened to him, as certain acts put it, the four ways of the world. This case was rare. Neither the Roman nor the Germanic tradition was favorable to it.

In Rome, not only did the offspring of the freed man have to wait until two generations had passed before having access to the rights of a citizen; the practice of the slave owners ordinarily kept them dependent on the author of the manumission and his successors, nearly indefinitely. Among a great many German nations—Franks, Saxons, Lombards, Bavarians—the slave, freed from servitude, could not thereby simply become a member of the tribe. He remained *lite* or *alduin*, from father to son, confined in an inferior legal status and, at the same time, attached to his former master for posterity. In order to tear him loose from this status, if one thought it fitting, a new manumission was required. Also, in a troubled society such as that of the barbarian kingdoms, within states where the protection, theoretically exercised by the central power, seemed in practice quite far away, almost negligible, absolute independence would most likely turn out to be other than an advantage. Hence, a man (mostly the common man) found it less difficult to accept a master than to live in fear of finding himself without a defender. And for whom would this isolation be more fearful than for the former slave, who was without any legal family?

A Lombard charter, giving testimony to the freed slaves themselves, puts these words into their mouths: "Vulpo, Mitilde, their sons, their daughters and their offspring have said that they did not want the four ways and were satisfied, for their future freedom, to receive it under the supervision and protection of the priests and deacons of Santa Maria Maiora of Cremona." Formulae of this sort are rarely completely sincere, but we can believe that in this case the writer was not too unfaithful an interpreter of Vulpo's mind and the minds of many like him. The interest of freed men, like that of the owners of slaves, contributed to the general application on manumission "with obedience," an obedience that, of course, assumed a hereditary character. Sometimes the former master himself kept the benefit of these new powers; at other times, he gave his rights to a third party that, more often than not, was a church. Already an act of piety in itself, a manumission became, in this case, doubly so, since it accompanied a donation to the servants of God. The *obsequium* not only consisted of a general duty of subjection, with more or less vague outlines and a promise of support in return, ordinarily it comprised very precise obligations, at times specified by the act of manumission itself, at others prescribed by a group custom known to all. Traditionally, the lites, the freed men of Frankish law, and probably their cousins under other Germanic legal systems, paid to their lord, one by one, a sort of annual tax in kind or in money, fixed once and for all. In barbarian societies, this taxation slowly became very widespread. It became the custom to demand it of all kinds of dependents, above all of freed men, without distinction between the modes of their manumission. Often the lord kept a certain part of the inheritances for himself, and at times he levied a tax on the occasion of marriages. Most important, the freed slave had most often been a tenant farmer after the time of his slavery. Having left his servitude, he naturally kept his landholding, subject to the customary obligations. This is why freeing a slave was at times expressed in terms of making a *colonus* out of him, that is to say a tenant farmer, who was free but still very strictly subordinate to the master of the land.

Now certainly, in the Roman world as in Germany, masters had always been able to obtain various benefits, on the order of material revenue as well as social influence, that were reserved for them by a liberty that was so judiciously granted and bestowed through their efforts. It is hardly necessary to recall the part that freed men played in the patronage of Rome, the mainstay of the aristocracy's power. But the particular conditions of the High Middle Ages made these advantages more evident than ever, at the same time as they tended to attenuate the inconveniences that had for so long been their counterpart. More and more it was in the indirect form of rents and duties that people were inclined to make use of servile labor. Once free, the tenant farmer did not in practice produce less than when he was a slave. Taxation, levies on legacies and on marriages, evidently compensated for the services that one ordinarily only asked of slaves.

Did the master sometimes ask more for manumissions than that the freed men no longer cost him anything? Did they perhaps put a price on freedom? The slaves, eager to see the legal and moral barrier between themselves and free men lowered, possessing in addition, if they were *casati*, a small personal hoard, were probably capable of purchasing a thing that was so precious in their eyes. In fact, charters of manumission do not seem to have ever mentioned any price paid. But the example of what later passed for slavery teaches us that in this kind of action, in which people wanted to preserve the appearance of a pious act, people were extremely reluctant to mention anything so mundane, even though it corresponded to reality. It is, therefore, possible that manumissions sometimes provided their granters the chance to add a supplementary increase to the periodic rents that they levied on the man and his land, to be collected once. However, we could not say for sure if this is how it was, nor could we determine any kind of frequency with which it happened. What is certain is that, from these real or seeming acts of generosity, the master derived benefits of another kind which, even though they had no monetary value, were nonetheless held in great esteem. In the society of these first few centuries of the Middle Ages, which was in many ways anarchic, relations of personal subjection had taken on a great deal of importance. The price of power and prestige was to group around oneself a large number of dependents—not slaves but free men who could sit in juridical assemblies and who were qualified to appear at the host. Manumission "with obedience" became foremost in the greatly varying range of relations between lords and followers, and even gave some of its characteristics to several of these relationships whose original reason for existence was different. Therefore, everything tended to increase their number: ordinary self-interest, the desire to be a leader, and concern about the life beyond. It is no surprise, then, that there were so many of them.

Thus, slavery was like a reservoir that constantly emptied itself at the top, at an accelerating pace. For slaves no longer to exist, however, these losses had to stop being replaced, or at least had to be attenuated at the bottom. In other words, the very recruitment of the slave population definitely had to dry up. For make no mistake—if masters no longer had the same interest as before in the maintenance of large groups of slaves, they still employed domestics, household artisans, and boys and girls as farm workers on their lands, not to mention concubines. They were inclined to seek these types of personnel from the slave trade. It is probable that this trade, after the Carolingian era, slowed up its supplies. But only the following centuries were to see, if not its complete cessation (which never took place during the Middle Ages), at least its diminution, to the extent that in most of Europe, slavery was practically to disappear and, even where it remained, was to become reduced to the role of a fairly insignificant supplement as a source of manpower.

Now that we have come to this point of the evolution, we must first warn of an ambiguity, to which the sources contribute only too well.

Let us leaf through the charters of the eleventh and twelfth centuries. Often we will see this old word servus designating a class of men, a word that dictionaries deservedly have taught us to translate as "slave" insofar as ancient texts are concerned. The vernacular languages, for their part, speak of *serf* in French and *servo* in Italian, and their agreement with the Latin of the acts assures us that the scribes, always to be suspected of an excess of purism, while continuing to apply a classical term to the reality of their time, were at least in this instance, only conforming to everyday usage.

More generally, under different names—there is nothing so variable as the juridical vocabulary of the Middle Ages—a whole population of humble people, much more numerous than the servi of the Frankish era had been, appear in these texts as if deprived of "freedom," as if plunged into servitude. They did not exist in certain countries where the development of the social structure had followed completely other ways, such as in the low lands that, from Frisia to Dithmarschen, lie along the shores of the North Sea, or in the Scandinavian peninsula. But they were spread over some vast expanses in Germany and Italy as well as in France and England. Within this population, groups of people from very diverse origins had come to mix. Many of the descendants of free coloni had joined there with the descendants of slave-tenants and of many manumitted "with obedience." At times this was after the express giving over of oneself, supposedly spontaneously, but which most had consented to only under the pressure of threats, from the need for protection, or more simply from hunger. At other times, and doubtless more often, it was the effect of a slow slipping process. This group, moreover, had by no means an absolute juridical uniformity. In Germany, especially, we can distinguish in it many subclasses, defined by different juridical characteristics. But one common characteristic dominated these shadings of difference: the strongly felt separation from men who were qualified as "free." Had slavery, then, made immense progress from the ninth century onward? Certainly not. What had changed was the very content of the notion of freedom and servitude, which is only its antithesis—to the extent that a whole crowd of men who would have passed as free came to see their condition thenceforth considered as unfree.

Constant warfare, the breakup of groups of ancient lineage or those thought to be so, and the already palpable weakness of public power had greatly enhanced relations of personal dependence in societies emerging from the invasions. The definite weakness of the state after the eleventh century made them, for several centuries, the only social adhesive that counted, kinship being thenceforth confined to a small circle of kin. It was natural that in order to establish the place of an individual in society, one was above all concerned about the nature of the particular subjection in which he was inevitably held by another more powerful than he. Now, among the originally manifold human relations that people saw beginning or continuing, two categories came rapidly to be distinguished. One was that of relations established by man, in principle, by his own will, even if he could not break them in his lifetime. Such relations in the upper classes as those of vassalage, whose transmission in practice from generation to generation was very frequent and nearly the norm, were never obligatory according to law. Others were those he found already formed as of his birth from his mother's womb, to which he could only conform until his death, and whose inescapable burden he then in turn bequeathed to his children. Among the peasants, there were always, in every country, those who while renting their fields from a lord and living on the territory where this chief exercised his powers of command, thus bound to him with duties that were frequently very burdensome, were however his subjects only by dint of circumstances—possession or residence—that did not touch them as people. If they abandoned their tenure—abandonment was legal for them—the attachment was totally broken. These *hôtes, manants,* and *vilains* (*Gäste, Landsassen* were the terms in Germanic law), were considered to be free.

In the opposite sense, there was nothing so common as the case of the descendants of freed men. Their fathers had been granted a freedom conditioned upon obedience. Since submission accepted in this fashion was hereditary, their sons would one day cease to be among the ranks of free men. As for the slave-tenants, the erasure of the juridical characteristics of slavery from their condition, which was already apparent at the beginning of the Middle Ages, was nothing but the nearly inevitable result of their actual situation, which put them so far apart from the slave. It is scarcely surprising that people progressively lost the habit of making a place for them apart from the dependents of other origins, whose subordination similarly increased, especially because the institutions of public law, having either disappeared or been profoundly altered, from then on, ceased to maintain the ancient barrier between the free man—the only qualified member of the population, the only subject to recruitment to tribunals and the army—and the slave who was foreign to the city. The current language, which is a faithful mirror of this confusion of ideas where the historian very frequently discovers the struggle between the new and the old, manifested a great loosening of terminology after the Frankish era. Poorly instructed scribes labeled free tenants as *servi;* even the Carolingian monarchy eventually allowed this. As for Visigothic law, a council in Spain did not hesitate to characterize as "servitude" the condition of the freed man who had a master. But official documents generally kept better track. There was still a semilearned law that with some success could impose respect for the ancient juridical classifications. Later on, the absence of all legislation, of any teaching of the law, of any juridical centralization, favored, on the contrary, their renewal.

This extension of the notion of the word "servitude" to all the dependencies that weighed on a man from the day of his birth and because of it, took place, of course, without people's being aware of it. This can be easily explained because slavery formed in a way the prototype for this kind of relationship. Not that the specific duties of the serf, in their details, dated back to the state of slavery; they were much more often borrowed from that of the man freed with obedience. Heredity itself suggested the analogy. Attached to this condition by a nearly physical destiny, the serf, like the slave, could only expect his liberation from the express consent of his lord. People kept the old term "affranchisement" for this act, and in the details of its formulary it continued to replicate certain of the characteristics of the manumissions of slaves of the Frankish era and even of the Roman age. It was the very social disfavor that was, it seems, insurmountably attached to the epithet "servile" that facilitated its application to any hereditary subject of another man, for this very absence of choice seemed to be a mark of inferiority. All serfs were made to suffer certain civil and ecclesiastical disabilities, by which formerly the slave had been affected, such as the refusal to accept his testimony against free men and the refusal to admit him into the holy orders. The name "serf" was a slander that tribunals punished when it was wrongly called. One was above all a serf of a lord, but one was also simply a serf, that is to say, a member of a class placed at the very bottom of the scale of human values. Certainly the subjection that was characterized this way was singularly rigorous. Everyday language gave it full justice when it gave to the serf these names full of significance: in France *homme de corps*, in Germany, "a man held as property by another," and in England "a bound man" (bondman). The subjugation was translated as various duties whose total weight was undoubtedly very heavy.

However, this serf, so despised and placed in a state of strict dependence, was not at all a slave. He did not present the same legal characteristics, since he could possess land by rental or even as full-fledged property to give, sell, and under certain conditions, inherit; since, also, he served at the host and sat at tribunals; and since above all his obligations were, in principal and except when violated, strictly limited by custom. Even less did he represent the characteristics of the slave's economic order, because his labor power did not belong to his lord. In every country, actually, certain lords persisted for a long time in demanding the right to requisition the labor of their serfs in times of pressing need. After all, among all the dependents of the manor, serfs were bound to a particularly commanding duty to help. On occasion, this pressing need could be formidable, but it did not claim in itself anything more than an implementation that was exceptional by definition, and we cannot see that it was frequently followed by other consequences. Serfs doubtless owed their lords a large part of their time, but—with the specific exception of a serf's duties—this was most often much less as serfs than as tenants, and at the same rate of levy as their neighbors, when the category of the tenures was similar.

Above all, whatever the origin and extent of this obligatory work, it was, like all other duties, fixed in its duration and, at times, in the nature of its use, by the normal customs of each manor. These were customs that, after the Frankish era and perhaps after the Roman age, in practice modified the condition of the slave-tenant. The German *Tageschalken*, whose work duty was on a daily basis, seem at first sight to have been very close to slaves, and they were in fact very humble people, scarcely casati, almost farm hands, whose holding was seemingly confined to their cottage and its garden. But even there the similarity was only on the surface. Did each Tageschalk, whatever his sex or age, come every day to take his place in the team of workers of the lord? Or rather, was not each household from this class—men, women, and perhaps already grown children—required to furnish one worker every day? The point is not clear, though the second solution, which is the most far from slavery, remains the most probable.

Also, such duties were extremely rare. In France, I knew of no such example. Nearly everywhere, the heaviest duties required only a few days of work per week. In a word, serfdom or rather the seigneurial system of which serfdom was only one aspect, scarcely placed a quantity of manpower at the disposition of the lords which remained very appreciable, or even numerous, for very long. The stock of labor that was supplied this way constituted an inextensible supply. The slave had been an ox in the stable, always under his master's orders; the villein, even if he was a serf, was a worker who came on certain days and who left as soon as the job was finished.

The fortunes of words themselves suffice to assure us that serfdom was something quite different from slavery. Servus and the Latin derivatives of the word had, as we have seen, slipped bit by bit into a meaning vastly different from their ancient content. The dissolution of the old social frameworks had also impaired various equivalent terms whose evolution followed fairly different lines anyway: the Germanic *Knecht* and *Schalk*, its synonyms, had passed on the Continent to the attenuated meaning of "servant." In England, the meaning of "knight" had changed to that of "armed follower" and later to "horseman." The Gallo-Roman term *vassus* or *vassalus*, which was originally Celtic and which certainly had formerly designated a slave, came to apply to a free retainer, our term "vassal." In their original, pregnant meanings, these terms were to be replaced by a new semantic creation: this was, in variable phonetic form, the very word that in modern French provided the word "slave."

The word's history itself is very unclear and lacking in sufficiently advanced studies. It seems to have appeared in the tenth century, about the same time in Germany as in Italy, and from there to have spread through the rest of Europe fairly slowly, for reasons we shall see. Naturally—and this is one of the reasons that makes this development so difficult to trace—it was adopted much more quickly in everyday dialects than by the Latin of the charters or the chronicles, which was essentially conservative and obstinately attached to classical usage. Its introduction into everyday vocabulary evidently marked the difference between the new model of serfdom and a condition that according to the ancient schema really made a man an object belonging to his master. It also attests that alongside the serfs there still existed slaves in the full sense of the word.

Moreover, these two conclusions do not exhaust the questions we can ask of linguistics. The word "slave" became only secondarily the label of class. It was primarily an ethnic name. This, too, we have kept in French, with its original meaning, but under a slightly different form: when talking of peoples we speak of Slavs. Certainly the alteration of the meaning is explained by the origin of a large number of men subjected to this condition. We can say more generally that if there were still some slaves in Western and Central Europe in the eleventh and twelfth centuries, these slaves were nearly all foreigners.

Actually, this fact was in no way foreign to the most deeply rooted customs. Aside from some exceptional cases, such as penal slavery, slavery for indebtedness, or, where the power of the father was the strongest, the sale of the child by the head of the family, neither the Mediterranean nor the German world had ever considered the enslavement of a fellow citizen as permissible. Most slaves were either captives or the sons of captives who came from nearby societies that were fragmented by a crowd of little tribes or, under the Roman Empire, who were fetched from the vast reservoir of its barbarian frontier. What was new was that in the Middle Ages the notion of "foreigner" took on a different, a completely confessional meaning.

States had been broken up into an infinity of tiny pieces. But above them, and encompassing immense human masses, a new city had been born, the *civitas Christiana*, Christianity, all of whose members belonged, in a moral sense, to a single nation. Of course, peace did not by any means reign there: far from it. However, the law of the Church and, more deeply, the religious conscience, did not allow a conqueror to reduce the conquered to slavery when the conquered was his brother in Christ. Here we are touching on the strongest action that Christianity had ever exercised, in a way that was actually somewhat indirect, upon the progress of human liberty, and perhaps upon the social structure in general. Even while favoring manumissions, it had not condemned slavery; it never ceased to accept its imposition upon pagans, infidels, and even upon schismatics within Christendom who were considered to be deprived of true Christian communion. It tolerated keeping baptized slaves under the yoke, if only because they themselves or their ancestors had been foreigners to the true faith at the time of their enslavement. However, in limiting the area where masters and slave traders could legally supply themselves to the space beyond the boundaries of the Catholic world, if it did not entirely dry up the recruitment for slavery, it at least reduced the source to a very thin trickle.

Of course, practice only slowly conformed to these feelings, whose influence naturally came into conflict with the old traditions of the *razzia* and the urgings of the spirit of gain. There is nothing to indicate that the slaves called *barbaricini*—probably Sardians—of which there was a great deal of trading in sixth century Italy and some of which Gregory the Great purchased, were not Christians. If Smaragdus, the Abbot of Saint Mihiel, thought he had to urge Charlemagne to forbid "further reductions of people into captivity" in his Empire, it is doubtless because acts of this sort had passed before his eyes. Even when the Anglo-Saxons had become Christian, internal conflicts that often set one of their various kingdoms in opposition against the others continued nonetheless for many years to supply captives for the market, sometimes captives of high birth. Also, England was definitely the country where slavery, properly so called, kept an important place in economic life for the longest time in all of Western Europe.

A continual guerilla war raged there between Saxons and Celts, who were Christians of course, but whom adversaries willingly considered foreign to Roman orthodoxy. It is not an accident if we can see so many slaves and freed men there carrying Celtic names or surnames such as "Scot," or if, according to usage that perhaps goes back to the time when the Germanic conquerors of the island still practiced paganism, the word "wealth" (meaning Welsh) came to take on, in everyday speech, the meaning of "slave." Thus fed by the very close presence of a population whose enslavement appeared legitimate, Anglo-Saxon slavery also owed its long duration to the particular characteristics of the society's general evolution. The development of the relations of personal dependence, in a regular system that could be substituted almost entirely for other social ties, was much slower than on the continent, and did not achieve its full development before the arrival of the Norman kings. The institutions of Germanic public law marked a greater power of resistance. The traditional classification of human conditions—maintained, besides, by the continuity of the written law and of legislation—fell less quickly into disuse. Indeed the Anglo-Saxon *theow* was fundamentally that juridical entity that had become so exceptional on the other side of the Channel: a slave. Serfdom, which there as elsewhere had to absorb so many former slaves, was scarcely established before the Norman conquest, no more than was the regime of the fief and vassalage—and the coincidence is significant.

War was not alone in providing the primary material for slavery: we are told that often fathers put their own children up for sale. The trade retained a large scale of activity. At the time when French clerks were editing the Domesday Book, people remembered very well the time when, in various internal markets, people "sold men." But the island also exported large numbers of boys and girls in the tenth and eleventh centuries to Italy, Ireland (notably from Bristol), and perhaps Spain. The girls were sometimes fattened ahead of time to increase their market value. Similarly, after they were converted, the seagoing hordes of Scandanavia continued to sweep the winding and barbaric coastline of the Nordic countries to gather human booty there. Frisian laws, as late as the eleventh century, considered such misadventures as a normal event whose juridical consequences had to be foreseen.

However, the movement of new ideas slowly made its way, here sooner and there later. It is very characteristic that the wars that tore asunder the Western world after the last years of Louis the Pious scarcely seem to have led to reductions in slavery. Without doubt, servile livestock remained among the merchandise most actively traded in this time of fairly infrequent exchanges. People not only traded from country to country inside Latin and Germanic Christendom, they also traded outside, but it was no longer people of Catholic birth who were sold this way. From what countries outside Europe (in the restricted sense in which we use this word) did people draw for these foreign slaves, either to keep them or to make money from them?

At the time we are studying, many and probably most arrived by land from the eastern confines of Germany. It is well to remember that Germany, at this time, was far from being its present size. In the East, until the tenth century, it scarcely went beyond a border generally marked by the Elbe, the Saal, and the Böhmerwald. In the course of this century the conquests of the Saxon dynasty only ended by extending the line of defense—definitely not what one would call a border—from the Saal to the middle reaches of the Elbe, and to enlarge slightly the zone of protection for the outposts that held its flanks on the right bank of this river. Beyond that began the world, hostile more often than not, of the Slavic-speaking peoples.

Two indigenous states had been formed there from the tenth century onward which were quite vast, relatively well organized, and in addition were Christian from quite early on: Bohemia and Poland. Outside of these, though, and for the most part between Germany and Poland itself, large expanses remained, occupied by a scattering of peoples who had remained almost entirely pagan, and who were ceaselessly at war among themselves and especially with Christians. This land, blessed as it was with warring raids, was an admirable reservoir for slaves. The lords of the German markets not only used their captives for their own benefit, making them into agricultural workers, tenant-farmers, domestics, and concubines, they also sold them and drew substantial profits from this trade. The Slavic princes who were already converted were similar: tenth century Prague, according to Arab travelers, was one of the great markets of the slave trade.

The supply from these far off countries fed a commerce of wide scope. In fact, it does not seem that within Western Christendom itself the area of expansion spread much beyond the Rhine. In France I do not think I have ever come upon them or seen any mention of them in the texts. We should not be so unwise as to conclude from this that nobody owned any. This would deny the possibility of new discoveries, which are that much less improbable because research is difficult and because people have not sought very extensively. Even supposing that the silence of the documents was not to be remedied, neither their abundance nor their precision, unfortunately, are sufficient for isolated facts not to have passed through their meshes. It is nonetheless striking that the very word "slave"—a juridical term, but still conveying at the beginning a very strong ethnic flavor—penetrated the domain of the French language very late. It scarcely appeared in it until the thirteenth century, and was then applied to people of an unfree condition who were perhaps Slavs, but who certainly had not been born upon the frontiers of Germany.

Everything indicates that the captives of this area, if they existed in France—we know nothing about them—were there, at any rate, in very small numbers. Probably this merchandise, which had to be fetched from too far away seemed to be too expensive. The very rarity of slave manpower had gotten most masters out of the habit of using them, and the society of the time provided other means for procuring needed labor. On the other hand, on the Rhine, until about the year 1200—that is, at a moment when the progress of the German conquest and that of Christianity began singularly to restrict the hunting grounds—one still found girls of the Slavic race in noble households, frequently as slaves. Around the year 1000, men and women, *servi ancillae*, figured among the imported merchandise that was tolled on the Alpine roads to Italy. Were these people Slavs or were they English? How can we decide? What is curious is that if the French castles scarcely sheltered any captives taken in the German territories, certain caravans that crossed the country from one part to another bore them fairly frequently. For as early as the tenth and in the eleventh century a good number were exported toward Muslim Spain, which was wealthy and was used to the employment of slave labor. Verdun, at the halfway point, was one of the active centers of this trade. Before sending the young boys they had bought across the Pyrenees, the merchants frequently castrated them to raise their price in th estimation of the harem-masters. Others were most probably sold in the Levant. Among the slaves that Venice shipped on her vessels, to Byzantium and doubtless also to Egypt, it is hard to believe that there were none who were from this source.

The ports of the Western Mediterranean and of the Adriatic were exporters of human flesh; were they also occasionally importers to their own hinterlands? There is no doubt about it after the middle of the twelfth century. The slave, at the time, was one of the ordinary items in the return cargos from the long voyages to the Orient and Africa. Slavs or Tartars snatched from the banks of the Black Sea, "olive-skinned" Syrians or Berbers, and Blacks of the Maghreb were to come during several centuries and populate the bourgeois households of Italy, of Provence, and of Catalonia with their humble presence.

These are certainly the kinds of people whom documents around that time, all from the South, call "slaves"—for the first time in France. By then, though, the conditions of the Mediterranean traffic had profoundly changed. From then on the craftsmen of Western cities exported their products to consumers beyond the seas, and the sales allowed in return the acquisition of all kinds of merchandise, including human merchandise. Prior to this revolution in the economic current, exchanges were not only much less active, the heaviest burden for the West was borne of the rarity of export goods. To procure the exotic commodities for which it had an overpowering demand, it had either to sacrifice its gold or, precisely, its very own slaves. It could hardly import any. In spite of everything, here and there the West doubtless succeeded in procuring some few, with raids on the nearby Slavonic coast helping to supply the market in Venice, which evidently did not send all of its booty westward. At the end of the eleventh century, the Crusades made the great lords familiar with slavery. One of the surprises to the Latins had been to find its practice widespread in Syria. Guibert de Nogent was all the more strongly offended that many of these slaves were Christians. Later on, Beaumanoir thought that he should set aside, in his descriptions of juridical statutes, a place for this servus "of foreign lands," so different from the servus he knew from his own experience. Imitating these foreign examples, some lofty personages, such as Gaudri, the Bishop of Laon, enjoyed maintaining Negro slaves in their following. All that was a very little matter. At war, Europe could demand a small amount of slave labor in the Slavic territories that its soldiers were ravaging. Economically still weak, it could not expect any appreciable numbers of them from international commerce.

The countries beyond the Elbe, however, were not the only lands where Europe touched civilizations that were foreign to Christianity. We should consider Muslim Spain, that Spain whose slow reconquest was one of the great facts of history. Of course, the inhabitants of the conquered lands were not ordinarily reduced to slavery. On the other hand, most prisoners made on the field of battle were, on both sides. Did the Christians export some of these *cautivos* outside the country? It is difficult to know. They definitely kept a large number for themselves, making them work in the household or in the fields, and submitting them to a condition that was very much, in the literal sense, that of slaves. The Iberian kingdoms, which were to do so much to spread slavery in the New World, had known it all the time on their own soil.

Thus Western and Central Europe, taken as a whole, was never free of slaves during the High Middle Ages. But from the ninth to the twelfth century, slaves always remained very few in number, even fewer than they were to be later on, after the resumption of large-scale Mediterranean trade. They were unknown in entire regions, such as France. Even where they were relatively numerous, enfranchisements came rapidly to thin their ranks because the same arguments that in the preceding era had increased these grants continued to be heard. Neither the lords of the European markets nor those of Leon, Castile, or Aragon managed great plantations that could use numerous slave gangs. And we know how easily, by the natural force of things, the slave-tenant ceases to be a real slave. Where the particular conditions of the country permitted the enslavement of captives without infringing the prohibition of the Church, slavery allowed well-to-do people cheaply to satisfy the manpower needs of the household, and on occasion, perhaps, of a workshop. In other instances, it provided the merchant with a convenient commodity that would help him make useful exchanges with foreigners. But as a force of production, slavery did not count any more.

A profound and slow transformation of the very foundations of the economic structure took place, but it is important to note that some of its consequences went beyond the economic sphere. Whatever the misery of certain classes and the disdain in which the fortunate of this world held them—a disdain preserved for some of them by the very survival of the epithet "servile," perverted, as we know, from its ancient juridical meaning—it was certainly remarkable that no man, no real Christian at any rate, could thereafter legitimately be held as the property of another. In breaking with slavery, the Middle Ages, whose social customs were not kind, neither destroyed nor intended to destroy inequalities of fact or birth, but it did give them a more humane tenor, so to speak. More easily apprehended are the demographic consequences. The importance of slave labor in the Roman world and the size of the scope of the trade led to a melting pot of peoples, whose importance can hardly be exaggerated. How many free families on the soil of Gaul, in the fourth and fifth centuries, were descended from slaves, slaves from the most far-off and diverse lands? Deprived of this foreign immigration, societies without slaves have had their blood renewed much less often. From this viewpoint, it is as if European civilization, like many others, became stabilized and closed in on itself in the course of these centuries.

CHAPTER TWO

Personal Liberty and Servitude in the Middle Ages, Particularly in France.[1] *Contribution to a Class Study*

Throughout medieval Europe men spoke of personal liberty and of servitude, i.e., of the deprivation of liberty. The courts investigated carefully, sometimes agonizingly, who was free and who was not. But, depending on the country, the social strata, and above all the era, the realities supposedly represented by the words "liberty" and "servitude" varied profoundly. I propose to retrace here, at least in broad outline, the history of these changes of meaning. I prefer to concentrate on French data that have been particularly accessible to me—or, more precisely, on certain French data. For indeed the researcher has to make a selection, governed both by the very nature of the data and their availability. Actually, the selection is not as clear nor as solidly founded on logic as would have been desirable.

We are well aware that French society in the Middle Ages was far from unified, but the precise determination of its diverse regional boundaries is still one of those most urgent tasks awaiting the historian. An excessive respect for administrative or political frontiers has masked this necessity for far too long. In the absence of a true social geography, only the most obvious contrasts can be pointed out. It is undeniable that, to the south of the frontier zone separating the two great groups of Gallo-Roman speaking peoples—the French bloc and the Provençal bloc—the structure of human groups generally appeared quite different from those further north. Without excluding either the kingdom of Burgundy or the two Lorraines, the following observations will mainly apply to the France of the *langue d'oïl*. I will look at the Provençal or Aquitanian Midi only to provide contrast. Finally, I will attempt to place French evolution within the general curve of European development.

It is hardly necessary to add that, even thus limited, this study, based upon a necessarily incomplete documentation, can only aspire to being a sketch, wherein many lines will be drawn with an uncertain pencil and where many others are certainly destined to be corrected by a more thorough inquiry.[2]

SLAVERY AND SERFDOM: A HISTORICAL CONTRAST

To grasp the general shape of a curve, first it is wise to consider two points sufficiently distant from each other. The beginning of the ninth century and that of the thirteenth offer themselves naturally for this role. Here are two relatively well researched areas separated by a large, obscure gap. Profound juridical and political transformations marked the intervening period that witnessed the death of many things and the creation of new ones. One may say that, in more than one sense, it witnessed the birth, along with French society, of France itself. But this intense gestation is hidden from us among the mists of a tradition extremely poor in written documents. It would have been impossible to begin in this twilight.

Under Charlemagne, then, and under Philip Augustus, there lived and labored on the soil of France men who in both reigns were designated in Latin as *servi*, men who in both reigns were considered to be deprived of that juridical characteristic known as freedom. But what a contrast between their actual conditions!

In reality, as we shall see later on, as early as the Carolingian era, the old notion of the deprivation of liberty had already been subjected to noticeable changes both in every day practice and in the common speech. But the *servus*'s condition, according to official law determined in statutes and capitularies and whose classifications dominated the polyptiques, can be defined in relatively simple terms.[3] Properly speaking, and in conformity with the Latin usage of the word, it was slavery.

Before Frankish society had been formed in the burning crucible of the invasions, both Germans and Romans possessed slaves. The rules of law and the economic utilization of human cattle presented marked differences between these two civilizations, but the fundamental features remained the same. These can be found in the Carolingian state, heir to this double juridical tradition. The servus was the object of a master who disposed arbitrarily of his person, his work, and his property. Of course, the Roman theory of wages, the humanitarian laws of both pagan and Christian emperors, above all the inevitable transactions of daily life, all had alleviated and were still modifying the rigorous ancient principles; these did nonetheless remain alive.

Furthermore the servus was not truly a part of the people. In the view of the mass of free men, he was like a foreigner deprived of all rights. Should he be killed or wounded, the master received the compensation. Should he commit a crime against his own master, the latter was allowed to judge and penalize him as he saw fit. Should he injure a third party, the master again took up the responsibility. The latter could sometimes even rid himself of that burden by handing over the guilty person or occasionally even by freeing him.[4] Only free men sat on the periodic courts that acted primarily as judicial assemblies. The servus could be armed by his own master, serve him as a guard, even accompany him to the feudal levy. Personally he was not subject to the obligation of military service toward the king or the emperor.[5] Finally, with the exception of those whose social status elevated them above their juridical status, the Carolingian servi as a group did not take that oath to the sovereign upon which was based, in law, the nation's allegiance. "Frank" and "free" are two words that for centuries were employed by the French language indiscriminately and interchangeably, thus perpetuating the memory of that far-distant time when the deprivation of liberty meant essentially the rejection from that great political unit that, irrespective of origin or ethnic law, was called the *populus Francorum*.

In the Capetian era the condition of those whom, for convenience's sake, I will call henceforth by their French name, "serfs," was completely different. The distinction introduced by the term "serf" is, of course, deliberately fabricated, since the Latin documents of the thirteenth century as well as those of the Carolingian period say servi; furthermore, since the Carolingian era, the servum of yesteryear was changing into the *serf* of the Romance language. But the obviousness of this artifice is precisely what removes any danger from it.

How was the serf recognized? The courts on many occasions—for cases regarding bodily possession were very frequent—had to ask precisely this question. In the twelfth and thirteenth centuries they established and regularized the laws of the servile status. Guided by their decisions and in a more general manner by documents regarding acutal practice, we must now try to resolve the problem.

Each serf was rigidly subordinate to a seigneur. The forms of this subjection are what above all defined his status. But here, the social fragmentation characteristic of "feudal" civilization rendered juridical procedure and jurisprudence particularly delicate. What was most striking about the duties characteristic of the serf's dependence upon his seigneur was their extreme variability of detail according to locale.

In the twelfth and thirteenth centuries a general law common to the whole kingdom or even to a vast region did not exist. In each case, custom, usually oral, proper to a small group gathered about a single seigneur and his manor, regulated the servile bond. On July 16, 1240, Renaud le Charpentier promised the monks of Saint-Martin-des-Champs to behave thereafter as their *homme de corps*—that is, as their serf, the two terms being then absolutely synonymous—in accordance with "the ways and customs of the village of Sainte-Gemme where he was born."[6] Many texts—such as an important decision of Parliament in 1263[7]—similarly illustrate that the "custom of the country" (*consuetudo patrie*) determined the servile condition. Undoubtedly the word country (*pays*) should be interpreted strictly, since even today, despite literary usage, peasants equate village with *pays*. Later, in the fourteenth century, some manuscripts from the *Grand Coutumier* added the following two maxims to the description that Jacques d'Ableiges had tried to give of the servitude in Champagne and in Brie: "Diverse are the duties owed to different seigneurs, according to the peculiarity of servile conditions or of locales.... Therefore, should you have to deal with such things in some country, first ask those who know its customs."[8] Modern historians could possibly also profit from these instructions.

Examined more closely, however, this juridical mixture appears to be nothing more than a jumble of nuances. Actually, almost similar traditions ruled neighboring groups, or those belonging to the same seigneur but not necessarily in close proximity to one another. It is thus often legitimate to speak of the servile custom of certain regions or of specific seigneuries. But throughout France as defined above, even with its infinite diversity of adaptation, the essential traits of a similar status, of a similar conception of servitude can easily be discovered. Similar social needs and the consensus of opinion imposed an overwhelming uniformity of principles.

In the eyes of the law, three duties, when brought together, essentially characterized the servile condition.

The first was a true tax that the adult male or female serfs paid yearly "from their heads"* to their seigneur. Fixed once and for all by tradition, this *chevage*—also called rent, *census de capite*—sometimes was paid in kind, such as hens or wax. Most often it was stipulated in silver deniers—ordinarily four deniers, sometimes less, very rarely more. But it must be well understood that, according to almost universal practice, the tax, although stipulated in currency, could in practice be paid in the equivalent amount of commodities or even workdays.[9] However computed, the tax was always quite modest.

The devaluation of money increasingly depressed the economic value of the chevage. This explains why, around 1150, a great number of seigneuries, at least in some regions such as the Ile-de-France, allowed it to lapse. As early as the end of the twelfth century the serfs of Sainte-Geneviève, for example, had ceased to pay it, although judges determining personal status took care to keep a place for it on their questionnaires.[10] Undoubtedly, if one judges from the description of the monk Guiman of Saint-Vaast of Arras[11] some had retreated before the difficulties and expense of such rent collections. However, the most perceptive administrators, such as the canons of Chartres, persisted in demanding this small payment. In Champagne, in many localities, it was maintained until the end of the Middle Ages.

Despite its slender amount, its very periodicity made the chevage valuable. Notoriously contrary custom excepted, the regular subjection to this tax signified servitude and its attendant compulsory obligations. When around the mid-thirteenth century the men and women de corps of the treasury of the Church of Laon "hid" their chevages, it was in order to escape the *mainmorte* and *formariage*, the two other responsibilities characteristic of the servile condition.[12] Again, in 1261, the fear of losing these two sources of royal revenue prompted a complaint against the bailiff of Vermandois who was accused of neglecting to collect the *denerée* of wax owed annually by the royal serfs.[13] Apparently those serfs living under foreign domination were most likely to avoid the rigid control symbolized by this tax. Thus, while the seigneur might relinquish

---

* Before its payment, the *denier* was placed upon the serf's head to denote his true servility.

the chevage for serfs living on his own land, he might insist on receiving it from those who lived elsewhere.[14]

This symbolic meaning of the chevage is understandable only because it was considered the indication, par excellence, of servitude, *pensum servitutis*.[15] It was not always so, as we shall see. But, as early as the end of the eleventh century, this doctrine was firmly established in most places. Around 1300, through disuse or formal agreement, a man might have abrogated the responsibilities of mainmorte and formariage. Yet the continued obligation of this trifling chevage symbolized his servitude, which only enfranchisement could change.[16] One of the traditional names for the serf was *homme de chef, homo de capite*, or still, in the crude Latin of some writers, *censualis*. The monk Guiman in 1170 designated the serfs of Saint-Vaast as such; charters issued by the Counts of Flanders (at least one of which was drawn up in the same monastery) called them quite simply *servi*.[17]

This connection between chevage and servitude could as well be found in most of those countries in which juridical conditions analogous to French serfdom had developed. "So that the serf (servus) should not hide in the shelter of any negligence," proclaimed an Italian constitution of Otto III in 996, "we order that each one henceforth, in order to attest to his servitude, pay to his master or his representative one denier on the Kalends of December."[18] A pious anecdote perfectly characterizes the importance that French seigneurial opinion attributed to this minor obligation. A serf belonging to the abbey of Fleury-sur-Loire refused to admit his status. According to customary law he claimed the right to test his case by judicial combat. Saint Benoît, flying to the aid of his flock, stunned the imposter with a miracle. According to the historian of the abbey, he changed the rebel's shield into a denier, the symbol and substance of the chevage.[19]

The two other duties concerned the familial status. They were much more lucrative and therefore much more durable. They lasted as long as there were serfs, i.e., until 1789. But the circumstances calling for their collection being much rarer, it was often quite difficult to prove their existence in the absence of the chevage, which would have immediately justified their application.

First, a matrimonial rule, the significance of which has to be carefully outlined. On some lands the serf had to pay a usually quite modest wedding tax to his seigneur, who, in some cases, at least, may have usurped it from the parish fees. It is clear that its enforcement in these rare areas[20] did not empower the seigneur to decide on the nuptials themselves. Undoubtedly, the seigneur could occasionally force girls and boys to marry according to his wish. All dependents, whatever their social rank, were at that time exposed to attempts of this sort. The history of the Plantagenets and even that of the Capetians illustrates the weight of such burdens on the life of noble vassals. The regulations in numerous urban charters attest fervently to the fact that the free bourgeois also had great difficulty in escaping such obligations.[21] On the whole, this right was only an abusive consequence of the bond of protection. By its very nature, the authority of the lord tended to replace that of the family. The recognized legitimacy of some of his interventions—witness the role of the seigneur regarding the orphaned vassal—only made it more tempting to extend them beyond the permitted boundaries. Evidence seems to prove that of all those persons subject to diverse forms of seigneurial authority the serfs were in fact the least often affected by these forced nuptials.[22] The matter is easily explained. Servile poverty nullified the profitable trade in heirs or heiresses so common among the bourgeoisie and the nobility. In any case, in the legal view, these constraints remained plain transgressions. Juridically, as well as almost always practically, the marriage of a serf was free within a prescribed group, but within that group only. It was this limitation that figured among the primordial and quasi-universal characteristics of his status.

In fact a strict law of endogamy regulated the lives of serfs. It was not enough for the two spouses to be serfs,[23] they also had to have the same seigneur. Any marriage "outside" this group whose members were attached to a single lord by exactly similar bonds was a formariage, and was rigorously prohibited—except, of course, with special authorization that was only rarely granted without a fee. The usually high price for this authorization made it inaccessible to most peasants.[24] Moreover, before the projected union could take place between the subjects of two different seigneurs, the latter were obliged to go through some delicate transactions. Gradually established practices or formal agreements on occasion, it is true, eliminated in advance any difficulty between two neighboring lands. For example, the seigneurs acknowledged that the woman and the children, or perhaps the latter only, would serve the husband's seigneur.[25] Or each spouse could remain under the domination of his or her respective seigneur while all their children would derive to one of the two, designated once and for all.[26] Some churches—such as Saint-Denis, Saint-Germain-des-Prés,

Saint-Florent of Saumur—sporadically went so far as to claim all children from any formariage arrangement contracted by one of their serfs.[27] Royal officers sometimes instituted a similar claim. Neither group met with consistent success.[28] Almost always it was necessary to reach an agreement limited to a particular case. Sometimes a seigneur would cede one spouse in exchange for a laborer of approximately equal ability and wealth. The transaction entailed some risk, since, as we shall see, the seigneur always hoped to inherit the property of his serf. To receive a poor handyman in exchange for a wealthy peasant would certainly incur a heavy loss. Easier transactions occurred when two unions were formed simultaneously. Then each seigneurie supplied one of the spouses for each couple. Most of these human barters implied preliminary negotiations between families. These were particularly frequent in the least miserable part of the servile population, notably among families of seigneurial sergeants, who, elevated by their wealth and prestige far above the peasant mass, hardly found suitable matches within their native villages.

Most often the seigneurs authorizing the formariage, leaving aside the spouses's status, were content to divide the children among themselves. Difficulties then arose with an uneven number of children. Customs or contracts offered a great number of solutions. In Beauce, custom decreed that in a case involving royal serfs, the King always took the firstborn even if no other birth occurred.[29] Elsewhere a remarkably liberal tradition granted an only child the right to chose his own master.[30] Or else, the two seigneurs agreed that, in case of an uneven number, the last born would enter a religious order to serve only God.[31] All these complications provided many obstacles to formariages.[32]

In fact, despite some exceptional local practices that then became customary,[33] one cannot doubt that the serfs of a single seigneurie were almost always obliged to marry among themselves. This instigated consanguineous unions. Everything indicates that, in defiance of Church law, they were quite widespread among serfs.[34] Indeed, the necessity of ending this sin sometimes motivated enfranchisements, granted, incidentally, for a fee.[35] There was worse yet. Even admitting the scandalous violation of canonical principles, the circle of licit alliances remained restricted enough to condemn a great many serfs to inevitable celibacy, spurring "corruption"[36] and "moral degeneracy" among the young girls.[37]

Finally, there is the problem of the inheritance. For the moment, let us leave aside the problem of the last will and testament, which was only gradually established and was always in question. When the serf died intestate, his natural heirs were not, as for the free man, the only ones whose claims had to be considered. The seigneur sometimes opposed them. This was known as the right of mainmorte. The "hand" of the serf, i.e., his power over his own goods, was, in certain cases, and on all or part of his patrimony, considered to have "died" irrevocably with him, so that he lost any power to divide his estate among his kin.[38]

Two general systems developed. They can be defined within wide geographical areas, which should be better determined in the future and which, despite occasional cases of cross-contamination, differ along clearly defined lines. This contrast marks one of the most curious enigmas in the history of serfdom.

Widespread in Flanders, Picardy, and Basse-Lorraine, the first system also was reminiscent of the most generally observed contemporary customs in both England and Germany. It allowed the seigneur to appropriate a part of the inheritance with every death. But his right was exercized only on the movables, the *catels*. As usual the norm varied according to different customs. Sometimes the appropriation was a fraction of the movable wealth determined in advance: one-half—such was the rule in Flanders[39]—or two-thirds.[40] Elsewhere—following, at times, some mitigating circumstances—it was limited to an object or an animal (the "best" catel), which the seigneur chose about as he wished. Or still, conforming to a tradition with Carolingian origins but also developed later,[41] as in Saint-Trond, a fixed amount of wine or of money constituted the collection.[42] According to the custom of the time, equally valuable commodities could readily replace cash payments. In the end, the seigneur, who always inherited, received rather little each time.

Throughout the greater part of France a totally different principle operated. Although the word "mainmorte" was, as we have seen, generally used, it was to this second type of seigneurial succession, or *échoite*, that it more especially applied. If the serf left descendents, the patrimony returned entirely to them, but on one condition. These heirs must have always lived in common with the deceased. Rather than transmitting individual goods, a collective possession was perpetuated. The system rested then on the practice of the familial community that, widespread throughout the European peasant class, especially retained its vigor in France.

Did the elimination of the child placed "outside bread" (*hors *pain, forisfamiliatus*) date from the introduction of serfdom? Or rather, was its appearance a later substitute to an age when all descendents could inherit without restriction? The documents are so obscure that a precise answer remains momentarily impossible. From the thirteenth century on the principle was clearly manifest and apparently readily observed,[43] with the usual disputes and compromises on details.[44] In a society where ordinarily unwritten customs contained so many uncertainties, where the absence of any juridical centralization hindered the establishment of a truly forceful jurisprudence, could there be many juridical codes that did not suffer from many adjustments? Formerly, only the child who, through enfranchisement, had ceased to belong to the servile group was specifically eliminated. The seigneurs always resisted the transfer of servile property into the hands of a freeman.[45] However, it would be imprudent to conclude anything from the silence of the texts. The customs of familial community, of the *freresche*, was so general for centuries that the exclusion of the heir who had escaped from it was only rarely formulated. According to all appearances, the rule, perhaps not universally respected, was always considered natural and desirable. But, only the need arising from the great demographic revolution of the twelfth century made it specific. It is probable that the increasing population multiplied the cases of rupture between children and parents. Furthermore, the seigneurs began to exercise more rigorously their right of *échoite* since vacant lands became less numerous and available labor more abundant. A confiscated tenure would now rarely revert to wasteland.

In some other places, in the absence of progeny, the brothers of the deceased serf could inherit, provided they had never divided the family patrimony.[46] Born thus from ancient community customs, the fixed servile inheritance patterns contributed, where serfdom persisted for a long time, to the perpetuation of these traditions, hindering the fragmentation of the estate, but also the colonization of new lands and, in human terms, depleting peasant lineages.[47]

On the other hand, if a serf left no heirs, nor even collateral descendents, or if both had broken away from him before his death, then the seigneur gathered all the goods, whatever their nature—with the exception of the widow's dowry, her share in the despoliations,[48] and the rights of creditors on the movables.[49] Together with the movable objects, the house and the land reverted to him. Most often the lord tried, as much as possible, to resell the whole to other serfs, and frequently to the collateral heirs. Thus, as is usual, practice being transformed into respectable custom, the relatives of the deceased received, in some places, a veritable privilege of preemption.[50]

Thus understood, i.e., throughout most French provinces, the mainmorte only occurred intermittently and generally at long intervals.[51] But its exercise involved the temporary absorbtion of a whole patrimony into the seigneurial domain. Thus sprung up seigneurial expectations of considerable profits and, for servile families, a feeling of insecurity which appears to have been very intense.

There remains the last will and testament. For a long time ignored by all strata of medieval society, it was first slowly reintroduced only under the singular form of legacies to churches and remained clearly distinct from a deathbed bequest. It raised some particular difficulties for the serf since any act encroaching upon the heriditary goods of future generations threatened his heirs as well as his seigneur, the eventual beneficiary of the mainmorte. This was particularly true where the mainmorte, when applied, spread over the whole of the inheritance. In the latter localities, at least, a principle existed, as stated in a decision of Parliament in 1263, that "the *homme de corps* does not possess the same free testamentary right as the free men of the same country."[52] In the eleventh and twelfth centuries, it was commonly admitted that a serf could only validly will his property with the authorization of his seigneur, even if his eternal salvation was at stake. This always happened when the seigneur was a monastery or a cathedral chapter and thus would be the recipient of the legacy. In other cases, the church involved tried to obtain, either by particular agreement, or once and for all, the indispensable consent.[53] Of course, since it was proper to respect the just claims of the family, the serf as well as the free man could only will a part of his heritage. Unfortunately, the old texts neglected to specify its amount.[54] The use of these pious arrangements, considered then as one of the most sacred Christian duties, became increasingly common in the thirteenth century, even among the servile population. It was noted with manifest surprise, in 1253, that a serf had died intestate.[55] Of course, many seigneurs continued to put obstacles in the way. Between 1227 and 1240, Jacques de Vitry preached against those masters who "similar to maggots on corpses" appropriated the mainmorte but refused "to give aid for the souls of the dead."[56]

However, custom led to the recognition that the serf possessed a real testamentary capacity independent of any seigneurial intervention. In 1247 a female serf of Sainte-Geneviève of Paris, promising the canons not to subtract anything from her goods "by last will and testament" or on the death bed, reserved for herself, however, the ability "to make a legacy by last will in the same way as the men of this church are accustomed to do": meaning, certainly, a legacy of piety.[57] Gradually, among so many tentative procedures, a disposable share was fixed, normally smaller than that of free men, but extremely variable according to regions or even seigneuries. At Meaux, around the end of the thirteenth century, on the land of the bishop, and at Lagny, in 1262, on that of the abbey, the share was one-third of the movables. In the Beauvais region, according to Beaumanoir who probably generalized somewhat, it was five *sous* or their equivalent value, no doubt in movables only. In Champagne, it was also five sous if we are to believe the different customs that perhaps were inspired by Beaumanoir,[58] but a fifth of the real property and a third of the movables according to another writer.[59]

These differences were quite natural in a new institution that, having appeared here sooner, there later, arose everywhere after the establishment of the overall design of the servile status. What matters is that in almost all places the serf's will henceforth was considered legitimate. But the legacies thus permitted were exclusively—Beaumanoir,[60] as well as the census of the bishops of Meaux specified it quite clearly—legacies "for the soul." Any other testamentary arrangement without seigneurial consent was long considered forbidden to serfs. It was certainly such purely temporal "last wills" that, in 1247, as we have seen, the canons of Sainte-Geneviève intended to prohibit in the same act allowing a "legacy." Again, in 1370, a serf of the chapter of Meaux made her last will and testament at the expense of her natural heirs without gaining the approval of the canons. The clerics upheld—truly by "mercy" if we accept their word—the legacy "for the remedy of the soul," but sought and obtained the anulment of the others.[61]

It is perhaps surprising that I have left aside two obligations frequently considered characteristic of servitude. The first, the "arbitrary" tax (*taille*), was thought of as a purely servile symbol as early as the fourteenth century, at least in some areas such as the Champagne. The second, the "attachment to the soil," a clumsy formula by which, in the last centuries of the Middle Ages, and especially under the Ancien Régime, various jurists, too slavishly copied by much more recent textbooks, sought to express some new features that in their time had appeared in the ancient status of serfs. A very simple observation should suffice to justify this silence. Up to the end of the thirteenth century, neither criteria can be found in the definitions that jurisprudence had given of the servile condition on different occasions. It should, however, be interesting to explain with more precision why these obligations cannot be included.

The taille was a tax generally paid in money and roughly proportionate to wealth. In everyday language it assumed different names according to time and place. Besides that of taille, which in all likelihood issued from a fairly realistic image—the seigneur "tailled" the taxpayer, i.e., he cut into their goods—there were courteous and somewhat hypocritical terms such as demand (*demande*) or request (*queste*). Or, on the contrary, some brutally sincere words, such as *tolle* (from *tollir*, to take), which the Latin documents translated as *exactio*. Very frequently one also said *aide*. To the historian this last synonym is the most instructive. Indeed under these different names the taille was only one type of the general obligation of the aide, then one of the major aspects of the social order. A multitude of social bonds wove their entangled network among men. The kinds of subordination varied greatly between two persons according to their rank, the tacit or expressed clauses of contracts, and the custom of the group. In their simplicity the general principles were immutable: the lord commanded and protected, the inferior obeyed and "aided" from his person as from his property. To seek in the taille, in the institutions of the preceding epoch, a unique importance, would be equivalent to inventing an insoluble problem. A pecuniary form of the aide, the taille was owed wherever and whenever one man called another his seigneur, a name both vague and weighty. The vassal paid it to the seigneur from fief; the "villein," "hôte," or "peasant" paid it to the landed seigneur whose *censive* he held or under whose justice he "bedded and rose"; the lay advocate who claimed he protected the goods of the saint, their master, often demanded it, rightly or wrongly, from churchmen; the king, when there truly was a king, endeavored to levy it on all the French; finally, the serf was subject to it from the seigneur of "his body."

In a time when scarce currency circulated slowly and when even with payments in kind—the taille was very rarely paid in goods—exchanges naturally operated with much difficulty. This tax of dependence, often capriciously disguised as a gift, was for a long time only appropriated in those rare moments of extreme need. The necessities or possibilities of the moment determined each time the sum the seigneur deemed worthy to demand. Originally, its periodicity and collection was always "arbitrary"—to employ the expression created later by feudal lawyers.

In the course of the twelfth century, some momentous economic transformations occurred. The role of metallic currency accordingly increased. The seigneurs increasingly resorted to the taille that their dependents, now more than ever, seemed able to pay. But, the ability to resist it varied among the contributors. Early on, the vassals had sought to fix and limit the applications and obligations of the aide, both militarily and monetarily. They generally forced through the principle that restricted the right to collect the taille to well-defined cases determined by group custom. Whether serfs or free, the peasants were much less adept at forming an effective opposition—not that they did not try. The repeated demands of the seigneurs appeared to be all the more abusive to them as these were not justified by a long tradition. The principle of the tax was ancient, but the frequency of its application was a novelty, in itself contrary to the law founded on custom. Why should the peasants not have opposed it when even within the seigneurial class the most scrupulous clerics judged these unceasingly renewed tailles as illegitimate?[62] Some revolts occurred, but they were mere flashes in the pan. On most seigneuries in the thirteenth century collections were made increasingly frequently, until they became an annual event, and even occurred several times in the course of a year.

At the same time, however, the seigneurial rights underwent a profound transformation. The recording in writing of customary burdens became habitual, thus removing their quite variable and arbitrary character. The subjects demanded this regularization. On the whole the seigneurs did not oppose it. Not only did they charge heavily for the act of registration, but the certainty of income assured their peace of mind. Thus, everywhere a new taste for judicial clarity became widespread. In their own way the "charters of custom" are an episode in the intellectual history of the period. This movement could not fail to affect the taille itself. From the twelfth century, in fact, and especially beginning in the thirteenth, one sees a multiplication of decrees stipulating the subscription to the taille, i.e., etymologically its "delimitation" (*abornement*) or its limitation (*abonnement*). Henceforth its periodicity would be fixed—almost always annually, on this point seigneurial pressure had triumphed—and, exception made for special circumstances anticipated in advance, fixed also in its ammount. Each year the men of the village paid in the aggregate the same sum that, divided among real property, finally appeared as a supplementary landed rent.

At least, such was the case on many estates, but not on all. Here and there, with more or less regional frequency, the arbitrary taille remained in force. And gradually servitude began to be associated with it.[63] This juridical confusion is easily explained. In law the annual subscription to the taille was absolutely distinct from affranchisement or "manumission," which transformed the serfs into free persons. This concession, particular to a specific form of the aide, was granted either to men who had always been free; or to former serfs freed many years earlier but who since their enfranchisement had continued to pay the taille under its early form; or finally to actual serfs. In practice, however, the annual subscription and the abolition of servile duties was often the object of the same charter, over which the seigneur and his subjects had long bargained. Where the peasants lacked the strength or necessary wealth to gain their enfranchisement in the course of time, usually they had equally failed to obtain the stabilization of the seigneurial tax. Therefore, around 1300 most individuals who continued to pay the arbitrary taille were in fact servile.

It was tempting to generalize and to take this juxtaposition as a juridical characteristic, particularly since the commonly held view of the idea of the deprivation of liberty was undergoing a change that worked in the same direction. The notion of serfdom elaborated in the tenth, eleventh, and twelfth centuries became more obscure; and the conception grew that lack of freedom meant, above all, obedience to the arbitrary will of another man: liability to forced labor "at his pleasure" and also, according to a much more frequently applied criterion (for the *corvées* unspecified by charter or at least by universally respected custom were in reality quite rare), payment of the taille at his will. The two images of servitude and arbitrary taille joined inseparably at this point. Forced to admit the existence of taille payers "high and low" who, however, had clearly escaped the mainmorte, and therefore were not serfs, a Burgundian jurist in the fourteenth century could only extricate himself from this apparent contradiction by applying the classificatory formula "free after death but serfs in life" to these unorthodox beings.[64]

Around 1200 we are still rather far from these tardy manifestations. The serf's status in regard to the taille only offered one peculiarity: as a serf he invariably owed it to the seigneur to whom he was personally attached; but he also owed it, as a hôte, to the man whose land he inhabited or whose fields he cultivated. If, as happened in some cases, these were two different individuals, the serf risked having to pay twice.[65] But this was only an infrequent consequence of his own status, and not a properly defining characteristic. When the free villein held property from two seigneurs, he likewise suffered this double imposition. Neither the taille, a universal charge on all dependents, nor the arbitrary taille, since any taille originally had merited this epithet, had any specifically servile characteristic.

"I give to Saint Martin," Sir Galeran de Breteuil dictated in 1077, "all my male and female serfs of Nottonville ... in such a way that anyone, male or female, from their lineage, even if he goes to another place, near or far, village, burg, fortified town, or city, will still remain united to the monks by the same bond of servitude."[66] Twenty years later a former mayor of Marmoutier promised "that he will never cease to acknowledge himself as serf of Saint-Martin, and even if he should decide to live under another seigneur he would never bring shame to the monks or to their assets."[67] In 1128 the deacon of Notre-Dame of Paris mentioned incidentally "our serfs who live on the lands of other seigneurs as well as the serfs of others who live on our lands."[68] In 1174, ceding the village of Artenay and two neighboring hamlets to Saint-Aignan of Orléans, Louis VI placed under the domination of the canons together with "the serfs and servile women who reside in these places," those men or women who "living outside nevertheless depend on the provotship of Artenay." With one exception, however: the King reserved for himself a certain Hugue le Vieux who possessed houses and fields at Artenay. Henceforth he would hold them from the chapter under the same obligations as other tenants. Thus this act mentioned the existence of serfs of Saint-Aignan who would be hôtes of other seigneurs and a royal serf who would be the hôte of Saint-Aignan.[69] Around 1250 the abbot of Saint-Germain-des-Prés, claiming the people of Esmans as his serfs, observed that they "could fix their residence under any seigneur they pleased," providing that they remained subject to the monastic mainmorte and formariage.[70] In 1273, claiming the mainmorte of one of his homme de corps who had lived on another seigneurie, the abbot of Saint-Denis recalled "that it had been impossible to stop this individual from living wherever he wished."[71] This legal rule equally applied when, about ten years later, Beaumanoir noted it in Beauvais where the serfs, he said, so long as they did not escape the duties of their condition, "can go serve or live outside the jurisdiction of their seigneurs."[72]

The problem of "the attachment to the soil" prompted such strange misunderstandings in the current literature that it is advisable to look first to the texts, or at least to the more striking ones. From the eleventh to the thirteenth century no document listed the obligation of a fixed residence among servile characteristics. On the contrary, a great number (as we have just cited) mentioned or anticipated the case of the serf who left the estate of the seigneur of "his body,"[73] not in order to condemn or prevent this departure but rather to note again that the serf, indissolubly attached to his own master, no matter where he went, remained subject to the financial and physical burdens expressing this very personal bond. Thus most seigneurs owned varying numbers of "itinerant" (*forain*) serfs outside the territory they dominated, who caused them great anxiety. Throughout dossiers of procedure, royal privileges, agreements, we glimpse tenacious efforts to safeguard the chevage and the taille,[74] a true servile justice, on these distant subjects. We perceive how good administrators watched for events leading to profits from a fine for formariage or from a substantial échoite of mainmorte. Of course, this incurred many difficulties and expenses.[75] These collections operating on a foreign seigneurie depended on the often doubtful good will of the master of the estate. More than once such seigneurial consent was given for a percentage of the take. This became so often necessary that, in a number of places, these demands became customary.[76] Other lords encouraged their neighbor's serfs, who had become their hôtes, to "disobey";[77] or, as at Borrest, the canons of Sainte-Geneviève, while admitting claims on the movables, instituted in principle that no other person, no matter how high his place—"neither the King, nor his cupbearer, nor even any bishop, church or knight"— could ever raise the mainmorte on the real property of their *mouvance* (fiefs).[78]

Of course, recourse to a superior jurisdiction could restrain the recalcitrant. For a long time political conditions had made this impossible. By the second half of the thirteenth century people became accustomed to bringing disputes of this sort before Parliament.[79] But the procedure was slow and costly. No doubt in the long run many of these "itinerant" serfs escaped the hold of a too distant authority. Those who did not succeed provided little income to their seigneur. Almost always the holder of the seignorial rights over an estate, anxious not to have as a tenant a person of equal rank, required that the property seized by the right of mainmorte should be sold within a year and a day. Sometimes he only tolerated one of his own serfs as buyer, hardly a favorable condition for a fruitful sale.[80] Frequently the seigneurs acted bilaterally to exchange their rights, each one ceding those of his serfs living on the land of the other.[81] It is not surprising, therefore, that toward the beginning of the great enfranchisement movement, the first concessions of liberty were often granted to groups that lived beyond the frontiers of the seigneurie.[82]

In truth, it is not certain that all nonresident serfs had been emigrants. Around the tenth or especially the eleventh century, sometimes even later, many free men willingly subordinated themselves to a powerful man. The most formidable seigneurs thus undoubtedly received allegiance from persons entering voluntary servitude, or who claimed to do so, who had not been their peasants and would never become such. Likewise the donation of one's self to a church was inspired by pious motives. One cannot doubt, however, that among servile families residing outside the land of their master, most had originally lived there. These departures seriously threatened seigneurial interests. To prevent the multiple disadvantages inherent in this, the simplest method would have been to prohibit them. The seigneurs did not reach this conclusion until very late, however. The prohibition against outside residence seems to have first been formulated in the Aquitanian Midi where, as we shall see, the specifically servile tenures were long separated from the whole—a custom foreign to more northern regions. There, despite new discoveries, this rule seems not to have operated until the fourteenth century.[83] Further to the north, this rule, as far as present research can tell, did not appear until the sixteenth century; from then on it is found in various regions.[84] Everything points to the fact that it was not always faithfully respected.[85] Since it did give the seigneurs a most useful juridical weapon, why had recourse to it not occurred sooner?

For such a juridical conception to be applied to the serfs it would have had to have been created during the period of the formation and expansion of serfdom—roughly from the tenth to the twelfth century. Yet the tradition of the preceding period shows no sign of it. Naturally the slave lived wherever his master wished. But, as we shall point out later, most serfs were not descended from slaves, and the fundamental features of their condition suggest precedents quite different from those of slavery.

The *colonus* of the late Empire had been rigorously fixed to "the clods of earth" of his tenure. But the barbarian kingdoms ceased to observe this aspect of imperial law. Carolingian texts never refer to it.[86] The same reasons that earlier had brought about its demise continued to suppress its resurrection. In all societies where the rule of attachment to the soil functioned, more or less badly—whether Roman colonate, French serfdom since the end of the Middle ages, or, closer to our time, in Eastern Europe those forms of peasant subjection we habitually, and somewhat unfortunately, also call serfdom—it was only effective with the intervention of a sovereign authority. It was always singularly difficult to stop a man from leaving. The medieval baron could hardly place a long line of troops around his borders. But where a superior jurisdiction existed, it could call upon a new master who had received the fugitive, or upon the community that had given him refuge, and demand restitution. The weakness of the state had everywhere led to the downfall of this restraint, as in the barbarian kingdoms, or had hindered its establishment for a long time, as in Poland.[87] Let us imagine for a moment the obligation of residence required in principle in feudal France: the parceling out of justice, its reciprocal impenetrability, the absence of any power capable of imposing its will upon the multitude of local dynasts, all would have irremediably emptied it of any practical value. This is why no one even thought of formulating such a rule. Deprived of a learned framework and of a written tradition, born from custom and fixed by so many multiple detailed decisions, the rights of persons in these times, despite all uncertainties and contradictions, was at least profoundly realistic. Later, the knowledge of Roman law would revive the image of the colonate. Political conditions allowed the absorption of one of its rules, henceforth capable of being translated into action. Having become strong enough to capture a fugitive, the royal or princely courts thereby prevented anyone in the seigneurial class from maintaining an interest in the preservation of the ancient freedom to circulate. Thanks to them it became increasingly difficult for anyone to welcome the outsider, to remove him from the authority, even distant, of his legitimate master. The landed seigneurs began to fight against the possessors of serfs, not to further attract immigrants, but on the contrary to repel them in order to prevent the consequent foreign intrusions.[88] Then and only then was the serf truly bound to the soil.[89]

However, the seigneurs had never been entirely without recourse against the departure of their serfs, which was so prejudicial to their interests. Against treacherous but weaker neighbors who made attractive offers, reprisals were always possible.[90] Most often, when recourse to a supreme authority was out of the question, agreements could take its place. The two contracting parties could forbid each other from receiving their respective subjects. Such agreements were always numerous, but they rarely applied exclusively to serfs.[91] Most often they included all peasants, free as well as unfree.[92] The seigneur dreaded the depopulation of his land and became particularly worried if a new settlement on newly cleared land arose next to his own village. He was against emigration in principle, without distinguishing between the juridical status of the emigrants. It is almost superfluous to add that these contracts were not always scrupulously observed. Moreover, lacking sufficient generalization, they could hardly guard against specific dangers. Many seigneurs hesitated to make or respect them because the hope of enrichment in human labor at the expense of neighboring estates prevailed over their own fears of a slow depopulation of their lands.

One other recourse was available to the master concerned about preventing desertions: the confiscations of the emigrant's tenure, or even of his movable goods if he left any behind. Properly speaking, this did not stop departures, but it did make serfs think twice before yielding to temptation. Actually two cases must be carefully distinguished.

If the serf was going far away without any hope of return, his fields inevitably would lay fallow, and the best established customary rules justified their confiscation. Indeed it was commonly accepted that the rights of the tenant lapsed on the day when he ceased to improve his land and thus reduced the dues on it to nothing. In 1201 some men of Saint-Germain-des-Prés—serfs probably—left the village of Esmans and settled in Flagny, which belonged to Queen Adèle. It was stipulated that they would lose their lands held from the abbey if, during a year and a day, they failed to cultivate them.[93] The novelty resided in the precision and the brevity of the stated period; the principle itself was never in doubt.

Often, on the other hand, the serf did not wander far from his birthplace. He wanted to retain his real property there, as he was confident of its continued exploitation either by himself, his family, or by subtenants.[94] Confiscation, if it happened then, had all the force of punishment. In addition it served as one of the constant principles of seigneurial policy: to recruit, as much as possible, tenants exclusively within the same seigneurie, the only persons truly under control.[95] In fact we find this principle increasingly formulated since the end of the twelfth century. But often no distinction was made between the types of personal status of the emigrants, just as in the agreements by which the seigneurs mutually forbade sanctuary to each other's subjects. According to an act of 1167 all hôtes of Saint-Germain-des-Prés, without specification of status, who sought asylum in wartime at Montchauvet in the castle of the lords of Montfort would lose their tenure if they failed to return in peacetime.[96] All peasants or *masoyers* (*mansionarii*) of the abbot of Saint-Basle, by an agreement of 1171, incurred the same penalty if they took up residence on the land of the archbishop at Sept-Saulx.[97] Clearly determined in Burgundy in the first half of the thirteenth century by a series of decisions from the ducal court as well as by miscellaneous customary charters, the rule was extended to "men" of certain abbeys, without any more precision,[98] and to the "taillables" of others;[99] indeed authentic acts of franchise included it.[100]

Nevertheless, serfs were already treated specially. Prompted by usages in "France around Paris," but naturally interpreting them in a sense favorable to baronial interests, northern crusaders united to Simon de Montfort instituted customs on conquered Albigensian land on December 1, 1212, by which the immovables of all the taxpayers, free or not, could be seized should they leave the seigneurie. The criterion drawn from the tax of dependence par excellence was the same as in Burgundy at the same time; the serfs however—the serfs alone—were in addition deprived of their movable goods.[101] Conforming more closely to the principle that was to be adopted in the future, a privilege given by Philip Augustus to the Chapter of Soissons in 1183 marked the antithesis: while the king included *"hôtes* sleeping and rising" as well as serfs in this agreement not to accept dependents of this church in his villages and diocesan communes, the serfs were the only ones whose "possessions" could be appropriated if they went to live on royal land outside the diocesan boundaries.[102] Again, and even more clearly, two charters of Gascon customs, those of Fousseret (1247) and Montoussin (1270) stipulated that anyone established in the bastide could carry his own movables; as for the lands held from another seigneurie he kept them if he was not a homme de corps; he lost them if he was a serf.[103] This increasingly became the general rule. Sometimes, as in most charters of franchise from the Dauphiné, the free man also had to divest himself of his immovables if he left, but he could obtain authorization to sell them at a profit.[104] The return of the tenure to the seigneur at the moment when the tenant ceased to reside on it was thought to involve serfs exclusively, and at the same time became for them a precept of common law. We would like to be able to describe more precisely the stages of this development, but preparatory works are lacking. We touch here upon one of the most shameful characteristics in the historiography of serfdom. Borrowing from recent writings—often in the last analysis from the jurists of the Ancien Régime—a preconceived idea of the institution, and projecting backward in time this same image, too many scholars have failed to seek the evolutionary traces (which they deny in advance), in the living witness of the texts. In this case the result is fairly clear.

His movements heavily constricted by the new rule, the mainmortable of modern times found appreciable compensations in the arrangements it included—not everywhere, however. Where regional or local custom remained faithful to traditional principle, the serfs, even though departure meant deprivation of any further claim to the house and field, could not get rid of any of the burdens attached irrevocably "to his bones," to borrow an image from Guy Coquille. But elsewhere the same abandonment of his plot (*déguerpissement*) freed him from all bonds. The servile stain stigmatized the property rather than the man in this case. Some tenures were considered as reserved for serfs, and to reside on them was to recognize that status.[105] By a natural consequence—not universal but frequent—departure from those tenures equaled freedom.[106] Nothing was more foreign to the feudal age than this territorial servitude.

Indeed, beginning in the Carolingian era, any relation between human status and the land had disappeared. Of course, ninth century "polyptiques" still referred to "servile" manses. This epithet alluded to a conception of serfdom equal to that of ancient slavery. This was merely a memory maintained by certain peculiarities of tenure without relevance to the tenant's person. Once slaves had received these farms from the master the dues or services attached to these lands continued to intimate specific characteristics from its earlier occupants. On the other hand, nothing now prevented the holder from being, in fact, a free man. Likewise many servi lived on *ingénuiles* (free) manses. The exhaustion of Carolingian seigneurial organization abolished even those memories. From the tenth to the thirteenth century the language of the charters totally ignored any expression of servile tenure or any similar formula. The serf was a tenant like any other, subject only to certain changes or appropriate disqualifications imposed upon him by his personal status and, in common with his neighbors, to the obligations attached to his land.

At least such was the case in the France of the *langue d'oïl*. Perhaps it was different in the southeast. There from the thirteenth century on, a whole category of serfs called *de casalage* seemed to be of servile status only by virtue of the tenures they occupied. But nowadays the evolution of southern seigneuries almost absolutely escapes us. The status of men de casalage appears shadowy.[107] All the more reason for being completely unable to decide whether this tie between personal status and that of the land is of recent or ancient vintage. One must be content to circumscribe this overwhelming problem within the clearest lines possible.

However, even in the north, the seigneurs did not favorably view the passage of goods from the fief from one of their serfs to a free man. Not only was the latter less narrowly controllable, but to allow such a transfer was in effect to renounce the mainmorte on the goods involved. From the eleventh century on, as has already been said, enfranchised children tended to lose any claim to servile inheritances. To be truthful, it cannot be a coincidence that the oldest examples of such attempts or measures all involved tenures of a special type. These were small "fiefs" belonging to seigneurial sergeants, men delegated to exercise some part of the master's authority. The lord attempted to choose his representatives exclusively among his more amenable serfs; along with the office, he reserved to them the lands that constituted their salary.[108] Later, however, the rule assumed a general scope. The enfranchisements of the thirteenth century often prohibited any claim to the inheritance from a mainmortable kin. It was a step toward the specialization of servile tenures.[109]

Here and there, by the way, we encounter clearer traces of this tendency, so favorable to the interests of the ruling classes. Any tradition of actual right over a tenure demanded a formal act of *mise en saisine* (seisin), in which the seigneur or his representative participated. At a time when this principle still was fully in force, it was perfectly legitimate, whenever the property concerned was formerly possessed by serfs, to grant the right to this land only to persons who were serfs or who agreed to become serfs. Thus between 1032 and 1084 a certain Bertrand l'Agneau, in order to purchase a house in the abbatial burg from a serf of Marmoutier, had to become a monastic serf.[110] Sometimes a complete group of tenures, as a whole and once and for all, followed this rule. To believe the sergeants of Louis VII such was the particular custom weighing upon certain lands from the royal mouvance bordering Etampes around 1158. Only royal serfs could occupy them. That year it was noticed that a number of purchasers who were not of this status had obtained parcels of land there. These were later confiscated.[111] In order to keep them they would have had only one recourse, as described later in a text of 1179, to accept the law of servitude.[112]

However, the abnormal character of the situation in this little canton of the Ile de France is highlighted by the very act abolishing its singularity: the charter of customs of Etampes of 1179. The reasons impelling the bourgeois to have such an arrangement inserted in their privileges are quite clear: since they were large purchasers of real property adjacent to town, they wished to get rid of any obstacle prejudicial to the extension of their landed fortune. If, in this region where the Capetians owned vast seigneuries and many serfs, other royal lands had also been forbidden to free men, would not our bourgeois have sought to have them also liberated? Or, if by chance this had been refused, would the officers charged with drawing up the charter in the name of the prince have neglected to introduce the necessary reservations? The tenures mentioned in these two texts of 1158 and 1179 were called *huitièmes* (*octaves*) which could hardly be anything but an allusion to a tax equal to an eighth of the harvest. Yet, throughout the surrounding countryside, such produce taxes seemed characteristic of the colonization of newly cleared land widely undertaken by the mid-eleventh century or thereabouts. These were probably a portion of domanial land that, previously uncultivated, had been distributed to colonizers picked from royal serfs on the condition that it would never leave the servile group.[113] No other similar example of restriction on the transfer of lands has been noted for the same period, nor in the following century. And even such cases as that of the churchmen of Marmoutier forcing a particular purchaser to acknowledge himself as their serf are extremely rare and all the more striking since acts registering such admissions have always been among the most jealously preserved.

Thus, although the clearest principles of good seigneurial administration pushed for the formation of specifically servile tenures, and the most stable customary arrangements furnished the means to this end, one discovers, up to the end of the thirteenth century, only a few isolated cases as evidence of such efforts, and these were never united into a cohesive juridical system. Assuredly, the frequency of purchase of servile lands by free men was too low to attract much attention, for in the greater part of France most peasants were serfs, and besides, the economy hardly favored commerce in real property. When, in the course of the thirteenth century, the circulation of money increased, even in the countryside, to an hitherto unknown level, and when, at the same time, following a greater number of affranchisements, a larger number of free families than ever before lived in the midst of servile neighbors, the seigneurs vigorously attempted to provide against transfers that insiduously undermined their rights of mainmorte, indeed even of formariage, both of which were generally proportionate to the wealth of the taxpayer. However, the danger had always been felt, since the servile condition had never included all the dependents. In any case, even if we assume that these numerical considerations suffice to explain the slow evolution of the tenures, they appear powerless to explain another developmental delay, equally characteristic of the history of serfdom. It took many years before the confiscation of property in cases of abandonment of the land became established as a rule. Yet this was the only effective defense against the emigration of serfs. Actually the two phenomena are inseparable.

Certainly, at that time, the idea men had of the servile bond, then in full vigor—this essentially personal bond, of man to man—long prevented its dependency upon the possession of land and made it unlikely that one took very seriously the abandonment of a tenure since the bond was kept intact. But, besides this common juridical thinking, whose influence is guessed at rather than clearly specified, purely material circumstances, easier to seize upon, exercized a probably decisive action. As long as land was more abundant than men, the weapons that the seigneurs might be tempted to turn to in order to reserve the tenures for their serfs or to compel them to reside there would have risked being not only singularly ineffective but there was grave danger that they would have turned against the seigneurs themselves. The fugitive or evicted purchaser could, almost certainly, find identical property elsewhere. On the other hand, what should be done with the confiscated land? Reunite it to the demesne? This would be a paradoxical solution at a time when seigneurs, deliberately abandoning the enlargement of their reserve of direct exploitation or even the maintenance of its former size, only dreamed, for the most part, of its division through repeated leases. Install a new tenant there? But who could be sure of finding one who would settle there? Rather than incurring the risk of leaving fields fallow for many long years for lack of labor, it was best to allow the emigrant, if he could and would, to cultivate it from afar or else to accept a free man as its occupant. Later, when increased population swelled the labor force and the resultant colonization movement rarefied empty spaces, circumstances changed. If the seigneur seized the tenure, he could easily rent it again, sometimes at a profit, or even lease it with a time limit, thus permitting rent increases. Now the serfs knew that once dispossessed they risked wandering at length before finding a new residence, likewise for the buyer or heir who refused to accept serfdom as a condition of investiture. Formerly a simple threat, confiscation now could prove intimidating; once accomplished, it did not infringe on seigneurial revenues and perhaps increased them. The new rules—prohibition of certain tenures to free men, and for the serf the loss of property as a prohibitive fine for departure—gradually entered into seigneurial practice, and practice in turn became law.

Around 1200 then, chevage, prohibition of formariage, and finally mainmorte were the only burdens indicative of serfdom. But to enumerate and describe these exterior characterisitcs does not fully expose the profound essence of serfdom.

The bond uniting the serf to his seigneur was strictly hereditary. It was attached to the man from the moment of birth and except for enfranchisement it followed him everywhere until his death. It was so indissoluble, from master to subject, that anciently, when a seigneur gave or sold a serf, he often began by freeing him. The momentarily liberated individual then, in a formal ceremony, placed himself under the servitude of a new master.[114] This strict bond was perceived as riveted to the person; with honest realism unaccustomed to the refinements of law, it was represented by the physical being, hence the widespread synonym for serf: homme de corps, man of the body. Of popular origin, but quickly adopted by the jurists, this formula was a vivid expression of the rigor of the subjection.[115] In a picturesque commentary on this term an abbot of Vézelay, claiming that a certain André du Marais was his serf, commented in 1166: "he is mine from the soles of his feet to the top of his head."[116] The serfs in turn expected from their seigneurs that most precious commodity in a troubled society: protection. To believe Guiman, the men of Saint-Vaast of Arras, quick to hide and renege on servile payments when all was calm, were, when "the time of tribulation and oppression by the rich" occurred, eager to beg for the "patronage" of the saint and his representative, the abbot.[117] In exchange the "men" owed obedience.

Like all feudal institutions, serfdom developed in a rough atmosphere replete with daily abuses of the law. It is with some reason that alongside of "deceit" Jacques Flach should rank "violence" as a significant characteristic of eleventh-century juridical life.[118] To give a too well ordered image of servile status summed up in a few articles in a code would mean that the historian had failed to communicate all the brutality and arbitrariness permitted in practice when one man had power over another. Provoked by an inhabitant of his village whom he claimed as his *culvert*—the word designated a condition analogous to serfdom and by the first years of the eleventh century tended already to be confused with it—Joël of Mayence in 1124 threatened this recalcitrant subject with despoliation of his land and even death by fire. Undoubtedly more than one member of his class thought and expressed the same thing. It was, however, certainly against the law. Thus, nothing of the kind happened; a monetary settlement ended the quarrel,[119] like so many others, but not all. We possess a genealogy drawn up in the eleventh century of a servile family in the Angevin region, evidently used to establish a servile claim. This is a peaceful judiciary document of the kind found more than once in the archives, but here is the last notation: "Nive who was murdered by Vial, her seigneur."[120] A criminal act, assuredly, a simple news item that at the same time like a flash of lightning illuminates a highly colored background too often hidden by the cold language of the charters. At the beginning of the twelfth century, due to the scarcity of wine in the cellars of Saint-Père of Chartres, the monks, rather than buy wine abroad, suspended the customary distributions to their sergeants. The latter complained that this decision deprived them of part of their salary. The court, probably composed of the vassals of the abbey, decided against them "for this reason above all," said the account drawn up by the monks, "that several of the sergeants being attached to us by the bond of servitude, it was lawful for us, in case of need, to use them for our tasks as we see fit."[121] The decision was probably not impartial; jurisprudence presents few similar cases. Servile duties were already fixed then by custom that in principle was imposed upon the seigneur as well as his own men. The rigorous conception of servile dependence expressed in the decision of the Chartrian judges reveals nonetheless the ideas circulating among seigneurial circles.[122]

The power of this bond was interpreted by much more regular juridical practices. Around 1224 the sons of the lord of Gallardon had mutilated two serfs probably employed as artisans by the chapter of Chartres. For want of a superior authority capable of ruling on such differences between two highly placed persons, the affair was submitted to one of those frequent arbitrations, in this case under the aegis of the chancellor of France, Guérin Bishop of Senlis. Three sanctions, characteristic of penal law of the period in general, and that of the serfs in particular, were imposed on the criminals. Disturbing the peace was punished by public penitance. An annual compensatory rent had to be paid to the victims now incapable of earning a living, proof that the serf, differing from the slave of yore, was endowed with his own juridical personality. Finaly, beside a sum of money, the culprits handed over a serf from Gallardon, a shoemaker by trade, to the canons since their own artisans could no longer work. Thus the wound sustained by the homme de corps injured as well his own seigneur.[123]

Above all, the particular judicial situation in which the serf was placed attested to the narrow bonds of his dependence. Generally, nothing was more complicated or less efficacious than feudal judicial organization. Many reasons contributed to perpetuate such chaos. This one among others: on all sides the personal and real bonds became confused, too often encumbering the question of predominance and leading to legal conflicts. The surface of the kingdom was split up in multiple divisions of low and high justice, the latter a little less numerous since some of them contained, each, several seigneuries of small judges. But different categories of dependents partially escaped these territorial authorities: the vassals subject to the lord who had received their homage; the sergeants—functionaries, if not simple domestics—whose employer claimed to be under his sole authority; finally the serfs who everywhere fell under the hand of their own masters. Undoubtedly, this last rule suffered in practice from some difficulties. If the serf had left the estate, upon which his seigneur exercised direct authority, it was no easier for this distant superior to arraign him before his own tribunal than, for example, to levy the taille or collect the mainmorte from him. In a laudable attempt at simplification, Parliament declared around the middle of the thirteenth century that henceforth the royal serfs "would be judged by the seigneurs whose lands they inhabit."[124] So much wisdom was exceptional. Truthfully such a renunciation of distant jurisdiction on the "outsider" might be an abdication of that authority that was the very essence of serfdom. It might risk the loss of mainmorte patrimonies in the profitable game of compensation and confiscation. Energetically defended by many barons and churches, the principle that made the original seigneur the obligatory judge of a serf, wherever he may be, remained very much alive until the end of the thirteenth century and beyond, not without the usual diversity from small locality to small locality wrought by the custms "of the country" and by formal agreements. Some documents seem to give the seigneur the right of jurisdiction without any exception, over his absent serfs.[125] This surely exceeds reality. For a current maxim held that any landowner could judge his tenant concerning his tenure. Under such imprecise formulae undoubtedly were dissimulated rules of authority similar to those clearly specified elsewhere. Sometimes the serf's seigneur took cognizance of all lawsuits regarding property.[126] Above all, it was commonly agreed (with the single exception here and there of a flagrant offense) that "bodily" or "blood" justice—i.e., crimes involving the death penalty[127] with the usual corollary permitting, for whatever reason, a judicial duel[128]—could only be applied to the serf by the seigneur whose homme de corps he actually was. Evidently, no one had to ask if the master was a high judge, i.e., if he exercised similar power over simple hôtes. Little mattered the place of the crime or the rank of the seigneurial court in the oridinary judicial hierarchy.[129] The serf's flesh belonged only to the one to whom he was attached by a quasi-physical bond.

However, this serf who was so rigorously subordinated to another man was not a slave, as the very obligations characterizing his status attest. Within certain limits fixed by custom, which the seigneurs could not transgress without abuse of power, he was the master of his person and property. In principle he could marry within his own group according to his wish. As a victim of a violent act he had the right to a special indemnity, which was not confused with that benefitting his own seigneur. The chevage in particular was distinct from ancient slavery: to demand each year a perpetually fixed part of a patrimony was to imply the existence of this patrimony and that its possession was guaranteed by more than simple tolerance.

In fact we even find alodial landholders among the serfs. One difference singled them out from alodial landholders of free birth. The latter could dispose of the land without anyone's permission. On the contrary, the serf had to obtain the consent of the seigneur who received his servile dues. Not that the latter, properly speaking, had any right to this fraction of land freed by definition of any mouvance. But any diminution of his homme de corps's wealth was subject to his approval because it might infringe on his inheritance privileges.[130]

Most serfs, however, just as the immense majority of humble people, only owned houses and fields in villeinage, i.e., subject to the superior right of a territorial seigneur to whom they paid, as property holders, different taxes and services.[131] Most often the seigneur of the land and the seigneur of the man were one. Nevertheless, they could be different, as we have already seen on several occasions. Juridical wisdom in this case knew quite well how to mark the necessary discriminations between the personal bond and the material bond. "I give ... a manse at Estiveau which holds the villein Espiuns, with all its appurtenances, except for the villein himself, his wife, sons, and daughters farming the manse, for they are not mine." Thus reads a charter drawn up in Cluny between 1049 and 1109.[132] Simply, when this duality of dependence occurred in earlier times any delivery of the tenure needed the consent of both seigneurs. The consent of the landed seigneur was always required. As for the personal seigneur the necessity of his intervention (here as for the alods) proceeded from his role as eventual heir.[133] Later, the weakening of the servile bond seems to have rapidly lead to the practice of neglecting this second authorization. Subject to the indispensable seigneurial investiture, these property transfers were perfectly legal, and the charters furnish more than one example of them. "As *hommes de corps* they could buy, sell, give away their property, save the right of the church," proclaimed a judgement by which Henri, Bishop of Senlis, forced the inhabitants of Rosny-sous-Bois, between 1182 and 1185, to acknowledge themselves as serfs of Sainte-Geneviève.[134]

By far the greatest number of tenures in villeinage (those of serfs as well as others), maintained a perpetual character protected by custom. From the eleventh century on, a number of texts classify those serfs under the name, *heredes*—i.e., possessors of hereditary title—or style their lands as inheritances.[135] Others show the serf inheriting from his father[136] or endowing his daughter.[137] Further, the very exercise of the rights of mainmorte, in those cases where the seigneur was in competition with the kinsmen, assumed the existence of regular inheritance procedures that, as we know, went for the most part according to normal customary rules.[138] Such an institution was absolutely opposed to the very notion of slavery.

The serfs, besides, had access to the most important social functions from which the servi had once been excluded. The public tribunals of yesteryear were changed into seigneurial courts on which the serfs readily sat as judges.[139] Sometimes, as at Corbie, they were all convoked to the judicial assembly,[140] or else if, as at Saint-Vaast of Arras, appearance constituted an obligation proper to certain tenures, such specialized property was ordinarily in the hands of serfs.[141] This was, after all, a kind of office attached to a land. We know that the seigneurs always preferred to pick their sergeants from among their own serfs. The barons took their serfs into combat with them. Philip Augustus called to arms the hommes de corps of the royal churches as well as his own men.[142] In fact, serfdom was so widespread at this point that if courts and armies had had to rule out servile men, one can hardly conceive how they could have been constituted. The barriers that in the Carolingian period had so brutally separated persons deprived of "liberty" from the rest of the people, had come down very far.

In any case thirteenth century jurists generally recognized this antinomy between slavery of yore and contemporary serfdom in its daily application. Writers of mediocre intelligence such as the author of *Jostice et Plet* could well disguise patchwork borrowings from the servile law of the Justinian code. On the contrary, the best were bothered by the very word servus, which, depending upon whether one found it in ancient Roman texts or in contemporary charters, had highly different meanings. Beaumanoir deemed it necessary to begin his study of serfdom with a description whose features are obviously borrowed both from books on ancient slavery and from accounts told to him of certain slaves in his own time in "foreign lands," Syria or the Levant, no doubt. He said in substance that there were "serfs" whose seigneur could take all their property and be responsible only to God. But, he hastened to add, these were not the serfs in Beauvaisis whose condition was fixed by custom.[143] In order to prevent any misunderstanding and although everyday language, unafraid of confusion with Roman law, continued to use daily the word serf, many notaries henceforth carefully avoided servus, judged inconveniently equivocal, and replaced it in deeds by various synonyms, notably homme de corps.

In Europe, slavery, in the strict sense of the word, had not entirely disappeared. Religious precepts forbade anyone to subject prisoners of war to this state when they were of the Catholic faith. On the other hand, it was permitted without difficulty for infidels or schismatics. Even baptism would not save them or their descendants. Too far removed from the two great sources of this traffic in human cattle, the Slavonic east and the basin of the Mediterranean, northern and central France contained few slaves. Here and there, some high baron, such as Gaudri, Bishop of Laon, might have a Negro in his following. In Mediterranean France, on the other hand, especially when, around the twelfth century, the renaissance in overseas commerce expanded the use of this exotic commodity, as well as of many others, the number of slaves was not absolutely negligible. They served as domestics. By the end of the thirteenth century and perhaps in imitation of the Italians, they were called by a name that recalled the origin of many of them and that gradually slipped from its ethnic meaning to a purely juridical one: slaves, i.e., Slavs. Progressively the word penetrated the French vocabulary, dissipating the ambiguous terminology that not long before had troubled Beaumanoir. Between slavery and serfdom, which the great jurists had labored to distinguish, everyday speech henceforth marked the contrast of a vigorously accentuated trait.

However different the serfs were from the slaves of old, they were still deprived of that concept called "liberty." And from this deprivation resulted several serious consequences. As early as the fifth century, the Church had closed entrance to holy orders to slaves; how could a priest be the object of a temporal master? It treated serfs in the same manner until enfranchisement, when they ceased to be serfs. In both cases the words were similar: *servus, servitus*. That alone had sufficed, no doubt, to entail assimilation since any distinction would have meant an audacious break with the letter of the texts whose antiquity made them particularly respectable in the eyes of the canonists. The idea was further dismissed since, although serfdom had none of the characteristics of strict slavery, the subjection of the homme de corps to his own seigneur was strong enough to be incompatible with the independence necessary for servants of God. This ecclesiastical incapacity seemed so significant that it readily figured, along with mainmorte and the prohibition of formariage among the criteria of servile status recognized by the law.[144] It perpetuated the idea of a sort of hierarchical inferiority where, vis-à-vis free men, the serf was confined.

Serfdom in fact presented this double character truly essential to its nature of being at one and the same time a bond between men and a class institution. The serf was not only a subject who depended on a more powerful man, he seemed tarnished by a "stain" that made him contemptible: *servitutis dedecus*. His name was an insult whose incorrect use drew down severe punishment from the courts.[145] Throughout France serfs could not testify—at least in the lay courts—when the litigants were free men. This law was only bent in favor of royal serfs and those of certain churches where custom or a formal concession from the king recognized this privilege. There again, precedent, comprised of general rules and their exceptions, went back to the laws regarding slavery such as they existed in the Frankish period.[146] This abased state was not expressed only by juridical criteria, far from it. If it is always true, even in our own day, that a feeling of membership in the same social class means, first of all, accepting intermarriage between two families, then the *servaille* (as one said willingly, when one did not belong to it) certainly did not form an absolutely unified class in this sense. It counted among its members some rich as well as many poor, and especially within this immense majority of humble people, a few individuals whose power of command, reflections of seigneurial authority, stood way above the crowd. Numerous acts attest that the lineages of servile seigneurial sergeants—equivalent in France to the *Dienstmänner* in Germany—tended to marry exclusively among themselves from seigneurie to seigneurie. Sometimes, endowed with a kind of solid prestige, they succeeded in uniting with free lineages.[147] But there is no doubt that the servile population in its entirety stood out as a distinct human bloc from the rest of society because of its matrimonial practices. From the servile ranks a complaint, which the dryness of the texts cannot stifle, rises up to the historian rummaging in old archives. The free peasants, their neighbors, refused to marry them. To marry a male or female serf meant in fact, according to almost universally observed custom, demotion into serfdom; in any case it was condemning the children to it. And no doubt self-serving motives can easily explain the repugnance to submit to this yoke, or to allow one's kin to submit—this resistance often came from the parents. The parents and half-brothers and sisters on the father's side would lose thereby all hope of collecting one day an inheritance henceforth tainted with mainmorte. But it is also probable that the idea of group honor was also present here.[148]

Finally, in order to leave this rigorously inherited condition, a single legal road lay open to the serf: enfranchisement. By its very name, manumission, by its rites sometimes—there were enfranchisements *par le denier* as late as Louis VI,[149] some manumissions "in ecclesia" around the same time[150]—and often by its formulation, enfranchisement was presented as the direct heir to acts of liberation for slaves whose principles Carolingian law had borrowed sometimes from Roman and sometimes from German tradition.

Why then did several marks of ancient slavery remain attached to men who were not slaves? Why were they still declared strangers to liberty?

THE GENESIS OF SERFDOM AND THE IDEA OF LIBERTY.

Before getting to the heart of the problem we should clear away some equivocation and one oversimplistic explanation.

It has been evident to historians that the medieval serf's status did not correspond to those characters often held by legal theoreticians—mostly inspired by the Roman example—to constitute the absence of liberty. Anxious to avoid what they regarded as an abuse of language, some have believed it necessary to define this condition, which seemed to slip away from the habitual juridical framework, by a hybrid expression that they themselves forged. They used the word "half-free" and they extended this same epithet to different classes of the Frankish period, notably to the coloni. Such a formidable confusion—for the colonate sprang from completely different ideas from serfdom—would suffice to denounce the awkward formula. The main danger, however, resides in its anachronism. In the Middle Ages—and no more under Philip Augustus than under Charlemagne—no one ever used it. In law a man then was free or he was not. One could in a particular case doubt if he was one or the other, for personal status was often difficult to establish. One could even, at times, especially when serfdom was being formed, wonder if certain forms of subjection were compatible with liberty or not. But no intermediary solution was envisaged. "Although on earth," said one Saumur charter of the eleventh century, "the human race issued from the same origin ... nevertheless the law of the tribunals has willed that some are called free, others are either serfs or culverts."[151] The historian should not substitute his own doctrine for that of the past. Confronted with a juridical term, his role is not to seek whether this word was well or badly used; a linguist might as well decide that the French were terribly wrong when they gave the meaning of the Latin *arare*, for example, to the Romance descendants of *laborare*. Rather his job should be to establish period by period the chain of meanings according to the eminently changeable times. With regard to the serfs whom everyone called unfree, to speak of half-free, willfully neglecting the role of evolution which should be studied, is to mask the very problem of serfdom.

Is it, however, quite exact to think that the contrast between liberty and its counterpart was clearly felt and perfectly marked? Some have doubted it. The idea of liberty, they say on the contrary, lacked true juridical precision for medieval men; it carried an infinity of gradations: man was not absolutely free, he was more or less free. This is simple misunderstanding founded on the inevitable, omnipresent ambiguity of language. In an organized society the individual is never fully free in the absolute sense of the word, even more so in a medieval society where there were multiple powers of authority. The concept of personal liberty—"corporal" liberty was the term in the Middle Ages[152]—is quite another thing. I consider myself to be a free man, but as a university professor, while I am "free" for example vis-à-vis the state to use my vacation as I please, I am not free to fail in my teaching during the school year. When I have to interrupt that activity I must ask the competent authority to "free" me from it. Forgive me for these truisms. It must be understood that they would have appeared as such to the men of ancient France. The same double usage was familiar to them. They willingly designated under the rubric of "liberties" or "franchises" those charters that, without modifying the personal status of their beneficiaries, whether they were serfs or not, freed them, wholly or partly, from miscellaneous obligations such as the corvées, the seigneurial right to hospitality, the seigneurial right to merchandise on credit. They knew very well that these were not manumissions, and did not ignore that to be of free status and to be free to do something constituted two different juridical realities.

By still another bias this too emphatic word, liberty, was sometimes diverted from its precise meaning. Clerics drew up all ancient charters, and one idea above all was dear to these pious redactors: true liberty was obedience, so long as it was to God, his saints, and to the devout communities that represented them on earth. "To pass from the subjection of a secular power to the seigneurie of the church is like becoming quasi-free since it means escape from the scorpions of domination in this century," wrote a bishop of Soissons in 1175.[153] A little more than one hundred years before, a monk from Vendôme wrote: "Freedom according to the world is not liberty; it is only a fallacious image. True nobility is voluntary submission to the Creator."[154] These feats of language appeared all the more natural since in virtue of the immunity claimed with more or less success from the temporal powers, the ecclesiastical seigneuries qualified themselves willingly as "libertés"—meaning exempt lands. For Guiman, if marriage with one woman from another "law" was forbidden in principle to the men of chevage (*censuales*) of his abbey (men whom we know the chancellaries never hesitated to treat as serfs), the reason was that the hereditary dependence was transmitted by the womb, and the children issued from such a union escaped the liberté of Saint-Vaast.[155] Some scholars have stumbled over the obliging fictions of church notaries because they took them much too seriously. And wrongly so. For the compilers never claimed to express juridical realities. The monks who contraposed the "free servitude toward the Creator" to the "servile liberty of the world"[156] did not wish to conceal that secular law firmly considered the former as plain servitude. The same act of Vendômois subjection already cited, which shows a lad so joyfully surrendering an empty image of liberty, took care to expressly mention that "in regard to men" subordination adorned with these flowers would not be entirely a "nobility" but, with no possible equivocation, "a servile yoke."

One could argue that serfs appeared to be deprived of personal liberty only as the result of a kind of habitual vocabulary. Let us suppose that the condition of the slave gradually eased; incapable of following a slow, almost imperceptible transformation, speech patterns persisted in their error and continued to apply the servile epithet to men who, step by step, arrived at a stage where they no longer merited it. If such was truly the case, nothing could be more foolish than to search for a new content to the idea of deprivation of liberty as it existed in the twelfth and thirteenth centuries. Such an idea would be properly void of any substance. Such an explanation evidently rests on two postulates: that the serfs thus conceived as the heirs to a name whose meaning became progressively anemic descended in their immense majority from servi of former days who were legitimate carriers of that title, and that serfdom itself was only an ameliorated slavery. Yet neither one nor the other thesis withstands the tests of reality.

There were few servi in the Carolingian period. Since the Roman era, multiple enfranchisements had thinned their ranks. Conceived as a pious deed, these acts of liberation were also favored by developments within the social structure and the economy. The great latifundia cultivated by gangs of slaves had never completely covered the soil of the Roman world; still they were abundant there. Everywhere a different exploitation founded on tenure replaced the old system: the tenant paid taxes and by means of the corvées furnished the largest part of manual labor necessary to improve the lands reserved for direct cultivation, which were still quite large. Besides, the strength and prestige of the powerful rested on the number of free dependents gathered about them rather than on the number of slaves they owned. Yet the great majority of manumissions, granted under the condition of "obedience" (*obsequium*), left their beneficiaries in a narrow enough subjection vis-à-vis the old master or eventually a church to which the latter had given his rights. The enfranchised, on the other hand, often already a tenant when still servile, usually saw no reason to abandon the land that had supported him, even had he been able to. At any rate he was at least as useful as a slave. However, to the handful of servi enumerated on the seigneurial rent-lists toward the end of the Frankish period, were opposed, some centuries hence, the innumerable serfs of Capetian France, with the exception of Normandy. Several statistics sharply illuminate this contrast. At Thiais, in the Parisis, around the death of Charlemagne, of 146 heads of families dependent upon Saint-Germain-des-Prés there were 11 servi; nearby at Villeneuve-Saint-Georges they constituted 14 out of 132. Under Philip Augustus almost all the population were serfs in these two villages. At Esmans in Senonais at the beginning of the ninth century there were no servi; in the thirteenth century—even with the intervening enfranchisement of 1289—almost everyone was a serf there.[157] There is no doubt: around 1200 the greatest number of serfs, had they been able to trace their genealogy back to the reigns of the great Carolingian emperors, would have discovered as ancestors coloni, *lites*, enfranchised small free-holders, in a word, men considered then as legally "free."

As for the fundamental burdens of serfdom, several reveal themselves as entirely foreign to the slaves of old, not only by their very spirit, as we have already seen, but also by their history.

Let us leave aside the prohibition of formariage, an inevitable consequence of hereditary dependence: Who would have received the children of a marriage between husband and wife belonging to two different seigneurs?[158] Thus the oldest examples we know of this rule relate to colons in the Eastern Empire at the time of Justinian and on the domains of the Roman Church at the time of Gregory the Great; from the reign of Charles the Bald the rule covered all the subjects of the seigneurie—*mancipia* said the capitulary; the context proves here that the term must be understood in its wider sense—in a word to men who, destined for the most part to found servile families, were not, by far, all servi.[159]

The history of the chevage is quite instructive. It is encountered as early as the Frankish period, being paid, as later on, in silver, wax, or workdays. But although owed already here and there by truly servile persons, it hardly pertained only to them; the greatest number of subjects who paid it belonged legally to the free class. It constituted, in fact, the characteristic tax of the *mundium*, i.e., of the protection and authority exercised by a powerful man over his subordinates. Most enfranchised notably paid it to the old master to whom they remained attached by hereditary obedience or to a church to which this person had delegated his own powers. Along with them were many humble people who, believing that they were retaining their freedom, placed themselves under the domination of a stronger or richer man.[160] It is also to those two categories of dependents that the first cases discovered of fixed taxes on inheritance are applied in the ninth century.[161] Just as the servile class included many people without slave origins, so did serfdom as an institution present a great number of traits that did not even vaguely reflect ancient slavery.

The originality of the character of the new servitude clearly stands out in the following evolutionary detail, which has all the value of a crucial experience.

Among the descendants of the enfranchised "with obedience," which a rigid subordination attached with their posterity to the original master or to his beneficiaries, the greatest number undoubtedly had gradually slipped into serfdom. In several regions, however, some of these families while being under similar burdens to those weighing on the serfs had preserved at least verbal vestiges of their ascendants's status. The Latin charters called these people *colliberti*, in French, *culverts*, i.e., etymologically, "enfranchised."; and they were considered a class different from the serfs and were probably judged superior. According to their distant origin, they should have been looked upon as free. To deny this quality to sons of the enfranchised was apparently illogical. However, since juridical classifications were not solely based on precedent, but on the contrary reflected above all the present, while distinguishing by a kind of concession to the past the culverts from the serfs, they were considered, on the same basis as serfs, to be unfree. We have seen how vigorously a Saumur charter marked them with this stain. The principle was universally recognized; in order to leave their status, as for others to leave serfdom, it was necessary for them to obtain a new manumission without taking any account of the earlier enfranchisement. By the essential features of their rank they appeared deprived of the characteristics that henceforth determined freedom. In the course of the twelfth century even a purely nominal discrimination between culvert and serf gradually disappeared. The two names became synonyms and the culverts thus melted into the servile mass, already welding together so many miscellaneous elements.[162]

Without doubt then, throughout the ages, the resonance of the word liberty and of its opposite had changed. It is advisable to inquire into the new realities behind the old expressions.

By scrutinizing more closely the Carolingian texts and preferably those documents closest to daily practice, we easily perceive that the idea of servitude was already undergoing transformations. It is language, through its subtle shifts of meaning, which offers us the clearest mirror of these apparently unconscious changes. To designate the slave, Gallo-Roman speakers willingly used an old, probably Celtic word, latinized into *vassus* or *vassalus*. Under the Carolingians the term gradually came to signify commended men of free condition, a new kind of dependence in many respects and for which, consequently, the traditional vocabulary did not furnish any adequate expression. As for the slave's status itself, two abstract noun, in classical Latin, were used practically interchangeably: *servitus, servitium*. During the barbarian era and more particularly in the Carolingian period, both frequently appeared altered from their strict meaning. Servitus denoted dependent relations that, by definition, left personal liberty intact: the "obedience" of the enfranchised in sixth- and seventh-century Visigothic texts[163] and under Charlemagne in documents originating from the Frankish state (here, precisely, they concerned lites, most of whom were enfranchised or descendents of enfranchised)[164] in a charter from 926 the bond, singularly more lax, which united a person of high military class (*miles*) to the abbey from which he had received land *in precarium*.[165]

But the evolution of servitium above all proved profound and lasting. Favored perhaps by a widespread use in classical Latin of the corresponding verb *servire*, it resulted in definitely emptying the word of any specifically servile content. Here and there no doubt the redactor of a capitulary, influenced by his reading of classical authors, maintained its old meaning.[166] These were exceptional cases. Ordinarily, servitium indicated the obligations proceeding from a subjection, whatever its nature, especially, but not exclusively, the obligations of deed rather than those of payment; the French "service" probably perpetuates this last meaning. With a free man, the correct term was *officium*, but it had fallen into disuse. A commended person who expressly maintained the earlier liberty of his condition in his new status, pronounced the following scandalous contradiction in the ninth century: "*ingenuili ordine tibi servicium ... inpendere debeam.*"[167]

A similar distortion had affected the very word servus. Certainly, it kept in many texts its precise juridical value. But usage obviously tended to attribute to it at the same time a broader and looser meaning. Under this name were jumbled all dependents of the seigneurie: coloni, lites, enfranchised, even humble retainers, as well as slaves. As early as 745, Pope Zachary had thus used it.[168] The two meanings of the term—one conforming to strict law, the other to everyday speech—are illuminated by the clumsy frankness of a Bavarian charter. "I give" said a certain Hilderoh " ... two of my servi employed as honey gatherers; one is free, the other is a servus and both their women are slaves."[169] Likewise the expression for "servile works," *opera servilia*, had come to designate the tenant's corvées in general, so that without bothering about contradictions, an abbot of Saint-Gall could write in 821 about a precarial holder of free status and his family: "they owe us the same servile work as other free men [of the same place]."[170] A similar extension of meaning characterized the history of *mancipium*, once a very strong synonym for servus. As early as the eigth and ninth centuries it was applied to free and enfranchised subjects.[171] But here the disappearance of the original semantic content was carried so far that finally among the only Gallo-Roman speakers who had saved it—those of *langue d'oc*—the word lost all relationship with any personal status whatsoever: *massip* in Provencal meant an employee or a valet. Protected no doubt by its obvious bonds with *servir* and its derivatives, serf escaped this complete debilitation. Throughout its evolution, class value affected it, but this value changed.

The tendency to assimilate all seigneurial dependents to the servi quickly went beyond the level of language. In other words the uncertainties of the vocabulary only mirrored an imperceptible evolution of juridical ideas that sooner or later had to influence practice. A great number of tenures on the seigneuries of Frankish Gaul were occupied by colons. However narrowly subjected these were, more than ever, to the authority of the master whose fields they cultivated, they nevertheless were regarded, in conformity with Roman tradition, as officially free. They swore an oath to the king. In cases of crime they were arraigned directly before the comital *mallum*, the only exceptions being for those who lived on an estate immune from comital or other jurisdiction, but the same reservation generally held for all free men. They sat, beside noblemen, on a tribunal of immunity, constituted certainly in the image of a tribunal of public law. However, the practical shackles attached to their independence prevented—as had been already the case in the late Empire—their classification as equals with other free men. Alaman law, which defined the Church's colon *liber ecclesiae*, declared no less expressly that in marriage he could not be coequal with a woman born in true liberty.[172] The language of the seigneurial rent-rolls so attached to traditional classifications, betrays some curious uncertainties as early as the ninth century. The polyptique of Saint-Rémi flatly treated the colons as ingénuiles (free), but that of Saint-Germain-des-Prés, while distinguishing them very clearly from the servi, and while qualifying the manses originally assigned to them as ingénuiles, set them in a special category apart from purely free men. Previously, what distinguished them from the latter had been the bond to the soil which made them "slaves of the land," rather than of a man. The disappearance of this rule led, on the contrary, to their being considered as primarily the subjects of a seigneur who, one readily said, borrowing from Germanic legal language, held them under his *mithium*. They shared this subordination with tenants of servile birth. The latter, due to the very fact that each one was assigned his own practically hereditary farm, in practice increasingly deviated from the original condition of slavery. Gradually the confusion between these two classes gained ground. From the end of the fifth century perhaps, by the sixth in any case, when a master wished to liberate his colonus from the burdens weighing upon him, he often borrowed the rites and the name of enfranchisement. Later, Charles the Bald applied corporal punishment, until then, with only a few exceptions, reserved for slaves, to coloni guilty of miscellaneous crimes.[173] In the ninth century (unfortunately it is impossible to be more precise), an official document—not, in fact, a great legislative ordinance but a simple response given by the Palace to a juridical question raised by a *missus*—declared that marriage between colons belonging to different masters must be submitted to the same principles governing the servi; for, added the text, expressing by a formula borrowed from the Breviary of Alaric a conception that certainly seemed to more and more correspond to the realities of the time, "there are only two kinds of men: the free and the *servi*."[174] The last stage of this evolution is, once again, to be revealed through the history of language. Servus, collibertus, even mancipium survived in Gallo-Roman speech, while colonus did not.

In sum, the impression one receives from Carolingian documents is one of dissonance, eternal no doubt in its nature, but rarely so perceptible. On one hand traditional law was still eminently respectable and forceful; on the other hand stood day-by-day law. Legislation and seigneurial rent-rolls, undoubtedly imitative of fairly archaic models, drew their inspiration from social classifications inherited from the past. Not, incidentally, without many hesitations witnessed especially in the divergencies one sees from census to census. Witness, for example, the groping evident in the charters of immunity, painfully enumerating the different status of men living on immune territory,[175] or again the imprecise list that a council of 813 tried to make of the "different ranks" within the bosom of the Christian church.[176] This catalogue of juridical values was horribly complicated in and of itself, if only because of its sometime Roman, sometime Germanic origin. Try to imagine the difficulties involved in classifying the enfranchised "with obedience." If he belonged to Frankish law he must in principle be ranked among the lites; sometimes, in fact, he was. Often, however, one was content to call him *libertus*, just as in Roman law. But as the enfranchised from one or the other law, in fact, remained tenants, and became free tenants, they were also sometimes called colons.[177] Between these different human categories whose members lived side by side and frequently intermarried, some contamination of law and language was inevitable. Witness the word enfranchisement, applied to the act discharging a colonus from his obligations, or the ecclesiastical application of the rule forbidding the slave entrance into holy orders to the coloni and to the enfranchised *cum obsequio*.[178] However, in this chaos, new relations appeared to which justice was, more or less, awkwardly rendered. The authors of the polyptique of Saint-Germain-des-Prés carefully noted whether a particular individual was a colonus, a lite, a servus, or quite simply "free." But the main preoccupation of the clerics was to find out whether the person thus counted depended or not on the abbey; for, to speak as they did—using a term whose meaning was evident in a Merovigian edict[179] and whose great force was maintained throughout the Middle Ages—in the presence of each peasant, it was necessary for them to prove that he was the "man" of the saint. The two terminologies, one more suggestive and traditional, the other more simple and realistic, began to intersect each other. Was it a matter of a particularly narrow subordination? It was readily expressed in the most rigorous vocabulary of the former subjection: slavery, from whence came the new meanings of vassus and servitium and even servus. But here, that word stained with an indelible mark of inferiority, although it included many dependents who were not slaves remained limited to a relatively humble social stratum.

The tenth and the eleventh centuries were periods of great social disorder and renewal. The king no longer demanded the oath from his subjects. Although the judicial organization continued to carry the marks of the system formerly vigorously established by the Carolingians, the great majority of courts were seigneurial, if not in origin, at least in function and spirit. Most Frenchmen recognized only their seigneur as a military leader; it is through him that the troops destined for the royal host itself or for the great territorial princes were raised. For a long time the institutions of public law, treating men qualified as free quite differently from those who were not, had helped save some practical strength for the ancient idea of liberty, despite the irresistible evolution of the bonds of dependence. Now this too disappears. Social rank could be determined only through the particular aspect of the single bond still retaining a concrete value; that which more or less rigidly subordinated a man to his seigneur.

Besides, the old written laws—Roman or barbarian laws, ordinances of Frankish sovereigns—had gradually slipped into oblivion. Their integrity was no longer maintained through teaching since almost nowhere in France, as opposed to Italy, were these texts regularly commented upon. Certainly the rules once handed down continued to affect practice; but they exerted influence only insofar as they were picked up by custom, which often deformed them. Tribunals judged without reference to the texts. For the most part the men who sat on courts did not know how to read. Even if they were, perchance, capable of it, or if they decided to call upon a reader, they still, ordinarily, could not refer to the ancient laws since they could not understand the terminology. Copying or paraphrasing a ninth-century rent-roll, a Chartrian monk a little after 1078 was astonished to encounter dues absolutely different from those he was accustomed to.[180] Deprived of all stable components of a juridical framework—schools, textbooks, legislation—deprived in effect of the solid supports that in the same period prevented the Church, this society apart, from deviating excessively from traditional roads and preserved its ecumenical character, the laymen's law during these troubled and ignorant centuries left considerable room for arbitrariness, uncertain jurisprudence, and the infinite variety of local usages. On the other hand, it showed a flexibility often refused to more sophisticated legal systems that remain much narrower prisoners of past formulas. It responded easily to the social needs and the exigencies of common opinion. Similar, as I have already observed elsewhere, to a language lacking literature and grammarians—like Latin after the collapse of the Empire or English after the Norman Conquest up to the thirteenth century—it simplified its classifications, notably those regarding personal status. Around 1200 in documents illustrating different types of status, there is no longer that incredible complication shown in the ninth century seigneurial rent-lists.

But simplification does not imply imprecision. In the Carolingian period the idea of servitude confused with that of dependence could have lost all its value. Soon, however, the perception grew that two profoundly distinct categories of subjection had developed side by side. One was not inherited and in principle at least assumed the free consent of the subordinate. The other, on the contrary, bound the man willy-nilly, from his birth, and in fact because of it.

In the first group were ranked primarily the military vassals allied to their seigneur by the old gesture of homage, accompanied by an oath of religious character: the *faith*. This double rite only obligated the two persons who met face to face. Ill advised certainly was the seigneur who, deprived by death of a vassal, failed to demand new homage from the deceased's sons: to allow such gradual exhaustion of his powers of command rapidly diminished his own power and prestige. Besides, how could the sons not want to swear fidelity to the seigneur whom their father had served? Once the seigneur was lowered into his grave, how could the vassal not willingly rally around the dead lord's heir? Not only did the need for protection counsel such steps, not only did an obscure sentiment of family loyalty frequently motivate them, but an economic consideration ordinarily prompted them more than any other motive. Most vassals lived on fiefs held from the seigneur upon condition of homage; any refusal to swear allegiance involved the loss of these estates or the right to receive them in inheritance. Although vassalage became increasingly patrimonial in character, it remained, in law, a mutually lifelong bond that the death of one or the other contractor sufficed to break. To retie the knot, a new homage was necessary each time.

Between the landed seigneur and the peasant who, without being his serf was still his villein or his hôte (i.e., held from him land on which he owed taxes, services, and the general obligations of aid and obedience), the relationship was equally deprived of any truly hereditary mark. In fact, as soon as a man abandoned his fields, dependance ceased. No doubt this abandonment risked being just as prejudicial to the villein as the loss of his fief was to the vassal. Unless the peasant yielded to the temptation of the advantages offered to the colonizers of a "new town," he rarely left, and his sons did not lightly renounce the rights that custom granted them on their father's land. In spite of the obstacles that seigneurial powers here and there erected to limit this procedure, departure generally remained legitimate. The villein's best interests could well tie him to his own seigneur, or the villein's son to his father's seigneur, but no juridical obligation stopped them from breaking the bond whenever they wished.

Other ties of dependence existed, however, that attached the man's "body" from the moment of this "body's" birth. Unless expressly lifted, they followed him wherever he went. Through this entirely unvoluntary attachment that imposed a sort of carnal fatality, the individual who was enclosed within seemed, despite different conditions, reminiscent of the ancient slave. Whatever his ancestry, whatever the particular name by which he was called—most often serf, but also culvert—he was still considered to be deprived of liberty. On the contrary, this liberty was granted whole to the simple villein and to the vassal who were not constrained by heredity.

It goes without saying that the division between the conditions of those thus inclined toward servitude and those apparently escaping this stain was not made all at once nor without many uncertain applications. Voluntary subjections, or those presented as such, posed a particularly delicate problem. In these troubled times numerous . Frenchmen swore allegiance to a seigneur: some were pushed by hunger, or anxiety over the persecution of evil neighbors, such as the lady from Lorraine who gave herself one day to Saint-Mihiel;[181] others were attracted to a church by piety or gratitude;[182] and finally no doubt there were persons simply incapable of resisting pressure exerted through promise or threat. Relatively high ranking persons, possessors of minor seigneuries, or dubbed knights whatever their fortune, swore lifelong homage "from the mouth and hands." But most men who sought placement in the shadow of a powerful lord belonged to a more modest station. Not that these protégés of inferior category were destitute; some manifested a certain affluence and even carried the then vague predicate, "nobles."[183] Without sufficient qualifications or cleverness for admittance in the group of military vassals, they had to pledge their posterity along with themselves. They invariably promised to pay the chevage and often recognized also that their new seigneur could exercise rights over their inheritance, marriage, or formariage.

Many acknowledged unequivocally the servile nature of this contracted bond. Following in words if not in the reality of the burdens undertaken by the many free men who in the Frankish period had become slaves, they bowed their heads "under the yoke of servitude." Others, on the contrary, while submitting to almost identical and similarly hereditary obligations, strove to preserve their "liberty." Sometimes its retention was expressly stipulated; at other times—particularly since the eleventh century—silence enveloped this burning issue. According to the chancelleries, and especially according to seigneurial policy, one or the other conception carried the day. While certain abbeys—for example Saint-Mihiel—appeared quite late to have accepted personal traditions where nothing in the terms of the contract prevented the new subject from continuing to consider himself as free, it is not accidental that the monks of Marmoutier uniformly gave to such contracts the form common to the numerous enslavements that are found in their archives.[184]

Such a state of perpetual dependence was less and less willingly accepted as compatible with the concept of liberty, however. While the chevage in times past was the indication of protection given without injury to the personal status of the protected individual, it now tended to become a sign of servitude, understood in a new sense. Distinguished persons now "blushed" under this obligation thus this "noble lady," subject of Saint-Bavon, who wished to substitute a common man for herself to pay the dishonorable tax.[185] Almost the whole evolution of serfdom is inscribed within this change in the social value of these few deniers. The evolution of the gift of one's self is a delicate problem since—as Nélis has clearly demonstrated for certain Flemish and Lotharingian estates[186]—many acts were rewritten from old notices and even from memory at a period remote from the actual event. However, the dossier remarkably well preserved by the monks of the abbey of Mont Blandin in Gand allows us to draw some plausible conclusions. Although the clause safeguarding liberty was formulated in an isolated act as late as 1050, it is not difficult to follow the progressive applications of the servile vocabulary to these *tributarii* as early as the beginning of the eleventh century. The "commandés" (*commendati*) that one can find here and there in the countryside in the eleventh and twelfth centuries[187] were undoubtedly descendents of free men who had thus voluntarily placed themselves under the mundium of a great lord. It may be that the ancestor, such as the poor fellow who appears in a famous Touraine formula,[188] had carefully specified the "free (ingénuile) character" under which he wanted to keep his subordination. His grandsons, however, appear to us to be very close to serfs; and charters, whenever they mentioned them, hardly failed to so place them. Some carried burdens analogous to mainmorte.[189] Finally, qualifying the rank of individuals who were treated as servi by the phrase *servitude et commendise*, a text from Sens well illustrated this definitively established confusion around 1160, at least in that region.[190] Still, where the old name, *commandés*, survived, something remained which set these heirs of free subjects slightly apart from serfs.[191] Elsewhere they certainly had become nothing more than serfs, sometimes in entire groups. Around 1200 one believed that such had been the fate of the immigrants who had come to populate the town of Ardres in Picardy around 1060. Originally free, but narrowly enough subjected to a seigneur whose domination they themselves had sought, they gradually came to be thought of as serfs.[192] It is hardly possible to verify this account, but it is not unreasonable in itself; under a system of law in full transformation and controlled by no written code, properties such as freedom or servitude could easily be lost or acquired through simple usage. From one to the other a transitory zone subsisted for a long time, a grey area in which oscillated certain forms of subjection with ambiguous labels. Depending upon whether juridical opinion inclined more readily toward one side or the other, in a given region the number of persons designated as serfs was more or less considerable at the end of this period.[193] The study of these uncertain statuses, one in which the profound texture of the new social classifications is particularly well revealed, finds especially convincing evidence in urban collectivities.[194]

In many towns no personal and hereditary bond ever seemed to have been tied between the inhabitants and their seigneur. In Paris, for example, nothing of the kind was evident, at least as long as one remains within the very nucleus of the city, for serfdom was established in the abbatial burgs of Saint-Germain-des-Prés and Sainte-Geneviève which, situated outside the third-century city walls and long more than half rural yet were erected in an area already somewhat built up in Roman times and where no doubt there had always been some habitations.[195] In other urban groups, on the contrary, even among those that were direct descendants of imperial towns, narrow bonds of dependence, attached to a man from birth, developed. There is no need for surprise at this. The truly thorny problems, even though they have often gone unnoticed, are how the ancient cities were conquered by the landed seigneurie whose Roman ancestors had been so rustic and how this soil, formerly juridically free from taxes, from investiture, in a word from all the superior rights of the territorial seigneur, had been subdued. But that many townsmen, just as peasants, could not live without a protector or lord, nor without granting him obedience in some corporal way that was extended to their posterity, is quite in conformity with the social evolution of the period. Sometimes this subordination acquired the clearest accentuated character both in form and in substance. Subject to the mainmorte, among other burdens, the people of Orléans were royal serfs until their final enfranchisement under Louis VII in 1180.[196] Likewise, the court of the counts of Flanders considered the people of Bourg Saint-Vaast, by far the most important section of the town of Arras, as serfs of the monastery. Elsewhere, some fluctuation can be noted. At Tournai, the major part of the population was composed of "men of Sainte-Marie," subject to the chevage, to a marriage tax, and to a fixed mainmorte from generation to generation. As was natural, in the survey of capitulary laws (the "register of white leather") established for the most part a little before 1285, they were normally called serfs. One of the authors however felt obliged to add this apparently singularly contradictory remark: "the payment of the rent which the serf makes ... is a sign and a manifestation of liberty." No doubt he had in mind this idea of ecclesiastical "liberty" which we attempted to analyze earlier. Perhaps, however, he only yielded to his inclination because he felt repugnance at ranking home-owning bourgeois among the serfs. Since the beginning of the commune, the "men of Sainte-Marie" were only attached to the chapter by payment of traditional dues, which was henceforth nearly empty of significance and ready to fall into desuetude: and this is apparently what happened, without any formal enfranchisement, as early as the following century.[197] At the extreme end of this wide spectrum that went from an openly designated servile status to an identical but unnamed status are placed the conditions in Amiens. Their very singularity invites exploration.[198]

In Amiens the hereditary obligations of most inhabitants toward the cathedral church corresponded exactly to those at Arras or Tournai: chevage, inheritance taxes, and formariage. All of them incidentally, as in most of these northern towns, were fixed in amount and were small enough sums. At least such was the case in the twelfth century: it is possible that this followed an annual subscription (abonnement) to these taxes granted early to these rich bourgeois who were much more accustomed to common action than were peasants. Nevertheless, the subjection that these burdens conveyed was strongly worded for the time: men who submitted to it were known to "belong to the church." Like serfdom this subjection was thought to be contagious between spouses.[199] But was it ever specifically called servile? We have found no text, so far, to prove this. But from the silence of the documents that have come down to us—simple strays from so many lost dossiers—how could one dare to draw a negative conclusion regarding written usage, which could be so variable, or even less regarding oral usage, which is almost impossible to grasp? What is certain is that if the condition of the Amiénois was ever considered contrary to liberty—we must be resigned to ignorance on this point—it very quickly broke away from this stigma, and this due to an evolution that illuminates the peculiarities of the urban milieu.

The seigneur willingly granted certain favors to the most narrowly attached subjects of his dominations—those who paid him the chevage and corollary taxes from birth. Notably at Amiens, as at Arras, Corbie, and Tournai, he granted the exemption from or a decrease in the *tonlieu*, levied on all traffic in merchandise.[200] And, as commerce became the preponderant occupation of townspeople and the source of ever-increasing wealth, these rebates of taxes carried on the very operations of business appeared increasingly attractive. Immigrants, more numerous every day, tried to secure such advantages for which no price was too dear, even if they had to take on the same obligations as the old inhabitants. Twice in the course of the twelfth century, a knight who held in fief from the monks of Saint-Vaast the collectorship of the chevage owed to them was convicted of improperly accepting as serfs of the abbey certain intruders, merchants whose only purpose was to escape the tonlieu. The mayors of the chapter of Tournai were accused of similar abuses in 1130.[201] Urban communities sometimes intervened so that the seigneur could not refuse to welcome these newcomers; then in their first expansion they wanted only to be totally open. Such was the case at Amiens. Although the royal charter of 1185 made no mention of this, the church claimed to admit into the commune only those persons who, according to the norm mentioned above, were "its own," and it maintained a register to insure this. In November 1226 the bourgeois obtained, for a goodly sum, two concessions from the church; a slight decrease in the chevage and, more precious still, the promise to henceforth register on its "tables" anyone offering to swear an oath to the commune.[202] In other words, any immigrant who consented to union with the collectivity by an oath of mutual aid and who was acceptable henceforth enjoyed exemption from the tonlieu, it being well understood that he would then assume the three traditional burdens as a condition. These burdens were found then to weigh on ever more numerous men, with very different origins, and whose situation appeared most often only slightly comparable with the common conception of a serf. The three charges were redeemed on June 9, 1391. Obviously, however, although they were similar to those borne by the servile population of the countryside, the idea would never have come to the thirteenth- and fourteenth-century Amiénois to consider them as signs of servitude or even as marks of a particularly strict dependence. People submitted to these charges, as to many others, without reflecting on their original justification. Thus a condition in principle close to serfdom failed here to be lastingly classified as such because its fundamental obligations, gradually detached from their original content, were at length conceived as being only the price paid by a fairly mixed urban population in exchange for commercial advantages.[203]

However instructive these aberrant cases may be, we should not forget the much greater simplicity of the normal evolutionary types. Beginning with the twelfth century especially, under the influence of both the renaissance in jurisprudence and the general intellectual revival, a new need for rigorous juridical categories became widespread. The ideas of liberty and servitude crystallized. Many uncertainties of detail were eliminated. This conformed to the clear pattern established by the developing society from the end of the Carolingian period. Nothing is more significant than a name that the Anglo-Norman texts used at times as a synonym for serf, *nativus* ("nief"): the man whose status is acquired by birth. For common opinion in the feudal age, not to be free meant not to be able to choose one's own seigneur.

Both the remnants of the past and the first hints of the future prevent us from ever faithfully describing a particular era's law, which, being a human device, is therefore eternally changing, as a rigorously logical system. The image we shall attempt to present here would be too inexact if we did not give a word or two on how the first symptoms of the future evolution began to alter the juridical conception of serfdom at the very moment when, around 1200, custom and jurisprudence had just imposed upon it some particularly distinct contours.

The enfranchisement movement that reached great amplitude in the thirteenth century, brought with it some confusion in the definition of servile status. While not daring to refuse grants of liberty, some seigneurs could not resign themselves to abandon all the profits they had realized until then from serfdom. The act of manumission itself stipulated the preservation of some of these ancient rights. Such was often the case in Flanders and in Hainault with the more or less mitigated right of the best catel.[204] It would then have been difficult to continue to hold these charges, which henceforth wieghed upon men who had just been granted freedom, as indices of a lack of freedom.

Elsewhere, in Champagne notably, many serfs escaped the mainmorte only through redemption or simple regulation. They remained subject to the other obligations of their status, particulary the formariage and generally the chevage.[205] In addition, some of them continued to owe the arbitrary taille that was generally considered a servile charge. Others, on the contrary, had obtained its annual subscription under various regulative agreements. A mandate of Philip VI to the bailiffs of Champagne on September 5, 1338, shows the royal administration's struggle with this chaos.[206] This was brought on by the necessity to resolve one of those serious boundary problems constantly posed by the coexistence of still very strong seigneurial powers and a monarchical authority increasingly desirous of greater power. Which categories of Frenchmen could the king rightfully draft directly into his army, or as a consequence—a consequence often more oppressive in practice than in its premises—compel to pay a replacement tax? The document is in fact only one of the first links of a long chain of similar arrangements with which it would be most interesting to retrace the vicissitudes of the classification of persons as seen from this particular point of view. Unfortunately, the components for such a study have never been gathered together, and we must be content here to cite the example of 1338 and to recommend similar ones to the zeal of other scholars.

The text distinguished, among seigneurial dependents, several classes characterized by criteria so different that not a few overlap. These classes were divided into three groups in order of the decreasing rigor of the subjection. At the top came the *"taillables high and low"* and "those who owed mainmorte"; neither one nor the other were in any case *semons*. Next came an intermediate tripartite group: men of formariage; men *de jurée*—i.e., probably those who had received a rudiment of communal autonomy along with miscellaneous privileges from one of the charters of customs so widespread in the region; and finally, men of the taille whose contribution, in principle annually subscribed, still remained suceptible to certain limited variations fixed no doubt by the same subscription. These were simply drafted, pending an inquest that would take place upon the "return from our present war." As for those who subscribed to a taille, which could not be increased or decreased, as well as all the subjects and rent payers who did not fall into any of the preceding subdivisions, the king would extend his *arrière-ban* (general levy) over them without reservation. The words "serf" and "homme de corps" were never pronounced in this enumeration. No doubt it would have been too frustrating to decide whether or not to rank a man "of formariage" who no longer owed mainmorte into this status. In fact, and in conformity with strict law, opinion in Champagne was long reluctant to admit that, except in the case of a formal enfranchisement, the sole suppression of inheritance taxes sufficed to free from this traditional stigma a born serf who nevertheless remained subject to other servile obligations such as the chevage. Gradually usage brought some uncertainty: was not the mainmorte the heaviest and consequently most typical servile burden? In the fifteenth century a lawyer of Reims refused to consider that chevage and formariage alone were marks of servitude.[207] Serfdom did not disappear only through expressed manumissions; the simple crumbling through disuse of the heretofore well knit bundle of characteristic burdens gave more than one man his freedom.

Most serfs, however, except for those who were more and more frequently enfranchised, remained tied to the bonds of their status, subject, if not always to the chevage, which in many regions had fallen into oblivion, at least to the mainmorte or to the best catel as well as to the prohibition of formariage. But despite the survival of these traditional obligations the new serfdom gradually became sharply distinct from the old. Among its symbolic burdens as we have seen, submission to dues or arbitrary service such as the taille and the corvée "on discretion" took their place. We have also seen how this new serfdom assumed a landed rather than a personal character, thereby often bringing restraints on residence, still most often transmitted to the man via his tenure, and therefore susceptible to being lost with it. Finally, less and less clearly conceived as "men" of their seigneurs, the serfs as a whole appeared to belong to a hierarchically inferior social group. Some of them, especially among the seigneurial sergeants, elevated themselves to the knighthood. Under Saint Louis or Philip III a decision of Parliament declared, on the contrary, that the seigneur who dubbed his own serf by the same act enfranchised him:[208] it posed in principle the incompatability of the status of the two classes.

It is evident that this evolution was connected to that involving the entire society at that time, reducing vassal homage to just an obsolete pretext for petty fiscal taxes and transforming the knightly order into a hereditary nobility. On all sides the sentiment surrounding personal bonds of dependence, recently so strong, began to weaken. Class gradation formed the plan for the reconstructed human edifice. Many aspects of the new serfdom were embryonic in the customs or practices of the earlier period but only took shape under the impetus of a social and political atmosphere quite different from that of the past. We have very clearly observed the development of ancient principles with regard to the history of servile tenure. That of the role attributed henceforth to arbitrary burdens is no less instructive.

There too that idea had some far-reaching roots. In the Carolingian period the servi readily owed to the seigneur the corvées "each time they were ordered." On the other hand, those owed by free tenants were most often fixed by custom. No doubt the changes that eventually totally affected the internal organization of the seigneurie and the status of the dependents generally erased this distinction. Almost everywhere custom fixed the services with no account taken of the differences among the personal status of the subjects. However, the old notion that a man deprived of "liberty" was thereby forced to respond to any requisition had certainly not completely disappeared from public opinion: witness the decision of the Chartrian judges authorizing the monks of Saint-Père to use their serfs "for all their works." Favored, as we have seen, by the parallelism between exemptions from the taille and enfranchisements this idea easily assumed new vigor.

Besides another similar prejudice had strengthened this idea in current opinion: some services, judged dishonorable, were held to be servile criteria. In the beginning of the thirteenth century, free men who lived at Gonesse on the king's land had tenures burdened with a particular obligation: they had to escort to Paris any offenders arrested by royal justice.[209] Burdens of this type were not exceptional; similar ones weighed on all the "men and hôtes" of Saint-Germain-des-Prés as late as 1275;[210] on the millers in fourteenth-century Blois;[211] and again on miscellaneous tenures in seventeenth-century Brittany.[212] It goes without saying that nothing in them involved personal status. They occurred among the infinite variety of the corvées described in the seigneurial rent-rolls, from that of the waggoners, for example, to that of the messenger. However, this job of valet of justice seemed despicable enough. The conclusion in Gonesse and its neighborhood was that it was incompatible with the dignity of a free man; the peasants who had to do it were wrongly treated as serfs within their own circle and could no longer find marriage partners.[213] A decision of the royal court toward the end of the reign of Louis VIII or the beginning of that of Saint Louis was necessary to manifest their liberty to everyone. Thus, the image of servitude held by the common people did not always correspond to that adopted by jurisprudence. To construct their successive theories, judges and jurists drew largely from current notions, but they had to pick and choose among this confused and contradictory mixture of ideas. Among the elements thus rejected, some fell definitively into the rank of popular delusions; others, favored by the course of evolution, resumed life later on.

OUTSIDE OF FRANCE: HYPOTHESES AND RESEARCH FRAMEWORKS.[214]

The social structure of other medieval western and central European countries has often presented very profound differences, but also a deep seated unity that responded to practical common needs and to similar directions of the collective mentality. Nothing would be more tempting than to be able to compare parallel developments in neighboring countries with the evolution of the idea of personal liberty in France. But, for the moment, the task goes beyond the modest possibilities of an isolated scholar, particularly since, as usual, there is no agreement among scholars as to what should be investigated. A few observations, or better, some rather discontinuous conjectures limited only to certain national laws must then suffice simple landmarks for an inquiry that we wish could be pursued of a common accord by scholars of all countries.

The extension of the idea of servitude way beyond its original concept of slavery, its application to all relationships of hereditary personal subjection, and to these only, seem largely European phenomena. In Germany, the *Miroir de Saxe* ranked the *Landassen*, also called *Gäste*,[215] among the free men. We call these manants and hôtes: we recognize under a foreign garment the French words readily used to designate the tenant and the villein. Sometimes the villein in general, serf or not, sometimes more precisely the pure villein bound to his seigneur only by possession of a tenure, was consequently considered endowed with "liberty." Eike von Repgow took the two terms in this restricted sense and evidently, if he held the landsassen or Gaste as free, his reason was that their subordination did not touch the person. Like the French *culverts*, the German *Laten* or *Lazzen* (the *lidi* of the ancient French texts) who were, as they, descendants of enfranchised "in obedience," slid gradually into servitude. Further, as for the culverts, but even more generally, their name was extended in different regions to all servile dependents without regard to origin. A study, with precise dates, of the numerous acts by which persons of different rank placed themselves under the protection of a church and agreed to pay the chevage to it would no doubt show with some exactitude in Germany as well as in France the oscillations, then the establishment of the new concept of the deprivation of liberty. The fate of the German *Muntmen* seems exactly parallel to that of the French commandés. The characteristic burdens of servile status—chevage, inheritance rights (most often under the form of the best catel),[216] prohibition of formariage—were found to be nearly identical on both sides.

No matter how extensive these analogies, it would be a grave mistake to see only similarities between the two evolutions. Certainly in most of its characteristics, the new servitude in Germany was very different from the old; however, more than a vestige of the old was retained in many places. One was the mark of dependence, which was reminiscent of slavery since the subject's tasks depended on the master's inclination rather more strictly than in France: some groups owed daily corvées; in numerous others, celibates were obliged to serve as valets in seigneurial houses, or heads of households had to accept different tasks, if required. A still more characteristic feature affected the place of the individual in society: he was unable to participate in juridical tribunals of the count or of the hundred reserved only to free men. The seigneurial sergeants, those *Dienstmänner*, despite their high prestige and power, were often excluded from these tribunals, if not as leaders of these proceedings, at least as judges. There was more: in Swabia at the beginning of the twelfth century, servile persons were not only deemed unworthy of sitting at the regularly convoked court, sometimes they could not even be judged by it, as if they deserved punishment but not justice.[217] Between liberty and its absence, German public law persisted in erecting a barrier that in France, with the single exception of the rule relating to the testimony of serfs, had almost entirely fallen down. As heirs to the Carolingian system that in its turn had especially regularized ancient Germanic custom, the very institutions of public law generally had a much hardier life in Germany than in France. And the German social structure had not been transformed as radically by the accession of a new regime of dependence. The same bonds corresponded in both countries but were appreciably less generalized in Germany than in France. Likewise many more allods existed in Germany, a greater number of average men, notably peasants, possessed liberty, in the recent as in the older meaning of the word: men capable, especially in the North, of manning the tribunals alone, who knew how to maintain the traditional cleavage between the free and the nonfree.

Thus, precisely due to this lesser emphasis upon the idea of personal attachment, which, in France, seemed to overshadow other criteria, and also as a consequence of a sort of inveterate taste for class gradation—a feature particularly distinctive of medieval German law—the fusions of the diverse status of hereditary subordination into a single servile group was never pushed in Germany as far as it was in France. One cannot find a single word there which, by its extension over immense masses of dependents, is the exact equivalent of the French "serf." In sum, something always existed there of the complexity that had characterized the classification of human status in the Carolingian epoch. Among the subjects that in view of the inheritance of their status were all considered to be deprived of liberty, the documents relating to the exploitations of the seigneuries ordinarily distinguished different subgroups that, variable according to place, possessed their own customs. At the very bottom figured normally the *Tagewarden* or *Tageschalken* (*servi quotidiani*), the closest to slavery as we have defined it, since, according to custom absolutely ignored in France in the same period, they owed a corvée each day; this daily repeated service often exempted them from payment of the chevage.[218] Above them were servi, considered a less humble rank because of greater limitations on their obligations.[219] Payment of the chevage—in wax, for example, or in money—created new nuances. Sometimes hesitation occurred in recognizing as clearly as in France that within this old tax of protection was a characteristic absolutely contrary to liberty, and the men who owed it formed a stratum superior to that of the servi proper.[220] At the top of the edifice were placed generally the servile sergeants who penetrated into the hierarchy of the holders of fiefs. Facing this organized variegation, how alien the scholar accustomed to handling French rent-rolls must feel!

The change of meaning, which made the name servus into a human category strongly distinct from slavery, was possible only because only a very few slaves remained in the greatest part of western and central Europe—too few, even where they could be found, to furnish anything other than domestic service, with one exception, however. In Catalonia and Roussillon the proximity to the Moorish countryside increased the number of captives who were reduced to slavery and who henceforth played a considerable economic role. In these countries, as in France, bonds of hereditary subjection were formed among which was the *exorquia*, the exercise of a true mainmorte. Various expressions designated men subject to it by the end of the thirteenth century, primarily *homines de remensa*, which alluded to a rule of land attachment whose *remensa*, or redemption, was always possible. They were never called servi. That old word still applied to the still-present slave.[221]

Of all European countries, England was certainly, around the beginning of the thirteenth century, the one where relations of hereditary dependence had assumed the closest form to French serfdom. The Norman Conquest had played the same simplifying role in England as the collapse of the Carolingian regime had in

France nearly two centuries earlier. A more complicated social classification than that found in the Domesday Book could hardly be conceived. Truthfully, the image was no doubt even less clear than the model, the work of French clerics who, inquiring into the realities of English life, could not have failed first, in reflecting on their observations, to use their own native languages, i.e., one of the French dialects, and then, to translate into bad Latin the results of this first work. The famous Book of Judgement (over which so many generations of scholars have grown pale) has all the inconveniences of a poorly executed double translation. But the complication certainly was already in the facts themselves: the old categories of Germanic law, more or less altered, intersected with classificatory principles of an entirely different nature derived from relationships of personal subjection that were much less well classified than on the Continent in the same period. Thirteenth-century documents described a society with a much clearer design. The action of Norman law, the frequent use of its terminology, furthered the resemblance to French institutions. Slavery, which had survived in England longer than in the kingdoms issuing from the Frankish state, had finally disappeared. The fief or bondman equaled the French serf.[222] As in France, he was called servus in Latin; this name, of course, was that which in Anglo-Saxon England had been applied to the *theow*, to the slave. But the conditions were very different. A characteristic trait: whereas according to Anglo-Saxon law only the master had the right to the price of a murdered slave, by the beginning of the twelfth century, the *Leges Henrici* compelled the murderer of a servus to pay a double indemnity, one to the master, one to the family.[223] Evidently, the conception of the absence of liberty developed along the same lines as in France. In both countries the burdens were similar: inheritance rights, prohibition of formariage, inability to enter holy orders, often also chevage. English law, however, added one more burden that, ignored on the whole in France, had its parallel in the Catalan *cugucia*, a brutally evocative name: if a female serf had allowed herself to be seduced she had to pay a special tax on her condition, the *leywite*, to her seigneur. The villein was like the French villein, i.e., a tenant and a free man if he was only a tenant.

But in the course of the thirteenth century, the line of demarcation separating the free from the nonfree was displaced once more. Since the preceding century, English royal justice was affirmed with a vigor that other European countries hardly knew; it extended its sovereignty over the entire kingdom, with one reservation, imposed by the power that was retained by seigneurial powers. From the beginning the king could not intervene between the seigneur and his tenant, pure villein as well as bondman. Numerous men, most of whom were not bondmen, were excluded, therefore, as a general rule from recourse to state jurisdiction. By returning to the old distinction that Germanic public law erected between free men who had access to its tribunals and slaves who knew not its justice, this inferiority appeared as a mark of servitude. And although here and there the bondman was distinguished from the mass of villeins, the latter in their majority were considered henceforth deprived of liberty;[224] tey were often subjected to the old servile burdens, and their status in any case was considered strictly hereditary in the future.

But among persons who held lands for rent from a lord were some of too elevated a social rank to be excluded from the benefit of judgment by the royal courts. How was one to determine, among the mass of tenures, those which, deprived of this recourse, were henceforth the only ones meriting the name, villeinage? In their distress the jurists called upon another criterion that, besides varying according to local customs, was generally inspired from the very burdens that weighed on the soil. Some of these burdens, degrading in nature, the rural corvée most often, sometimes the submission to *banalités*, were acknowledged as a sign of villeinage. There is hardly a juridical construction more worthy of attention in the history of medieval personal rights. Above all, it was the work of educated practitioners; its perpetually tentative procedures, the very contradictions that it has been impossible to dwell upon here, reveal a jurisprudence in search of itself. All of it betrays the work of a thought process that freely adjusted reality as it chose. And yet it was based not only on very concrete needs—the desire to fix precise boundaries to royal justice, necessary for its very effectiveness and the protection of seigneurial interests—but also on formerly widespread common opinions that it revived, such as the idea that a servile man by definition did not belong in public tribunals and the old idea of dishonorable services that we have seen beginning in the popular prejudices of France. Nothing is more instructive than such a mixture.[225]

Thus we find ourselves brought back from all sides to the same lesson. Human institutions being realities of a psychological order, a class exists only through the idea we have of it. To write the history of servitude is above all to retrace, in its complex and changing development, the history of a collective notion, that of the deprivation of liberty.

CHAPTER THREE

The "Colliberti".
A Study on the Formation of the Servile Class[1]

THE FRENCH CULVERTAGE

Colliberti and culverts

Archival documents reveal the existence in eleventh- and twelfth-century France of a class of men called *colliberti*. At least such is their Latin name, their scholarly name. The vulgar appellation appeared, more or less clumsily latinized, in several eleventh- or twelfth-century notices;[2] numerous literary texts, Provençal as well as French, directly attested to them by the end of the eleventh century. Ordinarily in Provençal as in French the word used was *culvert*, or else later, dropping the l *cuvert*; sometimes in French, watering it down: *cuilvert, cuivert*. Some etymologists, perplexed by the phonetical difficulties raised by the derivation *collibertum-culvert* have sought an explanation in an alleged popular etymology born from a fairly indecent pun. I have refuted that hypothesis elsewhere.[3] But perhaps the fear of similar equivocation has influenced a singular usage introduced in modern history books. Rather than the medieval and authentically French word, most authors have preferred a term modeled on the Latin: *collibert*. This barbarism has had much too long a life. Not only does it shock anyone at all familiar with the ancient language; more seriously it inevitably masks the semantic relationship that unites the culvert of the chansons de geste to the collibertus of the charters. While we must always try to discover under the artificial language of the notaries the thoughts of men of yesteryear, will we allow ourselves to be stopped here by scruples of elegance or of false modesty? In the following I will speak bravely of culverts.[4]

But France is not the only European country where documents reveal the existence of colliberti. They are found beyond the Alps in Italy, especially in Sardinia, and beyond the Pyrennees in Navarre. Culbert seems to have been the vulgar word in Navarre. Those of the Italian or Sardinian dialects are unknown to us; the texts only show that just as in French and Provençal, the words derived from a late Latin form with u in the initial syllable, such as culibertus, rather than from the classical Latin collibertus. The phonetic problem posed by the culverts is not properly French, it is Roman. Likewise the juridical problem comes under the purview of comparative history. But it will be proper for us to choose as a point of departure the study of the French *culvertage*.[5]

The culvert class

First we must go back to the eleventh century. Toward the beginning of this century the culvertage, as a particular social condition, was already well formed.[6] It disappeared gradually between 1100 and around 1140.

Its full development then coincided with that particularly obscure period that separates the Carolingian age from the great literary and juridical renaissance of the twelfth century—a period of diplomatic agraphia when the formalism dominating the life of the law most often rendered useless the compilation of charters; a troubled period when the little that was written (notices rather than charters), badly conserved and subject to all the vicissitudes of war and pillage, has too frequently perished. In other words our sources are rare and mediocre.

Among other drawbacks this poverty removes any hope for a precise determination of the geographical distribution of the culvert population. When the total number of documents is so small, the lack of information on colliberti in a particular region may well be the result only of a stroke of bad luck. By reason of this uncertainty drawn from the facts themselves, another is added whose origin lies in the necessary imperfection of erudite scholarship. Despite intensive research, I, no more than any of my predecessors, cannot entertain the rash claim of having inspected all the archives and the cartularies that could transmit the desired information to me. However, in spite of the inevitable inexactitudes, it will be useful to point out on a map of France the information that has filtered through our poor texts. The groupings obtained are, as one begins to see, too compact to be considered only the result of chance.

Obviously culvertage never extended throughout the former kingdom of western France or in the noticeably different territory that corresponds to present-day France. But it was widespread over a very vast region whose surface area and contour are as follows: To the north, the Beauvaisis;[7] to the East without doubt the Meldois,[8] in any case the Gâtinais;[9] then the Parisian region up to the boundaries of Normandy;[10] further toward the West, the Perche,[11] Vendômois,[12] Maine,[13] perhaps the neighborhood of Dol;[14] all the country around the middle Loire, Bourbonnais, Berry,[15] Nivernais,[16] Beauce,[17] Blésois, Touraine, Anjou,[18] plunging toward the Southwest, Poitou, Saintonge, Aunis;[19] and toward the center, the Limousin up to the outskirts of Tulle;[20] therefore neither Flanders, nor without doubt the greatest part of Picardy;[21] nor Normandy,[22] Brittany, Lorraine; nor perhaps western Champagne; nor Burgundy or the Rhône countryside; nor the Midi of the Southwest to the south of Tulle. It is only after further research that we will be able to seek an explanation for this distribution; but it is clear here and now that if this essay was not attempted, the study of the distribution would remain incomplete.

Any statistical survey naturally is impossible. The impression that the texts give—and we cannot speak of anything other than an impression—is that the culverts were everywhere less numerous than the serfs. Mentions of them are particularly abundant in some cartularies of the West: Vendôme, Touraine, Anjou, Maine. But since the same collections also include some remarkably copious information on the servile class in the eleventh century, the only conclusion that can be drawn from this relative richness is that the great ecclesiastical establishments in these provinces established the records of their peasants with a care that at the time was rather rare.

One cannot doubt that there truly was a culvert "class" in the eleventh century. The culverts were not free men nor, in the proper sense, serfs. They occupied a separate place in society. The testimony of the texts is absolutely precise on this point. Should one of the sergeants charged with gathering the revenues of the fairs of La Chapelle-Aude steal any of it "he will pay the fine" stated the regulations of the fairs in 1065, "according to the law under which he lives, whether he is free, serf or culvert."[23] Between June 21, 1040, and April 1, 1046, Bouchard, treasurer of Saint-Maurice of Angers, approved in advance any donation to be made to the church of Saint-Marcel of Briollay by any of his men, "knight, serf or culvert."[24] In the course of the same century, Renaud

Montier, buying a half-arpent of vineyard from Saint-Serge of Angers, promised never to sell it "neither to a customary man of the count"—meaning a free peasant obliged simply to the payment of taxes of "customs"—"nor to one of his serfs, nor to one of his culverts."[25] In numerous villages, as shown in the acts of donation, men called serfs and others called culverts lived side by side;[26] they were not confused one for the other. Sometimes a dispute would arise: was such and such an individual free or culvert? Or else was he culvert or serf? These lawsuits were brought before the courts, which applied methods used ordinarily in quarrels concerning personal status: the oath, the judgment of God, the judicial duel.[27]

It is not surprising, moreover, that the culvert was considered quite different from the free man. He was inferior to him in social dignity since he indeed lacked liberty. Let us avoid the concept of "half-free" artificially forged by some German historians. In the eyes of his contemporaries the culvert was not at all *halbfrei*. He was completely immersed in servitude. This very term is used by innumerable decrees. A charter of manumission kept in the Black Book of Saint-Florent of Saumur states: "Although all the human race issued on earth from a same origin and that according to heaven's law all those who carry the Christian name are united in Christ, nevertheless the law of human tribunals has judged that some are called free, the others *serfs* or *culverts*."[28] A curious judiciary episode illustrates well this opposition of the two notions, liberty and culvertage.[29] A certain Alon, knight and husband of a noblewoman, was from birth a culvert of the monks of Bourgueil, at least so the religious claimed, for Alon denied it. A lengthy lawsuit followed. Finally, in 1114, Alon, appearing before the chapter, recognized the right of his seigneurs. He was asked then to swear an oath of fidelity. He agreed to it; but as soon as the formula was pronounced, he added: "That is a free man's speech, as I have already stated not long ago."[30] It appears that these few words deservedly put everything back into question and Alon was sent to prison to meditate on the necessity of not introducing reservations into his faith. The culverts were such strangers to liberty that only one legitimate means of acquiring it lay at their disposal: enfranchisement. Through manumission they left their class and at the same time, having become like "sons of free (*ingénus*) fathers,"[31] they shook off the "yoke of servitude." Thus in some documents (rather rare before 1060) the same individuals were treated first as culverts then as serfs: *servus, ancilla*.[32] Careful notaries avoided this manner of speaking: it was ambiguous. But it was not absolutely inexact. In a general sense, if one wished, culverts were serfs, but not serfs like the others. They were unfree people of a superior rank.

This difference in degree appears clearly in the lawsuit that unfolded in 1070 or 1071.[33] Audrai, serf of the monks of Marmoutier, had married the culvert of a seigneur called Hugue. Four sons were born of this union. Hugue's heir, Guillaume, claimed half of them. This was to demand the application of a very simple rule that governed the division of children issued from parents belonging to two different seigneurs. The monks refused. The suit was carried before the court of the seigneurs of Montoire, Guillaume's suzerains. The judgement stated that the marriage of a serf with a culvert did not give rise to normal apportionment: the children had to "follow the father," i.e., all became serfs as he was, and belonged to his seigneur. We do not positively know the reasons invoked in this decision, but it is not difficult to reconstruct them. The parents, one a serf, the other a culvert, were not of equal rank and, therefore, came under the well-known maxim according to which the "worst" (in this case, the serf) "always won." By virtue of this axiom, when a free man married a culvert, the children remained in the culvert status.[34] If anyone doubts that such was indeed the idea behind the decision of the judges of Montoire, the lawsuit's sequel should suffice to convince him. Guillaume was loath to accept a sentence so unfavorable to his interests. However, he did not contest its principle. He tried to find a means of turning this same principle to his advantage; he affirmed that Audrai had not been a serf but a culvert of the monks. Thus, the equality being reestablished between the spouses, the game of division no longer suffered from any obstacles.[35] It appears that this late claim was only a lie. It is not less instructive for that.[36]

The culverts' position midway between serfdom proper and freedom is illuminated by the use made of their name in the Domesday Book. The word collibertus appears no less than 858 times, but only in passages relating to fourteen counties forming a cohesive group encircling Wessex and the western part of Mercia. It is not found in any other text relating to England. It was certainly not indigenous. A term familiar to the foreign clerics—no doubt these were not Normans since culvertage was unknown in Normandy; they were probably from Maine—who drew up the descriptions for these counties, it served them as a translation for a word from the language of the vanquished estimated by the clerics to be too barbaric or too difficult to understand to be simply reproduced. Occurrences of this kind are not rare in the great English land register. As a result of a similar transposition, its authors believed they saw, throughout England this time, innumerable *bordarii*—also a word from western France—who later on completely disappeared from the documents.[37] These clerics twice carefully indicated what the original term they claimed to render by collibertus was *bur*.[38] Despite the obscurity enveloping personal status at the end of the Anglo-Saxon period, we are certain of two things: the bur was of a superior status to the man absolutely deprived of liberty, the *theow*, whose name was readily translated into Latin by servus (the clerics thought, in French, serf). However, the bur's status betrayed several servile traits, notably that, when he died, all his goods returned to his master. This double character sufficed to evoke the idea of culvert status in the eyes of persons accustomed to the continental society.

What then placed the culvert above his companion in servitude, the simple serf? Three possibilities offer themselves at first. The culvert could differ from the serf in his juridical condition, in his economic situation, and in the nature of the seigneur to whom he belonged. Let us examine each of these hypotheses in turn. The comparison will focus only on servile law as evidenced in eleventh- and early twelfth-century customs of northern and central France. The peculiarities of southern serfdom do not have to be taken into account since culvertage was unknown in the Midi. By the end of the thirteenth century the serfs's condition throughout France had evolved considerably, but there no longer were any culverts.

That the juridical condition of the culverts was at all points identical to that of the serfs

We already know that, just like the serf, the culvert was considered to be deprived of liberty. What was, exactly, the meaning of this notion? The word servitude, in the eleventh century, no longer had its ancient meaning. The serf was not the object of his lord, but he was his *homme de corps*; in other words, he was attached to his lord by a personal bond, one impossible to break—unless by regular enfranchisement—and one strictly hereditary. It was a very strong bond that contained, to the profit of the seigneur, various restrictions of familial and successory rights and, in general, involved some obligations of aid and of submission which were only felt the more heavily and were the more susceptible of extension as they were ill-defined. All these features made up an image that did not appear to be that of liberty. The very hereditary nature of this condition was in itself a sign of servitude. Let us not forget that the other great personal relationship, that of vassalage, had always been conceived by the Middle Ages as being, in law, limited to the duration of the life of either the vassal or the seigneur. It is quite apt that the technical name for serf was in old English *nativus* (*nief*): that person who is another's man, not by choice as a vassal, but by birth. By the very fact that he was not held to be free the serf was thought to be occupying an inferior rank in society. This "stain" that soiled his condition, the rigor of the bond that riveted him to his seigneur preventing anyone from ever believing him capable of spiritual independence, his very name making him the natural heir to the ancient servus— all these things had led the Church to apply implacably to him the traditional rule that forbade the slave, except when enfranchised, entrance to the holy orders, a humiliating disqualification that constituted, at one and the same time, one of the most distinct characteristics of serfdom and the most striking index of the baseness of this status.

Such were the general lines of the servile condition. Let us now reexamine this picture in all its details and let us compare its elements point by point with what the texts reveal on the culvertage.

The hereditary nature of the bond? We know of many gifts of culverts; almost always the man or the household is expressly ceded together with "his fruit."[39] In 1063, Foulque le Normand, seigneur of Petit-Montrevault, demanded from Count Geoffroi le Barbu several culverts. "He said," recounts the notice, "that his grandfather Roger le Vieux had received as a gift from Count Foulque l'Ancien the fathers of these culverts—two brothers named Froger and Aitard—*and that as a result the descendants of these two men, by law, belonged to him.*"[40] One is born a culvert as one is born a serf: not culvert, or serf, in general, but culvert, or serf, of a particular seigneur.

The strength of the bond? In 1124 a man called Guérin le Prudhomme lived in Mayenne; once a culvert he had been freed by the seigneur of the locality, Gautier. But Gautier's son, Joel, who had just succeeded his father, claimed this enfranchisement was not valid because, though he had been old enough to be a horseman and in the "age of reason" (*intelligibilem etatem*) at the time when the act was concluded, he had not been asked to give his consent to it. Guérin owned a field near the chapel of the Saints Etienne, Laurent, and Vincent, which Joel had given as alms to the monks of Marmoutier. These churchmen needed the land for construction; Guérin refused to give it to them, "neither for a prayer nor for a price." "Greatly irritated against him" related Joel, "I told him that he was my culvert, that I could sell him or burn him and give his land to whoever I wished, as being my culvert's land." Joel was a violent man; it became necessary, in order to prevent him from carrying out his threats, to have some reasonable men, among whom were the bishop of Mans and the abbot of Marmoutier, push him by force into an "interior room" of the castle. No medieval custom ever recognized to a seigneur the right to "burn" his culvert, no more than his serf, nor even to despoil one of the other of his tenure without some court procedure. In fact, no fire was lit and no confiscation took place. All was settled by agreement, onerous enough for Guérin in any case. He agreed to donate to the monks the field that they desired and, by means of this concession and a gift to Joel himself, obtained from the latter a definitive enfranchisement.[41] Among the bad words pronounced by the seigneur of Mayenne in the heat of anger one must above all remember that the word culvert, as well as that of serf, evoked in the mind of a man of the eleventh century the idea of an extremely rigorous dependence, a favorable theme for the exaggerations of an impassioned temperament.

When a seigneur sold or gave a plot of land, he often ceded at the same time the serfs or culverts who lived on it. But there is nothing unique in this. One did likewise with free tenants,[42] indeed with vassals.[43] It was a simple means of noting the cession of seigneurial rights, whatever their nature, over these men. Besides, what value did the land have without the men to work it? On the other hand, it happened that a seigneur parted with a serf or a culvert "with all his property."[44] If this involved real property, the formula indicated the alienation of the rights of the tenure; if it involved movables or immovables, the formula had for its principal object the renunciation of the former seigneur to any claim on the inheritance, a renunciation that was a matter of course, yet was all the better for being specified. These turns of language, as well as some other similar ones, have sometimes been used to prove the existence either of a "servitude of the soil" analogous to the ancient *coloni*, or of a sort of slavery, because of the sale or gift of "men." In truth, such terminology was not proper to persons of the servile condition; they expressed quite plainly in concrete terms some very simple realities. I mention this here only to avoid the errors that have sometimes occurred in the interpretations of such texts.

The serf, in a general way, owed from his person obedience to his seigneur. This rather vague notion was therefore susceptible to many different applications. It was not universally believed, for example, that a seigneur had the faculty, if he so desired, to hold his serfs, willy-nilly, on his land. It has not often enough been noticed that none of the ancient definitions of serfdom given in jurisprudence or in charters up to and including the thirteenth century made any mention of an obligation of residence. However, some seigneurs believed themselves within the law to demand it and attempted to enforce it. The same conception was sometimes applied to culverts. Between 1060 and 1064 the monks of the Trinité de Vendôme on whose lands culverts belonging to some other seigneurs had come to settle, prided themselves on having attempted to expel them "so that the constructions raised by them would not attract on us the evil deeds and reprisals of their seigneurs." It is true that Count Foulque l'Oison, the monks' *voué*, was less scrupulous; he forced the culverts to remain and to build houses, solely to be disagreeable, said the monks, in reality no doubt so as not to lose the profits that a shrewd baron could expect from a new town.[45] We touch here on the fundamental reason that, in the eleventh century, made the "attachment to the soil" unrealizable and, consequently, in a jurisprudence nearly deprived of doctrine and lacking any practice, inconceivable: the absence of a central authority capable of imposing its will on all the seigneurs, as the state of the later Empire imposed its will on the various *domini fundorum*. To go from one seigneurie into another only entailed the crossing of a road, a stream, the boundary of a field, sometimes a purely imaginary line. Once the step had been taken, no one could recapture the fugitive. It is true that the wronged seigneur could more or less arbitrarily confiscate the fugitive's tenure. This was a paltry remedy: land then was not rare; labor, on the contrary, was not abundant. The dispossessed peasant was almost certain to find a new farm together with a new seigneur. Count Foulque had more than one competitor. But the abandoned tenure often remained uncultivated.[46]

Ordinarily, the seigneurs' efforts were applied less toward stopping their serfs from leaving than toward maintaining over them, once they had left, the integrity of their rights. It appears that this was just as difficult to accomplish. *Forain* (i.e., belonging to another area) serfs and culverts appear quite early in history. Toward the end of the eleventh century the vicountess of Tulle Ermengart owned several men of this condition who lived on the land of Saint Pierre of Uzerche. She eventually gave them to the monks of Saint-Pierre. It seems this was not the most generous gift she ever made for, in practice, there was little that could be gained from these men.[47]

Serfdom was a condition of the man, not of the land. As a tenant, the serf or the culvert blended in with the totality of the peasantry—the *hôtes*—on the seigneurial land on which they possessed houses or fields. Their property was subject to the same real taxes as that of their neighbors, and, as with the latter, could only be passed on, in case of transfer, through the agency of the seigneur or of his representative. Local custom protected their possessions, along with those of other tenants, and in practice considered these to be hereditary. As we shall see somewhat later, the only difference between serfs and other tenants was that the serf's or culvert's personal seigneur (*de corps*), who might not necessarily be the same individual from whom the tenure depended, figured among that serf's heirs. This form of tenancy was known generally, beginning in the twelfth century at the latest, under the name, *censive* or "tenure in villeinage." It was not specific to any one class of men but was open to the free as well as to the nonfree, and even on occasion to knights and to religious communities. Further, this was not the only form of tenancy available to culverts. In fact, I do not know of any example of alodial holders among culverts,[48] but since nothing stopped their elevation to the rank of sergeants—seigneurial functionaries or artisans—there are occurrences of culverts possessing tenures burdened not with a tax but with a service, in other words, fiefs.[49]

However, this strict separation between the condition of the man and that of the land could not be maintained in all cases without at times involving the seigneur in some grave difficulties. Toward the end of the eleventh century, a culvert of Saint-Aubin of Angers, named Geoffroi, who was provost of the monks,[50] contracted a marriage with a culvert who belonged in part to the count of Anjou and in part to Robert le Bourguignon, and had three daughters. The two youngest were assigned to the count and to Robert who freed them; they were married and each had one son. Then Geoffroi died, leaving as his only heirs the two grandsons issued from his younger daughters. Simon, whose mother was the older of the two sisters, first claimed the property that had formed his grandfather's "fief." When, for reasons we shall explore presently, he withdrew this claim, his cousin Maurice in his turn presented himself, demanding not only the provostship's fief but also the exercise of the provostal dignity itself. The monks had recognized in principle the rights of the first heir. They turned down the second's claim on two grounds. First, his demand had come too late. Second, they had a reason of a more general order: the enfranchisement. According to the monks, Geoffroi's daughters had thereby lost all rights to the paternal inheritance.[51] This ruling, had it been generally observed, would have been extremely favorable to seigneurial interests. Around the same period, the monks of Marmoutier tried to impose a similar rule on their serfs.[52] Later, especially in the thirteenth century, it became one of the typical clauses in acts of manumission. But in the particular period we are discussing, it was still not part of common law. The court of Hubert de Champagne, Maurice's seigneur, before which, after a sort of private war, the lawsuit was finally carried, did not accept either of the monks's arguments. Maurice was declared the legitimate heir, not, it is true, of the office, but of the lands. Nevertheless, the judgment posed one further question: was the plaintiff obligated, by virtue of taking possession of his grandfather's inheritance, to swear allegiance to the monks as their culvert? Could one, in other words, allow property, once owned by a culvert family, to pass into the hands of a free man? Such a ruling would have been gravely prejudicial to the seigneur who would thus lose his eventual rights over the inheritance. But this case was an extraordinary one: could one force the monks either to cede the fief of the provostship without remuneration or to accept as their provost a man who did not owe allegiance to them? This point was never decided. Maurice, fearing the "dishonor of servitude" preferred to compromise. This is what his cousin Simon had already done when faced with the same threat. Maurice, besides, was made to pay dearly for his renunciation by the monks, a fact that takes away some of the force from the lesson that the monk who authored this account claimed to draw from the episode: "One cannot be *ingénu* (free) when one owns a culvert's 'fief.' "[53]

An often uncertain jurisprudence, perpetual hesitations over the competence of various tribunals, above all the difficulty in obtaining the execution of even the most definitive judiciary decisions without compromising with the other party—all of these gave the customs of the eleventh century an extremely blurred character.

At least we can clearly grasp here how the notion of the servile tenure was gradually introduced. The seigneurs became accustomed to take advantage of the right that was generally attributed to them of controlling transfers of property and refused their consent to those transfers that had as a result the passing of a serf's land to a man of a different condition.[54] But the evolution that had as a result the making of servitude a part of real law took several centuries. It seems clear that in the eleventh century the ecclesiastical communities were strict on such matters only when the succession concerned one of these families of sergeants—provosts or monks—whose insubordination, always about to emerge, risked becoming formidable if one allowed them to escape from servitude together with their fortune and even their obligations. The incidents described above concern a lineage of this sort. It is truly remarkable that the author of this account, stating a general principle, did not apply it to any tenure but to a fief, i.e., a tenure that served as the salary for a sergeant, as for a vassal. Similar declarations from the same period that I have been able to gather, and concerning serfs proper, have to do with mayors or descendants of mayors.[55] Here again the abundance of available, arable land long constituted an obstacle to the desires of seigneurs by preventing them from being as selective as they would have liked to be in their choice of tenants. This state of affairs did not end until the great colonizations of the twelfth and of the first half of the thirteenth centuries. By then culverts no longer existed. The servile tenure proper does not appear before the end of the thirteenth century at the earliest. There never was any "culvertile" tenure.[56]

The serf's position with regard to the law was quite different from that of the free tenant. The feeling was that his only natural judge was his own seigneur. This conception was particularly strong when the case involved a capital crime. Ordinarily, cases of this sort—later grouped under the convenient name, high justice—were reserved for the courts of certain high barons. But when the accused was of servile condition it mattered little whether the seigneur to whom he was attached by the bond of servitude did or did not possess the right in common law to judge capital crimes. In all cases, the trial had to be tried before him. At least such was the requirement of the most generally widespread custom, one that appears to have been considered normal and legitimate.[57] The serf's "body" belonged to his seigneur: who else then could dispose of his life? This rule was in force, theoretically, no matter where the serf happened to live; his particular seigneur's justice—at least his criminal justice—followed him everywhere. This was not applied only to serfs. Similar rules affected other groups of dependents: vassals, or even simple servants or sergeants. The principle of personal dependence everywhere transcended that of territorial dependence in the vassalage era.

Culverts, again in this case, were placed together with the serfs. In Méron the monks of Saint-Aubin of Angers owned a portion of land; blood justice did not belong to them but to the seigneur of Montreuil-Bellay. Nevertheless, the latter, as stated in a ruling handed down toward the end of the eleventh century, "will never have the blood of the men of the *mesnie* of Saint-Aubin or of its culverts."[58] On the lands of Saint-Florent of Saumur, the provost of the count of Anjou, either alone or in cooperation with the monks's provost, exercised several rights of justice, "with the exception" prescribed in 1062 by Count Geoffroi le Barbu "of the serfs or of the culverts of the monks, who in all cases will have to answer to the prior or to the abbot."[59] The same principle is true for the judicial duel, allied by a natural association of ideas to blood justice. At La Chapelle-Anguillon, in Berry, two seigneurs, Humbaud and Gilles, on the one hand, and the monks of Saint-Sulpice of Bourges on the other, generally held common pleas for duels; however, when the litigant demanding battle was a serf, culvert, or sergeant belonging to one of the collaborating authorities, then the latter became the sole judge.[60]

Each and every year the serf owed his seigneur the *chevage*. This was a fixed tax, usually in money, and it weighed on all servile heads. The amount itself was negligible. Nevertheless, it was to the seigneur's great advantage to demand its regular payment, thereby protecting himself against any future restriction of his rights over his serfs. To pay the *chevage* was tantamount to admitting servile status. Thus, when a man acknowledged his status as the serf of a churchman, either because he voluntarily gave up his freedom or because he finally accepted, after long disputes, to confess his hereditary servitude, he presented himself to the representatives of his master with the deniers of the chevage on his head, or else he placed them upon the altar. "Martin," says a notice from Vendôme regarding a person who had just made himself into a serf, "placed on the altar the charter [with which he was giving himself] and at the same time, as a testimonial, performed the offering of the four deniers, *which expresses the servile condition.*"[61]

Again the culvert, as well as the serf, was subjected to this particularly characteristic burden—the *pensum servitutis*.[62] A notice from the cartulary of the cathedral of Angers tells us that Eude, son of Bernier Bruneau, after having long denied his condition, "in the presence of the Bishop Renaud le Jeune has confessed that he was the culvert of Saint-Maurice and as a symbol of this vow has placed four deniers into the hands of the bishop."[63] Four deniers was the classic price for the servile chevage as well as for the culvertile chevage. However, a different amount could be fixed by custom for both classes. The culverts of Saint-Cyr of Nevers, or at least some of them, only paid three *oboles*.[64] But this is of little importance: it was always the same tax, and to all intents and purposes, a symbolic one. The culvert, as the serf, deserved the name *homme de chef*.[65]

Most often, seigneurs did not interfere in the marriages contracted by their serfs within the servile family. Only the *formariage*, potentially prejudicial to their interests, was subject to their consent. The formariage was the union of one person of servile condition either with a spouse of more elevated rank or with a spouse belonging to the same class but the subject of another master. A similar obligation was imposed on culverts. It is expressly mentioned, in a notice originating from Saint-Michel of Beauvais, among the burdens from which a culvertile family sought in vain to be relieved.[66] A serf from the abbey of the Trinité de Vendôme one day married a culvert belonging to a seigneur named Fromond Turpin, without the latter's knowledge. When this was discovered, Fromond complained. As he was pious, he finally gave the culvert to the monks and, according to the text, agreed to "forgive the fault."[67] A culvert of Saint-Maurice of Angers had given his daughter to a freeman, under pretense that she was free. The canons thereupon started a lawsuit; the husband took fright and repudiated his wife.[68]

Under what circumstances did the seigneur inherit from his serf? The prevailing custom in this respect in the thirteenth century in the greatest part of northern and central France is well known: it was called *mainmorte* or *mortaille*.[69] Although the modes of application could vary locally, the general principle was imposed everywhere. The serf had for sole heirs among the members of his family those of his descendants living with him in common or, when absolutely necessary and following some more liberal customs, those of his brothers still living with him. In all cases other than these, which in fact amounted less to a succession than to the perpetuation of a community, the seigneur received the inheritance. This institution, called *mainmorte*, is without doubt the most characteristic of French serfdom. In England, in Germany, even in some of northern France, the institution evolved in a completely different direction. The French seigneur, who had rarely the occasion to exercise this right, seized the entire fortune of his serf when the opportunity presented itself. On the contrary, his German, English, Hainault, Flemish, even Artois equal, each time a serf died, collected a part of the succession. However, with the exception of an apparently small number of servile families in Germany who were subject to either total confiscation or to very heavy successorial dues (the *Vollschuldigen*),[70] the latter seigneurs only received a small part of the inheritance. It was reduced either, as at Saint-Vaast of Arras,[71] to a small sum of money or, more often, to the best head of cattle or to the best of the movables (*Besthaupt, Kurmede, heriot, meilleur catel*).[72] What was the situation in eleventh century France—the north excepted? Three points appear certain regarding culverts. Their inheritance was, in some cases, struck with a duty benefiting the seigneur which a Beauvais notice, as early as the eleventh century, called mainmorte.[73] This is one of the oldest examples of the use of this word, perhaps the oldest. The descendants' rights, as a rule, took precedence over the seigneurs'. Several documents mention the culvert's "inheritance."[74] A notice from the *Cartulaire de Noyers* shows a culvert being given, together with his *frerage* (*omnem fraternitatem suam quae ei eveniebat*)* i.e., his brothers, his share in the paternal succession.[75] The seigneur's rights normally took precedence over those of the collateral heirs.[76] It is clear that the same principles hold for serfs at about the same time.[77] Was it necessary for the descendants of a culvert, in order to inherit, to have lived in common (*à feu et à pot*) with the deceased? The example given above by provost Geoffroi's heirs seems to prove that it was not. It is most probable that this restrictive rule was not applied to serfs either at that time. One sometimes conceives of the history of servile succession as a regular curve: first the seigneur takes all, then a part only, then—but only on the condition that there were descendants and that these had lived in common with the deceased—nothing. This is to believe too firmly in the continuity of progress, or better, it is to misunderstand economic realities. The seigneurial system was founded almost entirely on tenures

---

* The brother's share that came to him.

laden with taxes and services to the profit of the seigneur. Naturally, it was to this latter's advantage never to allow the cultivation of these little agricultural farms to be interrupted. To confiscate the fields was impractical: the seigneur could do nothing with them. He could not conveniently join them to his domain: for want of slaves and of a sufficient number of agricultural workers—who had to be nourished or paid—the cultivation of the domain was mostly ensured through the tenants' *corvées*. Any increase of the domain's size at the expense of the tenures ran the risk of depriving the seigneur of the labor essential to cultivate it. To sell the confiscated property was equally impracticable: there was little money in the countryside.[78] The wisest course of action was to maintain the serf's or culvert's children on the soil by leaving them the inheritance. Only the collateral heirs were set aside because, in law, according to an old idea that we have to discuss further, the seigneur was thought to be closer to the deceased than they were, and also because in fact, being normally already provided with their own land, there was no advantage in increasing their tenures perhaps beyond their capacity to work them. Later, with the spread of currency and the increasing rarity of fallow lands, a land market was created. We know that in the thirteenth century the results of mainmorte were generally sold, often to the relatives of the deceased.[79] The seigneurs, always preoccupied with preventing tenures placed under theirdependence from passing into the hands of persons foreign to them—for example to former subjects who had emigrated—made the principle of the succession reserved to the community prevail. In conformity with these habits—the strength of the economic familial bond is attested to, in France, by the institution of the kinship right of preemption[80]—this principle assured the perpetuity, on a single agricultural enterprise, of the group attached to its cultivation.[81]

Deprived of "liberty" how could the culvert obtain access to holy orders? "No serf or culvert henceforth may be made a cleric, if he has not beforehand received freedom from his seigneur in the presence of the proper witnesses," the councils of Bourges and Limoges[82] prescribed in 1031. In order to enter religious orders, canon law did not require, as for ordination, the enfranchisement of the serf; it was content with the seigneur's consent.[83] The same rule was applied to the culverts. Toward the middle of the eleventh century a culvert's son died, in Noyers, as a monk. The rest of the text shows that his seigneur—a layman—had seen with favor this pious act; nothing indicates a previous manumission.[84] But the seigneurial consent was indispensable. When a culvert who belonged to the cathedral of Le Mans was welcomed, without the canons's knowledge, into the abbey of Saint-Vincent, the chapter became disturbed and demanded an indemnity.[85]

One road was opened, however, to the culvert desirous of ridding himself of all these shackles: the enfranchisement. We possess a rather large number of acts of this sort relative to culverts. They are in all details similar to the charters of the same nature and of the same epoch touching upon serfs.[86] Thus there existed, among the forms used by notaries, some models with two entries, allowing the blotting out of the inapplicable term, servus or collibertus. In the preamble, the two terms were often left to coexist.[87] Some ancient collections—a compilation originating from Orléans in four manuscripts,[88] another from the same source, known in a single example kept at Donaueschingen[89]—furnish, it is true, some special formulas for culverts. But these do not deviate from the ordinary type of servile manumissions. Whether applied to culverts or to serfs, the gift of freedom was considered to be a pious act. This idea provided the theme for innumerable preambles, and it was not without some moral force. When Aldeguer de Jaunac died under the cowl toward the end of the eleventh century, his three brothers, heirs to his property, thought to insure the repose of his soul by enfranchising all his culverts.[90] But the seigneurs were not always so disinterested. Decency generally forbade, in charters of manumission, any allusion to the price offered or received. It would be naive to conclude from this that manumissions were in fact universally gratuitous. Guérin le Prudhomme only obtained his delivery from culvertage by first paying to Gautier de Mayenne a sum large enough to allow the latter to build a stone charter near the castle's gate. Then, a little later, Guérin still had to compensate his new seigneur, Joel, with a second indemnity.[91]

One must not believe either that in the eleventh century the enfranchisement always had the definitive freedom of the beneficiary as its purpose. Sometimes the only reason was to legalize a change of servitude. When one seigneur ceded one of his serfs, by sale or as a gift, this operation produced a double effect: first the rupture of a personal relationship and then the formation of a new relationship of the same order in favor of a different master. One hardly allowed such strong bonds to be unmade and retied without a solemn ceremony. It was generally found necessary, therefore, for the former seigneur to mark the abandonment of his rights through a regular enfranchisement. Then, frequently, perhaps always, the momentarily enfranchised person, with an oath conceived according to these visual forms that were indispensable for the juridical conscience of the time, acknowledged his servitude toward the new master.[92] From this follows the fact that acts of donation or of sale of serfs, in ancient times, are so often drafted on the model of manumissions, likewise, habitually, for culverts. See, for example, the charter by which the castellan of Saumur, Hugue Mange-Breton, apparently gives—in reality sells for twenty sous—one of his culverts to the monks of Saint-Florent. It opens with a long preamble: the evocation of the Natural and Christian liberty, the theory of servitude issued from the *lex fori*, a eulogy of enfranchisement as "pious work," all the commonplace words that can be found at the head of so many manumissions. Then the apparatus follows in which the same stereotypes reappear here and there: "I, then, Hugue, surnamed Mange-Breton, moved by the love for this veritable salvation and for this true liberty, for the good of my soul, the souls of my parents, and that of my wife Hersent, I have freed a man named Lambert, surnamed Fantin, from the yoke of culvertage under which up to now I held him bound and, from my own power and from my own seigneurie I make him pass under the power and the seigneurie of the servants of God, the abbot of the monastery of Saint-Florent and his monks."[93] Any mention of the oath of servitude is missing from this example; that is because this charter emanates from the seller whose role ended with the enfranchisement. But here is a notice saved in the register on which the monks of Marmoutier transcribed the acts relating to their serfs and culverts. It begins by recalling that Hubert, son of Avejot, sold to Saint-Martin and to its monks his culvert Pierre Bonardin. In this case it is the very fact of the sale which concerns the monks who care above all to protect themselves, by recording the price paid, against any claim from a dishonest seller. It is of little importance how the bond between the culvert and his former seigneur was broken. On the other hand, it is extremely useful to record the formalities that created and sanctioned the new relation of servitude to the benefit of the saint: thus the notice continues by recounting how Pierre presented himself with four deniers on his head "and thus offered himself into perpetual service to God and to Saint Martin."[94]

Studied in detail, with as much precision as the bad state of our sources allow, the judicial condition of culverts appears to us to be exactly similar to that of serfs. It does not provide the

THE "COLLIBERTI" 111

touchstone we were searching for. Let us, therefore, explore other roads.

That the culverts were distinguished from the serfs neither by their social situation nor by the quality of their seigneurs

Between 1060 and 1068 a monk of the abbey of Maillezais in Aunis named Pierre undertook to recount the history of his community.[95] The neighboring region was a country where culvertage was practiced. Maillezais itself had received in 1003 from the duke of Aquitaine, Guillaume le Grand, a few culverts[96] whose descendants, attached to their hereditary status, probably still lived in Pierre's era and appeared by their "intractability" to have caused some concern to the religious.[97] They were subjected to the same taxes and to the same constraints as the serfs with whom, however, they were not confused. What was the origin of this difference between two classes of men that were on all points comparable? Pierre believed it to be his duty to present an explanation:

> At the extreme end of the island in question [that of Maillezais, in reality a peninsula or perhaps a knoll emerging from the swamps] on the banks of Sèvre stood a few huts [at the time of Duke Guillaume Fièrebrace, father of Guillaume le Grand]. There lived a race of men subsisting on fishing whom our ancestors called "culverts." This word has come to be [also] applied to a whole category of serfs, but, it seems, by derivation from the name given to the fishermen. Since the opportunity presents itself I am going to attempt to penetrate the sense of this term. *Collibertus*, according to some, comes from *cultu imbrium* [the use of rains]. The race of culverts perhaps earned their name in the popular tongue, which is capable at times of creating veracious appellations drawn from common things: in fact, when the rains swelled the Sèvre, our men, leaving their sometimes distant homes, hastened toward the river to fish. In any case one thing emerges from the popular tales about these people: they are irascible, almost ruthless, cruel, incredulous, intractable, almost strangers to the human race. A nation coming from the Aquilon, the Normans, used to come up the river, despoiling and killing all it came across. The tales tell that, under this nation's sword, in a vast massacre, a great multitude of culverts was destroyed.[98]

The sole interest of this document is to show us that the monk of Maillezais did not know any more than we do. The problem that occupies us already bothered curious spirits in the eleventh century. They were not able to resolve it other than through imagination. In any case, these fantasies are well suited to a supposedly historical tract from which exact history has almost nothing to draw. One is surprised to find that such stories could ever have been taken seriously. Yet these tales have influenced some scholars who retained the idea that culverts formed a poor, contemptible, perhaps backward class. In 1847 Francisque Michel gave them such a role in his *Histoire des races maudites*. This is an odd way in which to present the rank of culverts in the social hierarchy, which is below free men, it is true, but is above the serfs.

In 1878 Karl Lamprecht proposed an exactly contrary interpretation. According to him, the culverts had been "the richest and best considered" among the serfs.[99] It is incontestable, in fact, that a number of documents show some members of the culvert class occupying relatively superior situations—a fact that should suffice, if need be, to ruin the theories born of the mad lucubrations of Pierre de Maillezais. Guérin le Prudhomme, culvert of the seigneur of Mayenne, owner of a plot of land in the *castrum* of the same name, wealthy enough to pay very dearly for his enfranchisement, has all the appearance of having exercised the lucrative trade of pawnbroker[100] together with his friend Chotard who helped in his enfranchisement. Other culverts were artisans: blacksmiths,[101] carpenters,[102] tanners,[103] shoemakers,[104] masons.[105] They especially figured among the functionaries, the "sergeants" of ecclesiastical or lay seigneuries, where they filled either some functions of an economic order—millers,[106] bakers,[107] salt-makers,[108] laundrymen,[109] shepherds[110]—or even were entrusted with administrative duties such as those of forester,[111] surveyor of roads,[112] provost,[113] or mayor.[114] As all seigneurial *ministeriales*, these culverts held fiefs.[115] Thanks to their high positions, they gained power, consideration, and often wealth, and some of them sought to slip into the free class, indeed even to go higher still. Alon, culvert of the monks of Bourgueil, was a knight; he married a woman "free and of noble origin"; he tried, in vain incidentally, to pass for free.[116] Toward the end of the eleventh century, the ambitions of a culvertile family caused much anxiety to the monks of Saint-Vincent of Le Mans. First, Garnier, provost of the abbey at Sercy, claimed his freedom in a plea held at Chateau-du-Loir; his suit was dismissed.[117] His brother Rahier was more enterprising still and probably was more powerful. One day he armed his relatives, enlisted some "robbers," and beat back the abbot who, by authority of the courts, had come to seize his land. Despite this outrage, the death of one of the abbot's men, and the wounds inflicted on three others, Rahier succeeded, as a result, in having himself enfranchised. He henceforth rendered "the service of knight" to the monastery for the fief of *Apouchard*, which he had purchased. He gave hommage and faith "as a freeman." Unfortunately, having later omitted to observe the conditions that were imposed on him by the act of enfranchisement, he was, in conformity with the stipulations of this very act, condemned to fall back into culvertage; we do not know whether this judgment was ever executed.[118] All these facts are interesting, but is there anything inherent in them which places the culverts apart from the serfs? Artisans were not rare among the latter, and neither were sergeants who often manifested an extreme independence vis-à-vis their seigneurs and many of whom strove to enter and, in fact, did enter the ranks of the knighthood. This is all part of the history of the "ministeriality," which is common to serfs and to culverts. *Ministeriales* of both classes are more frequenly evident, particularly in older documents, than are men of similar servile condition but of less wealth. This is quite normal: ministeriales entered into formariage more often in order to find spouses who were their equals in dignity and in property, and they did so more easily because they were wealthy enough to indemnify their seigneurs.[119] Being richer and more eager for independence, a greater percentage among them purchased their enfranchisement; they also were quicker to enter into disputes. But ministeriales are not the only servile men to appear in the documents. The greater number of the many culverts recorded as having been given or sold were most probably humble peasants. There were many nuances within this single juridical class, and this was true for both the culverts and the serfs.

Pierre de Maillezais was not the only one in his time to be intrigued by the problem of the culverts. Another explanation has been recorded in a hand that appears to date from the eleventh century on a manuscript of Saint Augustine, preserved today in Munich. It is worth the trouble to cite it in its entirety.

> What is a *collibertus*? He is called *collibertus* who, first slave (*mancipium*) and serf, then devoutly given by his seigneur—who wished thus to redeem his sins—to a private (?) place,

that is to a bishopric or to a monastery or to some consecrated church, is therefore pledged to ecclesiastical liberty, not to be henceforth entirely free and independent (?), as are the enfranchised (*liberti*), but in order to belong to the divine service, under the laws of the ecclesiastical manse, and following conditions that he can in no wise transgress. In other words, if I have a serf, he serves me as my own man; he is neither enfranchised (*libertus*) nor *collibertus*. But if I give him for the good of my soul to the altar of a saint to which he pays each year a rent fixed by me, or else for which he accomplishes in person a daily service, he will henceforth no longer be my serf, he will be (my) *collibertus* (or "coenfranchised"), that is he will be included in the same liberty as I, according to my hopes, for I am also the serf of God and of the saint to whom I have given him.[120]

One must divide this text into two parts. On the one hand is an attempt at an etymological interpretation, a tentative one in any case: the word collibertus is first compared with the idea of *libertas ecclesiastica*, then, a few lines later, endowed with a pious significance in which the culvert and his first master are presented both as joined into God's slavery and in the hope for a final liberty. This is pure intellectual legerdemain of the kind that had already tempted more than one cleric;[121] it is less stupendous on the whole than the ideas Pierre de Maillezais toyed with, but it is equally unworthy of serious consideration. On the other hand, the text presents a factual statement, one that is at first glance more impressive as coming from a contemporary. It can be formulated as follows: "one calls culvert a serf who passed from the domination of a lay seigneur to that of a church." Alas! Social historians have too many opportunities to perceive that nothing is more difficult for an author than to describe correctly the society in which he lives. The testimony of the texts is unimpeachable. Despite our etymologist, there lived all about him in his own era numerous culverts whose masters—kings,[122] great princes, or simple seigneurs[123]—were simple laymen.

Here is another interpretation, a quite recent one: Let us suppose, says M. Petit essentially, in a treatise full of important information, that a man of servile condition places himself, as a provisioner or as a tenant, in the service of a person other than his own seigneur. Under the subjection of his new employer, he is nevertheless still attached to his first master by a bond that nothing can break save a gift or an enfranchisement. Our man remains his first master's serf; but in order to distinguish this "servitude at a distance" from the more general term, language has created a specific word: one says that our emigrant is the "culvert" of his distant seigneur. This original and ingenious theory unfortunately comes up against objections that appear insurmountable to me. First it expressly refuses to account for the genesis of the word collibertus, the primitive meaning of which—coenfranchised—is certain. Its etymology, as Pierre de Maillezais and the author of the note written on the Munich manuscript understood it, cannot be precisely determined. But this is not a good reason to deprive oneself of the means for an excellent investigation, which the serious study of a semantic evolution offers. What can one say of a historian who would write on serfdom without asking himself why serfs carried the same name as the ancient slaves? Second, what emerges clearly from the care with which authors of documents note the culverts's places of origin is, thinks M. Petit, that the culvert was a foreigner; authors rarely concerned themselves with such matters when they were dealing with serfs. However, this observation, borrowed from Grandmaison, rests on an unconvincing statistical analysis. I have studied the figures as best I can from the *Liber de Servis Majoris Monasterii*, cited by Grandmaison and by M. Petit. Of thirty-nine individuals (children or women placed under the dependence of a head of family not included) designated as serfs or servile women, I have found eleven mentions of origins; of thirty-one culverts, twelve. Inevitably the proportion could not be the same for both classes; and the total number being small, chances were high that the difference would be large. By chance the figures happen to lean in favor of the culverts (38% against about 28% for the serfs). M. Petit himself seems to recognize that the rule does not hold in other manuscript collections. Moreover, if culverts are only immigrated serfs one does not understand why so many documents make of them a class of men apart, better yet, as shown in the rules relating to mixed marriages, a class clearly superior to that of the serfs proper. Then, the foreigner, says M. Petit, is "a priori suspect"; this is why "culvert" becomes an insult. This last remark, as we shall see, is correct. But if culvert truly took on its insulting value because of its synonymy with foreigner, how is one to explain that the innumerable literary texts that use it as an insult never indicate, even by allusion, this particular nuance, never couple culvert to any other term meaning foreigner, whereas one finds it frequently joined to serf or to expressions recalling the chevage? Why would popular language have so rapidly and so completely allowed this word to lose such a fundamental significance, one that must have been so alive?[124] Finally, above all, many documents tell of culverts sold, given, or enfranchised, or simply of culverts living on a land and attached to their condition from father to son, without ever hinting at this duality of seigneurs, which, according to M. Petit, was characteristic of the culverts. To take only one example, a decisive one, Guérin le Prudhomme, culvert of the seigneurs of Mayenne, then enfranchised by them, lived in Mayenne and owned there a plot in the *castrum* and a meadow along the river; there is no indication that he had ever left the seigneurie of his birth.[125] In fact the serf who is separated from his native land or from that of his ancestors had a name, one that M. Petit knows well, and one that is very clear: serf forain, foreign serf. There is no other name.

In summary, the enigma remains total, but at least we can now specify its terms. I would put it as follows: among the nonfree, next to the serfs, there are, in the eleventh century, families whose members carried hereditarily, as proper to their condition, the name of culvert. The persons thus designated paid the same taxes as the serfs; they were subject to the same hardships, held by the same bond; they could belong, as could the serfs, to any seigneur; they differed from serfs neither by profession, nor by wealth, nor by place of residence. The similitude between the two categories was so exact that no one knew quite why one had to distinguish one from the other. However, it was known that a culvert was not a serf; it was believed that he belonged, in law, to a more elevated class. Such a paradoxical situation can only be explained as the result of the survival of an ancient concept. The idea that comes naturally to mind is that servile and culvertile families, no longer separated by any distinction, were at least distinct in their origins. Such is in fact the hypothesis that is imposed on us. We shall take it up shortly, but first, it is fitting to complete the image of French culvertage by following up to the end, that is to its disappearance, the curve of its evolution, and then to place it within the European framework.

The fusion of culvertage with serfdom

In the course of the first years of the twelfth century, the colliberti gradually disappeared from archival documents. Even in Touraine and Anjou, where they seem to have remained longer than elsewhere, I do not know of any act mentioning them as a distinct class later than 1163.[126] They simply were no longer thought about. In 1106 still, Philip I, granting to the abbey of Morigny in Beauce the much desired privilege of assimilating its nonfree dependents to the royal serfs who were habitually provided with various privileges and notably with the right to testify in court even against freemen, took care to include expressly in this grant the monks's culverts together with their serfs.[127] In 1120, Louis VI, renewing this arrangement, only mentioned the serfs.[128] It would be equally absurd to suppose either that the descendants of the culverts of the preceding era had all perished or that their seigneurs had agreed to ruin themselves by allowing them all to be raised to the rank of free men. It is obvious that they blended in among the serfs.

The distinction between serfs and culverts no longer rested on any tangible characteristics. It was normal that this distinction tended to disappear. In the second half of the eleventh century, uncertainties of vocabulary were multiplying. In decrees, the same individuals were called alternatively culverts or serfs increasingly often.[129] An enfranchisement formula from Orléans, handed down in two manuscripts dating from the first half of the thirteenth century (although the formula is undoubtedly more ancient) states: "I, B., of such and such a place, now and forever have delivered from all obligation of *culvertile* service a *serf*, called B"[130] (emphasis added). This growing imprecision was marked with a particular clarity in the rubrics of the cartularies composed around this time: sometimes, at the head of older decrees mentioning culverts, the rubrics speak of serfs; sometimes the inverse error appears.[131] Obviously the two words were constantly used one for the other. One no longer knew how to classify the children issued from marriages between persons belonging to these two classes, since the difference in rank between them had ceased to be perceived. Toward 1100 a serf of the monks of Noyers married a culvert of Robert de Fresneau; according to the rule the children should have belonged to the religious. However, the latter, uncertain of their right, agreed with Robert to submit the question to the judgment of men knowing the law and agreed beforehand to accept the decision of these experts, even if—and this they seemed to foresee—they ordered an equal division.[132]

Finally, as we have seen, the term "culvert" ceased to be used in the documents. Once there was no longer any distinction made between culvertile and servile families in daily usage, notaries used only serf. Any precise technical language cannot allow synonyms. A little later, incidentally, the very term serf, itself guilty of too imperiously evoking the memory of ancient *servi*, was in its turn ostracized from the charters and normally replaced by homme de corps.[133] Yet neither serf nor culvert ever completely disappeared from common speech. They were still in use in the thirteenth century, along with their derivatives. They simply were used as synonyms.

"Culvert" is rarely found, it is true, in juridical texts, since they hew to a certain purity. However, in the countries of the Loire where culvertage seems to have been particularly tenacious, the old word returned, hauntingly, under the pen of men of the law. The *Coutume de Touraine-Anjou* distinguished two categories of *aubains* (*escheats*): those who made "seigneurage" to the baron and paid him the four deniers of the chevage (one knows that the condition of the aubains was, in many respects, similar to that of the serfs; it had, according to a manuscript of the Grand Coutumier, "the flavor of servitude");[134] and those who had neglected this precaution. The baron inherited, in all cases, all the movables from the latter. From the others, if they had any children, the baron only received one-half of the movable succession. Some manuscripts call the aubains who are subject to the chevage *cuverz*.[135] The *Livre de Jostice et de Plet*, written in the Orléans region, made much use of cuvert, cuverte, cuvertage. Most often it is to render, from the Latin models—*Corpus Juris Civilis*, or *Decretals*—which it follows quite closely, expressions such as *servilis conditionis, ancilla, servitus, servitium*.[136] One passage, however, is independent of any translation, and none puts more clearly into focus the equivalence between the two words that served to designate the nonfree class. "A female serf" recounts the customary, "married a church serf; later her seigneur enfranchised her, but the husband remained a culvert."[137] In Poitou the use of the word culvertise to designate, in some seigneuries, the servile chevage is followed in the documents up to mid fifteenth century.[138] An ancient formula of oath, kept in a rent-roll dating from 1300, shows the canons of the cathedral at Chartres swearing, upon their entrance into that office, that they are "of free condition, neither culverts, nor the sons of culverts."[139] The popular usage sometimes even spread as far as the apostolic or royal chancelleries. On February 3, 1245, Innocent IV, granting to the monks of Saint-Benoît-sur-Loire the privilege to follow henceforth, in court actions regarding avowals of servitude, the procedure of the enquiry rather than the ancient one of the duel, designates the recalcitrant subjects from whom the religious will have to claim their right not, as normally in bulls of this type, under the name of serfs but under that of "culvert, otherwise called homme de corps." The bull, following usual practice, probably simply reproduced without modification by the curia the texts used by the Orléans abbey for its request.[140] In 1213 the chancellery of Jean sans Terre, writing in Latin but thinking in French, no doubt in western French at that, threatened with "*culvertagium* and perpetual servitude" those rebels who will not answer the feudal levy.[141] The use of culvert rather than serf spread even outside the original region where culvertage had existed. On December 3, 1254, Raoul, count of Gruyère, declared he renounced any right he possessed over a man of Morlon and his sons, who had become bourgeois of Fribourg, and evidently were his old serfs "under the term of [service of] their body or of service of culvert."[142]

But it is especially among the literary texts that it is necessary to look for common usage. In the texts of the twelfth and thirteenth centuries, examples of culvert, culvertise, and so forth are innumerable. To seize the perfect synonymy of serf and culvert, to feel the narrow association of ideas which bind the chevage—the servile tax par excellence—with the word culvert, let us read, for example, how, in the *Chevalerie Ogier de Danemarche*, Charlot insults the Danish hero:

> Ogier dist-il, fel quvers renoiés,
> Sers, de la teste rendans quatre deniers*[143]

or else, in *Renaud de Montauban*, here are the evil words Roland addresses to Ogier, who is decidedly under a dark cloud:

> Fix a putain, coars, mauvais sers acatis,
> Par .IIII. deniers l'an estes aculvertis.†[144]

For the antithesis culvertage-liberty, here is Hélinant's short maxim:

> Morz fait franc homme de cuivert‡[145]

---

* Ogier, he said, you are a crude culvert, a traitorous serf, giving four deniers from your head.
† Whoreson, coward, evil, mercenary serf, for four deniers a year you are a culvert.
‡ Death makes a free man of a culvert.

or still the chanson of the barons whom Saint Louis has forbidden the judicial duel:

> Douce France n'apiaut l'en plus ensi,
> Ançois ait non le pais aus sougiez,
> Une terre acuvertie.§[146]

This exact equivalence between culvert and serf was rendered possible by the fact that in usual French form, the end result of a profound phonetic transformation, nothing in culvert served to remind the speaker of the idea of liberty originally included in the very radical of collibertus. On the contrary as soon as one returned to the classical Latin form, the etymology, having become visible once again, showed a veritable semantic antinomy, one that was embarrassing to the theoreticians of language. Evrard de Béthune, who composed in the twelfth century or perhaps toward the beginning of the thirteenth a treatise on Latin grammar which had an extraordinarily lively and lasting success, was very careful to explain to his readers the different meaning of the narrowly connected terms:

> That one who is deprived of liberty is called *colibertus*,
> That one who from serf became free is called *libertus*.[147]

For a freeman there is no worse opprobrium than to be called a serf. In the lists of legally punishable insults published by some municipal regulations, serf figures prominently. And, to be called a serf or a culvert is all one: the example of poor Ogier of Denmark has just shown us such a tautology. One could as well, in this respect, use culvert by itself. The pejorative use of the word is very old; it is attested to in Provençal as early as the *Chanson de Sante-Foi*,[148] in French since *Roland*.[149] Later it developed marvelously. There is no more familiar insult to epic heroes. It seems to carry with it not only the idea of a contemptible characteristic in general, but more precisely a nuance of cowardice, as if courage was thought to be the privilege of a noble birth or at least of a free one. This insulting meaning was only derivative, but it rapidly became the most usual. Was the evil pun to which I made allusion at the beginning of this paper a function in this? In any case it could only have been conceived very late; it is certain that the "e" of the adjective "vert," once closed, did not start

---

§ Sweet France is no longer called thus, which was thenceforth known to its subjects as a "culvertized" land.

to open before the thirteenth century, rendering thus acceptable to the ear an assonance with the always opened "e" of collibertum culvert. Besides, no ancient text, to my knowledge, speculates on this equivocation, which has appeared so luminous to some etymologists. There is no need to have recourse to it; the semantic development is easily explained in itself. The outrage was not to tell one's enemy: you are subject to such and such juridically determined servile burdens. It was to cry out to him quite simply: you are not free. Empty of precise juridical content, culvert thus all the more strongly suggested the raw concept of the deprivation of liberty. Gradually, however, the first meaning of the word was lost; it ceased being synonymous with serf, which alone was maintained in the vocabulary of the social institutions. Culvert then became only an insult, stripped of any concrete association, and thus an insult without flavor. It was abandoned in the fourteenth century. I have not found any example of it after Eustache Deschamps.[150] After the first half of the twelfth century there no longer was a culvertile class. Two centuries and a half later, no one spoke any longer of culverts.

ITALIAN "CULVERTI"; SPANISH "CULIBERTI" OR "LIBERTI"

It would have been impossible for me to undertake by myself a study of the Italian *colliberti* based on extended scrutiny. Luckily, in Italy itself various scholars have gathered and diligently commente upon the principal texts. Their research will guide ours, without necessarily imposing upon us exactly similar conclusions.[151]

The documents are divided into two groups of different age, and it is necessary to differentiate them with more rigor than usual. The first date from the Lombard or Frankish period, the others are spread out over the eleventh to the thirteenth centuries. Only those from the earlier epoch must be retained for the moment, to be compared with the more or less contemporary texts found in France. They allow us to compare—let us use the properly medieval forms—the Italian *culverti* with the French culverts. In peninsular Italy, a single mention, in truth a somewhat enigmatic one, has up to now been found. In the time of the abbot Beraldo III (1099-1119), two ruffian seigneurs, Morico and Carbone, odiously molested the monks of Farfa, in Sabine, and their subjects. Beside the usual pillage and murder, these bandits committed all sorts of pleasantries of the worst taste. In particular they were accused of having had the rite of the offering performed, for the fun of it, by their "culvertes" in the church. This is the wording of the abbot's complaint.[152] He meant to say, I think, something like servants, or serfs, and at the same time, concubines. Is it necessary to see, in the use he made of this term, a reference to the language of the French or Provençal literary texts? Aside from the fact that neither in French nor in Provençal can one find the use of culverte in the sense of woman of pleasure, such a borrowing, at this date, is not very probable. Must one believe, on the contrary, that the word designated or had designated a juridical class in central Italy? On the basis of a single, and so obscure, example, it is hard to decide. It is better to leave the question open.

In Sardinia, on the contrary, there is no hesitation. One finds culverti there as a servile class up to the first years of the thirteenth century. Away from the social currents transforming the peninsula, this large island was a favorable terrain for the maintenance of archaic institutions. It is necessary to note, however, that when the culverti were in evidence there (twelfth and thirteenth centuries) their name was less a juridical reality than the survival of an old linguistic habit. They were hardly to be distinguished from the servi: "The culverts, that is the serfs and servile women," state two charters of 1108 and 1119;[153] "my culvert, that is to say, my serf," one reads elsewhere.[154] As in France, culvertage in Sardinia blends with serfdom. There also, the difference in the words must originally have corresponded to some difference in fact.

Spain, to the north of the Ebro, has also known culiberti and gave them a place apart in society, one analogous to that which the French culverts occupied. In 1087 Sanche Ramon, "king of Aragon and Pampeluna," proclaimed himself ready to protect the monastery of Our Lady of Yrache against all violence, whether exercised by "a seigneur or a knight, a cleric, a villein (*rusticus*), a culvert (*culibertus*), or a bourgeois," and ratified the donations made to that house "by kings, knights, clerics, and even culverts."[155] The *fuero* of Tudela in Navarre, probably written, in its present form, between 1247 and 1270 but based on some more ancient models, states as follows: When a man arrives from "beyond the harbors," if he arrived by horse and holds on to both horse an weapons for a year and a day, he will have the rank of a freeman (*infanzon*) and will not pay rent to the seigneur. If he has not arrived by horse and has not settled either in the house of a knight or in that of an infanzon, he will be a villein subjected to the king or to the seigneur. But if, deprived at the end of a year and a day of both horse and weapons he had nevertheless made his first entrance on horseback, he will be neither an infanzon nor a villein, but a culbert and he will pay each year two sous to the king or to the seigneur.[156] It is not certain, not even probable, that the culvertage must be considered as an indigenous institution in Aragon and in Navarre. The word's form, as given in the *fuero*—culbert, without the final "o"—attests to a verbal loan from the Gallo-Roman. Northern Spain, after the great devastations of the High Middle Ages, was largely repopulated by *coloni* from beyond the mountains.[157] Undoubtedly they carried with them the idea and practice of culvertage. The juridical principle thus transmitted from without was implanted in the local law and acquired there some new aspects, as shown by the classification of immigrants in force at Tudela and for which one would seek in vain the parallel in France. At least this is what appears to me to be the likely evolution of the term. But it is fitting to leave to Spanish scholars, placed near the sources and capable of interpreting them, the task of explaining the problem.[158]

Besides, it may be legitimate to compare the French colliberti with the liberti that some documents from Leon dating from the tenth and twelfth centuries show us as subject, despite their name, to a veritable servitude. A judgment from King Bermude, rendered on June 22, 999, decided that the children born from mariages between certain subjects of Saint James of Compostela and those of a seigneur called Vegila were, as in the past, to be divided equally between the two masters. The individuals placed under this essentially servile rule were called *servos et libertos*.[159] The bishop of Mondonedo, Rudesindo II, in 943, and the seigneur Oduardo Vimorez, on April 24, 1123, enfranchised, following the customary forms of manumissions, first a *liberta*, second a *libertus* together with his sons.[160] To enfranchise an enfranchised person—the expression is somewhat contradictory. But the same oddity already appears in those French decrees where culverts also were granted the franchise. *Libertus* or *collibertus*—the fundamental meaning of the two words is the same. Both carry the original idea of a liberty received and definitively acquired. How did collibertus in France (together with northern Spain) and in Sardinia, libertus perhaps, in the kingdom of Leon, happen to designate a quasi-servile class that, in France and in Sardinia, ended by blending completely with serfdom? In this verbal paradox is the key to the problem. It is now necessary for us to go back in time in order to discover an explanation.

THE ORIGINS OF CULVERTAGE

The colliberti *in Rome and in the barbarian kingdoms*

In Rome, from the time of Plautus,[161] one called colliberti the enfranchised persons of a single master. The word did not express only a relation of fact; but the memory of servitude once suffered in common; a similar submission and similar services rendered to the former master, now become the patron; and often some collective burden imposed by this very patron all contributed to the creation of bonds between these men who had received their freedom from the same hands, for some at the same moment. These bonds were at once juridical and sentimental, and they were frequently sanctioned by religious usages. The colliberti were held to be all equal, so much so that Ulpian believed it necessary to specify that, despite this equality in principle, they were nonetheless subject, among themselves, to the obligations of filial piety.[162] Business relationships—*societas lucri quaestus compendii*—were naturally established among them.[163] The same *columbarium* welcomed their ashes. They rendered each other funeral honors, sometimes in touching terms: "Between me and you" says an inscription consecrated by a collibertus to the memory of his companion, "my religiously venerated co-enfranchised, I know that disagreement was never raised.... We purchased our liberty in the same house and nothing would have separated us had not this day, marked by your destiny, accomplished it."[164] Frequently the patron gave them a legacy in common, either through pure benevolence or, more frequently, with the condition that they place his tomb under their collective veneration. Their group was then conceived as a true civil society, a *corpus*.[165] Even when their legacies were attributed individually, there were cases when these shares, with the death of each beneficiary, had to return to the common mass to be divided again between the survivors.

Neither the name of collibertus nor the usages just described disappeared after the invasions. But here two difficulties of a linguistic order must be cleared up before going further.

We have seen earlier how the author of an anonymous gloss in the eleventh century brought together the word collibertus and the concept of Christian freedom. Others had done the same before him. Delivered from sin by their common Redeemer, "called by Him to freedom" in Saint Paul's words,[166] Christians and pious souls could not have given themselves a name richer in meaning than coenfranchised. *Collibertus* thus penetrated into devout language. Whether Gregory the Great placed it in the mouth of Saint Peter haranguing a poor monk,[167] or whether it was used by some clerics of Saint Anastasia of Ravenna as a religious qualificative for other members of the community,[168] it amounted quite simply to something such as "brother in Christ." It is idle to seek, as has been done at times, to clarify with such texts the juridical history of culvertage.

Yet this mystical meaning was very closely related to the original significance. We are drawn much further from the first meaning by a graphic mistake, a true parody that for want of having been recognized as such, has been the cause of much trouble for some scholars.

In classical Latin, *liber* and *libertus* represented two distinct notions. But, as the two words were similar in appearance, inexpert scribes of the barbarian era sometimes confused one for the other. *Liberta persona* was a Frankish formula designating a free person.[169] The same parasitical "t" is found inopportunely inserted in the writings of several manuscripts of the Germanic laws.[170] In its turn, collibertus was sometimes taken in the sense of "equal in liberty," not in the common language, protected as it was against this confusion by the pronunciation and the phonetic transformations themselves, but in the both artificial and incorrect Latin of the jurists. The law of the Bavarians said of the free man who had sold as a slave another free man that he had delivered into servitude his *conlibertus*.[171] It is in the Lombard laws that this usage appears most frequently; there it is particularly annoying because the Lombard charters of the same epoch mention, from time to time, some true colliberti, by that I mean some coenfranchised persons. It has been difficult to believe that contemporary texts—although of different nature and language—could give two such meanings completely opposite to the same word. Scholars have performed feats in order to reconcile the two definitions. However, one must yield to the testimony of the sources. Presently we shall rediscover the colliberti of the charters, and we shall have no difficulty in recognizing them as perfectly similar to their homonyms in Roman juridical texts. As for the meaning attributed to the word by the laws, how is one to be deceived by it? The laws of Liutprand prescribe, in the case of a lawsuit on the remaking of a pledge, the selection as surety of a freeman, whom his conlibertus will recognize both as free and as worthy of faith.[172] The same laws anticipated the case when an individual will have deposited some of his property in the house of one of his conlibertos, "freeman".[173] They allowed scribes to draw up the *cartae* according to Roman law, even if the party who contracted the obligations were of Lombard law, or inversely according to Lombard law if the party was of Roman law, on the condition that the conliberti forming the agreement desired it.[174] The laws protected the agreements made between conliberți or between parents (of whatever condition).[175] The edict of Rothari obliges a champion accused of magical practices to swear an oath between the hands of his parents or one of his conliberti.[176] Ratchis forbade the representation of others in court; whoever appeared improperly in the trial of his conlibertus will pay a fine equal to his own *wergeld*.[177] In all the preceding texts "cofree" is an acceptable definition for conliberti. Perhaps in some of them and in another passage still to be cited it is, nevertheless, necessary to note a nuance: not only are conliberti "similarly endowed with liberty," but they are "endowed with the same kind of liberty"; in other words, they are among free men of equal condition. A law of Ratchis prescribed that when a *gasindus* (vassal) of the king was the object of a complaint on the part of an *arimannus*—a simple free man—he must in the first instance himself examine these complaints; he is to proceed to this examination either alone or, if he is ignorant of the law, with the aid "of other conliberti" who know how to judge.[178] One must believe that these conliberti were also royal gasindi. The law had for express purpose the protection of the gasindus; it could not submit his case to anyone but his peers. Whatever the variations of details and the diverse obscurities in these difficult texts, two points seem certain. Sureties, possessors of entrusted goods, contracting parties, champions, representatives in justice, judges in the tribunal of the gasindus—all these people could not possibly have been former slaves. Nor can one see in them, as has been proposed, the members of agrarian communities: nothing here evokes such an idea.[179] The only probable explanation is that one already perceived by Benjamin Guérard:[180] the colliberti of the Lombard laws were only *colliberi* with a superfluous "t."

Let us return then to the true colliberti, products of a common enfranchisement.

The survival of practices that had unified economically and juridically the Roman collibertal group appears clearly, at least in Italy. Slaves were often enfranchised in a group, either in a will or otherwise. These manumissions sometimes gave birth to some true communities. One of these, in 797, stipulated that if one of the freed persons died without leaving any father, son, or daughter, or even a brother, he will have for heirs his colliberti.[181] Others, from the same century, forbid the enfranchised to alienate their lands, except among themselves.[182] As we shall see in greater detail in a moment, charters of this kind did not confer independence to their beneficiaries; having left servitude proper, these people still remained placed under the *obsequium* of a seigneur. Undoubtedly, the clearly understood interest of the seigneur led him to preserve and to reinforce the practices of solidarity bequeathed by the tradition of the preceding eras. In any case the arrangement forbidding any alienation of land outside the little society formed by the subjects of a single seigneur is found in other decrees, where it is not applied to enfranchised, for example in the charters of settlement.[183]

In Gaul the word colliberti, save error, is not found in the Merovingian era; but since it reappeared as early as the end of the eighth century and since, besides, popular language conserved it and transformed it according to its own rules, one cannot doubt that it had survived in practice. The texts do not show as clearly as in Italy the existence of juridical affinity between the coenfranchised. On the other hand, very ancient documents highlight the survival of another form of solidarity, born this time from religious works accomplished in common. On March 31, 558, the hermit Cybard, granting freedom to 175 slaves and placing a certain number of them under the protection of the church of Angoulême, stipulated that the latter were to present themselves on the day of the feast of the Chair of Saint Peter in the "temple of God" each carrying a candle in offering weighing one pound.[184] On March 27, 616, the bishop of Le Mans, Bertrand, made his last will and testament; according to custom he stipulated the enfranchisement of a great number of slaves, among others his domestic slaves (*famuli*), but not without imposing on the latter a very curious obligation: on the day of his anniversary, they were to present their offerings on the altar of the basilica where the bishop had located his grave; there, no doubt under the clergy's directions, each was to perform on that day the office with which he had once been charged in his master's household; then, the following day, the abbot of the basilica would join them in a great feast.[185] The *credo* had changed; the tradition of honors rendered, in a group, to the burial site of a patron by his old slaves was not lost.

Thus in Italy and in Gaul all kinds of practices preserved from oblivion the notion of a collibertal bond and the very name of colliberti. But it appears that at the same time this term took on a new meaning. If libertus disappeared from the Gallo-Roman and Italian languages, it is because it was replaced in practice by collibertus; the simple word ceased to be; the composite alone survived. There is nothing odd in such a substitution. Romance linguistics offers many such examples; in a great number of composite nouns the sense of the prefix, at first clearly perceived, gradually faded and finally vanished completely.[186] Of course, the fact that many liberti truly felt among themselves to be "coenfranchised" could only favor this shift of meaning, enlarging and attenuating at one and the same time the original significance. Two acts of donation, one from 757 in favor of the abbey of Gorze, the other from July 12, 764, in favor of that of Lorsch, included in the formula of pertinence the following enumeration: "with ... litis, libertis, conlibertis...."[187] One is aware of the frequency of redundancies, through the use of synonyms, in formulas of this sort. There is no reason to doubt that from the end of the eighth century, in Gaul, collibertus was only understood as the equivalent of libertus.[188] We are led then to the study of the enfranchisement.

The enfranchisement in the high Middle Ages; lites, aldions, enfranchised cum obsequio.[189]

In Frankish Gaul, in Lombard and Frankish Italy, during the high Middle Ages, innumerable slaves received their freedom. A great deal contributed to this trend: the teachings of the Church which made of enfranchisement a pious work, and whose voice was brough forcefully to the attention of the great proprietors in particular, at a time when they were preoccupied to insure, in their wills, both the transmission of their fortunes and the salvation of their souls; and the economic conditions that, for some reasons too lengthy to scrutinize here—only the fact is important to us here, and it is undeniable—made the wide use of servile labor increasingly less remunerative. These frequent acts of liberation were performed in extremely diverse manners. The Germans, since before the invasions, had developed a whole law of enfranchisement, likewise, on their side, the Romans. In the barbarian kingdoms, these two systems—the German one, moreover, varied according to peoples—coexisted, and sometimes influenced one another. Then, under the influence of the two mixed traditions, molded by the needs of a society in the process of organizing itself along new principles, a new, less disparate, legal system began to emerge. But this did not happen before the tenth or eleventh century. Until then nothing was more complex, more involved, than the regime of enfranchisements. However, within this chaos, a broad outline emerged with much clarity. However different in form the various types of manumissions were from one another, two large, well-defined categories based on the condition of the enfranchised can be defined without difficulty.

On the one hand, the master, if he so desired, had the faculty of giving to the slave his complete freedom, without any restriction. These are the *manumissiones sine obsequio*, the *ingenuitates generales* of the formularies of Frankish Gaul. On the other hand, the seigneur could grant only a *manumissio cum obsequio*, a *ingenuitas respectualis*. In this case the enfranchised remained under the domination either of his old master or of a new seigneur (often a religious community or rather the patron saint of that community), to whom the old master had remitted him. The enfranchised's position in the society was then slightly different, depending on whether the manumission had taken place according to Germanic law—such at least as the Lombard and Frankish laws—or conforming to Roman rules.

The Frank and Lombard societies had a place designated in advance for enfranchised persons remaining within the bonds of seigneurial dependence. Lombards and Franks in fact—the latter together with most of the peoples belonging to the western Germanic group—only exceptionally allowed former slaves, even once freed, into the ranks of fully free men. They created for them a special juridical category, unknown in Gothic and Burgundian laws. The Franks, along with the Saxons and the Frisians, called these people, depending on the dialect, *lata* or *la[z]za*.[190] The Latin sources of the imperial period transcribed this as *laeti* or *leti*. This is the name they give, by analogy, to German soldiers established in the Empire under the subjection of Roman authorities. Later, at the time of the barbarian laws, it is still to be found in the ancient texts, such as in some manuscripts of the Salic law: *leti, laeti, letones*, more often *liti, lidi, litones*. This "*i*" is obviously the result of a properly Romance evolution of the *e* or *ae* of the first Latin transcription. It is never found in the Germanic forms and, if it penetrated into some Latin texts written or copied in German countries, it was under the influence of the mode of writing then in force in Frankish Gaul. As for latinized forms with *e* and germanic ones with *a*—supposed to be long—they are explained easily by a Germanic *lēt*. The simplex can never be separated from the compound OHG, *frilazza, frilaze, hantlazza*, Goth. *fralêto*,[191] which can be found in the sense of enfranchised; it was related with them to the root of the Gothic verbs *lêtan*, OHG *lâ[z]an*, "to let, to loosen" and has the same meaning. The "lites"—I am using the form currently adopted by French historians—were then, properly speaking, "enfranchised" people.[192] In order to designate a similar class the Lombards used the word "aldion." "The aldion," states a gloss, "is a person enfranchised under condition of certain services."[193] This conception of the aldions, who were expressly compared to the lites by Charlemagne,[194] did not, it is true, at least after the occupation of Italy, include all of the enfranchised still subject to the master's power. The edict of Rothari allowed a Lombard to make of his slave, through manumission "of the four roads," a free man according to the law of the people (*fulcfree*) and as a result raise him well above the aldionate, while maintaining him under his protection, his *mundium*.[195] But there is no doubt that in practice most of the enfranchisements cum obsequio had as a result the creation of aldions. The large numbers of aldions attested to in the documents is in itself a sure proof of this. To pass from the condition of aldion or from that of *lite* to real freedom, it was necessary to obtain a new enfranchisement following some very solemn ceremonial forms.[196]

In any case, enfranchisement was not the only source for lidism and for the aldionate. The ancient law rigorously prohibited and provided with the harshest penalties the union of a free woman with a slave. This rigor softened with time and as a result it became necessary to regulate the condition of children issued from such marriages, which henceforth became customary. In order to find for the children an intermediate status between the mother's freedom and the father's servitude, the best solution seemed at the time to be to label them as aldions, as in Italy, or as lites, as in Gaul.[197] In addition free men could, voluntarily it seems, pass into lidism or into the aldionate.[198] Above all, in the beginning, lites and aldions, similar in that at least to the Athenian resident foreigners, counted among their ranks all the individuals who, without being slaves, were forbidden access to the city; next to the enfranchised were members of conquered peoples, incorporated into the state but not admitted to the privileges of the victorious.

All traces of this practice had not disappeared at the time of the invasions. The *wergeld* of the free Roman, in Salic law, was equal to the lite's.[199] The Lombard laws did not mention this, perhaps because they included the free Roman under the rubric of aldion. But while it was easy, in documents, to retain the ancient usages, the total assimilation of conquered populations within a social category placed in a state of narrow dependence upon barbarian masters was evidently incompatible with the new conditions created by the establishment of the Germans in the Empire. The lites and the aldions in Gaul and in Italy ceased to have their numbers increased by conquest; but they continued to be recruited largely among persons enfranchised according to Frankish or Lombard laws.

One scholar, Maurice Kroell, has, it is true, tried to demonstrate that lites were extremely rare in Frankish Gaul and that they disappeared early.[200] His argument rests essentially on the small number of references to lites which, he tells us, he has found in the texts. But, aside from the fact that he did not scrutinize every text (he has omitted, notably, the polyptique of Lobbes[201] and the collection of acts of the Merovingian period, *Actus pontificum Cenomanensium*,[202] which attests to the existence of lidism in Maine on two occasions), it is not clear that any certain result can be obtained in this manner. Litus was a barbarian word that the notaries did not use willingly, preferring to translate it. As is to be expected, they rendered it—as several texts show—by libertus.[203] How is one to determine when this very general term was meant to apply specifically to lites? Any statisticalstudy will forever remain impossible. We may grant without difficulty to M. Kroell that in all likelyhood lites, created under Frankish, Saxon, and Frisian laws, were more numerous in the territories occupied by these nations than in the territories inhabited for the most part by a Gallo-Roman population. But it is certain that their name became a sufficient part of the vanquished's language to undergo, as we have seen, a new vocal transformation. It is probable, also, as we shall see later on, that even in Gaul this personal status with Germanic origins was sufficiently widespread to leave traces in the subsequent period's law.

The Roman law of the later Empire did not set the enfranchised in a class apart. Only a few, the Latin enfranchised—*Juniani*—remained foreign to the freedom of the city. But, in these later centuries, they were certainly not very numerous. When Justinian suppressed this old institution, it had no doubt been moribund for some time. It remained without influence on the law of the barbarian period.[204] A manuscript from the *Formules de Tours* still mentions in its table of contents an *ingenuitas latina*;[205] but the decree is not to be found in the body of the text; it was probably considered practically useless. One can say that, as a general rule, ancient slaves liberated according to Roman formulas, except for the *obsequium*, remained with their patron only as a matter of individual choice. Later on, however, from the ninth century at the earliest, some decrees take note of such persons and attribute to them a quasi-technical term, *colonus*. We will have to return later to this particular case.

Whether enfranchisement was accomplished according to Roman or Germanic forms, the relation of the enfranchised cum obsequio to his former master or to the substitute this master had designated hardly differed in practice. This was a bond of dependence, a very narrow and hereditary one. The enfranchised and his descendants after him remained placed under the protection, the *mundium*, of their patron, and they were compelled in return to perform those duties of submission and of respect which were properly expressed, in the diplomatic language of the time, inspired as it was by Roman models, by the term obsequium. The pontifical chancellery, by a curious survival of the most archaic vocabulary of the clientage, said, with the same meaning, *salutatio*.[206] An annual tax, collected by head, was the most ordinary symbol for this subjection; as a rule this practice, a very ancient one for the *lites* and no doubt also for the aldions, expanded gradually, as we shall see, and included the beneficiaries of manumissions according to Roman law. Beside this kind of poll tax, a variety of burdens, different in each case, often very heavy, weighed almost always on the freed man, who generally continued as a tenant to cultivate his patron's lands, and on his posterity. These burdens, although most of them had an economic character, had on occasion, as we have seen, a religious side to them. When there was a written decree, these charges were sometimes but not always, specified in this document.[207] The strength of the bond created by this kind of enfranchisement and the contrast which opposed such enfranchisements to those of the other category are highlighted with particular clarity in a decision taken in 633 by the Fourth Council of Toledo which became first known at the end of the eighth century by the Church of the Gauls. The decision concerned the question of regulating the access to ordination. If "the patron has not retained any *obsequium*," then there is no difficulty: the enfranchised is placed on the same footing as the freeborn man. On the other hand, the council extended the absolute prohibition against the entrance into holy orders, traditionally applied to slaves, to those who "have only received the manumission under the reservation of *obsequium*," for, said the canon, "those are still attached to their patrons by a bond of servitude."[208]

What was the proportion between enfranchisements of either type? Any precise calculation is obviously impossible, but one can accept without fear of error that the manumissions cum obsequio were much the more numerous. In fact these were favored not only by the two Roman and Germanic traditions, but above all by the conditions of the time. This imperfect liberty created by this type of manumission served the interests of the manumitted most often and the manumitter almost always better than the granting of true freedom. In a troubled society, there is nothing more dangerous than isolation, and none was more isolated than the former slave who was deprived of his legal family. The need for him to be attached to a patron was so imperious that one of the essential rights recognized to the beneficiaries of enfranchisements *sine obsequio* was, almost always, to seek a protector for themselves wherever they wished. The former master was, of course, a most natural choice. A Lombard charter gives voice to the enfranchised themselves in these terms: "Vulpo, Mitilde, their sons, their daughters, and their descendants have said that they did not wish the 'four roads' and that they were content, for their future liberty, to receive it under condition of remaining under the guard, tutelage, and protection of the priests and deacons of Santa Maria Maiora of the city of Cremona."[209] Decrees of this nature are rarely entirely sincere; one must believe, nevertheless, that more than one person placed in Vulpo's situation did in fact go along with his choice. As for the masters, living in an environment where wealth, essentially landed wealth, rested on the use of the taxes and services furnished by tenants, where all power had for its base a patrimonial authority extended over a very large number of men, they were quite willing to yield to any reason—economic or religious—which counseled them to be generous with freedom only because the rules of law allowed them to retain the freed slaves in their dependence. The practice of enfranchisement cum obsequio, which is after all only one of the pieces of a social system entirely constructed upon relationships of personal subjection, is sufficient by itself to explain the progressive disappearance of slavery in the proper sense of the word.

The coloni: the word and the thing

The term *colonus* sometimes served in Frankish Gaul to designate certain enfranchised persons who remained under their master's mundium. Much later, some French notaries connected it with the term culvert. A brief search on the fate of this word in France will thus be necessary here, if only in order to clear the terrain of useless hypotheses.

Everyone knows that in the later Empire laws attached, by hereditary bonds, all tenants to the soil they tilled, whether they were slaves or of free condition. The free men were generally called coloni. They were also called, in the same sense, *adscriptitius*. However rigorous the lot of the coloni may have been, and it was very close, in many respects, to that of the slaves, they were nonetheless freemen, and thus very carefully distinguished, by this title, from true slaves (servi).[210] When the Germans penetrated Gaul, a great number of farmers belonging to this juridical category lived on the lands of rich proprietors there. What became of them after the invasions?

An imperial rescript had superbly proclaimed that the rule that attached the coloni to the soil was "eternal."[211] In fact in appears it hardly survived the great upheavals of the pre-Middle Ages, either in the East[212] or in the West. In Italy Theodoric abolished it expressly for the slaves;[213] an ephemeral abolition, incidentally, since the Byzantine reconquest reenforced the ancient law, further solidified and developed by the eastern emperors and by Justinian himself. The coloni proper were apparently not affected by the provisions of Theodoric's edict. In Gaul, in any case, no measure was taken in their regard. It was not the law, at that time quite inoperative, but the very social conditions of the time that lead, in Gaul as in Italy, to the relaxing of the shackles once imposed by the late Empire both on the proprietors and on the tenants.[214] Born from the needs of a very powerful state and bound to a juridical system that made hereditary characteristics of profession and of rank, the Roman institution of the colonate, in the exact sense of the word, could not help but be drawn into the collapse of that state and of that system. Of course, one can find, here and there, a few proprietors seeking to strengthen the bonds that were to hold the tenants on their land: On January 18, 721, Abbot Wideradus, enfranchising his serfs and placing them under the patronage of diverse religious communities, forbid them to go live on lands other than those on which he had established them and which he had given to these churches.[215] But the "eternal" succession of free farmers, from father to son, on the tenures, was no longer assured in practice, as is strikingly shown in the *Polyptyque de Saint-Germain-des-Prés*, in the first years of the ninth century. This document distinguished, in the customary way, three categories of hereditary manses: *servile, lidile,* and *ingénuile*.[216] The latter, according to all evidence, had originally been those of the coloni. Had the coloni remained fixed to their plot, one would expect to find them all on ingénuiles manses, and on these only. And yet this is not the case. Many coloni held serviles or lidiles manses; a good number of the ingénuiles manses were in the hands of servi.[217] And indeed Carolingian legislation, usually so careful in cases regarding social classification, never bothered to refer to the fundamental principles of the Roman colonate on this question; in fact these principles had been forgotten.[218] No doubt many families of coloni remained on their tenures; there was no reason for them to leave or for the proprietors to chase them away. But to the extent where coloni could make use of a hereditary right to their land against attempts at dispossession, this right rested henceforth not on a state law but on those local customs that gradually became the foundation for all the relationships within the seigneurie. And if the seigneur could still hope to compel his coloni, even against their will, to remain on their land—in fact a rather difficult thing to do—it was in virtue of the both vague and powerful authority he extended over all of the inhabitants of his land. The celebrated formula in Theodosius's law: the coloni "are the slaves of the land on which they are born,"[219] thus establishing through an audacious fiction a relation of dependence between a man and an object, was much too abstract to remain intelligible in an era where all social relationships tended to be reduced to the notion of submission and protection exchanged between two individuals.

However, there were always some coloni. They lived, as tenants, on the land of others; were subject to the seigneurial power, now expressed by the wholly Germanic word *mithium*;[220] and they continued to be, in principle, considered of free condition. These coloni took an oath of fidelity to the sovereign.[221] They depended, in law, directly on the tribunal of the state: while the servus when suspected of public crimes could only be conveyed before the *mallum* by his own master, the colonus, in a similar case, was only compelled to go through the intermediary of his seigneur when the latter had obtained a privilege of immunity.[222] The coloni themselves had jurisdictional capacity: in June 857 a certain number of coloni figured as judges, alongside "noblemen" in a case held by the provost of Saint-Martin of Tours where the parties were local proprietors and a priest.[223] The inventories of the domains that sometimes, as at Saint-Germain-des-Prés, gave them their proper name coloni, sometimes, as in most of the *villae* of Saint-Rémi of Reims listed them under the significant name *ingenui*,[224] and regularly placed them apart from the servi. The coloni themselves estimated it was to their interest to be distinguished from the servi, probably because they felt better protected than the servi against seigneurial despotism in matters of taxes and, perhaps, especially in matters of corvées.[225] In 801 the inhabitants of Mitry brought a suit against the monks of Saint-Denis before the royal tribunal—a suit that, incidentally, they lost—with the sole purpose of proving that they were coloni, not servi, and must not be burdened with "inferior service."[226] For the most part, these coloni of Frankish Gaul descended—one does not know how—from ancestors already called coloni in the late Empire. Others had entered into this condition voluntarily.[227] Finally there were occasions when enfranchised *cum obsequio* were assimilated with coloni, whenever the former had received their manumission according to the Roman form. In January 876 the priest Menlodinus, enfranchising his servus Gaubert and placing him under the authority of Saint-Bénigne of Dijon, declared him to be "a free colonus."[228] Likewise, between 951 and 962, the monk Gibert, granting freedom to five servi who henceforth would pay a chevage —the sign of dependence—to Saint-Florent, therefore made them pass "into the colonate," states the notice.[229] The *Polyptyque de Saint-Germain-des-Prés*, in contrast with the polyptyque of Saint-Rémi of Reims which listed enfranchised of all kinds (*liberti*, who perhaps are lites, *chartularii, epistolarii*), mentioned among the peasants who cultivated the lands of the abbey only lites, who were enfranchised according to Frankish law; it is probable that it ranked the enfranchised according to Roman law together with the coloni.[230]

Let us not be deceived, however. As early as the ninth century this distinction between coloni and servi, despite the efforts of the coloni to reemphasize it at times, had become very difficult to perceive. It was most probably remembered that the two conditions ought not to be considered similar, that the position of the coloni ought to be superior, that some men hereditarily belonged to one class or to the other. In fact, though, the two classes tended to be confused. The Carolingian legislation most often did not properly separate the coloni from the slaves; it was content to place the coloni in the first rank of slavery, above the masses but on an equal footing with the slaves of the Treasury, those of the churches, those who had received from their master an important function in his house or on his land—a *ministerium*—in short all the categories that formed a sort of servile aristocracy.[231] The reign of Charles the Bald marked an important step in the progressive rapprochement of the two classes: from this date, corporal punishments, which characterized the condition of servus and which the Roman legislation of the late Empire had extended to the coloni, only in particularly grave and clearly specified cases,[232] were officially recognized as proper also to the condition of the coloni.[233] A long time ago Guérard noted that mixed marriages, which were very numerous at that time, contributed much to the fusion of the lower classes.[234] It is necessary to add that the rules placed over unions of this sort show, better than any other indication, to what point the antique barriers had been erased. What must be done, a *missus* asks the imperial palace, when a man's female colona married the servus of another? Here is the reply: "Ask yourself, when your servus is united to the servile woman of another master, or when the servus of another master takes for wife your own servile woman, to whom among the two of you must this couple's descendants revert"—no doubt following local custom—"and follow this same rule in your case: for there are only two kinds of men, the free and the servi."[235] One could not hope for a clearer assimilation of the colonate with servitude. The last formula, it is true, by its too obvious resemblance to a celebrated saying of Gaius reproduced in the *Lex Romana Visigothorum*, betrayed a bookish recollection.[236] But basically it was indeed contemporary realities that inspired the solution indicated by the palace. The classification of persons in the Carolingian era owed its hopeless complexity and its uncertainty to a terminology imposed by tradition, or rather by two different traditions imperfectly adapted to new conditions. When one was faced with a practical problem, this confused hierarchy yielded easily to a very simple opposition between two great human categories.[237]

Once beyond the ninth century, the institutions of the state, in whose regard the colonus had never ceased to be considered a free man—as witnessed by the provisions for the oath of allegiance and for public justice—disappeared or definitely assumed the seigneurial form. The old traditional framework within which a relatively literate legal system also regulated by the state had attempted to enclose society were entirely broken. From then on, one lost the habit of considering the coloni as forming a distinct juridical class intermediary between servitude and the fully free man. There no longer was any mention of this concept in documents. Certainly most of the coloni blended into the servile class that, in any case, despite this epithet—and we shall have to return to this—represented a status quite distant from that of ancient slavery. The history of the vocabulary furnishes a perfectly clear testimony of the death of the colonate. In contrast to the words designating truly existing conditions such as servus, which became serf or collibertus which became culvert, and in contrast also with the general term mancipium, which, lost in French, was perpetuated, in the sense of servant, in the Provençal, massip,[238] colonus in Gallo-Roman lands, did not contribute anything to the vulgar tongue.

But it was maintained, of course, in the Latin of the charters, with a very different meaning, however, according to the convenience or fantasies of the notaries. I detect at least four such meanings: (1) In Rome the first definition had already been vague enough: cultivator, especially cultivator on the land of others, by opposition to the *dominus fundi*, but without anything inherent in the name itself to define the juridical relationship that united the farmer thus designated to the owner of the land. This meaning was without doubt never completely eliminated by the more precise value the term took later in the vocabulary of the later Empire. It is found in all periods of the Middle Ages.[239] Numerous decrees understand by coloni very simply tenants established on seigneurial land, whatever their personal condition or the modalities proper to their tenure. It is thus that in 1060 the count of Anjou, Geoffroi le Barbu, confirmed the renunciation, made by his uncle, Geoffroi Martel, on his death bed, of the evil customs that he had perpetrated on the "coloni of the churches";[240] thus in 1091 the knight Héliart gave to Cluny "a hemp field with the serf, colonus of this land."[241] It is useless to accumulate examples that could be multiplied infinitely.[242] Coloni was simply used as a translation for the French hôte or *manant*. Oddly, this very general meaning was the only one of which the vulgar tongue kept any trace. *Colonus* perished utterly, but a derived substantive, *colonica* became *coulonge* and was retained in certain regions, especially it seems around the Rhône or the Saône, in the sense of tenure. Some *coulonges* occupied by serfs are found rather frequently in texts from these regions.[243]

(2) Any man, whatever his condition, could be a tenant; but a free peasant—according to the medieval conception of liberty—was only a tenant since, in contrast with the serf who was placed in a state of personal subjection, the only bond that attached the free peasant to his seigneur was the possession of land depending upon the latter. Thus the double meaning of words such as hôte or villein, designating sometimes all the inhabitants of the seigneurie, sometimes more specifically those who escaped serfdom. Likewise for the colonus, the passage of one meaning to another was in this case made all the easier since the learned notaries no doubt knew of the original freedom of the Roman colonus. In 1179 Louis VII's chancellery quotes the men of Rosny-sous-Bois as claiming they were not serfs but "only hôtes and coloni" of Sainte-Geneviève.[244]

(3) Here is a meaning exactly opposed to the preceding one. Very early, notaries were reluctant to translate by servus the term serf which was current in common language: they felt more or less obscurely that the Latin servus had been an entirely different thing. They sought other equivalents and believed at times to find them among the terms found in the Roman juridical vocabulary that had been applied to conditions both different from full liberty and from slavery: *liberti, adscriptitii,*[245] and especially coloni. From the tenth century on, the use of this last word seems to have been particularly dear to the chancellery of King Lothar. On September 11, 814, Louis the Pious granted immunity to Sainte-Croix in Orléans: "We forbid," said the diploma, "any public judge to enter ... onto the possessions of this church ... in order to exercise a restraint upon the men of this church, either free or serfs serfs (servi)."[246] Between 954 and 972 Lothar renewed this privilege, but the formula was modified: "The men of this church both free or coloni." The antithesis, free or *ingénus* versus coloni,[247] is found again in three other diplomas from the same prince, of which two are for Saint-Benoît-sur-Loire and the third is for Notre-Dame of Paris.[248] In the eleventh century the charters or notices of Tours and of Anjou, especially those of Saint-Florent of Saumur, employed constantly *colonilis servitus* to express serfdom.[249] Thus colonus, earlier a synonym for free villein, is here a synonym for serf.[250] These are habitual games to this artificial and uncertain diplomatic language where one can witness *consul* designate alter-

natively a count or a municipal magistrate; servus mean in turn a serf, a sergeant, and—in the Mediterranean regions where ancient slavery still subsisted, or had taken on a new life—a slave; *famulus* and *cliens* any imaginable species of dependents.[251]

(4) What was written about serfs could hardly fail to be written about culverts. In documents from the same period and from the same source as those where serfdom was called *colonilis servitus* one finds this expression or other analogous ones applied to the culvertile condition, even with some predilection it appears, no doubt because of the vague assonance perceived by the notaries, such as the one between count and *consul*, between *colonus* and *collibertus*. Under the abbatiate of Ferri (September 1, 1022 to September 28, 1055), Gui de Thouars sold to Saint-Florent the culvert Audri, "who was attached to me," he said, "by the colonile servitude."[252] "I cede," said in 1035 a certain Marran, "to Saint-Florent a culvert called Aleaume ... in such a way that from today he will be subjected both to Saint-Florent and to the monks according to colonile law."[253] All the foregoing suffices to show that nothing would be more useless than to draw from these stylistic elegances any conclusions about the origins of culvertage. At the time when the clerics of Saumurs were devoted to *colonus* and the derived adjectives, these were only scholarly words, material for compositions and not living instruments of language. It is fitting to return now to some more concrete realities.

The fate of the enfranchised cum obsequio: the origins of serfdom and of culvertage

The medieval serfs inherited both the ancient servi's name and some of the characteristics of their condition. To conclude that they almost all descended from former slaves and that their condition was only an attenuated kind of slavery is seemingly a simple step. These two propositions, when looked at more closely, suffer from some grave difficulties, however.

In the ninth century the servi were few. In the twelfth and thirteenth centuries, on the contrary, before the era—which varied according to regions—of the great charters of liberty, the serfs formed in almost all of northern and central France the immense majority of the peasant population.[254] The domains of Saint-Germain-des-Prés furnish, on this subject, the elements of an instructive comparison. In the village of Esmans, in the Senonais,[255] at the time when the famous *polyptyque* was written (the end of the reign of Charlemagne or the beginning of that of Louis the Pious), there were no servi at all. In the thirteenth century, before the enfranchisement was granted in November 1289, serfdom weighed on all the inhabitants of Esmans.[256] At Villeneuve-Saint-Georges,[257] of 132 heads of family, the polyptyque counted 112 coloni, 1 "free" man, 5 individuals of unspecified condition, and only 14 servi; at Thiais,[258] of 146 heads of families, 130 coloni, 1 "free" man, 3 hôtes, a man of unspecified condition, and 11 servi. In 1249 and 1250 the general manumissions were granted to these two areas for the price of, respectively, 1400 and 2200 *livres parisis.* There can be no doubt that everyone there was a serf.[259] It is evident that the ancestors for these innumerable serfs of Capetian France cannot be sought uniquely among the handfuls of *servi* of Carolingian Gaul, and that, on the other hand, the coloni, lites, enfranchised of old, could not have had as unique descendants the very rare free villeins mentioned here and there by the texts. The composite origin of the servile class has long been recognized. I do not know, however, if one has always perceived clearly where this observation leads. It compels us to admit the existence of a social movement of wide import: from the ninth to the eleventh century, through a "slow and silent revolution," as Guérard has it,[260] the greatest part of the population of the French countryside fell or refell into a condition called servile. But this new servitude was quite different from ancient slavery.

There is no doubt that medieval serfdom borrowed some traits from slavery. First and foremost was the name. It is again necessary to note that as early as the Carolingian period the word "servitude" and all its synonyms or derivatives had lost much of their technical value. By then they only evoked the idea of a particularly narrow dependence. Guilhiermoz has shown very well the imprecision of the vocabulary of the vassalage, and of that of slavery or of serfdom.[261] In the tenth century even the *miles* who received a land in precarium from an abbey was called *servitus.*[262] A formerly powerful term such as *servitium* thus evolved and was forever stripped of any specifically servile connotation. This evolution goes a long way to explain how a class in which the descendants of coloni were certainly more numerous than the descendants of servi, nevertheless, received its name from the latter. Colonus would have suggested only the scarcely intelligible notion of a relation with the land; serf indicated a personal relationship.[263] Moreover, serf was the only term in use; an individual of this condition was often called the "man" of his seigneur. The *Polyptyque d'Irminon* already made use of this term to designate personal subjection, but it did not differentiate between coloni, lites, or servi, and called them all "men of Saint-Germain." The descendants of these people were, in fact, eventually all joined to the monastery by the "homage of the body,"[264] and they were called indiscriminately serfs. In those areas where slavery proper was maintained or reappeared, the popular language had to create a new word for this condition, and that new word was "slave." However the use of the ancient name to designate the medieval serf was heavy with consequences: it contributed to the maintenance of the notion of the inferiority of this condition and later allowed jurists to make dangerous comparisons with the rules of servility as fixed by Roman law.

The formalities and the vocabulary of enfranchisement was also inherited by the serfs from the former servi, likewise, for the incapacity to enter into holy orders. Here again, this extension of the characteristics of slavery to a much larger class dates back very far. In the Frankish period, it appears that coloni were allowed to be enfranchised.[265] Beginning in the same period, as we have noted, ecclesiastical legislation tended to refuse the ordination to enfranchised cum obsequio,[266] as well as to coloni.[267]

It is not necessary to refer back to precedents in ancient institutions in order to explain some of the other essential aspects of serfdom. These proceeded necessarily from the existence of a bond of hereditary dependence between the seigneur and his serf: the seigneur's justice following the serf everywhere; the substitution of the seigneur for the family as principal heir in certain cases as well as in the exercise of private vengeance; the chevage as manifestation of the seigneurial mundium, a point on which we shall have to return; the prohibition of formariage as the only means to prevent the difficulties brought about by the partition of children born of parents belonging to different seigneurs, a fact documented as early as the sixth century for eastern coloni[268] and for those of the Roman church,[269] and under Charles the Bald for the mass of the mancipia, certainly including coloni.[270] But it is above all the very nature of this bond so relevantly called "homage" that separates serfdom from ancient slavery: the relation of one man to another, regulated by the custom of the group, incorporation, despite much insubordination, exploitation, and violence, an exchange of aid for protection,[271] and not one man's right of property over an objectlike being. Fustel de Coulanges said that "serfdom" has "nothing in common with feudalism" and is "anterior" to it.[272] With a tendency to explain medieval society in terms of its antecedents alone, Fustel de Coulanges too glibly denied it any creative powers of its own. Benjamin Guérard, on the other hand, thought that the serf was, on the whole, "a vassal of an inferior degree."[273] I can only see one objection to this formula: it is incomplete. It is necessary to add that, in contrast with vassalage, serfdom was transmitted from generation to generation without the consent of those subjected to it; this is one of serfdom's fundamental characteristics. On the whole, however, Guérard is correct. Together with vassalage, serfdom emerged from a society where, considering the dissolution of the state and the loosening of classical and even familial bonds, only personal relationships of subjection and protection appeared to have any validity. The "homages," modeled, more or less, on ancient institutions (a collectivity has, per force, to work with the raw materials and particularly with the vocabulary handed down from the past), incorporating traces of ancient apprenticeships, clientage, slavery, and the status of enfranchised persons, were, however, original in their amalgamation of these various elements and particularly in the profound nature of the newly created bonds. Some of these bonds were of a superior order and of a contractual character (*ingenuili ordine*)[274]—the vassalage essentially—others, such as serfdom or culvertage, incorporated a hereditary obligation and the idea of a kind of baseness of status.

How did a mass of people who were originally not servi gradually enter into serfdom? A few were brutally thrown into this status one day by judicial decision, as was the case as early as 827 for the fourteen enfranchised of Oulx, in the Val de Suse, who were the victims of a thirty-year prescription (*trentenaire*) by the tribunal of a missus.[275] Many no doubt slipped imperceptibly into serfdom. A great number, however, changed their status voluntarily—by voluntarily I mean in law, for it is likely that, in fact, this "voluntary action" most often was imposed upon the individual by circumstances or even forced upon him by threats. This act was, in fact, quite exactly comparable to a commendation, with the difference, however, that it pledged both the individual as well as all of his descendents. Earlier, one could also be made into a lite or a colonus,[276] but most often, and exclusively after the ninth century, one was made into a servus. This practice can be traced far back in the history of Germanic societies; it dated from the time when serfdom was in fact slavery.[277] But in the tenth and eleventh centuries, the practice took on an incomparable extension. Documents from that period reveal the existence of a very large number of self-donations into serfdom. And there is little doubt that the texts only preserved the memory of a small percentage of the total that actually took place: although such acts were carried out along formal lines, a written record was not obligatory. This practice held such an important place in the juridical life of the time that some subtle clerics began to twist the clearest texts in order to justify this spontaneous abandonment of of freedom by referring to "Roman law."[278] This mass of free men entering into what was called serfdom certainly contributed to the changes in the conception the community-at-large had of this condition, and even to the changes in its very character. As early as the beginning of the ninth century, one witnesses small, free proprietors, in a contract with the abbey of Saint-Gall, foreseeing as an almost normal, probable, and apparently not particularly odious enventuality the subjection of their descendents.[279] In this new type of servile class, the enfranchised—lites, aldions, simple liberti cum obsequio—must have constituted one of the most important elements. Several texts from the Frankish period already call lites, servitus.[280] This is the name, as we have already noted, which is generally given to enfranchised cum obsequio by the Council of Toledo in a canon reproduced in most Italian or Gallo-Frankish collections. Further, the status of these men, bound from father to son to their seigneur, may have served, in one instance, as a model for the status of nonfree persons of a later period.

The obligation that was so characteristic of serfdom and of culvertage in France was the *chevage*.[281] Nothing smacks less of slavery than this tax in which the amount, fixed by custom for each family, was absolutely beyond seigneurial control. It was paid by men ranked into very different categories by a traditional, if already out of date, social classification: free men, coloni, servi.[282] It is difficult, perhaps impossible, for us now to understand why this tax weighed then on some men and spared others who appear to be of similar condition. But it is clear that it represented a narrow relationship of dependence to a seigneur, without regard to the original condition of the individual paying the tax. It is not without reason that, in the following century, a document from Lorraine calls such men *mundiales*, i.e., men placed under the mundium, the power of a seigneur.[283] Similarly, on the lands of Saint-Germain-des-Prés free men subjected to the monastery's *munborati* owed each year a predetermined amount of wax.[284] This payment of wax was to become, in time, one of the types of servile chevage. Its originally religious character is not to be doubted:

the wax was meant for tapers for the church, which were generally to be placed around a holy sepulchre. But it also had an economic character. Money was scarce; thus, in most cases when goods were purchased, the price was quoted in money, but it was paid in equivalent goods. The same practice was naturally applied to charges imposed upon poor people. They were obliged, for example, to pay each year "two deniers, in wax"; sometimes they owed "two deniers, or two days' work."[285] Whether payable in money or in goods, the meaning of chevage remained fundamentally the same. The chevage was a manifestation of the seigneurial authority and protection, and of the submission of the homme de chef. Which ancient institution, however, provided the antecedents for the chevage?

It seems natural to first look to the *capitatio* of the later Roman Empire. A state tax, the capitatio could have become, through concession or usurpation, a seigneurial tax. Let us examine this posibility. Under the common name of capitatio—everyone agrees on this point—the imperial administration gathered two taxes of different nature: one a real estate tax (the word *caput* here indicating a cadastral unit), the other a personal tax. The former cannot be considered: to the extent to which, after the state ceased to require it, the seigneur perpetuated this tax to his benefit, it must have blended within the mass of land taxes weighing upon the manse. There remains the personal capitation. We do not know precisely on which classes of the population it weighed. The only two classes of interest to our study are the coloni and the slaves.[286] In their regard, two main theories conflict. According to some authors, among which it is sufficient to cite Otto Seeck, the coloni and the slaves who owned tenures paid—directly or through the intermediary of the master, it matters little here—both taxes simultaneously: so much for the land, so much for their heads or for those of their families. It is possible to conceive, *a priori* that this tax, in its personal aspects, perpetuated and annexed to the seigneurial duties, might have generated the chevage. But documents dispel this notion. In fact, during the Frankish period, not only was there no longer any trace of a state personal tax on nonfree persons,[287] but most important, the testimony of the polyptyques is unimpeachable: those who paid the *cavaticum* are not, as the suggested hypothesis would necessarily imply, the whole of the tenants of Saint-Germain-des-Prés or of Saint-Rémi of Reims, they are not even all the peasants living in any given *villa*, but are, here and there, persons of all classes who are thus signifying a condition proper to themselves. If in ancient times coloni and tenant slaves had indeed been personally taxed, either this type of public charge had disappeared during the Frankish kingdoms or, at least, it had taken a landed character and could no longer be distinguished from other real estate taxes. On the other hand, if we adopt M. Piganiol's theory, whereby only nontenant slaves were counted by head, together with the other cattle, as part of the raw material of the great landed estates, the evolution appears clearer. In fact the slave, no more than the sheep or the steer, did not owe this type of capitulation: it was the master who was taxed in proportion to the number of servile heads in his *familia*; the slaves of this category, owning nothing by definition, could not reimburse him. When the state ceased to require it, the *capitatio humana atque animalium** simply disappeared. In any case the Roman fiscal system cannot explicate the chevage. We must look elsewhere.

I have already mentioned the fee paid, by head, hereditarily, by those enfranchised cum obsequio of Germanic law, lites, or aldions, to their patrons. This fee was called, among the Franks, litimonium,[288] among the Lombards by the common sense term mundium.[289] It was so characteristic of the status of these men and of their dependents that according to Frankish custom the abondonment of it by the master or the patron in a symbolic gesture—the throwing of the denier—constituted the essential rite of enfranchisement. By extension this fee was imposed on all enfranchised bound to a patron, whatever the form of their manumission. It is the *libertaticum*, the *libertinitatis munus* of the formularies. This "freedom tax" was owed *pro patrocinio et deffensione atque mundeburdo*.†[290] Those rare charters that have been preserved, particularly since the ninth century, specify the amount. Always small, it often seems to have been four deniers, this amount being attested for the litimonium, and the most usual amount in the polyptyques for the *cavaticum* in documents posterior to the servile chevage.[291] The status of the enfranchised cum obsequio, and earlier, the status of the lites, were better suited than the colonate, which was a purely landed bond, to evolve into the earliest type of a hereditary bond quite unlike slavery, and further to develop considerably in the course of time. The personal duty that earlier was indicative of the submission to a patron's mundium was used, as early as the time of the polyptyques, to

---
* Tax on people and animals.
† For patronage, defense, and protection.

indicate all kinds of mundium.[292] When institutions with sharper definitions finally emerged from the social confusion of the ninth and tenth centuries and when juridical thought became able to elaborate a new, more or less, stable terminology better suited to the comtemporary conditions, it became customary to consider any man who owed a payment "from his head" to his seigneur as belonging to this humble condition of hereditary dependence named henceforth serfdom. In the ninth century a number of personalities, enfranchising their servi, gave them the duty of paying a chevage to Saint-Etienne of Dijon on that saint's day. As early as the tenth century and during the eleventh, Saint-Etienne received as gifts men subjected to that very charge; however, these individuals were now called servi or mancipia.[293] At Saint-Pierre du Mont-Blandin, the status of the enfranchised placed by their former master under the mundium of the monastery visibly serves as a model to the status of free persons—called tributarii—who donate themselves to this house. The resemblance is not only to the chevage, which amount to two deniers in both cases, it also covers duties on marriages (six deniers) and the successorial tax (twelve deniers).[294] These tributarii remained free in principle. Indeed, they retained this handsome title for a long time. Yet, there also, the new classification finally triumphed. One can clearly follow the progressive application during the eleventh century of the servile vocabulary to this condition.[295] Certainly, the heirs of numerous enfranchised shown in the manumissions of the Carolingian era as subjected from generation to generation to the annual payment of a few deniers found themselves, due to this very obligation, ranked among the servile class.

Is it possible that these descendants of enfranchised, fallen once again into a new servitude, had no memories of their origin? We know that in the eleventh century, there existed in northern and central France, in Sardinia, perhaps also in northern Italy, and in northern Spain, some families with the hereditary name colliberti, in Spain sometimes liberti. These families were not thought of as free. Nothing in daily life distinguished them from the serfs who surrounded them. Yet, there was about them the feeling that they were not on the same level as truly servile families; they seemed to belong to a superior class. This idea slowly disappeared, for it had no concrete support; soon it vanished completely, and the merging of the two classes became complete. In the period that concerns us here, it still remained, tenaciously and inexplicably, as a pure memory. In fact, it was only a memory. All these culverts (to use the French term) were only, in all likelihood, the descendants of liberti from the early Middle Ages. Already almost identical with the rest of the serfs, they were still distinct from them by name and by rank. The mostly verbal relic of earlier times, culvertage remained in the eleventh century as a witness to one of the currents that had fed the great servile class.[296]

It is certain that even in culvertile regions, all those families who descended from liberti cum obsequio did not retain the privilege of a kind of social superiority. We still do not know why some were favored over others. But many areas, in and out of France, where enfranchised cum obsequio existed, did not have any culverts. Why? It is extremely difficult to explain such divergences. We are ill-informed about the evolution of various provincial societies between the Frankish era and the twelfth century. One can, however, guess at a few answers, clearly marking them as hypotheses aimed mainly at stimulating, I hope, further discussion and research.

In France the descendants of enfranchised men apparently succeeded in forming a distinct class, particularly in those regions ruled by Frankish law or subjected to its influence. In those areas, in fact, this class, placed between serfdom and complete freedom, was recognized early by custom; these were the lites on whose condition the status of the enfranchised in general was modeled. If culvertage is absent from the Midi to the southern Limousin and from the region of the Rhone River, it is perhaps because the Goths and the Burgundians had never allowed this intermediate category in their social hierarchy. The Aragon or Navarre culberts probably represent a French importation. There remains, in an originally Gothic region, the liberti of Leon. Spanish historians will have to supply us with an answer in this case.

Peninsular Italy and northern and central Germany, with which must be ranked Germanic speaking Flanders, provide us with a truly crucial case. There, with the possible exception of certain regions of Italy where culverti may have existed (we were not able to conclude this point with certainty), the Romance term designating enfranchised men did not survive as in France; the Germanic term did. One discovers aldions in Italy, sporadically until the middle of the twelfth century.[297] The case of Germany is still clearer and more instructive. In Frankish, Saxon, and Frisian lands, *laten, lazzen* were very numerous in barbarian times. The name remains throughout the Middle Ages and beyond.[298] It continued for a while to designate a distinct class. Then, at least in many areas, its meaning broadened. All persons who were not of free condition, whatever their origin, were called by this term.[299] This is the same history, albeit within a longer time period, as that of the culvert, which was, after all, the Romance equivalent of *lazze*. Thus, throughout western and central Europe, the vassalage era—from the ninth to the eleventh centuries—created original social institutions from ancient elements, to which were applied, with much hesitation and uncertainty, ancient words.

CHAPTER FOUR

*The Transformation of Serfdom:
Concerning Two Thirteenth-Century Documents
Regarding the Parisian Region.*[1]

Among those texts I have collected concerning the history of serfdom in the Parisian region, there are two that, at first glance, are striking by the singular character of some of their details. I wish to publish them here and to comment upon them. I hope the reader will see that their very oddness is instructive.

A king of France, either Louis VIII or Louis IX, granted some men of Gonesse[2] an exemption from the duties that they were formerly obliged to carry out for him and that resulted in their being considered serfs (no date, ca. 1223-ca. 1227).[3]

A. Lost original.

B. A contemporary copy, abridged, titled *Carta hominum de Gonessa*, Arch. Nat., JJ 26, fol. 120.

In nomine Ludovicus etc. Notum etc. quod nos, considerantes quod homines de Gonessa quorum nomina in carta quam eis consessimus plenius declarantur non poterant filios suos aut filias liberis personis in maritagio copulare, eo quod, sicut dicebant, imponebatur eis opprobrium servitutis propter hoc tantum quod adducebant latrones captos Gonesse apud Parisius et quod in mense augusti singuli eorum tenebantur per unam noctem granchiam nostram de Gonessa custodire, fecimus diligenter inquiri per dilectos et fideles nostros Hugonem de Atheiis et Johannem de Vineis prepositum Parisiensem quibus nobis obsequiis per hoc quod appellabantur servi tenebantur; qui, legitima inquisitione super hoc facta, ipsos erga nos in nullo invenerunt penitus obligatos, nisi in hoc quod adducebant latrones captos Gonesse apud Parisius et custodia granchie nostre sicut superius est notatum, propter que solummodo appellabantur servi. Unde nos, ob remedium anime clare memorie..., ipsos et heredes ipsorum in perpetuum penitus duximus absolvendos; et quiti a predicta servitutis nota, sicut predictum est, et absoluti penitus remanebunt: ita tamen quod nobis exercitum et equitationem et omnes alias redibitiones reddent sicut alii homines manentes apud Gonessam; et sciendum quod si aliqui prenominatorum manum mortuam nobis debuerint, in predicta non includuntur libertate, nec illos per presentem cartam volumus ab isto honere aliquatenus liberari. Propter hanc autem libertatem quam eis duximus concedendam, quittaverunt nobis et heredibus nostris in perpetuum totam campipartem et censum que apud Gonessam debebantur eisdem. Quod ut etc.

On first reading, this text is somewhat obscure. Let us try to reconstitute the events that brought about King Louis's intervention and to determine precisely the nature of that intervention.

There were in Gonesse, on the king's land, a certain number of men who, probably due to the tenures they held, were subject to the following two obligations: to escort to Paris thieves caught in Gonesse, and to guard the royal barn during the month of August, each man for a night. These services were not without remuneration: they were recompensed with a percentage of the *cens* and of the *champarts* of the seigneurie. This was a typical manner of remunerating seigneurial officers, or *sergeants*. In fact, it appears certain that the individuals brought to the fore in this document were low-rank sergeants whose functions, as so often happened, had become hereditary and attached to the tenure.

But the true origin of these charges were not known to the public. One, in fact, the duty of escorting prisoners, was probably considered somewhat honorable. Ignoring the reasons behind these duties, an unflattering explanation was thought up: rumor had it that these men were serfs. This rumor was quite detrimental to them: it notably prevented them from finding matches for their children among the free class. Indeed serfdom, following widely accepted custom, was thought to be contagious between kin; whoever, being born free, married a person of servile birth became, the very day of the wedding, a serf in turn and, therefore, subject to all the duties and juridical incapacities this status implied. In particular, his wealth fell under the weight of the rules of inheritance which allowed the seigneur to be heir to his serf [*mainmorte*], replacing, in some cases determined by local custom, his direct descendants, and everywhere and almost always, his collateral heirs. It was, therefore, in a free family's best interest to prevent unions that one day might jeopardize an inheritance. One must also point out that serfdom not only brought about very serious material inconveniences, but also a socially inferior and despised status. The "opprobrium of servitude," as our text has it, was a very heavy burden to bear. For all these reasons, a male or a female serf could not hope to marry except among his or her equals. Even when they purchased from their seigneur the right of *formariage*, that is to marry outside their own seigneurie, this was most often only to seek a spouse among the serfs of other seigneurs. They suffered from this matrimonial ostracism; several documents bear witness to their complaints.[4] The fate of Gonesse's pseudo-serfs must have been particularly worthy of pity. Being in fact free men, they certainly felt toward servile unions the repulsion common to their class; and the suspicion under which they suffered barred them from other free men; where could they turn? It is understandable that they wished to clear themselves of this calumny.

For it was indeed a calumny. The king received their complaints and wished to know why, in fact, they were called serfs. He, therefore, had two high placed persons begin an inquiry. The result was definite: the only cause for this unfortunate reputation attached to these individuals was the two duties detailed above. Jurists, then as now, have argued about the characteristics proper to serfdom, but none ever claimed that escorting thieves or guarding a barn were among these. There is more. The king, upon these individuals' request, decided to abolish the two unfortunate duties that had brought them so much trouble, in return for their abandonment of their percentage of the cens and champarts. This is the purpose of the text we are presently considering. But it was perfectly well known in high circles, for reasons I have discussed elsewhere, that the true condition of the king's subjects was always, in practice, extremely difficult to determine.[5] One had to avoid enfranchising a real serf, that is, someone subject to the mainmorte, by error. Thus, the letters of patent specified very clearly that if perchance one of the men mentioned happened to be subject to the mainmorte, he could not use the royal concession to escape this duty, and in general was not covered by this "liberty." This indicated unequivocally that the bulk of the men appeared to the investigators to be exempt from the most notoriously servile of all juridical incapacities. In a word, they were called serfs, but they were not.

Before deriving general conclusions from this text, let us go on to the second document.

Urban IV decided that clerics born either of mainmortable fathers or of fathers subject to the arbitrary *taille* must not be considered of servile status. He charged the bishops of Senlis and of Meaux with the duty to see to it this prescription was followed (Orvieto, November 13, 1262).

A. Lost original, described as follows by the compiler of the cartulary mentioned under B: "Collation a esté faicte à l'original des lettres escriptes en parchemin, saines et entieres, scellées de plomb et latz de corde, auquel plomb d'un costé sont impresséz le[s] chefz sainct Pierre et sainct Paul, et excript: *S. Pe. S. Pa.*, et de l'autre costé du d. plomb est escript: *Urbanus pp*ᵃ *IIII*."

B. Sixteenth-century copy, titled *Carta Urbani pappe quarti quomodo clerici nati ex regno Francie in terris religiosorum sancti Benedicti liberti sunt, et non ex servili conditione, dignitates enim obtinere possunt*,[6] in the cartulary of the abbey of Saint-Pierre of Lagny, Bibl. Nat., latin 9902, fol. 5 vo.-6 ro.

Urbanus episcopus, servus servorum Dei, venerabilibus fratribus Silvanectensi et Meldensi episcopis salutem et apostolicam benedictionem. In regno Francie, prout accepimus, circa nonnullos laicos est obtentum ut, cum iidem laici, constituti sub jurisdiccione aliquorum religiosorum aut secularium dominorum, clericorum vel laicorum, decedant, si nullos vel aliquos emancipatos habuerint filios, ipsi domini percipiunt omnia bona sua, tercia parte bonorum mobilium ipsorum decedencium, si de illa iidem decendentes in ultima voluntate disposuerint, dumtaxat excepta, vel nisi decedentes predicti fratres relinquant superstites cum quibus ea que habebant pro indiviso communiter possidebant. Si vero prefatis decedentibus supersint uxor et filii qui sub eorum potestate consistant, tantum medietatem omnium bonorum mobilium suorum que vulgariter in illis partibus mortalia seu manusmortua nuncupantur domini percipiunt eorumdem. Sunt et alii laici qui communiter[7] collectas dominis suis pro ipsorum dominorum voluntate persolvunt. Propter quod nonnulli asserunt quod liberi talium laicorum clerici servilis condicionis existant; sicque nonnulli prelati et capitula regni predicti statuisse dicuntur, super hoc prestito juramento et statuto hujusmodi, ut asseritur, per sedem apostolicam confirmato, ne dicti clerici ad beneficia ecclesiastica in suis ecclesiis admittantur, quamquam patres eorum dum sospitate fruuntur irrequisitis eorum dominis temporalibus bona sua libere ac licite vendant et donant, et alias de ipsis pro sua voluntate disponant, matrimonia contrahant et ad ferendum testimonium admitantur. Quia vero super hiis ad nos habitus est recursus, nos tales clericos qui nunc sunt et fuerint in posterum propter premissa seu eorum pretextu non servilis condicionis sed liberos existere decernentes, auctoritate presencium districte inhibemus ne de cetero ab aliquibus exceptio de servitute aut servili condicione occasione premissorum, in judiciis vel extra, ipsis clericis opponatur, nichilominus statuentes ut hii qui contra inhibicionem predictam venire temptaverint, exceptionem hujusmodi opponendo, nisi ab ea destiterint infra octo dies ab exceptionis hujusmodi proposite tempore numerandos, cadant a causis vel negociis in quibus exceptionem ipsam proposuerint, eo ipso. Volumus autem quod si hujusmodi clerici, recipiendo uxores vel alias, ad statum se converterint laicalem, quamdiu in hujusmodi statu permanserint, ad premissa jam dictis eorum dominis ac si non extitissent clerici teneantur. Quocirca fraternitati vestre per apostolica scripta mandamus quatimus per vos, vel per alium, seu alios, predictos clericos denuncietis fore liberos, et propter hoc non servos nec condictionis esse servilis, ipsosque posse, premissis ante statuto seu confirmacione hujusmodi nequaquam obstantibus, dum tamen alias sint ydoney, ad ecclesiastica beneficia cum cura vel sine curae personat[u] et quaslibet alias dignitates, episcopales et alias, necnon et ad quoslibet actus legitimos seu qui sunt publici juris admitti, nec permittatis prefatos clericos contra decretum statutum ad denonciationem[8] hujusmodi molestari, invocato ad hoc si opus fuerit auxilio brachii secularis, molestatores hujusmodi per censuram ecclesiasticam, appellacione postposita, compescendo, non obstante si aliquibus a sede apostolica est indultum quod interdici, suspendi vel excommunicati nequeant per litteras sedis ejusdem, nisi in eis de indulto hujusmodi plena et expressa de verbo ad verbum mencio habeatur.

Datum apud Urbem Veterem, idus novembris, pontificatus nostri anno secundo.

Here the general sense of the text is clear. The entrance into orders and, in consequence, the possession of ecclesiastical benefices, were forbidden to persons of servile condition. The Church never wavered from this principle. But what was meant by servile condition? One could hesitate on this particular point. The bull openly proposed to discard one definition that it judged to be false.

What Urban IV stated in substance, or rather what the petition that the bull most probably only paraphrased argued, was that there lived in the kingdom of France lay persons whose belongings were subject to special successorial customs. When, upon their death, they left no son or only "emancipated" sons—that is, sons who had left the family group—the seigneur inherited all their belongings. There were only two exceptions to this rule. On the one hand, these persons could dispose of a third of their movables through a will. On the other hand, if it happened that they left brothers who had lived together with them, in that case, the brothers inherited instead of the seigneur. Also, when the deceased left sons who, at his death, were still "under his rule" (that is still lived together with him), the seigneur only received as mortaille or mainmorte half the movables.

As we can see, this is a description of successorial law as applied to mainmortables—a somewhat scrambled description it is true. Not only does the bull's author reserve, wrongly, the term mainmorte to those cases when the seigneur receives only half the movables (the term, as we know, designated in an absolutely general manner the seigneur's rights over all servile inheritances); not only does he express himself so awkwardly that the allocation of movables to the seigneur appears to apply only to the detriment of sons rather than brothers, which is most unlikely; but, and this is more serious, he unfortunately introduces in his last sentence a mention regarding the widow. I have had to eliminate it from the summary above in order not to cloud the issue further; here it is now: "If these deceased persons," he states, "leave a wife and children who are under their rule. . . ." Yet it appears that in the thirteenth century the widow's rights, in the case of mainmorte, were in regard to the seigneur the same as in regard to the children in the case of a natural inheritance. In all cases, she received her dowry from the property and her part in the estate;[9] thus, it was completely unnecessary to cite her here.

As such, this exposition is very valuable. Naturally, we cannot give it too general an application. In such matters, local custom governed the application of the law, if not its principles. The customs described here must be considered to be proper to certain seigneuries, in a specific region; we shall see in a moment that this region was most probably the one spreading around Lagny, at the western tip of the comté of Champagne and of Brie.[10]

There was, the bull goes on to say, another category of lay persons: those who paid an arbitrary taille to their seigneurs. And some people considered as serfs the children of such lay persons (*tallium laicorum*, which, from all appearances, one must understand as describing both categories here discussed; but the text here again lacks precision). In virtue of this opinion some prelates or chapters of the kingdom refused to grant them ecclesiastical benefices. Wrongly, stated the bull. The lay persons concerned could, during their lifetime, without the consent of their seigneurs, sell or give away their possessions or dispose of them in any way; they could marry and give testimony in court. The sons of such men were, therefore, not servile. "We decide that they are free" and that in consequence they had to be given access, within the normal conditions of aptitude, to the ecclesiastical benefices and ranks.

An astonishing proposition! Two classes of men are thus declared juridically free by authority of the Apostolic See. On the one hand were those who paid an arbitrary taille, in my opinion, a perfectly tenable notion; or, even better, in the north of France in 1262, this was the legal reality. Originally the taille on free men as well as on serfs had always been "at will," for it was raised only on exceptional occasions. Gradually, as tailles became more frequent, the peasants obtained an annual subscription to it, particularly the free or enfranchised peasants. The arbitrary taille then began to be considered as a sign of servitude, particularly in Champagne. In Urban IV's era, this notion was abroad, but it had not yet acquired the force of law. If the bull had mentioned only those subjected to the arbitrary taille it would have had nothing special about it. But let us proceed to the second category of men considered as free, the mainmortables. Here the paradox is startling. There is no doubt that the ancient rules of canon law forbidding access to holy orders to *servi* had originally been conceived as applying to a class of men quite different from the mainmortables. The early servi were quite simply slaves. But the transition from ancient servitude to medieval serfdom was almost imperceptible. Although thirteenth-century French serfs—particularly Church serfs—could, in general, as our document states, bear witness in court; although they had, when alive, almost the same rights to dispose of their tenures as free tenants;[11] although their marriages (while still subject, in case of formariage, to the seigneur's consent) were really legal unions; in other words, although their condition was very far from that of slavery, neither customary law nor canon law held them to be free. And the Church had never hesitated to apply the venerable rules that excluded the nonfree, unless enfranchised, from all participation in the holy ministry. Naturally, this does not imply that in practice the rules could not be bent somewhat. There are several cases of serfs obtaining the tonsure without going through manumission. But these were undeniable transgressions that, until the fourteenth century, when made public, were most often severely punished. Later it was looked upon more tolerantly. The law, however, was never specifically modified. Thus, as a decision on principle, Urban IV's bull appears to be absolutely isolated in the history of servile institutions.[12]

And indeed it is probable that its author was aware of the extraordinary character of the statements he was putting to paper. His account, as we have seen, is far from being perfectly clear. In particular, it is hard to determine, on first reading, who are the individuals declared free: only those subject to the taille or, what I believe is the case, also the mainmortables; this obscurity was perhaps deliberate.[13] Yet, even in this somewhat veiled form, such a document, had it been widely distributed, would have certainly created violent protests. Nothing of the sort occured. I cannot find a single citation of it by a canonist. It was kept very quiet as perhaps the best way of making use of it. What were its origins? It probably was formulated at the apostolic chancellery upon the request of a well-placed person who suggested the idea. What were this solicitor's ambitions? Certainly he did not envisage a revolutionary opening of the doors of the militant Church to a whole social class: he would have come up against stony resistance. Everything indicates that he ends were less disinterested: he wanted to obtain a coveted benefice with this bull, for himself or for a protegé, in spite of any servile stain. He succeeded, I suppose, with the ecclesiastical authority concerned, which was perhaps also involved; an in order not to compromise the success of this affair, the wiser course was to avoid any unfortunate publicity. We shall probably never know who was the lucky beneficiary of this strange decree. It is to be supposed that he belonged, in some manner, to the Abbey Saint-Pierre of Lagny. The bull did not mention this community, but the document was kept in its charter box. Also Urban IV appears to have looked upon the monastery of Saint-Pierre, built on the borders of his native Champagne, with particular benevolence. No less than eight bulls[14] were written in its favor, an imposing number when one considers that Urban's pontificate lasted barely three years. It is not surprising that he would readily accede to a request from this house. But no matter, whether requested from Lagny or from elsewhere, the bull of 13 November 1262 merits consideration as a particularly striking example of the ease with which the roman curia made the best established juridical rules bend in favor of particular interests.[15]

One can also draw more important conclusions from this text.

What was a serf? Today's historians often ask this question, and rarely agree on the answer. It is interesting to note that, at certain periods of the Middle Ages, men who lived among servile populations also hesitated over this question. What is most important to know is the social milieux where such doubts were evident. I do not think the jurists were much bothered by these difficulties —I mean those jurists who practiced the law, not the authors of theoretical treatises who must only be consulted with great caution on this matter. When one asked a royal or seigneurial judge, in the reign of Louis IX in the Ile-de-France, what were the characteristics of serfdom, he answered approximately as follows:[16] the mainmorte (with the variety of details determined in each case by local custom), the formariage (that is the prohibition of formariage without seigneurial authorization), the inability to enter holy orders. In the preceding century, he would have added the *chevage*. In the thirteenth century, however, this duty had fallen into disuse. In the eyes of the common man the solution was not so clear. This is exemplified by the case of the men of Gonesse and, to a certain extent, by Urban IV's bull, which would not have been granted had the problem it so singularly decided been susceptible to a general solution.

Where did such doubts originate? It is not surprising, of course, that the peasants of Gonesse lacked a very precise juridical knowledge. Also, as I have mentioned previously, there were practical difficulties in determining whether a particular individual was or was not subject to specifically servile charges such as formariage or mainmorte. The opportunities for seigneurs to collect these taxes were so rare that the charges often fell into oblivion. This frequent uncertainty about the status of individuals had to bring about some equivocation in the very idea men had of the characteristics of serfdom. This does not explain everything, however. In the thirteenth century, in the Paris region, the institution of serfdom was in full transformation; this is why its outline, in the popular mind, did not appear with great clarity.

In some regions of France, we know, serfdom was maintained until modern times. But it lasted only by evolving. There are few common traits between the *homme de chef* or *homme de corps* of the eleventh and twelfth centuries and the "mortaillable" of the Champagne and Burgundy of the sixteenth century. This, is not surprising considering that during this time the whole of society in its constitution and even in its spirit had undergone profound transformations. In other provinces, serfdom disappeared earlier, around Paris, as early as the thirteenth century and the first years of the fourteenth. But even where, for reasons that are too lengthy to go into here, serfdom disappeared early, one perceives in it, at the very moment of its decline, the first symptoms of the metamorphosis that elsewhere modified its nature completely. The texts we have just studied allow us to capture a few of these tendencies.

I have already hinted at one of these. The bull of Laghy is in fact founded on ambiguity: it affirms at the same time the freedom of men subject to arbitrary taille—which is historically correct—and that of mainmortables—on all counts a notorious untruth. This probably willful confusion was only possible because public opinion tended to confuse the taille as belonging to the same group of obligations as the mainmorte and ended by considering taillables as serfs rather than mainmortables as free. The essential aspect of this, for the bull's author, was that confusion reigned.

The case of the men of Gonesse brings us to another aspect of the same evolution. The homme de chef of former times had always been considered as belonging to an inferior social class, but this was not, in the eleventh century for example, the most striking aspect of his condition. Above all he was known to be attached to his seigneur by bonds of dependence and of reciprocal aid far stronger than those of the free tenants. To him must be applied, in its full force, the admirable definition of Benjamin Guérard: the serf was only "a vassal of inferior degree"[17] (I would add "and strictly hereditary"). Toward the thirteenth century, the order was reversed. The strength of the personal bond, in all areas, was felt less vividly than before. The society was becoming hierarchical. What henceforth was to characterize the serf (beside the material inconveniences of his status) was his situation at the bottom of the social ladder. Inevitable errors grew from this. A few peasants, in a village of the Ile-de-France, subject to an obligation held commonly as demeaning, were, therefore, thought to be serfs. At least that is what their neighbors decided.

The knowledge of Roman law, spreading everywhere, threw much doubt in the idea learned people had of serfdom. Was the serf's condition modified, in practice, by this invasion of doctrines borrowed from the ancient society? The problem, one knows, is evident for the *Leibeigenen* of Eastern Germany. It, therefore, merits some attention from French historians. But here is not the place to study it. What cannot be denied is the influence of Roman juridical texts on the theoreticians of the law, on Beaumanoir for example. The same is true for the curia. One cannot doubt, after an examination of the terminology used by pontifical notaries, that they perceived very sharply the difference between the ancient servi and the contemporary serfs. Exploiting this widespread feeling, an adroit supplicant one day had the idea of having the Pope rule that ancient canon laws regarding the servi did not apply to serfs. This is the whole story behind the bull of Lagny.

There is no doubt that this declaration of principle was in flagrant contradiction not only with the law, but with custom. Had it been generally known, the scandal would have been great—less so, and less universally than a hundred years earlier. God's servant could not be a man's object; such was the main reason that earlier had excluded slaves first, then serfs, from the ranks of the clergy. As the relations between serfs and their seigneurs ceased to be thought of in terms of bonds of narrow personal dependence and came, more and more exclusively in men's minds, to be conceived on financial grounds, this argument lost its strength. In the fourteenth and fifteenth centuries, in those regions where serfdom survived, servile ordinations were apparently easily tolerated. The custom of the duchy of Burgundy, written in 1459, mentions mainmortable priests without embarrassment.[18] In the neighboring region of Paris, this change did not have time to take place. But there again the bull of Lagny, ahead of the development in practice, was well within the general lines of the evolution of servile institutions.

Texts such as I have just discussed are extremely useful. They reveal juridical heresies. And juridical heresies often prepare and explain transformations in the law.

CHAPTER FIVE

*Blanche De Castile and the
Serfs of the Chapter of Paris*[1]

Concerning the second regency of Blanche of Castile, an anonymous chronicle of the fourteenth century[2] reads:

> La reyne Blanche entend que les chanoines de Nostre-Dame de Paris avoient emprisonné plusieurs de leurs hommes et femmes de corps,[3] qui ne pooyent payer les tailles a quoy ils les avoient assis, et avoient moux de maulx en prison. Pour quoy la Reyne, meue de pitié, fist rompre les prisons et les délivra.*

The same account, a little less brief but, as we shall see, extremely inaccurate,[4] is in the *Grandes Chroniques*.[5]

This is the episode that we have undertaken to relate anew. We will be supported by documents that were contemporary to the events themselves, and that have remained unpublished until now.[6] As we go along, we will come across more than one detail that is interesting for the history of royal or seigneurial institutions, and even concerning the old landscape of Paris.

It may have been in the last months of 1249, in 1250, or at the beginning of 1251, when the canons of Notre Dame de Paris decided to levy a tax upon their land in Orly.[7] We do not know the date.[8] The peasants, who were serfs, refused payment of the impost demanded of them, and questioned its legitimacy. It seems that they were then brought before the capitulary court, as was natural. Sixteen of them were arrested and then, on June 13, 1251,

---

* Queen Blanche heard that the canons of Notre Dame had imprisoned several of their men and women serfs who could not pay the taxes for which they had assessed them, and who were suffering greatly in prison. Therefore the queen, moved by pity, had the prisons broken open and freed them.

were released provisionally, in the presence of the bishop of Paris and three canons. We still have the document, called one of "recrediting" (*"recredito"*), by which they promised, under penalty of one hundred pounds and with guarantees[9] to be at the prison of the chapter on the 28th of the following August.[10] Meanwhile, the people of Orly, who had had recourse to one of their usual intermediaries,[11] the Parisian bourgeois Philippe Boucel, carried on endless negotiations with the canons through his intervention.[12] After this time we should note the intervention of a royal functionary. One of the two provosts of Paris, Garnier de Verberie,[13] went to Orly several times and advised the people to yield.[14] He could not overcome their determination, and brought back from his endeavors the impression that they were supported in their resistance by the peasants of other lands that also belonged to the chapter. He put the number of peasants thus "bound together" (*"colligati"*) against their lord[15] at about two thousand. This was not merely a matter of purely moral support: according to the provost, the allies had helped the people of Orly cover their costs. What costs did Garnier de Verberie refer to? Perhaps de Boucel's intervention was not entirely gratuitous. Above all, though, it was necessary to account for the expenses that recourse to royal jurisdiction, which had to be the last hope of the serfs of Orly, was bound to involve. Actually, the serfs appealed to the regent queen, presumably after a definitively unfavorable judgment by the chapter. A certain number[16] of refractory peasants were thrown into the prisons of the chapter, to stay there until they decided to pay the tax.

Blanche of Castile, in conformity with the traditions of royal government, accepted the request to intervene.[17] She made a request to the canons to submit to an inquiry on the extent of their rights: we know that the juridical ideas of the time would not allow an inquiry to proceed without the assent of the parties involved. The prisoners would be set free until the time of the inquiry. The canons refused to allow the royal court to judge between them and their serfs. Let us cite the *Grandes Chroniques* here, since their testimony, even though it is always suspect, is the only one we can depend upon:

> Les chanoines respondirent qu'à lui (à la reine) n'aferoit pas de congnoistre de leurs sers et de leurs vilains, lesquiex il pooient prendre, ou ocire, or faire tel joustice comme ils voudroient. Portant comme plainte en fut fête devant la royne,

les chanoines emprisonnèrent leurs fames et leurs enfanz; et furent à si grand méseise de la chaleur qu'ils avoient les uns des autres que pluseurs en furent mors.*

This was to defy a strong government. However, it seems that in the following of the queen, and in Paris, there was a party, of which Garnier de Verberie was a member, which was hostile to any energetic measure against the canons.[18] Finally, the queen decided upon action—we do not know on what advice. The insinuations of Garnier de Verberie remain mute to us.

One day[19]—here again no precision about the date is possible[20]—the queen, accompanied by the two provosts of Paris, Garnier and Gautier le Maître, by the Castellan of the Louvre, Eudes de Machault,[21] by knights of the Hostel and by men of arms, went to the cloister of the canons, which extended to the north of the cathedral. The canons did not put up any active resistance; they seem to have left the cloistral buildings at the approach of the royal troop, which found all the doors barred before it. Apparently, they got inside the confines of the cloister fairly easily. At the time of the inquiry, whose subject was later to be these same incidents, only one witness[22] spoke of a door being broken in, concerning the entry into the cloister. The prisoners were locked up in a cell. Access to the cell was gained by way of the cellar, where the chapter kept the wine that it laid aside to distribute among the canons or for sale on the Parisian market.[23] The queen commanded that someone look to find the keys to the two doors, that of the cellar and that of the cell, which had to be opened to get to the peasants. It was already a serious matter to have violated the legal immunity of the cloister, which the canons had made the kings recognize so many times. The desire of Blanche de Castile seems to have been to avoid any violence, insofar as this was possible. When the *Grandes Chroniques* recount that not only did she order the door of the cell battered in, but moreover that she *"féri le premier cop d'un baston qu'elle tenoit en sa main,"* †
they are particularly distorting reality. We can follow Blanche step by step after the entry into the cloister.[24] After having given

---

* The canons replied that it was not her (the queen's) affair to deal with their serfs and their villeins, whom they could seize, or kill, or upon whom they could make such a judgment as they wished. However, since a complaint had been made before the queen, the canons imprisoned their wives and children; and they were so overcome by the heat that they had from one another that several of them died.

† "... delivered the first blow with a stick that she held in her hand."

the order to search for the keys, she entered the "church"—probably the cathedral, or perhaps one of the two little churches continuous to the cloister, Saint-Jean-le-Rond and Saint-Denis-du-Pas. She remained there some time, presumably busy at her prayers. Then she came back towards the buildings that served the canons as a capitulary room, doubtless hoping to find there one of the clerics. She left the building and found herself in a "passageway" ("*in exitu capituli*"), when she saw four of the prisoners who, having been freed, came to thank her. Addressing the castellan of the Louvre, who accompanied them, she asked how they had gotten hold of the keys. "*Madame, n'ayez cure*," answered the chatelain, and he added, referring to a hagiographic legend very widespread in the Middle Ages,[25] "*Saint-Léonard les a délivrés*."*

What had happened? All the witnesses are in agreement in naming a certain Guillaume de Senlis—whom we knew from elsewhere[26] to have been one of the crossbowmen of the Hostel—as the agent of the peasants' release. More or less helped by several men at arms, "sergeants" of the royal guard,[27] he had forced the first door—the door of the cellar—off its hinges and then broken in the door of the cell with blows of his axe. A townsman of Paris, Eudes de Roux,[28] who made a deposition at the inquiry, expressed the opinion that the men at arms "*n'eussent jamais fait une chose pareille sans ordres*."† According to him, either the castellan of the Louvre or a knight of the royal entourage, Pierre de Châtres,[29] had ordered them to commit this violence. If we are to believe him—and the matter that he reported was nothing if not extremely plausible—the castellan is to have said afterwards, "*il eût été mauvais que la chose n'eût pas été faite, pour laquelle la reine etait venue au cloitre*."‡ This meant that it would have been unfortunate if the prisoners whom the queen had come to free were not freed, no matter how. "The thing" thus having been "done," the peasants fled, some to the palais and others to the chatelet.

Is it so that, as the *Grandes Chroniques* tell us, the queen seized the temporal goods of the canons in the aftermath of these events? We must resign ourselves to ignorance. We have no more sources, actually, that are worthy of credence until the time when they came to an agreement. Furthermore, the royal jurisdiction was

---

* "Madam, do not worry ... Saint Leonard has freed them."

† "... would never have done such a thing without orders."

‡ "... it would be evil if that thing for which the queen had come to the cloister were not done."

not to have the final word in this matter. With the agreement of the peasants, the queen[30] and the chapter[31] set up three prelates as arbiters of the dispute—Renaud de Corbeil, the bishop of Paris, Guillaume de Bussy, the bishop of Orléans, and Gui de Mello, the bishop of Auxerre. The charters by which the parties declared that they would accept the arbitration of the three bishops are dated November 1252.[32] But let us not be deceived by the fictions of the chancellary. The agreement must have taken place well before the month of November, because the arbiters began their inquiry as of the month of March. On March 8, 1252, a notary of the officiality of Chartres, accompanied by a special delegation and possessed of *"articuli"* that were drawn up in good form by the chapter, visited Corbreuse[33] to interrogate the mayor of Notre Dame, Simon, who could not be summoned to Paris because of his great age and his infirmities.[34]

On November 27, a canon of Laon, Maître Luc, in the name of the three bishops, went to find the archbishop of Sens, Gilles Cornut, to obtain his deposition.[35] It is probable (even if we cannot prove the fact) that the archbishop had formerly belonged to the chapter of Paris, as had his colleagues: Gautier, his predecessor on the office at Sens and Aubri, the bishop of Chartres. The canons, three curates, two of whom had formerly served in the choir of the cathedral and the third of whom had been the secretary of a canon, a few bourgeois of Paris, the two provosts of the city, a plea-auditer at the Châtelet, knights and men at arms of the Hostel—all compared accounts before the investigators. Finally there arrived, "brought" by "the people of Orly," peasants who were residents of the surrounding villages: they came to testify in favor of the "neighbors." And their depositions, which contain obvious untruths, force us to presume that they had plotted with them beforehand.[36]

The bishops seem to have carried on two inquiries at the same time, causing the witnesses to be interrogated about two different orders of fact. On the one hand, they inquired about the incidents in the cloister. We do not know why, as it does not seem to have produced any repercussions after that inquiry. There was no question of the violation of the cloistral immunity, neither in the decision nor even in the two constitutional charters of the arbiters.[37] On the other hand, they devoted their efforts to the very basis of the dispute: they sought to find if the chapter had been within its rights in levying the tax upon the peasants.[38] This is what we, too, will seek, following after Renaud de Corbeil, Guillaume de Bussy, and Gui de Mello.

For the canons, it was a question of proving the legitimacy of their claim to collect the tax on the village of Orly. Now, what was the legitimacy of all seigneurial right based on at this time? It was essentially based on *custom*, that is to say, prescription. Perhaps it would be better to say upon tradition, because the word "custom" calls up ideas of respect and authority. In addition, these rights themselves, which a later era was to incorrectly call feudal rights, were called "customs" in the thirteenth century. The question before the canons therefore came down to this: how does one prove custom? First, through public knowledge: each witness would be asked about common opinion—"*requisitus de fama.*" Above all, the canons were going to aim at proving that they actually had, upon several occasions, in well-established cases, levied the tax upon their land in general and upon Orly in particular. That was the central point of their argument; the law proved itself through fact. At length they were to seek to establish their legitimacy upon three further bases. First, upon analogy: lay lords levied the tax upon their lands,[39] so how could the same rights be refused to the canons? The bishop of Paris taxed his peasants all the time. Now, the rights of the chapter could not possibly be inferior to those of the bishop, since their source was the same: they still possessed the charter that in separating the two domains testifies to the ancient community of the goods of the Church of Paris.[40] They further adduced royal confirmation: two kings (it is true that it concerned lands other than Orly)[41] had sanctioned the custom. Finally, they turned to account the acknowledgement of the men of Orly who once recognized the right of the chapter.[42]

What were the peasants to say in reply? They too were to call upon the facts. They wanted to establish that the tax was never asked of them up until that time. Or rather that the taxes that they paid—because they did pay them, and the fact was too obvious to be denied—were not levied by the chapter for the chapter. They had all been intended to payment of the royal impost, to borrow their own expressions, of the subsidy of the royal aid.

Actually, this is what they could argue, from an easily made confusion. Under the common name *taille* were included two fees that, while they were exactly similar in their method of collection, were nonetheless essentially different in their true character. One was a royal levy and the other was a seigneurial levy. Both were levies of assessment; the sum to be collected upon each land holding was fixed in advance, and it was the inhabitants themselves, or rather the delegates named by them and from among them[43] who divided up the levy within the land.[44] Both were levied by the chapter; the king could not directly collect the tax on the land of the canons, but the chapter transferred to him intact the sum collected upon its lands.[45]

The royal tax, which was sometimes called *les sous du roi*[46] appears in our text in the form of a tax for replacement of military service: it is the tax "for the host of the King." We are in a position to determine with some precision the moment when the levy in kind, as it were, was substituted for the military service demanded of the peasants.[47] Some of the peasants who were called to testify remembered having seen the men of Orly go to the king's host; these were doubtless men who were already aged. Another witness, Acon l'abbé, knew that the men of Orly were called in person to the royal army in the past, not because he saw it for himself, but because his father had told him about it. There was practically no one who had not heard of the practice. Everyone knew that a time had come when "the host had changed to a tax," "*mutatus fuit exercitus in talliam.*" Since this time the tax "in place of the host" had been levied by the king upon Orly. As for the village that concerns us here, this transformation of the methods of the royal government took place approximately at the end of the twelfth century. These facts seem definitely to confirm the views of M. Borelli de Serres[48] about the era of the transformation of military service into a levy. In any case, one can see that we are far from the theory that ascribes the honor of this innovation to Philip the Fair.

A little more than ten years before the incidents we just recounted, the collection of the royal tax was the occasion of an earlier conflict between the canons of Notre Dame and the government of Saint Louis. The affair turned out in favor of the chapter, a result that was perhaps not without influence upon the aspect it was to take on as it concerned Blanche of Castile. The matter took place while Eudes Popin was provost of Paris,[49] doubtless at the beginning of 1238.[50] The royal accountants declared, rightly or wrongly, that a sum of one hundred pounds was missing from the total of the tax paid by the chapter on behalf of Orly.[51] The peasants who, in testifying at the inquiry of 1252, remembered this story, accused the chapter of having dishonestly kept the missing sum. Whatever the case, the royal government[52] employed the simplest of methods to recover its funds: it had a certain number of the residents of Orly arrested and kept them in the chatelet until they brought themselves to decide to pay the hundred pounds, which they thus seem to have paid out twice instead of once. The chapter was enraged, all the more so because it was not in its first complaint against royal policy about this.[53] While it apprised Rome of the matter, it interrupted celebration of the divine service in the cathedral. Furthermore, it suspended the interdict thus placed on Notre Dame fairly quickly, but without bringing itself to lift it completely. The interdict was first suspended from March 24 to November 3, 1238, and then from July 26, 1241, to December 14, 1244.[54] We do not know how the matter would have ended if Saint Louis had not fallen seriously ill at the beginning of the month of December 1244.[55] Wanting to make his conscience at peace with God and His Church, he therefore declared, on December 14, that is, precisely the day before the date on which the divine service was to cease again in the cathedral of Paris, that he would remove himself from the task of deciding his quarrels with the chapter, in favor of two arbiters, whom the canons themselves were to designate.

The decision of the arbiters[56]—Archdeacon Eudes and the Canon Raoul de Chevry—was not reached until May of 1248. It was favorable to the canons upon nearly all the points (since it only found them wrong one time out of eight), and affirmed in particular that

> li bailli le roi firent contre le droit dou chapitre, de prandre, por la taille, les hommes des viles Nostre-Damme, mal tretier et despoillier; car li chapitres, a qui il apartenoit, avait fet, pour cele aide, taille sur les hommes et levée, et en avoit fete l'aide le roi.*

The king ordered the provost of Paris to submit to the decision of the arbiters.[57] But one cannot think that the peasants of Orly recovered possession of the one hundred pounds that they had unduly paid out.

Let us come back to the tax that the chapter levied on its own account. Our documents allow us to make an exact assessment of the nature of this fee, and of its fuctioning during the first half of the thirteenth century.

---

* "The king's *baillis* acted against the right of the chapter to seize the men of the towns of Nostre Damme for the taille, to maltreat and despoil them; for the chapter to which they belonged had taken and levied duty from the men for this aid, and had made of it the king's aid."

[The word "*bailli*" refers to a lay administrative staff under Royal orders. —Trans.]

The seigneurial tax was essentially an arbitrary imposition.[58] *"ad voluntatem,"* *"ad beneplacitum."* The chapter fixed the quantity of the levy and the date of its collection. It claimed the right to levy it once, and once only,[59] per year; in practice, though, this was a completely imaginary right.[60] In fact, this tax was nothing but an extraordinary source for the finances of Notre Dame, as the list of taxes collected since the end of the twelfth century, which we will put together below, will show quite well. The canons had recourse to it, at irregular intervals of time, when they needed money—"for their businesses," *"pro negotiis suis,"* as the accepted expression goes.

While most revenues of the domain of the chapter were farmed out to probendary groups of canons, the taxes, as exceptional levies, went to fill the central treasury, the *"deniers communs."*[61] These common monies themselves included a certain number of "offices," each one of which received its own revenue; the profit from the taxes was paid to that office that constituted the treasury of the chapter, the "chamber" collection was supervised by two chamberlains who were elected each year by the canons. The capitulary assembly first voted on the total sum to be required from the lands of Notre Dame; the chamberlains then set up their "schedules" upon which were written the sums to be collected by each of the provosts (generally about twelve) who shared the administration of the possessions of the chapter. We have seen that the peasants themselves determined the basis for the levy within each holding. Once the sum was collected, the mayor of the village took it to Paris. In compensation for his trouble, he took a certain amount of money[62] from it: twenty *sous* was deducted from the total of the taxation levied on the lands of his provostship.[63] As the money was paid into the hands of the chamberlains, the clerks of the interior staff of the cathedral, whom the chamberlains charged with keeping their accounts, wrote down upon scrolls the sums that entered the treasury. These scrolls, which were called the "registers of the chapter,"[64] served the chamberlains as expense and receipt books, in a general fashion. Preserved in the canonical archives, they served as evidence for the chapter: *"illis rotulis adhibetur fides a capitulo sicut adhiberetur ancientie scripture."**[65]

Of the taxes that in the twelfth century were demanded of the peasants of the Church of Paris, we only know of two, the first

---

* The trust of the chapter was given to those scrolls just as if it was given to ancient scripture. —Trans.

of which was levied between 1148 and 1163,⁶⁶ and the second in 1178.⁶⁷ We do not know the reasons that made the chapter decide to collect them. The canons declared before the investigators that the levy of the tax was a very old custom on the land of Notre Dame, that it had taken place "since very ancient times" ("*a longe retroactis temporibus*").⁶⁸ But it could have been of but little use to back up their assertions with precise facts, as their memories⁶⁹ scarcely went back to those of the taxes that they themselves had seen collected, or at least that they had heard their elders of the chapter talking about. Their historical memory was short, like that of most of their contemporaries. At least the facts that they cited are going to allow us to draw up a list of the taxes collected by the chapter during the first half of the thirteenth century.

Around the year 1212,⁷⁰ the canons began some large construction projects that involved no less than building or rebuilding the cloister, the capitulary chamber, the granary,⁷¹ and the cellar. They also were to finish the architectural body formed by the new cathedral and the new episcopal palace. To offset the expenses, they had recourse to a tax.⁷² Between 1198 and 1216 another tax was levied; it was intended for payment of the subsidy that Innocent III requested of the churches of France.⁷³ In 1219⁷⁴ the chamberlain, Maitre Aubry Cornut, ordered the beginning of construction of a "house," or rather of a group of houses, intended as housing for the canons, along the Rue du Fumier Saint Landri. He suggested that recourse again be had to the tax and the proposition was accepted. In 1221,⁷⁵ the chapter procured, by the same means, the money for the purchase of a tithe in Sognolles.⁷⁶ Finally, around 1232,⁷⁷ a new tax was collected, but we do not know what expenses it was to cover. Then, on the day of Saint-Rémi of the year 1247, the men of the village of Corbreuse, but of Corbreuse alone, had to pay the same fee; it was a matter of the chapter's paying a debt.⁷⁸

These repeated imposts must have weighed heavily upon the peasants. What is more, the basic characteristics of the arbitrary tax—a levy whose total always varied and of which no one ever knew when it would be demanded—would have been enough to make it hateful, and at the same time prevented it from having that air of evident legitimacy that their very regularity gave to other dues. It is a fact that its very principle was always contested by those whom they wanted to submit to it;⁷⁹ we will see that it was contested not only by them. The first of the taxes that the archives of Notre Dame mentions caused a conflict between the chapter and the peasants of Rozoy-en-Brie,[80] who refused to pay it, and who at length only agreed to accept the impost when it had ceased to be arbitrary and took on the form of a land rent, which was annual and fixed, of eighteen pounds of Provins.[81] In 1178 the residents of Epône,[82] who had already been taxed once during the year for the king's "lodging," refused to submit to the taxation of the chapter. They were condemned by the capitulary court, and this judgment was verified by an act of the chancellery[83] of King Louis VII. During the reign of Philip Augustus, the peasants of the village of Vernou[84] in turn contested the right of the chapter to levy the tax. They took their complaints to the king, who had the canons summoned before his court. Two delegates of the chapter, Hugues de Chevreuse and Nicolas de Chartres, the cantor of Notre Dame, journeyed to Melun, where the king was at the time, and where the trial took place. The canons won their case; Philip Augustus flew into a great rage against the peasants, and cried, "*Que maudit soit le chapitre, s'il ne vous jette en une latrine.*"*[85]

We have seen that from 1210 to about 1232, the chapter had recourse to the tax five times. Then, from 1232 to 1250—if we except a completely local impost at Corbreuse—we observe with surprise that it ceased to use this fiscal procedure. This anomaly cannot have failed to strike the investigators, as it strikes us today. Moreover, the witnesses tried to provide an explanation.[86]

Among the canons there existed a party that was hostile, on principle, to any levy by the tax. Previously, when the houses in the rue Fumier were built, the doyen, Etienne de Reims, had suggested that in order to subsidize the expenses, they rely on the regular resources of the chapter, which according to him were sufficient.[87] His opinion was not listened to, though later on, the majority belonged to the enemies of the tax. The depositions have preserved for us a faithful picture of the disputes that, it seems, frequently tore asunder the capitulary assembly. Many of the canons—Jean, archdeacon of Paris, Maître Elie de Cahors, Maître Pierre de Colombe,[88] Maître Henri the subcantor, and more than one whose name we do not know—wanted the tax to be levied. They did not exactly adduce arguments of a financial nature; they expressed the fear that too long an interruption in the collection of the tax would cause harm to the rights of the chapter, that

---

* "Cursed be the chapter if it does not throw you into a latrine."

these rights would come to "wither away" by the fact of the prescription. Others, however, "had pity" upon the peasants and were opposed to any tax being demanded of them. The names of principals of these "good men" (*boni homines*) have come down to us. They were the doyen Luc de Gif, Guiard de Laon, the chancellor of Notre-Dame, who was to die bishop of Cambrai, Eudes de Chateauroux, who was chancellor after him and who was cardinal-bishop of Tusculum and legate of the Holy See, the Cantor Nicolas de Chartres, the Subcantor Pierre de Maisons, Henri, who succeeded Eudes de Chateauroux as chancellor, Maître Jean le Noir, Maître Eudes de Garlande and Friar Jean de Montmirail. As one of their adversaries tells it, they said "that it was a sin to levy the tax when we could wait a long time to do so, because the men were poor." The reply was "that they were putting the Church in such a state that they would never be able to restore it." They added, ironically, "that they were not the men to know how to manage a land holding and that they should have taken on vassals," by which they meant that they should have enfeoffed their lands to knights who would know how to exploit them better than they. But the "good people" brought forward new "pious reasons," and they kept the majority until 1250.

These facts are very interesting. It seems that the most delicate moral consciences in the Middle Ages had a great deal of difficulty admitting the idea of the legitimacy of the levy, whether royal or seigneurial. The ideal king or the ideal lord was one who was satisfied with the revenues from his domains without asking anything from "extraordinary" fees. We know what scruples afflicted the pious Charles V on his deathbed. Similar scruples made the boni homines of the chapter of Paris act. Of the names that we gave above, it is interesting to recall those of two[89] of the greatest preachers of the century, Guiard de Laon[90] and Eudes de Chateauroux.[91] The designation of the first for the See at Cambrai and his death, and the departure of the second to Egypt, where he accompanied the Seventh Crusade as legate of the Holy See, doubtless helped to contribute to their party's defeat within the chapter.

The fact remained that this hesitation on the part of the canons concerning the legitimacy of their own pretentions could scarcely fail in some measure to compromise their cause before the investigators. But they had a last argument to exploit, a very strong one.

Around the middle of the thirteenth century, a wind of emancipation blew through the rural population of the Parisian region. All around, serfs sought to obtain permission to purchase their freedom from their lords. We should therefore not be surprised to see, at this time, the serfs of the seven "towns" of Sucy,[92] Créteil,[92] Chevilly,[94] L'Hay,[95] Bagneux,[96] Châtenay,[97] and Orly acting together, negotiating their freedom with the chapter of Paris, their lord.[98] There were repeated negotiations, sometimes undertaken separately with certain dignitaries of the Church of Paris, such as the doyen, the chancellor, the official or with ordinary canons, and sometimes with the chapter itself united in a general assembly. This is what certainly explains the disparity in the dates assigned to these negotiations by our different witnesses: the dates given[99] vary from 1246 to 1250. Since too many people came on the side of the peasants, it was decided that each village would send six delegates. We know the names of two of the delegates of Orly: Roger le Mâçon and Gerbout de Villeneuve,[100] the latter being a former man at arms of the provost of Paris, Nicolas Arroux. Above all, though, the serfs had chosen mediators who were more highly placed: there was a canon, Pierre de Boissy, the archdeacon of Bayeux; there was a knight in the service of the king, Pierre de Châtenay, called Maleterre; and finally there were three townspeople of Paris who were foremost among the Parisian bourgeoisie: Thomas Tiboud and Philippe Boucel, who were both responsible to the chapter for negotiating their wares on the Parisian market,[101] and Evroin de Valenciennes, who was noted in the history of Paris as the first provost of the merchants, and whose name has come down to us.[102]

As a price for their freedom, the serfs offered ten thousand Parisian pounds to be paid once, or an annual rent of four hundred pounds. We do not know which of these two methods of payment got the preference of the chapter. Moreover—and this is what was to be a very strong argument in the hands of the canons in 1252—they offered to buy back the right of the chapter to levy arbitrary taxes, by paying two thousand pounds to it once and for all, which would have been used by it for "purchase of rents." This proposal was rejected; the peasants then offered an annual rent of one hundred pounds, which was accepted. How would the serfs hope to raise such a huge sum as twelve thousand pounds? Probably the Parisian townspeople whom we saw acting in their name were moneylenders in addition to being negotiators, and they sought to profit from the manumission by sinking their capital into real estate taxes in the countryside.

The two parties involved came to an agreement on the advisability and even the conditions of the manumission properly so-called, and upon the repurchase of the arbitrary tax. But the chapter, as was the practice of most lords in such a matter, tried to have a complete enumeration of its rights "distinguished one by one" inserted into the charter of manumission. These rights were then to be established in writing for the first time, and the canons sought to profit by the occasion by extending a measure to the collection of the tithes, which seems to have been previously applied only to that of the *champart*. Our texts are explicit that that was the only cause of the final breakdown of negotiations: "no one was opposed to the manumission taking place, except that the chapter wanted to collect the tithe as counted in the fields, before the wheat to be harvested was gathered from the ground, which the men did not want."[103] The measure which the chapter sought to impose seemed irritating to the peasants, because at the moment of the harvest, it put the fate of their wheat at the mercy of a possible delay by the seigneurial officers, and they ran the risk of finding themselves prevented from gathering it in at the proper moment.

We can see the possible use the canons could make of the talks concerning the repurchase of the tax, to defend their cause before the investigators. We should add that the failure of the negotiations, certainly very painful for the serfs, must have had a good deal of influence on the revolt of Orly.

The three bishops delivered their decision on December 1, 1252, three or four days after the death of Blanche of Castile.[104] It favored the claims of the chapter. It recognized for it "the possession or quasi-possession of the right to tax the men of Orly for the affairs of the Church of Paris, and not only for the king's host." It seems quite likely that the bishops made their judgment in all fairness. True right was on the side of the canons, in a society where nearly all rights were based upon custom.[105]

Thus the royal intervention did not amount to a lightening of their obligations for the peasants. In the acts of manumission that followed, the chapter was careful to have a clause written, in which it noted recognition of the obligation to pay the discretionary tax, independently of the royal tax: "every year, if the chapter so wishes."[106] Finally, in May of 1263, all the serfs of Orly, numbering some 636, were freed. The act of manumission,[107] at the same time as it honored the claims of the chapter relating to the collection of the tithe, authorized the repurchase of the arbitrary tax at the cost of an average annual rent of sixty pounds.

The compiler of the *Grandes Chroniques* attributed the enfranchisement of the serfs of Orly to the intervention of Queen Blanche. It is interesting to recall his opinion: it shows clearly that the enfranchisement of serfs passed as a pious act, the sort with which a biographer willingly ornaments the life of a great queen. But his zeal as an official historian went too far this time. When the men of Orly were "liberated from the yoke of servitude and mortmain,"[108] the body of Blanche of Castile had been lying in the Abbey of Maubuisson for some eleven years. Her intervention between the canons and their serfs is explained very simply by the habits of a firm government, and by the strength of a long tradition that imposed upon all kings the need to make their right of jurisdiction respected, which was the principal basis of their authority. In this affair, as in so many others, the royal officials were more royalist than the king: the *châtelain* of the Louvre had the doors smashed in, while the Queen wanted to open them with the keys. But official chronicles do not retain these details: they attribute to kings all the great acts of their reign, even those that they did not wish. The picture is much more attractive when Blanche of Castile strikes the first blow upon the door behind which the prisoners are moaning.

Chapter Six

Serf De La Glèbe[*]

THE HISTORY OF AN EXPRESSION

In a famous passage of the Coutumes de Beauvaisis, Beaumanoir depicted lay society, as it appeared to his eyes, in a hierarchical order:

> L'en doit savoir que III estat sont entre les gens du siecle. Li uns des estas si est de gentillece. Li secons si est de ceus qui sont franc naturelment ... et li tiers estas si est des sers.[†][2]

This description is valid for France in the thirteenth century. It could not apply, without retouching, to feudal society during its entire historical development. In the first stages of feudalism there was no "gentillece" at all, that is, "nobility" in the sense in which Beaumanoir intends this word, which for him connotes a hereditary class that is vested with precise juridical privileges. The noble group only gradually emerged from the mass of free men, but one aspect of the sketch we just read retains general relevance. In France, or rather in Western Europe, during a long period of time, from the Carolingian Empire until dates that vary according to the region, but frequently very close to the modern age, there existed beneath free men a special category composed of people whom customs and laws considered lacking in full liberty. These "unfree" (to borrow a convenient expression from the language of the German jurists) men were distinguished from "naturally free" men in two ways: on the one hand, they formed a class that law and public opinion agreed was inferior; and on the other, they were

---

[*] *Serf de la glèbe*—both *serf,* "serf," and *glèbe,* "earth," "clod of earth," "soil," have been left in French when used as technical terms. —Trans.

[†] One must know that there are three estates among secular people. One of the estates is that of nobility. The second is of those who are naturally free ... and the third estate is that of serfs.

attached to their particular lords by extremely strong ties, so durable that only a very specialized juridical operation, that of manumission, could break them. At different times, sometimes one or the other of these two characteristics would seem to prevail; both were always present. Beaumanoir called the members of this class serfs, and this is the name that French historians still commonly give them.[3]

Now sometimes people add a qualifying term to this word serf. They say *serf de la glèbe*. It is true that this expression appears to be a little out of style. At least, informed medievalists avoid it without, however, explaining why. But it has enjoyed great success. Fustel de Coulanges, that unchallenged master of historical semantics, used it several times. In antiquity there was slavery and in the Middle Ages serfdom of the glèbe: this antithesis has furnished material for many dissertations. It was used to provide the subject for an academic contest, of which Michelet was the judge.[4] It has not completely fallen into disuse.

When did people decide to add the word glèbe to the word serf? Why did people get this idea? What did people originally mean by this verbal association? What were its variations? This is what I propose to research here. To illuminate the history of words is to throw a brighter light on the things that they designate, or the things that they conceal.

I need scarcely add that I do not at all pretend to offer the results I have arrived at as definitive. I know better than anyone what is incomplete about them and, as a result, conjectural. The vocabulary of old French law is singularly difficult to study. We must work by feeling our way. The documents are extremely dispersed; many have been published, but all are without glossaries. It is the same for narrative sources. The immense literature of scholarly law (Romanists, Canonists, and later feudalists) forms a dense underbrush where guides go wrong. We have no lexicon of French institutions: this is a serious gap from which linguistics and history suffer equally. It must definitely be filled some day. I hope that today this short study before us will be considered among those that will have served to clear up the material. My ambition is limited to this.

In the time of serfdom, what did people call those whom today we label serfs and sometimes serfs de la glèbe? We cannot ask that question in too general a form. The legal language of the Middle Ages was not fixed by any code, and it lacked uniformity.

It varied in different regions and at different times, and differed according to the people who spoke it. Notaries, lawyers, and troubadours did not always call the same things by the same words. Let us consult them one by one.

Let us first sift through the French literary texts. These are the documents closest to everyday usage. Here there is no doubt. The term used is the same one that we saw in Beaumanoir, and which deservedly has remained in the current historical vocabulary: *sers*, a special case of serf.[5] It is extremely frequent. However aristocratic the inspiration of the *chansons de geste* or the courtly love songs was, we can sometimes see in them the *"servaille"* moving in the background. Besides, the very contempt in which the men of the lower classes were held made their dishonorable name appear in the epics' verses, for the heroes willingly used insulting language, and serf was a cruel insult among the well-born.[6]

The etymology of the word is clear: sers was the Latin *servus*, which, to avoid any confusion, we call "slave" today. Not that medieval serfdom was simply an attenuated and softened version, as it were, of Roman slavery in a new society, a survival of past ages. The formula of Fustel de Coulanges, "serfdom ... has nothing in common with feudalism and antedates it,"[7] could not be accepted without reservations. A similar spirit animated all the institutions born in the disintegration of the ancient state: serfdom was a close relation of vassalage. However, since human institutions are not created out of nothing, the serf, so profoundly different from the slave, was after all only a gradually transformed slave. By an imperceptible transition, the word servus, to become sers, came to designate a juridical reality very far from its original meaning. The men of ancient France who pronounced this familiar term did not perceive that its meaning changed bit by bit, any more than they felt Latin turn into French on their lips.

However, a day came when reflective minds measured the road traveled and were shocked to conclude that the same term applied to two dissimilar things. The popular language, only moderately accessible to etymological considerations of this sort, was not at all bothered by them: the word serf continued to be honored in it. But notaries, who were thinkers, thought it would be well to reform their vocabulary. Here is how they did it.

Let us go through the documents, which are very numerous, where serfs appear. For a long time, in these texts, which at the time were compiled in Latin, the serf was called, as was natural, servus, and the female serf, *ancilla* or, much more rarely (because clerics were proud of classical expressions) *serva*. Around the beginning of the thirteenth century, these words fell out of use. They did not disappear completely, but they became rare, and this seems to have been the result of a uniform trend in the charters of nearly all of France.[8] This is not to say that the class of serfs suddenly disappeared at this time. In certain regions, we see it persist for several more centuries. But after that time, notaries sought to designate its members by new terms. Also, a great uncertainty prevailed over this almost-improvised vocabulary. Sometimes they wanted to recall certain specific duties: they said *homo* (or *femina*) *de manumortua, de forismaritagio et de manumortua*. Or they used formulae that translate the strength of the tie that attached the unfree man to his lord: *homo ligius, homo de corpore*. In legal documents in French, which were numerous after the end of the thirteenth century, they said *homme lige* and *homme de corps*.

This last term, especially, had success. With a certain brutality it restored the personal and nearly physical character of the lord's dominion. There is no doubt that it was not made up by the thinkers. We must see it in a popular artifact: "the male and female serfs, which we call *hommes de corps*," said a diploma of King Louis VII in 1180.[9] But the notaries adopted and expanded it a great deal. Homme lige pleased them less. This term, with a fairly mysterious etymology,[10] had a double meaning: they applied it to serfs at the same time as to vassals, or more exactly to those vassals who had given the most rigorous form of homage, homage without reserve. Thus, language, the interpreter of the collective consciousness, reconciled two forms of dependence that theoretical law, elaborated in the later days of feudalism by technicians, had accustomed us to consider radically distinct. Jurists would not have invented this ambiguity, which was certainly born in everyday usage; they did not welcome it. Almost everywhere in the language of the charters, homme lige was accepted only to designate a vassal. In the sense of unfree it was scarcely retained except as some local idiom, particular to certain regions (Bugey, Bordelais).[11] Homme de corps remained the master of the field. Writers, even in books of law, continued to use the term serf,[12] while notaries banished it, so much so that the people, used to the language of notaries, came at times to forget the juridical sense of the word, only to retain its injurious connotation. Under Charles VI the hommes de corps of Vermand complained that it was outrage that they had been treated as serfs.[13]

Whence came this striking ostracism of a word? Without a doubt, it came from the influence exercised by Roman law. The very moment when we see servus and serf disappear from the charters was when the formulae borrowed from the *Corpus Juris* penetrated in large numbers into diplomatic usage—at the beginning of the thirteenth century. This renaissance of sorts was especially the work of the officialites, whose task was then to edit most authentic legal documents. Pierre de Blois certainly confused the law of Justinian and the officials in the same anathema.[14] Now, the documents that issued from the officialities were precisely the first to reject servus; the other chancelleries followed the motion, sometimes only slowly.[15] The medieval serf resembled the Roman servus very little. Men brought up on ancient legislation could not fail to perceive it: the study of a beautiful technical language had given them the taste for exactitude, and it seemed intolerable to them to continue to use an improper term. In replacing it with new expressions, they were obeying a scruple of juridical purism. This scruple, moreover, found its very precise expression in certain texts, not, it is true (at least to my knowledge), in actions by officials but in certain documents equally established by learned jurists—the jurists of the papal court.

French churches possessed serfs in great numbers. This is why the popes, involved in so many matters, frequently had occasion to intervene in questions concerning serfdom. The unfree appear in many bulls. Under what name? This is what is curious.

French serfdom visibly embarrassed many stylists in the apostolic chancellery. They nearly always worked on petitions or on projects presented by the churches concerned, but they modified their wording. Their drifting vocabulary has certainly preserved the trace of their own incertitude. Sometimes we see them borrowing words from Classical Latin which they perverted from their original meaning: *originarii*[16] and *famuli*.[17] Sometimes they said simply *homines*, or *homines vestri*,[18] vague terms that, in the Middle Ages, served to indicate relations of dependence, whatever their nature was. When serfs were concerned they specified them, as we know, by a formula: *homines de corpore*. But this technical expression, foreign to good authors, displeased the Roman clerics for a long time. When they did decide to use it, they were careful to remark that it was a Gallic term. "*Originarii ecclesiarum quos homines de corpore patria censuit nuncupandos*," is written in a privilege granted by Gregory IX to St-Maur-des-Fossés;[19] they only sanctioned the word slowly and gradually. There remained servus, a perfectly Ciceronian term, and accordingly frequently accepted. But in this case, if those fond of good language could say they were satisfied, the jurists were not, for reasons that we already know. A bull of Pascal II explains this point clearly. The canons of Paris had for some time before obtained from Louis VI a diploma authorizing their serfs to bear witness in legal proceedings.[20] They asked the pope to confirm this favor for them, and their petition was accepted. The royal action spoke simply of serfs, servi. Rewritten by more learned notaries, the bull said, "... the *famuli* of your church, that in your domain the common people incorrectly call *serfs*."[21]

In addition, there are two papal documents whose comparison, better than any other example, will make us understand the change that took place in the thirteenth century in the terminology of serfdom. In 1245, Innocent IV legislated for the serfs of Saint-Germain-des-Prés, and the notary who drew up his bull did not like new expressions. He wrote, "You have *serfs* that, popularly, are called *hommes de corps*."[22] In 1289, the clerks of Nicholas IV sent out two bulls in favor of the chapter of Chartres. The pope claimed for his "dear sons" the canons all temporal jurisdiction "over their *hommes de corps* which popularly are called *serfs*."[23] The contradiction between these two actions is striking, and it translates, in a rather bizarre fashion, the evolution of the language. In the course of the thirteenth century, French notaries whom the apostolic chancellery followed slowly, replaced the word serf (or servus) which offended their erudition, with a name borrowed from everyday speech, homme de corps. Serf, formerly common to intellectual and everyday discourse, was only retained by the latter; the popular term became the juridical term, and the juridical term became popular.

Homme de corps, homme lige, *homme de mainmorte*—what more is there to say?[24] The terminology for the serf in the diplomatic language of the thirteenth century is particularly varied. However, one expression is missing in this abundance: it is the very one we are looking for: serf de la glèbe. It does not seem to have ever been pointed out in the charters of medieval France.[25] Should we then assert that nowhere, at any time, in no authentic act did it slip in? This would be unwise. We will see presently that Romanists and canonists were not unaware of it; it is possible that some time, by chance, some cleric who was educated from their works may have used his literary memory while drawing up some contract. No case of this sort has yet been discovered, though perhaps we will discover one some day. We will then have dug up a curious exception, and this will be all. Serf de la glèbe did not belong to the usual vocabulary of medieval notaries in France. This is a fact that cannot be doubted. These two words are not found joined together, either, among the jurists who wrote the great books of French common law in the vernacular. Neither Beaumanoir, nor Pierre de Fontaines, nor the authors of the *Livre de Justice et de plet* or of the *Etablissements de Saint Louis*, called unfree men by this term, any more than did the officials or functionaries of the royal chancellery. The historians of the nineteenth century who discoursed on the "serf of the soil" of the Middle Ages were thus using a term that the practitioners of the very age they were studying either did not know or rejected.

However, they did not invent it. What tradition did they receive it from? To learn this we must leave practice for jurisprudence, and leave France for Italy.

Around the end of the eleventh century began the teaching of Irnerius, the torch of the law, the *lucerna juris*, at Bologna. He explained the compilations of Justinian to his audience. The school which he founded shone on all of Western Europe. It was a school of annotators, of "glossarists" (this name has remained with them), who followed the Roman texts step by step to clear up obscure points, enriching the spaces between the lines and the margins of their manuscripts with commentaries.

Now Irnerius, in commenting on the digest, came across title V of the first book: *De statu hominem*. The legal experts from whom the extracts are compiled in this book divided men into two categories, the free men and the slaves (servi). This classification must have appeared incomplete to a commentator who knew the Justinian Code in depth. For in the code, testifying to a state of the law that was subsequent to the doctrine of the "cautious," as it is summed up in the digest, there appears a social group whose juridical status forms a sort of intermediary between freedom and slavery: the *coloni* or the *ascriptitii*. These two terms, frequently replacing one another in the ancient usage, seem to have been accepted as exact synonyms by the commentators. Irnerius, for the instruction of his students, sought to fill the lacuna that the ancient text presented to him. He made his endeavors in the glosses, which were collected. Here is one of them. I translate servus as serf, as a medieval writer would have done.

The condition of the *ascriptitius* is not such that by it one would be submitted to the *dominium* of others. By ascriptitius we must understand, essentially, not the serf of a person but the *serf of a glèbe (glebe servus)*.[26]

To my knowledge, that is the oldest example of this expression which was destined for such a great future. From Irnerius, it passed to his successors. Placentin, the first of the great glossarists who taught in France, uses it twice in the *Somme des Institutes*, like Irnerius in the form of a synonym or rather a paraphrase of the Latin ascriptitius.[27]

Then it spread to the canonists, who were also disciples of the professors of Roman law on many points. Toward the middle of the twelfth century, the monk Gratian had composed a selection of canon law, the *Decretum*, which soon took on a nearly official value. Let us open this illustrious compilation, and let us look there for the *Distinctio* LIV. All of the first part is devoted to the ancient ecclesiastical rule, which forbade the conferring of sacred orders on the unfree. In particular, Gratian reproduced in it a letter from a pope of the fifth century, Gelasus I, annulling the ordination of two *originarii* to the deaconate.[28] It seems that this word designated *coloni* who were fixed on the same domain from their birth. It could have appeared obscure to some readers, and it required a gloss. One of the oldest commentators of the *Decretum*, Paucapalea, contrived to explain it by the term ascriptitius. He was thereby led to give a definition of this latter term evidently borrowed from Romanist literature, and serf de la glèbe found its place there.[29] His gloss was accepted by the school, Master Rufinus copied it,[30] and Etienne de Tournai—a Frenchman who died in 1203—was inspired by it to write in his *Somme du Décret*, "The *ascriptitii* are those who are registered as attached to a property of land according to established conditions; these are called *serfs de la glèbe*."[31]

Thus for all these jurists the serfs de la glèbe is an ascriptitius or, as today's historians say more easily, a colonus, in the sense in which the legislation of the late Empire understood this term. From whence did this association of words come to them, or rather from whence did it come to the first of them, Irnerius?

If we believe the *Dictionnaire de l'Académie* on the subject, the answer to this question would not suffer from any difficulties. Actually, let us take the article glèbe in this venerable publication. We read this in it (after 1762): "Slaves attached to a domaine, to a land holding, were called *esclaves de la glèbe*." The glossarists, then, seem only to have delved into classical tradition. Unfortunately, it seems probable that the *Académie* is mistaken. I do not know of any text by the ancient writers where *servus glebae* can be found. We can scarcely doubt, until further orders, that Irnerius created the expression.[32] But he made it up under the influence of certain passages of the code and of the digest. Let us seek to rediscover his sources.

Around the end of the Roman Empire, politicians and jurists dreamed of a society in which each person had to be attached to his function by hereditary and indissoluble bonds, the *decurio* to his communal dignity, the soldier to his army, the farmer (whether of free or servile birth) to his field.[33] This farmer, thus attached to the land, was the colonus. The slave of ancient times had a man as his master; the colonus had a thing, the domain, as his master. A law of Theodosius, collected in Book XI of the Justinian Code, explains this point very clearly. I translate servus as serf: "They (the *coloni* of Thrace) are *serfs* of the land on which they are born."[34] *Servi terrae*: in writing servus glebae, Irnerius only substituted the word glebae for the word *terrae*.

Why did he make this substitution? In a sense it was perfectly legitimate. In the bizarre and emphatic language of the late Roman jurists, *gleba* (a poetic term) was an exact synonym for *terra*, to the extent that in the same text, reproduced simultaneously by the Justinian Code and the Theodosian Code, where the first reads terra we can read gleba in the second.[35] The Justinian Code did not say servus glebae but it could have. Let us continue through Book XI. In a law of Arcadius and Theodosius II, we find this phrase in reference to the coloni: "They cling so strongly to the glèbe that they cannot be torn from it even for an instant."[36] This law, the law of Theodosius, and perhaps still other glimmers of the *Corpus Juris* where the word gleba appeared,[37] were floating in Irnerius' memory when he wrote his gloss on the *Digestum Vetus*. From these mixed recollections—much more, it seems, than from any conscious and deliberate effort of style—was born servus glebe.[38]

As a paraphrase of a Roman term, ascriptitius, the expression serf de la glèbe had not been created by Irnerius to apply to the realities of his own time. It was the ancient colonus, not the medieval serf, whom he intended to designate this way. His imitators were not mistaken. For example, let us consider Etienne de Tournai, whom I quoted above. This commentator on Gratianus was not a pure theoretician. As abbot of Saint-Euverte d'Orléans, then of Sainte Geneviève de Paris and as bishop of Tournai, he was familiar with French serfdom. Besides his juridical works, we have preserved his abundant correspondence;[39] the archives of Sainte-Geneviève contain many acts passed under his rule as abbot.[40] The letters and charters talk often of serfs or of hommes de corps, but never of serfs de la glèbe. As a canonist, Etienne spoke the language of the scholar; as an administrator he spoke the language of an executive. He did not mix them together.

Others, it is true, had minds less neat. The clerics of the Middle Ages were proud of their erudition: obliged as they were constantly to use a dead language—Latin—and thereby used to misinterpreting, one way or another, the things of the present in an ancient form, they frequently sought the elegant or rare term rather than one that was exact. In a word, they were enthusiastic pedants. Finding an attractive phrase used by good writers, how could they not have been tempted to take it over, without too much concern for its meaning, in order to dress up their style with it?

All the same, let us be just with the French notaries. As we have seen, they let the expression invented by Irnerius lie unused in the manuals of Roman or canon law. The authors of common-law books did likewise. On the other hand, I know of two examples of the term which concerns us in the Latin literature of the thirteenth century, and I do not doubt that if we looked carefully we could find others. My two authors are Jacques de Vitry, a preacher, and Guillaume le Breton, a historian.

We have a series of sermons by Jacques de Vitry which are directed respectively to different classes in society. Among them there are two, *ad servos et ancillas*. These are not, as one might think, intended for serfs, but actually for serving men and women.[41] The ancient Romans scarcely asked anyone but their slaves to do domestic duties; this is why the language had no customary term to designate the free servant. It could not have been otherwise in the high Middle Ages, beause in nearly all of Western Europe slavery was then unknown. People had servants, and in French these were normally called *sergeants*.[42] But authors who wrote in Latin, wanting above all not to deviate from the classical forms, often used the words servus in this sense, without any precise juridical meaning for the purpose of the case.[43] This is what Jacques de Vitry did.[44] However, perhaps to avoid any equivocation, or perhaps more simply with the intention of displaying his erudition, he thought well to put at the beginning of his second sermon an elaboration on the different meanings of the word he used. He distinguished four categories of servi: those who did not have control over their own bodies (the slaves of ancient law), the ascriptitii, the originarii "born from ascriptitiae," the *conducticii famuli*, that is, servants. Speaking of the second, he gave the definition that has become classic in the school: "*Ascriptitii*, or *serfs de la glèbe* attached to the soil."[45] This exposition, drawn perhaps from some law book that I have not been able to find, was devoid of any relation to contemporary reality. Jacques de Vitry was not thinking of the serfs of his day.

This is not at all the case with Guillaume le Breton. We are indebted to this canon—learned and careful to show it—for two historical works, written in Latin and dedicated to the reign of Philip Augustus. One is a chronicle in prose and the other a sort of epic poem, the *Philippide*. In one passage of the chronicle, we see a nobleman of the diocese of Saint Pol-de-Léon appear to one of his peasants after his death. Guillaume le Breton wrote: "to one of his slaves, by which I mean a slave of his *glèbe*," "*cuidam mancipio suo, scilicet sue glebe.*"[46] This is not entirely the expression we are seeking, but is nearly so. The *Philippide*, on the other hand, presents it to us in its traditional form. On July 3, 1194, at the battle of Fréteval, Philip Augustus lost his archives. For our historian, it was a chance to describe them to us. They contained, if we are to believe him, among other precious documents, "writings by which one could ascertain ... who was *serf de la glèbe* and *serf de condition.*"[47] What differentiation did Guillaume make between these two aspects of serfdom? We do not know. For my part, I would be inclined not to take too seriously what might only have been a stylistic redundance. At any rate, that is, to my knowledge, the oldest text where we find French serfs called serfs de la glèbe.

Did Guillaume le Breton have imitators in his day? I would not dare deny it, but it is certain that his example was followed very little. In giving to medieval serfdom the name *servitude de la glèbe*, invented for the roman colonus, the thirteenth century could hardly have helped falling into the same mistake. This only came about later, and it remains for us to recount how.

Serfdom did not always remain the same. Toward the end of the Middle Ages it underwent profound modifications. Apparently, the same was so of all the institutions that made up the so-called "feudal" system. Unfortunately, we understand this waning of feudalism very poorly; its history has never been written. As for serfdom, here is what we may conjecture, without taking local variations into account.

The serf of early times was, in the full sense of the word, an homme de corps. Whatever he did, wherever he went, whatever land he cultivated, he remained attached to his lord by a bond that was indissoluble by anything less than manumission, that was hereditary, nearly physical; it was a bond, as Guy Coquille would call it, that stuck "to flesh and bones."[48] He remained always under the jurisdiction of his lord for certain misdemeanors, and he remained always indebted to him for the duties of his station. On the other hand, a free man who acquired a field from the possession of a serf did not on that account cease to be free. There were servile people, or rather servile families; there were no servile landholdings. Thus composed, serfdom did not appear as an anomaly. Nearly the entire social structure was founded upon analagous conceptions. Nothing seemed so strong as the bonds between man and man. But this system of personal relations broke down very quickly, because the collective ideas that supported them were worn away. We hesitate to give dates in such a matter, but we can say that from the beginning of the thirteenth century, in northern France, society had begun to change its appearance. Now, serfdom did not disappear along with the whole of the customs and juridical notions from which it had been born. It survived in many French provinces until the sixteenth century, and in some, until 1789; but it was slowly and deeply transformed. After that the servile "stain" adhered less to the man than to the earth. Whoever inhabited a certain contaminated holding became a serf, while whoever left it became free. Real serfdom slowly superceded serfdom "de corps."

The serf whose condition had taken on this new form remained quite different from the Roman colonus; he was not, strictly speaking, attached to the soil. By law nothing kept him from leaving his landholding if he wanted to. In fact, however, this freedom was somewhat imaginary—he could go, as long as he left all his possessions to his master. Departure for him meant poverty, and fearing that, he was bound by an economic necessity to his fields as strongly, or nearly so, as if he had been kept there by the most implacable law. How could one avoid comparing him to the colonus of the late Roman Empire? This was all the more natural a temptation since jurists, educated in the practice of ancient legislation, only asked from it precedents for what they saw around them.

In Languedoc, after the thirteenth century, the juridical situation of the serfs was similar in some respects to what it was later on in the North. There were servile land holdings that were called holdings of *casalage*.⁴⁹ Also, it was in a decree of Philip the Fair for the province, which was definitely drawn up by officials who were versed in the law of the south, that we see for the first time serfdom reconciled with the *ascriptitiat.*⁵⁰

The example caught on. Still under Philip the Fair in 1303, the notaries of the royal chancellery, called upon to draw up a decree applicable to the entire kingdom, used ascriptitius as a synonym for serf.⁵¹ This verbal association spread in juridical writings. In the fifteenth century, Gui Pape used it without hesitation.⁵² It became commonplace.

Let us consult Guy Coquille. This great jurist was from Nivernais. He was from a region where personal serfdom, at least in some of its features, persisted until modern times. Around him there lived serfs "de corps" and "de poursuite." In his beautiful language, which is rich and lively, he described more than once this serfdom "attached to the bones," "which cannot be shaken off."⁵³ However, following the theories of the school, this is what he wrote in his *Institution Du Droit Des François*:

> Les servitudes qui sont en France ne sont pas semblables a celles qui étoient en usage auprès des anciens Romains, qui faisoient trafic des personnes serves comme d'animaux brutes; ... mais bien sont semblables aux servitudes ascriptices et colonaires, qui rendoient les personnes attachées et liées aux domaines des champs pour les faire valoir. ... L'origine des serfs, que nous avons en quelques provinces de France, procede de cette usance ancienne des Romains, au temps qu'ils seigneuroient les Gaules.*⁵⁴

This doctrine was to do well in historical literature, that serfdom was born from the coloni and was practically the same as their condition. So many scholars refused to recognize in institutions of slavery anything "in common with feudalism": would not this above all be because people taught for so long, like two axioms, of the Roman origin of serfs and the German origin of vassals?

The serf seemed similar, or nearly so, to the Roman colonus

---

* Servitudes in France are not similar to those that were used among the ancient Romans, who carried on a commerce in unfree people as if they were brute animals ... but many are similar to the servitude of the ascriptitius and the colonus, which rendered people attached and bound to domains of fields in order to profit by them.... The origins of serfs, whom we have in some provinces of France, follows from this ancient usage of the Romans, at the time when they were lords of the Gauls.

because like him he appeared attached to the soil. Now the code said of the colonus that he was "attached to the *glèbe*." This is a pretty expression; why should the jurists who wrote about serfdom have given it up as an ornament to their discussions? They adopted it very early.

At the parliament of Pentecost in 1287, Philip the Fair, in giving satisfaction to the complaints of the barons, had determined "the manner of conducting and holding" the royal *bourgeoisies*. When in 1303 he promulgated the grand and fruitless decree of the reform of the kingdom, he added to it, as a sort of appendix, a new addition of this regulation. In 1287 the royal court had legislated in French. The solemn decree of 1303, however, was in Latin. To keep the unity of style it was, therefore, necessary to translate into this learned language the ten articles on the bourgeoisies which had formerly been written in the vernacular. The notary to whom this homework exercise was confided allowed himself one liberty. In Article 9, he read this phrase:

> Ne n'est aussi sa ententions que si sobgiet ne puissent poursuire a retraire de bourgeoisie leur hommes de cors ou d'autre condition.*

He translated it as follows:

> Nec est intentionis nostre quin subjecti nostri possint requirire, aut de prefatis burgesiis extrahere homines suos de corpore, *ascripticios, seu glebe affixos*, aut alterius servilis conditionis.

In French, the royal chancellery had spoken the language of practice, but in Latin the imitation of Roman law slipped in. Thus there appeared, apparently for the first time, in an official document, serfs "attached to the *glèbe*."[55]

This expression slowly entered into use.[56] At the beginning of the fifteenth century, Jean Jager, the king's attorney at Chateau-Thierry, wrote, "The serfs in Champaigne *sunt servy conditionati et quodam modo astricti glebe*."†[57] Around the end of the same century, Gui Pape, a lawyer of the Dauphinois, used analogous terms.[58] This linguistic habit ended by passing from Latin to French. The *Dictionnaire de l'Académie*, in 1694 sanctioned it: "Men of mortmain," we read in it, "are attached to the *glèbe*."

* And it is not his intention that his subjects not be able to pursue, in order to reclaim from the bourgeoisie, their *hommes de corps* or those of another condition.
† ... are in the condition of servi and in a certain way tied to the soil.

People got used to the association of these two words in their language: serf and glèbe.

But this was not yet "serf de la glèbe." Did this verbal association, invented by Irnerius long before, penetrate into French before the eighteenth century? I do not know, but in any case it did not take over everyday usage. Neither jurists such as Guy Coquille,[59] nor scholars like Etienne Pasquier,[60] seem to have known it, no did feudalists like Brussel or like Dunod, who "cooly and disinterestedly"[61] wrote the *Traité de la mainmorte* which is justly famous. Nor did Ragneau nor Laurier in their glossaries of French law,[62] nor did the *Dictionnaire de l'Académie* or that of Furetière.[63] It seems likely that it vegetated obscurely in the old books of the glossarists or the canonists, until one day when, by some chance, a writer of genius, who had frequented this literature a great deal, pulled it out and made it famous. This writer was Montesquieu.

In the *Esprit des Lois*, which appeared in 1748, we come across *servitude de la glèbe*[64] twice and *esclavage de la glèbe*[65] once. All three times it refers to the coloni rather than to serfdom. However, placed in a work that was so frequently read, commented upon, and discussed, the expression was, as it were, started on its career. In calling up an image that was precise, by the use of this word glèbe, which was a bit rare and pompous and flattered the classical taste, it could not fail to please. Very quickly writers who were less precise than Montesquieu applied it to the juridical conditions of the time. From 1762 on, the *Dictionnaire de l'Académie*, completely making over the article "Glèbe" from the old editions, discovered "serfs de la glèbe" in several provinces of the kingdom."[66] Doubtless technicians scarcely liked this new term, which was more poetic than correct. The lawyers Claude Serres,[67] Fréminville,[68] and Pothier[69] ignored it or wanted to ignore it. But the *philosophes* accepted it willingly: it appeals to the spirit, it seems that in uttering it one sees the peasant a slave of the earth, it carries a sort of indignant force. Voltaire[70] and the Encyclopédie[71] use it. In 1789, several *cahiers* demanded, as the Tiers of Belfort said, "that *servitude de la glèbe* . . . be abolished in the whole kingdom."[72] The Revolution gave satisfaction to this wish. Servitude de la glèbe only survived in the language of historians, where it was firmly established.

Let us quickly sum up the results of our research.

In Bologna, around the end of the ninth century, a professor of law, Irnerius, mixing up in his mind several passages of the Justinian Code, wrote glebe servus in a gloss. This is the way he designated the colonus, the asciptitius of the Roman texts. His authority was great; after him, Romanists and canonists picked up the expression he had created, and they used it in the same sense as he. With the exception of a writer without any juridical pretentions, it seems that no one in the Middle Ages—almost no one, at any rate—thought to apply it to the social conditions of the day.

However, in the fifteenth century, serfdom changed its character. People wanted to reconcile it with the condition of the coloni and thenceforth it lent itself to this reconciliation. Now the Justinian Code called the colonus "slave" (or "serf") of the land. Were they then to call the French serf this? No, because the word "land"* is ordinary, it does not strike the imagination. No one thought of digging up this dull verbal association from the old texts. However, taking up another passage of the code, people readily said, during the last centuries of the Middle Ages and later still, that the serf was "attached to the glèbe" because glèbe is a pretty word that belongs to the noble style and which flatters the fastidious.

In 1748, probably without paying much attention, and upon a chance memory from his reading, Montesquieu wrote, "Servitude de la glèbe." People read it. There was something both concrete and unusual about the phrase, something picturesque and distinguished. It roused people, and the enemies of serfdom adopted it. It was quickly accepted. Serf de la glèbe, in everyday use, became the eloquent synonym of the too-simple word "serf" without people distinguishing between periods of time.

Thus the historians of the nineteenth century often designated medieval serfs by a term that was, in this sense, unknown in the Middle Ages. One might say that this was a harmless oversight. It is nothing of the sort. Words have a singular force. Each draws after it a following of ideas and images which it imposes on the mind. To apply to serfdom an expression that was invented for the coloni is to fall into error. It would be hard to imagine two institutions more profoundly different than the condition of the coloni and serfdom—by which I mean serfdom during the classical period of feudalism. One was created by an absolute Empire, in order to satisfy the most implacable affairs of finance, and which

---

* The French word is *terre*, the Latin *terra*.

perished along with the state that thought itself strong enough to attach a man to the soil. The other was born in the very dissolution of the state itself, in the bosom of a society where practically nothing counted more than the most strictly personal ties of dependence. Let us not call serfs de la glèbe those whom the people of the Middle Ages admirably called hommes de corps.

SERVUS GLEBAE[73]

The expression *serf de la glèbe* has had a brilliant success. But is it very old? In an article that appeared in 1921 in the *Revue historique*,[74] I had thought that I had demonstrated that it was not. More recently, in a communication presented to the *Société des Antiquaires*, M. Martroye has taken up the problem again and has proposed, on one point at least, a completely different solution.[75] Our disagreement, as we shall see, concerns, in short, less the history of facts than of words. I thought, nonetheless, that it was worth while to submit the question to a new examination. In addition, there is a certain kind of superficiality in the reading of the texts which should not be allowed to pass without a word of protest.

First, let us sum up the two theses before us.

The history of the French expression that concerns us had seemed to me to be the following. In its French form, it is very recent: everything indicates that it was popularized by Montesquieu. In its Latin form, servus glebae, it goes back without any doubt, to a much more distant past, but not to antiquity. We come across it for the first time, it seems, in a gloss of Irnerius, who died shortly after 1125.[76] This professor of Bologna used it, moreover, exclusively to explain the condition of the Roman colonus during the imperial period and, very explicitly, as a synonym for ascriptitius. It was a scholar's term, without any tie to contemporary life. It was only later that some overeducated writers, first in Italy and then in France, thought up the idea of extending the rise of this happy association of words to their present time.[77] They called the serfs who lived around them on seigneurial lands servi glebae or rather *glebae affixi* or *astricti*. The transformation of the institutions of serfdom, which I need not retrace here, favored this verbal takeover, but the expression always remained quite uncommon. What remains is to ask how Irnerius came to create it. A law of Theodosius, included in the Justinian Code, said of the coloni of Thrace that they "are serfs of the land upon which they were born."[78] On the other hand, in the bizarre and emphatic language that the jurists of the fourth and fifth century used, gleba, a poetic term, is the exact synonym of terra. Irnerius knew this. A law of Honorius and Theodosius II, which he had read, since the Justinian Code gives it, speaks of the coloni in these terms: "they are attached to the earth so strongly that they cannot be separated from it even for an instant."[79] This law, and perhaps other glimmers of the *Corpus Juris* where the word glebe appears, were floating around in his mind when he compiled his gloss on the *Digestum Vetus* and brought him to write glebae where one would expect terrae.

M. Martroye does not accept these last conclusions. He has not directed his attention to the Middle Ages. He does not even contest that Irnerius was the first among medieval writers to speak of serfs de la glèbe. But he only identifies the glossarist as having "restored to its rightful place" an ancient term: "the expression servus glebae is that of authentic original texts of the fourth and fifth centuries" (p. 243). In these texts it designates the colonus.

Put this way, the question is one of fact, by its very nature. Do the legislative texts of the late Empire mention servus glebae? Yes, says M. Martroye, and he cites two of these texts. Let us look at them along with him.

The first is that very law of Theodosius relating to the Thracian coloni which I recalled above. We read in it, it is true, *terrae* and not *glebae: licet condicione videantur ingenui, servi tamen terrae ipsius cui natisunt aestimentur* (C.J. XI, 52). However, says M. Martroye, we only kow this law by means of the Justinian Code, whose lessons are always under suspicion of alteration: "the word *terra* was doubtless interpolated there (by Justinian commission) in place of *gleba*" (p. 242). In sum, a correction of the text is suggested to us, not without some boldness. What are we to make of it? For the moment, we can only reserve our judgment. The conjecture is only worth as much as the general thesis held by M. Martroye. It could not serve as the basis for this thesis. Therefore, let us provisionally set aside the law of Theodosius, and pass to the second citation.

It is a law of Valentinian, of 31 July 365, and it has been preserved for us by the two codes at the same time. Here is how M. Martroye analyzes it, according to the Theodosian Code (p. 240): ". . . upon whoever possesses the *servi* of abandoned holdings it places the responsibility of the tax of the *glèbe* of which they remain the serfs, the *servi*." There is no doubt that if this interpretation is correct, we have the expression we are looking for. Even better, we have it in the text provided by the older of the two codes. The Justinian Code (XI, 48, 3) says here terrae where the Theodosian Code gave glebae. Here is the above correction justified. The change that the compilers made in the Valentinian law could very well have equally been made in the Theodosian law. No one will deny the ingeniousness of this argument. But what are its premises worth? Let us place the document before the reader's eyes:

> Quisquis ex deserti agris veluti vagos servos liberalitate nostra fuerit consecutus, pro fiscalibus pensitationibus ad integram glebae professionem, ex qua videlicet servi videantur manere habeatur obnoxius.

One word causes some difficulty: it is *manere*. One would have expected a verb indicating the idea of origin. Godefroy proposed that it read *manare*, "to flow from," which the codes actually used in a figurative sense, but applying it, it seems, always to things and not to persons. I wonder if it would not be better to suggest *emanare*, which is very unusual but supported in the sense of "to remain far from," "to desert." Whatever the case may be, the general meaning is clear. We can render it thus:

> Whoever shall have obtained, from our generosity, slaves coming from desert lands and (thereby) placed in a situation analogous to that of wandering slaves must include in their tax declaration all the earth which these slaves have evidently left.

Where can one see that in this text coloni are called serfs de la glèbe? And where can anyone see that coloni are being mentioned in the first place? Servi are slaves. Without doubt after the fourth century, an irresistible social evolution tended to make the state of the coloni and that of slaves similar to one another, but in 365 this evolution was very far from being achieved. Legislation still distinguished servi very clearly from coloni or ascripticii. Were the servi of this law serfs de la glèbe? Naturally not. Applied to slaves, this expression would have been absurd. One could very well metaphorically call coloni "slaves of the land." Properly speaking, slaves belonged to a person, not to a thing. The text confines itself to mentioning a *glèbe*—it means a landholding—from which slaves come, who are objects of the emperor's generosity.

It says *ex qua*; M. Martroye has translated it as if it was *cuius*. Could it be that he is asking us for another correction? There is nothing to indicate it. Perhaps he simply read a little hastily.

Thus, there is nothing that we can conclude from the law of Valentinian. In particular, it does not furnish us with any reason for substituting servi glebae for servi terrae in the law of Theodosius. However, in support of this modification, M. Martroye brought up another aspect, which we now must examine. For him gleba is not, as I had thought, a poetic or, if you will, a literary synonym for terra. It is a very precise and almost technical term. As far as the original meaning goes, of course, this presents no difficulty. Everyone knows that gleba means "a clod of earth," properly speaking. However, says M. Martroye, "from the classical period on," a different meaning, perfectly clear, was introduced: gleba originally designated a parcel of land, or rather a cultivated plot, and terra never has had this meaning. Wanting to state that the colonus was the slave of the field, or of the domaine, the "original texts" could only say servus glebae. Later on, it is true, they changed glebae to terrae. This is because the word gleba had become odious: it evoked the memory of the *gleba senatoria*, a tax detested by the upper classes, which was happily suppressed in 450. It was necessary to wipe out, even from the vocabulary, this "hateful memory" (p. 242).

What judgment are we to make of this little lexicographer's design? Here again the testimony must be left to the texts. I am going to take up all those brought up by M. Martroye, one by one; I will translate them, and I think that this very translation, without commentary, will suffice to show that in no case does gleba have the meaning of "cultivated plot of land." In all the examples cited, except one—I will come back to this one later—the word simply retains its original meaning of "a clod of earth." There is no doubt that very often it creates an image, but to fail to retain its concrete meaning would be to lose precisely this image.

Titus Livius, IV, 11: *consenterant autem ut ... nec ulli prius Romano ibi, quam omnibus Rutilis dividus esset, gleba ulla agri adsignaretur*: "... before each Rutilian has taken his part of the territory (of Ardea), not one clod of earth should be taken away from it in favor of a Roman."

Cicero, *In Verrem, actio.* II, *lib.* III, 11: *iniquios decumanis aiebat omnes esse qui ullam agri glebam possiderent*: "... he accused anyone who possessed even one clod of earth of partiality to the *decumani*."

Cicero, *De Lege Agraria*, III, 1: *Si ostendo non modo non adimi cuiquam glebam de Sullanis agris, sed etiam, genus id agrorum certo capite legis impudentissine confirmari atque sanciri*: "If I prove not only that (by the proposed agrarian law) no one will be able to take away even a clod of earth from the fields assigned by Sulla but, even better, that this kind of possession is impudently confirmed and sanctioned by a particular article of this law. ..."

Virgil, *Aeneid*, VII, 746-747: *gens ... duris Aequicola glaebis*: "... the Aequi, whose soil is made of hard clods of earth ..."

Juvenal, XIV, 163-167: *tandem pro multis vix iugera bina dabantur vulneribus; ... saturabat glaebula talis patrem ipsum turbamque casae*: "... finally, as a reward for so many wounds they were scarcely given two acres of land ... this little clod of earth was enough to feed the father and the whole household ...."

Apuleius, *Metamorphoses*, IX, 35: *iamque tota frugalitate spoliatum ipsis etiam glebulis exterminare gestiebat*: "Having already despoiled him of all his harvest (?) he now sought to drive him from the poor little clods of earth (which formed his whole holding)."

Iavolenus, in *Dig*. X, VIII, 3, 13: *Si totus ager itineri aut actui servit, dominus in eo agro nihil Facere potest, quo servitus impediatur, quae ita diffusa est, ut omnes glaebae serviant*: "If a field in its entirety is made to serve as a passage for men or herds, the owner can do nothing who raises an obstacle to this service, which is spread over the whole field so that there is not a clod of earth which is not subjected to it."

However, gleba was not always retained in this concrete sense. Sometimes we find it used in the general sense of "land" or "soil." Is this a change of meaning? Not at all; it is a simple rhetorical device, "synecdoche," to use the accepted term, by which the part—the clod—is used to designate the whole, that is to say "soil." In good Latin, this seems to have been rare, at least in prose. Among the texts cited by M. Martroye, I only notice one example that is ancient—it is the passage I set aside above—and it is borrowed from a work of poetry. I am thinking of the famous verse of Virgil, *Terra antiqua, potens armis atque ubere glebae* (*Aeneid*, I, 531 and III, 164[80]). But the language of the constitutions of the late Empire was fond of figures of speech and disliked simplicity. It generalized the usage of gleba in the accepted meaning of "soil" or, with a slight extension, a large portion of soil, a domain.[81] In this latter sense gleba took the place of the classical terms *fundus*, *praedium*, or even *terra*. M. Martroye is in error, actually, when he denies (p. 243) a similar meaning for terra prior to the law of the Burgundians. A law of 387 speaks of *possessionibus ac terris*.[82] The adjective *glebalis* had the same success. When a special fiscal tax began to be levied upon the *clarissimi*, it was designated by the name *collatio glebalis*, from which current language more briefly made *gleba senatoria* or simply gleba. Also, in this case rhetoric was perhaps not the only cause for this recourse to a rather affected term: it is possible that they wanted to avoid the adjective *terrena*, which was reserved for the ordinary land tax (*iugatio terrena*).

As M. Martroye very correctly remarks, gleba is especially frequent in the Theodosian Code. The Justinian Code seems to say terra more willingly. We even have proof, by the law of Valentinian, that at least once those who compiled this latter code, in an imperial constitution, substituted terra for gleba. It is very probable that they did so several times. What reasons led them to do this? It would be difficult to believe that it was a sort of retrospective repugnance for *collatio glebalis*, which had been abolished half a century before. The explanation is obviously much simpler. These jurists hardly appreciated the rambling style that had had the favor of the imperial offices two centuries before. Most of the alteration that they introduced into the laws evidenced a great care for clarity and an active taste for correctness of language.[83] This is why for gleba which, to repeat, was a sort of poetic and metaphorical term when it appeared in any meaning other than that of "clod," they preferred, as a general rule, the good old word terra.

From the preceding discussion we can, it seems, draw two conclusions.

The first and basic one is this. The Roman juridical texts, such as they have come down to us, never considered coloni as servi glebae. Such an expression would not have been absurd since gleba which was, it is true, unknown in good Latin in the sense of "cultivated field," was nonetheless currently employed, in the bad Latin of the fourth and fifth centuries, as a synonym for words that designated the soil or the domain. If one likes hypotheses, one can suppose that it was sometimes used, but this cannot be proven. And since Irnerius apparently read approximately the same texts as we, we must admit that he himself fashioned, rather than recovered, the verbal association that he unwittingly willed to such a fine future.

The second conclusion touches upon method. It is not enough

to cite texts. One must translate them at least for oneself, often putting the translation before the eyes of the reader. To translate Latin, however, is always a fairly delicate exercise.

Notes

Chapter 2

[1] *Annuario de Historia del Derechio Espanol* (1933), pp. 5-101.

[2] The present study—based on a lecture given in May 1932 at the Semaine d'Histoire du Droit in Madrid—follows a number of studies on social classifications in the Middle Ages and, more specifically, on servitude. If only so as not to multiply the footnotes, I will have to refer on several occasions to the following earlier articles I have published: "Blanche de Castille et les serfs du Chapitre de Paris," in Marc Bloch, *Mélanges Historiques* (S. E. V. P. E. N., Bibliothèque Générale de l'école pratique des Hautes Etudes, Paris, 1963), pp. 462-490 [pp. 163-177 of the present volume]; *Rois et Serfs, un chapitre d'histoire capétienne* (Paris, 1920); "Serf de la glèbe, histoire d'une expression toute faite," *Mélanges Historiques*, pp. 356-373 [pp. 179-195 of the present volume]; "Les transformations du servage à propos de deux documents du XIIIe siècle relatif à la région parisienne," *Ibid.*, pp. 491-502 [pp. 151-161 of the present volume]; "Servus glebae," *Ibid.*, pp. 373-378 [pp. 195-201 of the present volume]; "Les 'colliberti': études sur la formation de la classe servile," *Ibid.*, pp. 385-451 [pp. 93-149 of the present volume]; "Un problème d'histoire comparée: la ministérialité en France et en Allemagne," *Ibid.*, pp. 503-528; *Les Caractères originaux de l'histoire rurale française* (Paris and Oslo, 1931), translated as *French Rural History: An Essay on its Basic Characteristics* (University of California Press, Berkeley and Los Angeles, 1966). The reader will forgive me if I repeat here some of the observations I have had occasion to present earlier—at times, to be truthful, in order to correct or modify them. Such repetitions are probably inevitable when one is, vis-à-vis a difficult problem, only in the beginning stages of an investigation that attempts to clarify, one by one, its various aspects. On French serfdom, I must mention the very rich article by M. P. Petot, "L'hommage servile," in *Revue Historique du Droit* (1927).

[3] These facts are so well known and so well established in their general outline that it is sufficient to refer the reader to general works. See, for example, H. Brunner, *Deutsche Rechtgeschichte*, under the word "Knecht" in the tables.

[4] *Histoire du Languedoc*, ii, no. 49 (819, 8 February).

[5] We know that in the Visigoth kingdom, on the other hand, a law of Ervig, in 681, obliged a master to bring to the feudal levy a tenth of his servi, under arms: *Lex Visigothorum* IX, II, 9. In the Carolingian state, I only know of one text where the service of servi in the levy is mentioned: it is a diploma from Louis the Pious to Hermoutier, 2 August 830. (Böhmer-Mühlbacher, no. 875); however, a capitulary of 802 (I, no. 34, c. 13b) mentions a mass levy for the defense of the coastlines, a very special case. M. Lesne (*Histoire de la propriété ecclésiastique*, II, 2, pp. 472 ff.) denies that church tenants—notably husbandmen—had, properly speaking, to serve in the armed forces; they served only as footmen. This thesis does not appear to agree with the texts.

[6] "*Juravit quod se tenebit et habebit tanquam hominem nostrum de suo corpore ad usus et consuetudines ville Sancte Gemme de qua fuit oriundus.*" Arch. Nat.

LL 1351, fol. 125, vo. It would be easy to cite many other examples. Thus, on 24 October 1291, a free woman, from Maisons-sur-Seine, having promised to marry a serf of the monks of Saint-Maur-des-Fossés, admits that she, and the children to be born of this union, will henceforth be serfs "*ad usus et consuetudines aliorum hominum ville de Domibus.*" Arch. Nat. L 458, no. 40.

[7] *Olim*, I, p. 181, no. XIII. (Parlement de la Saint-Martin d'hiver). On this affair, see also *Olim*, I, p. 446, no. XXIV, and Arch. Nat. LL 79, fol. 36, the notice stating that the recalcitrant serf had been delivered to the chapter by a royal sergeant, to be imprisoned for as long as the canons wished (6 December 1263).

[8] "*Jura enim diversa debentur dominis diversis secundum diversitates servillum condicionum aut locorum . . . Ideo cum de talibus habebis agere in aliqua patria, informa prius te per illos qui illius patrie consuetudines cognoscunt.*" These two sentences take place in the developments that form, in the Dareste edition, chapter 14 of Book 2. They can be read, among other places, in Ms Bibl. Nat. franç. 10816, fol. 175 and verso. (Text communicated by M. Olivier-Martin.) The same observation is found in several other medieval customaries, in all countries, in Germany, for example, in the *Sachsenspiegel, Landrecht*, III, 42, 2, concerning administrators (*ministeriales*); in England, in the *Rectitudines singularum personarum*, c. 21 (960-1060), in a very general form: "*Landlaga syn mistlice*"; or as it is translated in the *Quadripartitus*, "*Leges et consuetudines terrarum sunt multiplices et varie.*" See also Glanvill, *De legibus, Prologus*, Woodbine, ed., p. 24. One can easily conceive how much these very variable local customs defied any kind of systematization. Thus, we can probably explain why Beaumanoir spoke of servile duties—of mainmorte notably—in such imprecise terms, an imprecision foreign to his normal turn of mind, and a most curious contrast to his newly found assurance when he reaches those sections of servile law determined by a jurisprudence of more general character: emancipation, lawsuits over servitude, cases on descendancy, etc.

[9] To be truthful I know of chevage paid in workdays only in Germany, in the eleventh century (*D. D.* Conrad II, no. 216). But these are data rarely recorded by the texts, since they do not impinge upon the form of the law itself. In the Hainaut, in 1402, one finds a formariage settled in this manner: L. Verriest, *Le régime seigneurial dans le comté de Hainaut*, p. 272.

[10] Lasteyrie, *Cartulaire de Paris*, p. 429, no. 519 (26 October 1173-1 May 1179). Giard, "Etudes sur l'histoire de l'abbaye de Sainte-Geneviève," in *Mém. Soc. Hist. Paris* (1903), p. 110, no. II. Act prior to February 21, 1185, the earliest date one can accept for the death of Henri, bishop of Senlis, from whom the charter issues; after February 1, 1182, date of a bull from Lucius III. *Bibl. de Sainte Geneviève*, Ms. 356, p. 86. This last element of dating comes from the history of the dispute between the serfs of Rosny-sous-Bois with the abbey, on this subject. "De la cour royale à la cour de Rome: le procès des Serfs de Rosny-sous-Bois," *Mélanges Historiques*, pp. 452-461.

[11] Van Drival, ed., *Cartulaire de l'abbaye de Saint-Vaast d'Arras*, p. 177, and particularly p. 178.

[12] Act of the dean of Laon, canceling, in favor of these men, the mainmortes and formariages in exchange for an increase in the chevages, June 1255, in a royal *vidimus* of the same date: Arch. Nat. JJ 26, fol. 375.

[13] *Rec. des Histor. de France*, XXIV, p. 326, no. 179.

[14] A. Lesort, *Chronique et chartes de l'abbaye de Saint-Mihiel*, no. 32 (25 November 1006) and No. 33 (1024-1033). On the fact that the words serf and servitude are not found in these two acts, see pp. 77-78. The custom was frequent in England. See also an act of the bishop of Cambrai, Gérard I (1012-1051) in Wauters, *De l'origine et des premiers développements des libertés communales*, "Preuves," p. 1.

[15] Marc Bloch, "Les Colliberti," p. 106, n. 62. See *ibid.*, p. 105 for the role played by the deniers of chevage in the symbolism of enslavement, a very characteristic feature, but one that need not be taken up here.

[16] Emancipation by Phillip IV of Thierry de Montaigu, bourgeois of the communne of Bruyères-en-Laonnois, June 1309. Arch. Nat. JJ 42B, fol. 52 vo. As early as the Parlement of the octaves on All Saints Day 1272, a decree seems to indicate that among the serfs of Saint-Crépin of Soissons, although some, as is normal, had to pay the mainmorte without owing the chevage, others, and this is a very rare anomaly, paid the chevage but were not subject to the mainmorte. *Olim*, I, p. 414, no. XXIV.

[17] *Cartulaire de Saint-Vaast*, pp. 177 ff. Decrees of the comtes, pp. 182, 185. The first decree (1122) ends with these words: "*ego Gerardus monicellus sancti Vedasti scripsi*" (p. 185).

[18] "*Ut autem servus propter ullam remissionem non occultet, hoc nostro aedicto, Deo volente, in aeternum valituro statuimus, ut deinceps unusquisque ad ostendendam suae servitutis condictionem in Kalendis Decembris unum publicae monetae persolvat denarium aut ipsi domino aut eius ministro ad hoc offitium deputato.*" *Constitutiones*, I, no. 21, c. 2.

[19] Certain, ed., *Miracles de Saint Benoît*, VI, 2, p. 218 (toward 1050).

[20] For example, on the lands of Saint-Vaast of Arras in the twelfth century: *Cartulaire de Saint-Vaast*, pp. 178, 255, 362; in Hainaut, according to L. Verriest, *Le servage dans le comté de Hainaut*, Académie Royale de Belgique, Classe des Lettres, Mémoires in 8º, 2e série, vol. VI, (1910), p. 66; on the lands of the college of Bonne-Nouvelle in Orléans, in the twelfth century (see p. 293, n. 2); in the Maiche, in 1452, on the lordships of Magnat-l'Etrange and of Montvert: *Mém. Soc. Sc. Naturelles Creuse*, 2e série, XX, (1916-1918), p. 414; see also pp. 409 ff.

[21] Many examples in A. Giry, *Les établissements de Rouen*, II, p. 237, under the word "mariages." Customs of Saint-Antonin, toward 1144: *Layettes du Trésor des Charles*, I, No. 86. Customs of Montpellier, August 1204, in Ch. Giraud, *Essai sur l'histoire du droit français*, I, p. 65, c. 84. (Article reproduced in the customs of Carcassonne.)

[22] On the lands of the college of Bonne-Nouvelle, in the diocese of Orléans, a tax on servile marriages existed in the twelfth century, and was collected by the solicitor: de Vassal, "Recherches sur le monastère de Notre-Dame-de-Bonne-Nouvelle," in *Mém. Soc. Royale des Sciences d'Orléans*, IV, pièce justificative V. In 1110 the canons accused the solicitor of forcing serfs to marry whom he wished, unless they paid him a fee: *Ibid.*, p. just. C.

[23] I will not examine here in detail the solutions offered to the problem of status when the two parents were of different conditions. Two principles have been opposed: at times the opinion was that "the worse won"; at times servitude was considered transmitted matrilineally. The latter thesis was Beaumanoir's and seems to have generally triumphed in juridical literature. In earlier eras the difficulty did not often present itself, since one rarely allowed a free individual to marry a servile one without agreeing to be a serf himself.

[24] It is possible to gather together, from various sources, a relatively large number of documents regarding formariage payments. However, these are difficult to interpret, first, because most texts do not distinguish between two, quite different, cases: the purchase of seigneurial assent, or a fine (probably costing more) placed upon the serf who did not procure such assent, and second, because the sum paid is in itself of little interest since we do not know its relation to the total wealth of the payee, to which the formariage tax was, according to Beaumanoir (Para. 1458), and naturally so, proportional. Fines were very high, reaching, in law, as far as the confiscation of the whole of a person's belongings, according to a charter of 1070. (Mabillon, *Annales*, 1745 edition, V, p. 26.) A fine of 500 pounds was extracted a little before 1134 from a serf of Saint-Denis, who was, it is true, mayor of a village and had a somewhat exceptional fortune and social rank. There were such abuses that in 1385 the Parliament thought it necessary to overrule the Chapter of Laon in order to determine the amount of a fine. (Melleville, *Histoire de l'affranchissement communal*, p. 55, n. 21.) Sometimes the price for formariage

became the confiscation, after death, of half the inheritance: *Gesta abbatum Trudonensium*, XIII, c. 10, in *S. S.*, X, p. 316. As for the tax, as distinct from the fine, it amounted, in 1386, on the domain of Marizy-Sainte-Geneviève, to a third of all assets: C. Archibald, "Le servage dans les domaines de Sainte-Geneviève," in *Bull Soc. Hist. Paris*, 1910, p. 105. Naturally, and particularly in earlier times, the tax was often paid in land: E. de Lépinois and L. Merlet, *Cartulaire de Notre-Dame de Chartres*, II, p. 327, or with workdays: *Ibid.*, p. 290, n. 1. Elsewhere the tax was abandoned in favor of a fixed amount, such as in Saint-Vaast of Arras (*Cartulaire*, p. 178). Other examples are in Bloch, *Rois et Serfs*, p. 30, n. 3.

[25] Decree of Louis VI, 1124, before August 3: Lasteyrie, *Cartulaire de Paris*, no. 202 (women and children). Decree of Louis VII, 1155: Guérard, *Cartulaire de Notre-Dame de Paris*, II, p. 133, no. XLIV (children only).

[26] Agreement between the countess of Troyes and the abbey of Saint-Germain-des-Prés, including an indemnity to the monks who relinquish the children and the mainmorte: Arch. Nat., L 777, no. 18, and d'Arbois de Jubainville, *Histoire des ducs et des comtes de Champagne*, V, no. 1035.

[27] Fake diplomas of Dagobert I, Pépin, and Louis the Pious for Saint-Denis: Pardessus, II, no. CCLXXXVII; *Diplomata Karol*, I, no. 35; Böhmer-Mühlbacher, no. 661. Fake diploma of Charles the Bald for Saint-Germain-des-Prés regarding the marriages between the monks' serfs and those of the abbatial house: Poupardin, *Recueil des chartes de l'abbaye de Saint-Germain-des-Prés*, I, no. XXXI. Notice relating the failure of the claims of Saint-Florent of Saumur, 8 August 1011 to 8 April 1013: L. Halphen, *Le comté d'Anjou*, p. justif. no. 6. See for the culverts, M. Prou, *Recueil des actes de Philippe Ier*, no. CXLVII.

[28] J. Thillier and E. Jarry, *Cartulaire de l'église cathédrale de Sainte-Croix d'Orléans*, no. XLVI, 1116, before 3 August. R. Hubert, *Antiquitez de l'église royale de Saint-Aignan*, pr., p. 81. (Decree of Philippe-Auguste, November 1, 1204, to April 9, 1205, analyzing a lost diploma of Louis VI.) *Etablissements de Saint Louis*, II, c. XXXI, P. Viollet, ed., II, pp. 432, 436.

[29] *Olim*, I, p. 164, no. XIII, 1262, Parliament of All Saints' Day.

[30] Such was the case, in the beginning of the fourteenth century, in Nouans-sur-Loire, on the occasion of formariages of serfs of the Orléans chapter: election decree of the lord on 29 April 1329. *Arch. du Loiret*, G 244.

[31] Decree of Maurice de Sully, bishop of Paris (12 October 1160-11 September 1196): Guérard, *Cartulaire de Notre-Dame de Paris*, I, p. 53, no. XLV.

[32] According to canon law, how valid was a marriage concluded without the lord's assent, either between a serf and a free person, or between two serfs belonging to two different lords? This question, occurring often in practice, was discussed on several occasions, notably in the twelfth century, among French bishops. (See Ives de Chartres, *ep.* 121 and 242.) Ancient decisions saw the union as void; however, a bull from Adrian IV (1154-1159), collected in the *Decretals* (IV, 9, 1) proclaimed its validity. See a good exposition of the problem in R. W. and A. J. Carlyle, *A History of Medieval Political Theory*, II, 2, Chapter V. Two bulls from Alexander III, 30 July 1170, and 11 December 1170-1172. (*Rec. des Historiens de France*, XV, p. 890, no. CCLXXIV, and p. 894, no. CCLXXXIII) show him resolute in having his predecessors' decision respected, and although not willing to be absolutely opposed to the intended prosecution of formarried serfs, he is inclined to consider temporal sanctions without indulgence. However, lay justice does not seem to have so easily accepted the solution offered by canon law, if one is to judge, for example, from the harsh style of French Ms. 18419 which, around 1400, still holds that formariage unions are void (fol. 58 vo.; this text was kindly provided by M. Olivier-Martin. See Olivier-Martin, *Histoire de la coutume ... de Paris*, I, p. 96).

[33] In 1278, the Count of Chartres complained that, contrary to hitherto observed custom, the cathedral's canons were preventing marriages between their serfs and the serfs from the count's domain. Agreement of the Monday after the Feast of

Saint-Grégoire, 1278, ms. 1162, fol. 179. See also, in a much earlier era, the curious edict of the Count of Chartres, Thibaud, on 9 January 1083, where it is noted that a custom regarding the marriages of serfs from the count's abbey of Saint-Martin-au-Val with those of the cathedral chapter was developed before the Count of Eudes (Eudes II, 1004-1037) "*prohibuisset ne servi canonicorum sanctae Mariae conjugio miscerentur suis.*" E. de Lépinois and L. Merlet, *Cartulaire de Notre-Dame de Chartres*, I, p. 95, no. XVIII. Date corrected from the original, *Arch. Eure-et-Loir*, G 717.

[34] Bull of Honorius III, repeating the complaints of the men of Rosny who pretended to be free, while on the contrary, the canons of Sainte-Geneviève of Paris claimed them as their serfs, 13 February 1219. (*Mèmoires de la Soc. de l'Histoire de Paris*, XXX, 1903, p. 118, no. X): "*nunc a vobis ... adeo importabili onere deprimuntur ut, vicinorum locorum hominibus corum evitantibus copulam nuptialem, in tercio et in quarto consanguinitatis gradu matrimonialiter invicem misceantur.*" See also the testimony cited in the following note.

[35] Bull of Innocent IV authorizing the emancipation of the men of Wissous by the Bishop of Paris, 13 November 1247. E. Berger, *Registres d'Innocent IV*, I, no. 3445. (The bull evidently reproduces the request.) For the costs, see the emancipation act itself, July 1255, in G. Dubois, *Historia ecclesie parisiensis*, II, p. 491. Emancipation by the same prelate of the men of Moissy, July 1258: Guérard, *Cartulaire de Notre-Dame*, III, p. 168, No. CCXIII. For the costs, see the letter of agreement, Arch. Nat. LL 8, fol. 273. Emancipation by the abbot and monks of Saint-Denis of the men of La Garenne-Saint-Denis, November 1248: J. Doublet, *Histoire de l'abbaye de Saint Denys*, p. 907.

[36] Du Cange, Henschel edition, IV, p. 255, col. 2, at word "Manumissio"; and *Recueil des Historiens de France*, XXI, p. 141. In the twelfth century the Chapter of Saint-Germain-l'Auxerrois emancipated a female serf to allow her to marry a serf of Notre-Dame of Paris, and thus to enter into servitude under that church; this was, according to her father, the only husband he was able to find. The canons declared that they gave their assent for fear that this girl, in case they refused, "fornicaria fieret." Guérard, *Cartulaire de Notre-Dame de Paris*, II, p. 177, no. VII.

[37] G. Raynaud and H. Lemaitre, eds., *Renart le Contrefait*, II, p. 152, v. 37203 ff. See also p. 153, v. 37249-50.

[38] Thus the word "mainmorte" could then be applied to any total or partial confiscation of inheritances, whatever the origin of such a right might be. The general tendency, through a normal specialization of the language, was to restrict its use to the inheritances of serfs. However, in several regions, the feudal relief was also called mainmorte. Such was the case notably in Poitou and Saintonge, and in the Dauphiné: see Garaud, *L'abbaye Sainte-Croix de Talmond*, pp. 113 ff., and for the Dauphiné see the bibliography given (incidentally without a perfect understanding of the semantic phenomenon) by P. Viollet, *Histoire des institutions politiques*, III, p. 5, n. 6. The two juridical realities were quite different, both in principle—for feudal relief must be compared to similar laws on tenures—and in the social classes it involved. But the use of the same term to designate both naturally involved some ambiguity that lawyers, on occasion, used to their benefit; see for example, in an article by Louis Royer in *Revue Historique du Droit*, 1927, p. 261, the arguments of the Dauphin's people concerning the barony of Uriage. At the hearing concerning an edict of the bailiff of Orléans on 22(?) February 1299 (Ch. Cuissard, ed., in *Mém. Soc. archéologique Orléanais*, XXVIII, 1902, p. justif. VI) the *pueble* commonly called mainmorte the right that, by virtue of the obligatory character henceforth recognized of pious legacies, a number of ecclesiastical authorities claimed over the personal estates of believers who died interstate. Official documents, on the other hand, visibly avoided, in similar cases, this altogether too ambiguous term. See *ibid.*, p. justif. nos. III, IV, V, VII, and M. Prou, *Registres d'Honorius IV*,

No. 623. Even more curious is the use made of this word in the emancipation act granted by the abbot Suger in 1125 to the inhabitants of Saint-Denis. (Suger, *Oeuvres*, ed. by Lecoy de la Marche, pp. 319 ff.) He first describes the rights of the lord over the goods of his deceased serf in the previous order of things. Then, in the present order, where such rights are no longer in force, he describes the succession of the inhabitant, still subject to some restrictions, since only the family residing on the lands of the abbey are allowed to collect the mainmorte. (i.e. the inheritance).

[39] Enfranchisement of the comital serfs by Marguerite, Countess of Flanders in April 1252: Warnkönig-Gheldorf, *Histoire de la Flandre*, I, p. 358, no. xx. It seems to me reasonable to think that this decree, which appears to have had such far reaching effects—think of the size of the countess's domains—was in reality, as with the manumission of the royal serfs of Languedoc by Philippe Le Bel in 1299, only a prelude to a campaign of enfranchisement to be undertaken in place after place by commissioners. For other appropriations of half the movables, see L. Delisle, *Restitution d'un volume des Olim*, no. 716 (1289, Compiègne region); Arch. Nat., JJ 56, fol. 226 vo. ("Noyans," before the manumission of 12 December 1318).

[40] L. Delisle in *Notices et Extraits*, XXIII, 2, p. 154. ("Chailly," in the *baillage* of Vermandois, 1275, Parlement of All-Saints-Day). This formula is in this particular case applied to an *aubain* (foreigner) but is expressly likened to a serf or homme de corps.

[41] Shortly before 1138, the first continuator of the *Gesta abbatum Trudonensium* (XIII, 10, *SS.*, X, p. 316) protested against these fixed payments by which many serfs had replaced the best catel defined precisely by the text. On the other hand, see the example of the best catel considered as a concession: A. Wauters, *De l'origine* ..., Preuves, p. 233 (February 1275).

[42] For Saint-Vaast of Arras: *Cartulaire*, p. 178. For Amiens and Tournai, see below note 200.

[43] "The 'colliberti,' " p. 106 n. 69.

[44] For example, agreement of Saint-Germain-des-Prés with a girl *forisfamiliata*; Arch. Nat., L 809, no. 50 (June 1251). In the same seigneurie, on the contrary, see a very clear case of the exclusion of a son "separated" from his parents; L. 806, no. 48 (June 1225).

[45] See pp. 52-55.

[46] Such was the case on the lands of the abbey of Lagny in 1262. Bloch, "Les transformations du servages," p. 156. The rights of brothers and sisters living together with the deceased were also recognized in the beginning of the fourteenth century. In the villages of the Auvergne seigneurie of Montboissier, see the decree through which, on April 30 to May 5, 1403, the lord decides henceforth to recognize among the heirs all descendants, ascendants, and collaterals, without any restriction of common domicile. H. F. Rivière, *Histoire des institutions de l'Auvergne*, II, p. justif. no. xxxiii. Around the same date the rights of ascendants and collateral heirs having lived with the deceased were recognized by the abbey of Prébenoît in the Marche: A. Thomas, *Le comté de la Marche et le Parlement de Poitiers*, p. 222, no. cclxiv, 6 March 1433; see also no. cccxxxix, 8 July 1436.

[47] See J. Garnier, *Chartes de communes et d'affranchissements*, II, p. 513, March 1409.

[48] Olivier-Martin, *Histoire de la coutume de la prévôté et vicomté de Paris*, II, pp. 220 n. 1 and 276 n. 3; for the dowry see Arch. du Loiret, M, fonds de Bonne-Nouvelle (Saint Jacques's Day 1186); Arch. Nat., S 1337, no. 9 (August 1220; see L. Delisle, *Catalogue des actes de Philippe-Auguste*, no. 1988). For the despoliations see Guérard, *Cartulaire de Notre-Dame de Paris*, I, p. 435, no. xxiv (July 1234).

[49] *Rois et Serfs*, p. 33 n. 1. The enfranchisement of Orly, in May 1263 (Guérard, *Cartulaire de Notre-Dame*, II, p. 7) provides that the seigneur—in this case the chapter of Paris—will not be responsible for debts owed on the mainmortes that

remain in force until the full price for liberty has been paid. These debts will have to be dealt with by the inhabitants as a whole. It is useless to underscore the exhorbitant aspect of this arrangement.

⁵⁰ The sale of the mainmorte to relatives of the deceased is recognized in principle by a rule for the administration of the possessions of Saint-Denis (22 February 1174): Arch. Nat., LL 1167, p. 58: "*Ea vero que de mortuis manibus ad ecclesiam redeunt hiis dumtaxat vendi concedimus quibus jure cognationis competere videntur et post quorum decessum rursus ad ecclesiam reditura sunt.*" Practical examples abound: for Sainte-Geneviève, Bibl. Nat., lat. 5526, fol. 76 (1176-1192); Cartulary of the church of Meaux, Bibl. de Meaux, ms. 64, p. 196 (January 1254, new style); several testimonies in the inquest of 1244-1256 regarding the village of Esmans, published in P. Guilhiermoz, *Enquêtes et procès*, App. I, pp. 297, 298, 302, 304; Melleville, *Histoire de l'affranchissement communal dans les anciens diocèses de Laon* ... (1209). See for the diocese of Carcassonne, A. Cazaux, *Décadence progressive et abolition du servage de la glèbe*, p. 37 n. 3. For a gift to relatives, together with the apparent recognition of their preemptive rights, see R. Poupardin, *Recueils des chartes* ... *de Saint-Germain-des-Prés*, I, no. c (1116-1145). The same right is expressly affirmed, with the remittance of a third of the "just price," in the dues list (*censier*) of the bishop's land in Meaux toward the end of the thirteenth century; Bibl. de Meaux, ms. 64, p. 200. The very same arrangement is noted by P. Darmstädter, *Die Befreiung der Leibeigenen (Mainmortables) in Savoyen, der Schweiz und Lothringen*, p. 87, in Romainmotier (15th century?). Similarly, one finds a right of preemption, with the payment of a fee of unspecified amount, in 1408 in the valley of Charmey in the comté of Gruyère (*ibid.*, p. 102). Also in Alsace, with a generally lower price: Ch. Schmidt, *Les seigneurs, les paysans et la propriété rurale en Alsace au Moyen Age*, p. 73. However imprecise Beaumanoir's data on the mainmorte may be, it is clear that, in his view, they consisted mainly in a repurchase of the goods of the deceased by his relatives (para. 1452).

⁵¹ A mixed system was in force on the lands of the abbey of Lagny, toward 1262; when the deceased left neither children nor brothers still living with him, the seigneur seized all the property; otherwise he seized half the movables: "The Transformation of Serfdom," p. 156. This, obviously, is one of those cases of cross-contamination I spoke of above. Other aberrant cases can possibly be interpreted, without certainty, of course, as simple mitigations of the charges through concession of prescription: in Donchery-sur-Meuse, for example, in 1321, only half the goods are seized from the serfs called "de meiz demoyne," when there are no direct heirs (see below note 198). In Bryères in Laonnois in 1381, mainmorte is collected only from those serfs dying outside the commune (Douët d'Arcq, *Choix de pièces inédites du règne de Charles VI*, II, p. 129, no. 56). In Champagne, beginning in the fourteenth century, the mainmorte was often limited to the movables (G. Robert, *Les serfs de Saint-Remi de Reims* in *Travaux de l'Acad. Nationale de Reims*, CXL, p. 15 of the "tirage à part").

⁵² *Olim*, I, p. 182, no. xiii: "*non habent illam liberam testamenti faccionem quam habent liberi homines istius patrie*" (Parlement of the Winter St. Martin's day).

⁵³ The agreement concluded in 1126 between the abbeys of Saint-Germain-des-Prés and Saint-Jean of Sens is of particular interest due to its date and its preciseness: R. Poupardin, *Recueil des chartes* ... *de Saint-Germain-des-Prés*, no. lxxxiii. Most other documents fail to clearly distinguish between gifts and legacies.

⁵⁴ A. Salmon and Ch. L. de Grandmaison, *Liber de servis Majoris Monasterii*, no. cxi and app. no. xxi (the two decrees of 1064).

⁵⁵ A homme de corps of Saint-Germain-l'Auxerrois died "*intestatus, in campis*": Arch. Nat., LL 387, fol 35 vo. In the fifteenth century, the pious legacy had become so clearly an obligation, even for serfs, that the curate of Coulommiers took the right to levy automatically a third of the movable goods of the serfs, his parishioners, after their death: *Grand Coutumier*, II, xiv.

⁵⁶ Second sermon *ad potentes et milites*, Bibl. Nat., lat. 17509, fol. 106 ro.

[57] Bibl. Saint-Geneviève, ms. 356, p. 328.

[58] Bloch, *Rois et serfs*, p. 32 ns. 2, 3. On the fixed amount of five *sous* as the share that could be willed, see also, for Champagne: *Grand Coutumier*, II, c. xiv, p. 212; and for Lagny: "The Transformation of Serfdom," p. 156

[59] "Abrégé champenois des Etablissements de Saint Louis," in P. Viollet, *Etablissements*, III, p. 151, c. xxxii. On the variability of the rules relating to the serf's will, as late as the fourteenth century, see P. Guénois, *La conférence des coustumes* (1596), I, fol. 14.

[60] Para. 1331.

[61] Bibl. de Meaux, ms. 63, p. 1 (27 May 1370).

[62] See Bloch, "Blanche de Castille and the Serfs of the chapter of Paris," pp. 172 ff.

[63] As early as around 1250 one of the witnesses summoned by the monks of Saint-Germain-des-Prés in order to prove that the peasants working their lands in Esmans were serfs seems to place among the indices of servitude the arbitrary taille, which, as was commonly recognized, was traditionally applied by the abbey in this locality (Guilhiermoz, *Enquêtes et procès*, p. 300; deposition of Guillaume de Montceaux). In fact he was the only one to have this opinion, and his probably biased testimony is naturally open to doubt. But one can see an indication of things to come in this more or less willful error.

[64] Bouhier, *Oeuvres de Jurisprudence* (1787), I, p. 150, c. cxxv. This specifically servile value given to the arbitrary taille did not mean, of course, that among groups for whom the taille was fixed annually one could not find some, composed of unenfranchised serfs, who were considered bound to their original condition—this even in Champagne where the particularly early evolution had been practically accomplished as early as the beginning of the fourteenth century. See, for example, the people of Dompremy and Favresse, who owed a fixed tax, yet were still hommes de corps in the decrees of 1379 and 1402 published in G. Robert, *Nouvelle Revue de Champagne*, X (1932), pp. 230, 235, 239.

[65] See as examples of tailles levied by the seigneur from serfs living outside his lands: Sainte-Croix of Orléans in J. Thillier and E. Jarry, *Cartulaire*, no. cxlii (September 1204); see also nos. ccii and cciii; Saint-Aignan of Orléans in *Olim*, I, p. 1011, line 24 (9 October 1216); Saint-Germain-des-Prés in Arch. Nat., LL 1025, fol. 28 vo. (February 1224 new style); Saint-Faron of Meaux in Bibl. de Meaux, ms. 65, p. 160. (The exchange agreement which ended this right until then exercized by the monks on their serfs living at Barcy on the lands of the chapter of Meaux is dated March 1268, old style; it is later than a charter of January 1269 new style [*ibid.*, p. 213], since it must be dated 24-31 March 1269 new style.)

[66] E. Mabille, *Cartulaire de Marmoutier pour le Dunois*, no. xxxix.

[67] *Liber de servis Majoris Monasterii*, app. no. xlii, and E. Mabille, *Cartulaire de Marmoutier*, no. cliv.

[68] B. Guérard, *Carulaire de Notre-Dame de Paris*, I, p. 218, no. iv.

[69] Arch. Eure-et-Loir, G 1502; a mediocre edition by R. Hubert, *Antiquitez historiques de l'église royale de Saint-Aignan*, pr., p. 83.

[70] Guilhiermoz, *Enquêtes et procès*, p. 295; see at p. 302 the deposition of the knight Hugue de Pilliers.

[71] *Olim*, I, p. 936, no. xxx.

[72] Para. 1457. Beaumanoir only mentions one exception, a very normal one: the seigneur has the option, for a year and a day, to prevent his serf from settling at a place where residence itself grants enfranchisement. It appears that in such a case the seigneur often was satisfied to force the serf to formally acknowledge his status as such, notwithstanding any contrary privileges, and did not demand a change in residence which such an oath rendered useless. See a decree—a late one it is true: 7 June 1395—published by G. Robert in *Nouvelle Revue de Champagne*, x (1932), p. 237.

[73] To cite one further example, serfs are certainly the object of the following

decree of Count Guillaume II of Nevers conceding, in 1097, to the Saint-Etienne church of this town the borough called "bourg Saint-Etienne" (*Galla Christ.* XII, *instr.*, col. 334): "*quod si forte homines de terra mea pro tollenda conseutudine mea se mihi subtrahendo hanc terram ad habitandum delegerint, prior quidem habebit in eis conseutudines et justitiam suam sicut in caeteris hominibus suis ejusdem burgi, mihi tamen serviant sicut homines mei.*" A ruling of the royal court of 23 October 1132 (Luchaire, *Louis VI*, no. 497), unfortunately written in a very obscure style, recognizes for the men of the Laonnois, the right to change residence and to settle under whichever seigneur they choose—and this notwithstanding any contrary wishes from various seigneurs. These endeavors of seigneurial authority conform to a tendency which we shall see develop later, and their failure in face of the king, the guardian of custom, is very interesting. One can notice, finally, that in Saint-Trond, a monk, writing shortly before 1138, considers as equally plausible both hypotheses according to which the serf, subject to duties on his succession, dies "*sub nostro jure sive sub alieno*"; *SS.*, X, p. 316, c. 10. See also the texts cited above regarding the taille on itinerant persons (forains) and p. 48 and pp. 59-60 regarding mainmorte and justice.

[74] Louis VIII's instruction to the royal provosts of Paris, Corbeil and Moret, to aid the monks of Saint-Germain-des-Prés in the collection of the taille from their itinerant serfs (serfs forains) (see above note 65) is sufficient proof of the difficulties seigneurs had in this taxation.

[75] On the itinerant (forain) serfs of Saint-Rémi of Reims and the difficulties they caused the monks, see G. Robert, "Les serfs de Saint-Rémi de Reims," in *Travaux de l'Académie nationale de Reims*, CXL (1926), pp. 15 ff. However, the author may not have sufficiently distinguished between two juridically different cases: that of the landed seigneur who improperly attempts to impose his duties on persons who, while peasants on his land, are the serfs of another master; and that of the lay attorney (*avoué*) who, charged with supervising both a church's land and the nonitinerant serfs living on it, attempts to eliminate to his own benefit the authority of the church over both the land and the serfs.

[76] Notably in Champagne, where in the case of mainmorte the seigneur of the land seems often to have received a third of the collected échoite: decree of Thibaut II for Montier-en-Der, 1139, in d'Arbois de Jubainville, *Histoire des ducs et des comtes de Champagne*, III, p. 426, no. xciv (this right to be collected only when the monks have deemed it necessary to call upon the assistance of the comital sergeants). Agreement between Saint-Faron of Meaux and the seigneur of Crécy-en-Brie, 27-31 March 1250 or 1-31 March 1251, in *Layettes*, III, no. 3930; Decree, *Olim*, I, p. 212, no. 1, Parlement of the *octaves* of All Saints' Day 1265. For the serfs of Saint-Rémi of Reims, living in the comital newtown of Fresne-sur-Moivre, the partition, which covers formariages as well as mainmortes, is done by half: *Layettes*, I, p. 387, no. 1034, January 1213.

[77] Agreement between the bishop and the canons of Paris regarding the exchange of the bishop's serfs who lived in Orly on the chapter's land, for the chapter's serfs living in Saint-Cloud and Wissous on the bishop's land, 1100. Guérard, *Cartulaire de Notre-Dame*, I, p. 327, no. xx: "*dum ... episcopus eorum servos nolentes eis obedire, quia in villis ejus manebant, contra voluntatem eorum tuebatur....*"

[78] Customs of the seigneurie of Borrest (around 1250); Bibl. Sainte-Geneviève, ms. 351, fol. 132.

[79] See in particular three decrees, all in favor of the serf's seigneur: *Olim*, I, p. 933, no. xxv; p. 936, no. xxx; Arch. Nat., LL 157, p. 820; and Boutaric, *Actes du Parlement*, II, no. 2715 D (September 1290).

[80] See on this matter a decree, upon agreement, given by the bailiff of Senlis, between Saint-Arnould-de-Crépy and Saint-Denis, 8 June 1323; Arch. Nat., LL 1171, p. 144; and the arrangements in *Ancien Coutumier de Champagne*, c. xxx; this last text includes an obligation to sell only to a serf.

[81] Examples are too numerous to cite. Some instances are very ancient, such as

the agreement between the bishop and canons of Paris in 1100 cited above note 77. One can get an idea of the difficulties provoked by the existance of the itinerant (forain) serfs through a series of agreements between the chapter of Meaux and Saint-Faron: Bibl. de Meaux, ms. 63, pp. 153, 154, 186 (November 1222-May 1223). See also the information given on the activities of royal collectors of mainmortes and formariages in *Rois et Serfs*, pp. 82 ff.

[82] For the Paris and Orléans regions see *Rois et Serfs*, p. 22. Itinerant (forains) serfs, on the other hand, are formally excluded from affranchissement by the great charter given to the serfs of her domain by the countess of Flanders in 1252 (see above note 39).

[83] The prohibition against leaving the tenure—the *mayne*—is specified in the vows of servitude of *questaux*—i.e., serfs—of the Bordeaux region, 24 October 1322, 9 January and 15 May 1372, and 24 August 1384: *Archives historiques de la Gironde*, VIII, nos. xxv, xxviii; I, nos. xxxiii, xxxiv. See E. Lodge, *The Estates of the Archbishop of Bordeaux*, p. 87 (14th century); "Serfdom in the Bordelais," in *English Historical Review* (1903), p. 421 (no texts before 1322). For the Pyrenees region the same obligation is noted in the fourteenth century (since 1318) by E. Lodge "Serfdom in the Pyrenees," in *Vierteljahrschrift für Sozial-und Wirtschaftsgeschichte*, III (1905), pp. 27, 28. It is clearly there in the affranchissements published by Paul Raymond, "Enquête sur les serfs du Béarn," in *Bull. Soc. Sciences, Lettres et Arts de Pau*, 2e. série, VII (1877-1878), nos. 60 (4 January 1362) and 113 (1341). The Bordelais vow of servitude of 24 August 1384 goes so far as to give the seigneur the right to fix at will the residence of the *questal*. However, several items in Raymond's research (nos. 24, 65, 81, 152, 176, 195-200) specifically mention desertions. Besides, among those vacant tenures that Béarn officials so often took note of, many undoubtedly had simply been abandoned by their occupants.

[84] See for the Marche, L. Lassarre, *De la condition des personnes ... dans la Marche*, p. 71. For the serfs of Luxeuil, in the eighteenth century, see Dey, in *Bullet. Soc. D'Agriculture de la Haute-Saône*, 3e série, nos. 1, 2, (1869-1870), pp. 222, 223.

[85] See above note 82.

[86] See "The 'colliberti,' " pp. 134 ff.

[87] See J. Rutkowski, *Le régime agraire en Pologne au XVIIIe siècle* (extract from *Revue d'Histoire Economique*, 1926), p. 16, and *Histoire économique de la Pologne*, p. 104.

[88] Thus in 1308 the bailiff of the count of Blois opposed the settlement in that town of serfs of the chapter of Chartres: délibération capitulaire, 2 February 1308 new style, Bibl. de Chartres, ms. 10071, fol. 86.

[89] On the history of this expression, see Bloch, "Serf de la glèbe: The history of an Expression," and "Servus glebae," pp. 179-201. I find the expression *astrictus glebe* in the customaries of Gérone, written very early in the fourteenth century: *Anuario de Historia del Derecho Español* (1928), p. 476, c. 116.

[90] See "The 'colliberti,' " p. 101, on the worries of the monks of Vendôme.

[91] There are, however, some examples of this, at least since the second half of the thirteenth century: agreement between the monks of Saint-Faron of Meaux and the seigneur of Crécy-en-Brie, regarding the old castle of Crécy, 27-31 March 1250 or 1-31 March 1251; *Layettes du trésor des Chartes*, III, no. 3930; agreement between the same religious order and the chapter of Meaux regarding the land of Barcy, 24-31 March 1269, new style: Bibl. de Meaux, ms. 65, p. 160.

[92] Numerous examples: see Bloch, *Les caractères originaux*, p. 90. Sometimes the prohibition against accepting immigrants applied only to heads of families: R. Poupardin, *Recueil des chartes ... de Saint-Germain-des-Prés*, II, no. cccii (1202).

[93] R. Poupardin, *Recueil des chartes ... de Saint-Germain-des-Prés*, II, no. cci.

[94] A characteristic case of immigrants attempting "by force" to continue to cultivate their lands in a place they no longer inhabited is shown to us in a bull of Alexander III cited below, note 97.

⁹⁵ This concern is at the origin for the provision of the decree of "freedom" of Saint-Denis (see note 38 above) reserving to those relatives living on the monks's land the inheritance of the bourgeois even though the latter had gotten rid of the mainmorte. Similarly, there are clauses in enfranchising charters which relatively often prevent any legacy of immovables to persons foreign to the locality: see E. Bonvalot, *Le Tiers-Etat d'après la charte de Beaumont*, pp. 474 ff., and as an example the charter of Draize, October 1328, in *Nouvelle Revue de Champagne*, X (1932), p. 207.

⁹⁶ R. Poupardin, *Recueil des chartes . . . de Saint-Germain-des-Prés*, I, no. cxxxix.

⁹⁷ Varin, *Archives administratives de la ville de Reims*, I, i, p. 367, no. ccxiii. In the same Reims region a bull of Alexander III, 6 September 1168 or 1169 (*Rec. des Historiens de France*, XV, p. 868, no. ccxxxiv) shows us the full power of the seigneurs' right to seize the lands of immigrants; the text does not specify the latter's juridical status.

⁹⁸ J. Garnier, *Chartes de Communes*, II, p. 167, no. cccxxxvi (24 February 1236). See the texts of 1216, 1236, 1238 cited by Marc in *Revue bourguignonne de l'Enseignement Supérieur*, VI (1896), pp. 94-95. As far as we can analyze them, they are not more precise.

⁹⁹ J. Garnier, II, p. 132, no. cccxxvii (November 1232); p. 191, no. cccxlvi (May 25, 1242).

¹⁰⁰ J. Garnier, II, p. 134, no. cccxxvii, c. 2 (April 1233). The charter is presented as a manumission, without, however, any mention of servile duties; p. 262, no. ccclxviii, c. 11. 14, 17 (April 1246). (The suppression of mainmorte on the village of Saulx-le-Duc, which is the subject here, was expressly granted only in October 1285. See p. 266, c. 19; however, article 9 of the charter of 1246 seems to assume that the abolition was already accomplished.)

¹⁰¹ *Histoire du Languedoc*, VIII, p. 631, c. 27.

¹⁰² F. Delaborde, *Recueil des actes de Philippe-Auguste*, I, no. 80.

¹⁰³ S. Mondon, *La grande charte de Saint-Gaudens*, p. 131.

¹⁰⁴ E. Perrin, "La bourgeoisie dauphinoise, d'après les chartes de franchises," in *Annales de l'Université de Grenoble*, nouvelle série, II, no. 3 (1925), p. 191.

¹⁰⁵ Some customaries, in the sixteenth century, know no other source for the servile status than in the ownership of certain lands, those of the Marche, for example; see L. Lassarre, *De la condition des personnes . . . dans la Marche*, p. 35. In those areas where a personal serfdom remained, and where also mainmortable estates as distinct entities had been introduced, a problem could arise: what was one to do when such an estate was acquired by a serf depending upon a seigneur other than the one who ruled the land? From the fourteenth century on the custom in Burgundy recognized in this case that the land-owning seigneur could force the serf to give up the immovables (action in "vide-mains"); see G. Jeanton, *Le servage en Bourgogne*, pp. 116 ff.

¹⁰⁶ This was sometimes called the servile "disavowal" (*désaveu*). The meaning of the term is quite different in the two charters of the nobles of Champagne in May 1315, art. 9 and 6, *Ordonn.*, I, pp. 573, 578. In those two texts to "disavow" ones seigneur is for the serf to declare, in the appropriate manner, that he does not hold himself as serf of this master; the seigneur had a year and a day to prove his rights.

¹⁰⁷ See *Rois et Serfs*, pp. 100-101. The whole question is still to be studied.

¹⁰⁸ See "the 'colliberti,' " pp. 102 ff.

¹⁰⁹ It is significant to see the *Ancien Coutumier de Champagne* consider as an abridgment of "fief"—in the same way as enfranchisement—the authorization given by a lord to his serf to sell land to a free person. For this reason it insists upon the approval of the suzerain in such cases. [P. Pithou, *Coustumes au bailliage de Troyes* (1630 edition), pp. 517 ff; c. xiii; see c. xvii; this part of the coutumier was written toward 1253.]

¹¹⁰ *Liber de servis* (*Mém. Soc. Archéologique Touraine*, XVI), no. iii.

[111] Diploma of Louis VII, 1158, published by E. Menault, *Morigny*, p. 157. See A. Luchaire, *Etudes sur les actes de Louis VII*, c. 410: "*In territorio Stamparum quedam terre existunt, que Octave dicuntur et ex antiqua consuetudine eorum possessores regii serui solent esse. Et quoniam multi pro utilitate terrarum eas occupaverant qui non erant servilis conditionis, ipsas communiter saisiri fecimus.*" Among the lands that were confiscated, some had been purchased by the abbey of Morigny, which obtained their restitution.

[112] *Ord.*, XI, p. 211 (see A. Cartellieri, *Philipp-August*, I, p. 60, no. 45). The decree—a charter of customs granted to Etampes—declares henceforth legitimate the purchase of these lands by anyone, and adds: "*nec ob hoc emptor servus noster efficiatur.*"

[113] It would have been interesting to place exactly on a map this group of tenures. M. Lemoine, archivist in Seine-et-Oise, kindly tells me that unfortunately neither the cadastral surveys of Etampes, of Morigny-Champigny, and the neighboring communes, nor more ancient surveys, originating from the abbey of Morigny give any place names resembling this *Octaves* or "Huitièmes."

[114] See "The 'colliberti,'" pp. 109 ff. Add to the references cited: C. Archibald in *Bullet. Soc. Hist. Paris* (1901), p. 97.

[115] See "Serfs de la glèbe," pp. 183-184. Often the serf—as well as the vassal—is simply called his seigneur's "man." However, this expression, itself deprived of any juridical precision, only indicated a more or less narrowly conceived dependence. It can with certainty only be applied to serfs when the context allows it, as for example in the case where "men" are opposed to hôtes (i.e., simple tenants), or when the word *homo* is accompanied by an adjective, such as *proprius*.

[116] "Historia Vizeliacensis monasterii," in *Rec. des Histor. de France*, XII, p. 340: "*Andreas de Palude, nihil omnino ad te pertinens, meus est a planta pedis usque ad verticem, sicut proprius servus monasterii Vizeliacensis.*" It is impossible, of course, to know whether to attribute the remark to the abbot or to the author of the "Historia," Hugues de Poitiers, who was probably a witness to the scene, but it matters little.

[117] *Cartulaire de Saint-Vaast*, p. 177.

[118] "Deceit and violence" is the title to one of the chapters in *Origines de l'ancienne France* (I, 2, ch. XXIII).

[119] "The 'colliberti,'" pp. 99-100.

[120] "*Nivia quam trucidavit Vitalis senior suus*": genealogy of a text of the eleventh century, cover sheet of ms. 2041 in the Bibliothèque de Tours.

[121] B. Guérard, *Cartulaire de l'abbaye de Saint-Père de Chartres*, II, p. 371, no. cxlix (1101-1129): "*presertim cum plures eorum nobis essent famuli servitutis vinculo obnoxii, quos, si necessitas urgeret, licebat quolibet modo in nostris usibus insumere.*"

[122] I do not know whether one should attach any practical importance to two rules found in small customary written between 1235 and 1255: "*Li serf qui se sont aforcié de destruire leurs seigneurs doivent estre ars,*" and "*Li serf qui renie son seigneur doit estre mis en pardurable paine.*" Olivier-Martin, ed., "Les poines de la duchée d'Orliens," in *Rev, d'Hist. du Droit* (1928), p. 433, c. 64-65.

[123] This sentence is known to us through a confirmation of Louis VIII, Melun, May 1224, published by L. Merlet in *Mémoires de la Soc. Archéolog. de l'Eure-et-Loir*, II, p. 295. The mutilated individuals are mentioned in the text only under the rather vague juridical term of "men" of the chapter. One cannot doubt, however, that they were of servile status when one observes their seigneur indemnified through the transfer of an individual specifically called a serf. Similarly, the fact that this individual was a laborer appears to indicate—although nothing is said of it in the decree—that the victims also were artisans. A little earlier (1169), another decree, also regarding the misdeed of a member of this redoubtable Gallardon lineage, throws light upon the same principles: an indemnity to the seigneur (the chapter of Chartres); rent to the victims; and, in addition, due appologies in the form of homage

from the guilty party, his knights, and his seigneur. Unfortunately, the vague term "homines Beate Marie" does not allow us to formally assert serfs were the victims here, in the absence of any possible cross-checking, although it is most probable that they were. E. de Lépinois and R. Merlet, *Cartulaire de Notre-Dame de Chartres*, I, p. 179, no. lxxx. The bonds of passive solidarity which united seigneur and subject were also in force when the latter was of free status; see Bloch, *Les caractères originaux*, p. 88.

¹²⁴ *Olim*, I, p. 842, no. xi. Parlement of Candlemas 1271 (new style).

¹²⁵ Examples: (i) Decree of the court of the Count of Poitiers, 10 December 1032, recognizing to Saint-Maixent the right of jurisdiction, in all cases, "*de propriis hominibus.*" A. Richard, "Chartes . . . de Saint-Maixent," in *Archives histor. Poitou*, XVI, p. 109, no. xci. (ii) while granting in 1173 to the Count of Blois his rights in Sennely, Louis VII reserves, in favor of some churches of Orléans, two very distinct categories of jurisdiction: that which they exercise over their hôtes (free villeins) and their "men" (serfs) residing on their lands, and that which they have over their "men" only, when the latter live on the count's land. Thillier and Jarry, *Cartulaire de Sainte-Croix*, no. lxxxii. (iii) Arbitration decree between Saint-Mesmin and the lord of Beaugency, 30 May 1209. Arch. du Loiret, A 1095, fol. 250 (for serfs and for *commendaticii*). (iv) (With the exception of flagrant offences) L. Delisle, *Essai de reconstitution d'un volume des Olim*, no. 549, June 1284. (v) Two decrees of the Parlement of Paris for Faremoutiers, both of 24 March 1324, new style. Arch. Nat., X 1a, 5, fol. 381 vo. and 383 ro. (Boutaric, *Actes*, Nos. 7512, 7513). See a reference to this right, acknowledged to be the abbey's, in Dareste, ed., *Grand Coutumier*, II, c. xiv, and also Bibl. Nat., franc. 19816, fol. 187 vo. (vi) A petition from the monks of Sainte-Colombe of Sens against two servile families, in a procedural decree of 12 April 1326: Arch. Nat., X 1a 5, fol. 460. (vii) Chapter of Meaux: agreement in Parlement with the royal provost of Meaux, May 1320. Bibl. de Meaux, ms. 63, p. 356. (With a reservation for royal cases. The decree also concerns the determination of the jurisdiction of the provostship of Paris to which the church of Meaux, a royal church since the era of the counts of Champagne, happened to belong.) Decree of the Parlement, 21 February 1331 new style, and agreements of 10 October 1337 and of Monday after St. Vincent's Day 1340, following difficulties with the archdeacons of Mulcien, Meaux, and Brie (important for the history of ecclesiastical jurisdiction). As corollaries: the right of the seigneur to apprehend his homme de corps on a foreign land: decree of Philip-Augustus regarding the count and chapter of Chartres, March 1207; E. de Lépinois and L. Merlet, *Cartulaire de Notre-Dame de Chartres*, II, no. clxxvii. Obligation for the homme de corps, in every locality, to surrender to the call of his seigneur: Guilhiermoz, *Enquêtes et procès*, p. 302 (around 1250).

¹²⁶ Arbitration decree giving the canons of Orléans "*la justice et la connaissance de meubles et de chatiex de leur hommes et fames de cors,*" in Nouans-sur-Loire, and generally, it seems, on all the comital lands of the county of Blois. 26 September 1291. Thillier and Jarry, *Cartulaire de Sainte-Croix*, no. ccclxii; P. Viollet, ed., *Etablissements de Saint Louis*, II, xxxii, p. 444.

¹²⁷ Examples: (i) Decree of Marie, Countess of Troyes, and of her son, Henri, regarding the serfs of the abbeys of Sainte-Geneviève and Saint-Denis living on the territory of the commune of Meaux, 1184: Arch. Nat., 1 885, no. 57: "*homines predictarum ecclesiarum . . . manentes in villis que in carta comitis continentur, in quibus dumtaxat comes talliam et justiciam habebat, in dominio predictarum duarum ecclesiarum ita remaneant sicut ante stabilitionem communie fuerant, scilicet ut capitagia, forismaritagia, allevia interfectorum, sanguines et manum mortuam ipsis ecclesiis sive dominis suis ex integro reddant.*" (ii) Decree transferring a family of serfs to Thibaud, Count of Champagne, from Erard de Brienne, September 1227. *Layettes du Trésor des Chartes*, II, no. 1945: "*ita quod nos et heredes nostri habebimus . . . justiciam in omnibus possessionibus dictorum Hu-*

gonis Poilevilain et Coleti et heredum ipsorum . . . que sunt apud Erbice . . . ita tamen quod nullam prorsus habebimus justiciam . . . in corporibus eorumdem . . . aut heredum ipsorum . . . vel servientium ipsorum . . . nisi illi servientes fuerint homines nostri de corpore aut justiciabiles nostri." (iii) *Olim,* I, 550, no. xvii; Parlement of Candlemas 1263. (Theft). (iv) Decree of Parlement, March 1282 or 1283. *Bibliothèque de l'Ecole des Chartes* (1885), p. 474 (Riot). (v) Bull of Nicholas IV, in favor of the church of Chartres, 19 March 1289; Bibl. de Chartres, ms. 1162, fol. 34: "*cum dilecti filii capitulum ipsius ecclesie de antiqua ac juri consona consuetudine hactenus observata . . . in homines ipsorum de corpore qui servi vulgariter appellantur jurisdicionem omnimodam habeant temporalem, in illis maxime criminibus que penam sanguinis ingerunt, ubicumque illos in civitate, comitatu aut diocesi Carnotensi, etiam si in ipso maleficio, deprehendi contingat.*" On this affair, see E. Langlois, *Registres de Nicolas IV,* I, nos. 736, 737; and de Lépinois and Merlet, *Cartulaire,* II, no. ccclxxviii. (vi) Agreement between the bishop and the chapter of Meaux, 5 July 1289: Bibl. de Meaux, ms. 63, p. 295; and in part, Toussaint-Duplessis, *Histoire de l'église de Meaux,* II, no. cdxxvii (Justice *de facto corporis* flagrant offense excepted). (vii) Arbitration decree between the chapter of Chartres and the monks of Bonneval, 1294: de Lépinois and Merlet, *Cartulaire,* II, no. ccclxxxii (*causes de sang*). (viii) Agreements of the chapter of Chartres with the count of Chartres, 26 September 1306, and with the count of Blois, 5 July 1330; *ibid.,* II, nos. ccclxxxviii and cccxcii (*peines de sang*). (ix) *Olim,* III, 275, no. ii, January 19, 1309 (riot). (x) Agreement between the prior of Champigny in Vendômois and the chapter of Chartres, March 2, 1312, new style: Bibl. de Chartres, ms. 1007[1], fol. 82 vo. (*causes de sang*). (xi) *Olim,* III, 2, p. 1413, no. lv; May 8, 1319 (criminal cases). See for culverts: "The 'colliberti,'" pp. 104 ff.

[128] L. de Kersers, *Essai de reconstitution du Cartulaire A. de Saint-Sulpice de Bourges,* no. lxxii (July 1064).

[129] In line with this same feeling, serfs—or culverts—belonging to a church often more or less completely escaped from the lay solicitor's (avoué) jurisdiction, although it did range over the free tenants; see "The 'colliberti,' " p. 105 n. 59. And churches often claimed even spiritual jurisdiction over their serfs: witness the agreement between the bishop and the chapter of Meaux, 18 September 1309: Bibl. de Meaux, ms. 63, p. 326, and in part Toussaint-Duplessis, II, no. cdxliv (on the synonym of the term *hominibus* alone, used in the decree, with "hominibus de corpore," a fourteenth century note inserted at the top of page 327 of the ms.). See the agreements of December 2, 1320, and 26 September 1327; ms. 63, pp. 328, 341, Toussaint-Duplessis, nos. cdlviii and cdlxv. See also the decrees regarding the archdeacons of the diocese of Meaux, cited above note 125, no. vii, and a deliberation of the chapter of Chartres of September 2, 1303. Bibl. de Chartres, ms. 1007[1], fol. 31 vo. 130. On the alods owned by serfs and the manner in which they could be disposed of, see Bloch, "La ministérialité," pp. 511 ff. The serf's obligation, should he wish to dispose of his alod, to obtain the assent of his personal seigneur is once again formulated (although the word *alleu* does not appear; but the meaning is clear) in the customary of Toulouse of 1286, edited by Ad. Tardif, c. 148. This seems to clarify the event in Liége collected by F. L. Ganshof (*Les ministériales en Flandre et en Lotharingie,* pp. 391 ff.) without his giving them the interpretation I suggest here and which seems imposed by the documents from the custom of Hainaut of 1200 (*SS.,* XXI, 622; see "La ministérialité," p. 512 n. 3). Of course, there is no doubt that in other documents the word "alleu" shows aberrations of meaning which Ganshof has cleverly pointed out and of which I have, after him, given several examples in the work cited above.

[131] It is important to note that this term villeinage was, at least until the end of the thirteenth century, the technical name for a tenure for which the holder had to pay taxes and corvées. To Beaumanoir, the *censive* is, by comparison with villeinage, clearly only a particular case, characterized by the payment of an annual

fee in money (Para. 1443). Above all we must well realize that the term does not imply any social inferiority whatsoever: witness, among others, this item in a cartulary of Saint-Germain-des-Prés, from the second half of the thirteenth century, Arch. Nat., LL 1025, fol. 34 vo.: "*Hec littera est quod rex Navarre tenet in vilenagium domum suam.*"

[132] "Nisi tantum ipsum villanum et uxorem ejus et filios et filias qui ipsum mansum incolunt, qui non erant mei." A. Bernard and A. Bruel, *Recueil des chartes de l'abbaye de Cluny*, IV, no. 3024.

[133] *Liber de servis Majoris Monasterii*, app. no. XIV; and A. de Trémault, *Cartulaire de Marmoutier pour le Vendômois*, no. xx (1050-4 November 1060). This same right of expectancy of the seigneur over the goods of his serf explains two rather curious rules that, in the middle of the fourteenth century, are found in several mss. of the *Grand Coutumier* (notably Bibl. Nat., fr. 10816, fol. 190, 191). If a property put forward as security is seized, without contestation from the individual concerned, can the seigneur demand a "refinancing"? Yes, if it concerns a serf, but not if it is a freeman. On the other hand, can a lord put forward a complaint if his "subject" has been the victim of a disseisin (*nouvelleté*)? Generally not, except if the subject is his homme de corps.

[134] "*Possunt enim sicut homines de corpore emere, vendere, dare de rebus suis, salvo jure ecclesie antedicte.*" *Mémoires Soc. Hist. Paris* (1903), p. 110 (for the date, see above note 10). See on Esmans the text cited and discussed in "The Transformations of Serfdom," p. 157, n. 11.

[135] For example: serfs called *heredes*, see E. Chénon, *Histoire et coutumes du prieuré de La Chapelle-Aude*, p. 16 n. 3; serf's land called *hereditas*, see A. Bernard and A. Bruel, *Recueil des chartes de l'abbaye de Cluny*, III, nos. 2071, 2075; C. Chevalier, *Cartulaire de l'abbaye de Noyers*, no. cccl.

[136] Cases of serfs inheriting from their fathers are numerous as early as the eleventh century: for example, A. Salmon and Ch. de Grandmaison, *Liber de servis Majoris Monasterii*, app. no. XXIV (Mabile, *Cartulaire . . . pour le Dunois*, no. viii).

[137] See an odd notice in the Black Book of Saint-Florent of Saumur, Bibl. Nat., nouv. acq. lat. 1930, fol. 112; the formulation of the endowment was before the death of Abbot Ferri, 28 September 1055. Also Guérard, *Cartulaire de Saint-Père de Chartres*, II, p. 354, no. cxxx (1101-1129); M. Prou, *Recueil des actes de Philippe Ier*, no. cxli (24 February 1101).

[138] See, for example, a decree of Maurice de Sully, bishop of Paris 12 October 1160-11 September 1196); Guérard, *Cartulaire de Notre-Dame de Paris*, I, 53, no. xlv. Sometimes, however, the rules on the partition among the children of servile inheritances showed a few peculiarities: see a juridical text of the Champagne, probably from the end of the fourteenth century, edited by A. Giffard, in *Nouvelle Revue Historique du Droit* (1906), p. 627.

[139] For example, the *boni* who, in March 1260, formed the court of the mayor of the chapter of Paris at Orly are certainly serfs; the villagers, numbering 636, were only enfranchised in May 1263: Guérard, *Cartulaire de Notre-Dame de Paris*, II, pp. 3, 17 (original: Arch. Nat., S 344, no. 1).

[140] See J. Massiet du Biest, "A propos des plaids généraux," in *Revue du Nord* (1923), pp. 37 ff., and "Le chef-cens et la demi-liberté," in *Revue Historique du Droit* (1927), pp. 504 ff. The men paying chevage were certainly not considered free: witness the notice regarding the abbot's rights, toward the end of the thirteenth century, in A. Thierry, *Monuments de l'histoire du Tiers-Etat*, II, 430, c. 1, 2, 20.

[141] All information on these *homines de generali placito*—which for the most part comes from a law record book of 1023-1036—has been excellently gathered together by F. L. Ganshof in *Les ministériales en Flandre et en Lotharingie*, pp. 397 ff. See also, under a slightly different form, *Revue du Nord* (1922). The word serf does not appear. Guiman, as we know, does not use it either with regard to *censuales*, although they were called servi by the counts of Flanders and even by one of his

colleagues (see above note 17). A passage in the record book, regarding formariage, clearly proves that the men on the general tribunal were not considered to be free: "*si liberam feminam uxorem duxerit, nihil dabit, quia libertatem uxoris sue ad legem suam convertit.*" Also, with the exception of the chevage, from which they had been dispensated, and with exception made for a few details, the duties burdening them were fundamentally the same as those for censualis or servi. However, richer, at least at first, than most serfs (I suppose urban development must have redistributed wealth somewhat), they paid much higher taxes on marriage and mainmorte. The restriction to some tenures of the obligation to appear on tribunals is found throughout Europe; see notably for England: F. W. Maitland, "The Suitors of the County Court," in *English Historical Review* (1888), and Maitland, *Collected Papers*, I; W. S. Holdsworth, *A History of English Law*, 2nd. ed., I, pp. 5, 7.

[142] See A. Luchaire, *Manuel*, p. 468; Ch. Petit-Dutaillis, in *Bibliothèque de l'Ecole des Chartes* (1915), p. 548; and for the seigneurial levy, the perfectly clear passage in Beaumanoir, Para. 1687. No juridical conclusions can be made from the literary texts gathered by H. Lemaitre, "Le refus de service d'ost et l'origine du servage," in *Bibl. de l'Ec. des Chartes* (1914).

[143] Para. 1452.

[144] Thus the occasional interdiction against a serf sending his sons to school; to study meant for men at that time—particularly humble people—to prepare for a clerical career. This rule was often formulated in England, very rarely, it appears, in France. Yet one can find it in some vows of servitude in the Bordelais, 9 January and 15 May 1372: *Arch. Histor. de la Gironde*, VIII, no. xxviii and I, no. xxxiii. See, on 28 September 1395, article 27 of the charter of Montfaucon-en-Bigorre, which grants the inhabitants, together with the free right of marriage, that of education for their children (*Ord.*, VIII, p. 55). The acquitanian origin of these documents make plausible some influence from English law. However, see monk Guiman's text regarding the prohibition against entering holy orders applied to the serfs of Saint-Vaast: "*quicumque est de censu sancti Vedasti, si filio vel propinquo suo ad litteratum studia procedenti coronam fieri voluerit . . .*" *(Cartulaire*, p. 179).

[145] A few examples are cited in "Serf de la glèbe," p. 181 n. 6. There are others; see, for culverts, "The 'colliberti,'" pp. 93 ff. *Servitutis dedecus*: B. de Broussillon, *Cartulaire de l'abbaye de Saint-Aubin d'Angers*, II, no. ccccxxx, p. 40 (30 November 1113).

[146] The question was a subject of controversy with church tribunals: see the opinion sent to the archdeacon of Paris by Ives de Chartres, ep. 183; Ives agreed to admit the testimony.

[147] See Bloch, "La ministérialité," pp. 514, 519.

[148] Bull of Honorius III, cited above, note 34. Affranchissements of Pierrefonds by Philippe-Auguste, cited in *Rois et Serfs*, p. 58 n. 2 (1220). Guérard, *Cartulaire de Notre-Dame de Paris*, II, 11, no. viii (19 November 1268). J. Garnier, *Chartes de communes*, introduction, p. 179, n. 1 (read pp. 565 and 632 for 525 and 633; decree before 1409), and p. 221, n. 1 (1668). Finot, in *Bulletin de la Société d'Agriculture de la Haute-Saône*, 3e serie, X (1880), p. 477 (11 August 1622), XI (1881), p. 382 (5 August 1450), and p. 406 (17 December 1495). See also p. 349 about the pseudo-serfs of Gonesse, and the tragic story of a servant girl of Champagne which I told, after G. Robert, in *Caractères Originaux*, p. 116.

[149] Prou and Vidier, *Recueil des chartes de l'abbaye de Saint-Benoît-sur-Loire*, no. cv (before August 2, 1109). In Germany the last example dates from 5 January 1107: *Monumenta Boica*, XXXI, 1, p. 383. See Waitz, *D. Verfassungsgeschichte*, V, 2nd ed., p. 247 n. 2. On both sides, it appears that the rite underwent a similar deformation since the Frankish era; the serf henceforth was given to the king before receiving from him his freedom. The original meaning of the royal intervention had been forgotten. In Catalonia, there is still some mention in the thirteenth century

of enfranchisement through the denier in the customaries of Tortose; Olivier, *Estudios . . . sobre el derecho de Cataluña* (1876), I, p. 343 (cited by Th. Melicher, *Der Kampf zwischen Gesetzes- und Gewohnheitsrecht im Westgotenreich*, p. 137, n. 7). One must recall, incidentally, that enfranchisement through the denier, which made its beneficiary a member of the free population, a Franc in full right, was originally given only to the lite, not to the slave.

[150] Inscription of the cathedral of Orléans, reproduced by Mabillon, *Annales ordinis S. Benedicti*, Lucques ed. (1740), V, 500, and approximately dates by Bishop Jean's pontificate, either Jean I or Jean II, therefore 1096-1135. See the Council of Limoges in 1031, *Recueil des historiens de France*, XI, 504; and the texts of the eleventh century cited by R. Fage, *La propriété rurale en Bas-Limousin*, p. 133. (One may wonder, however, in this last case, whether it concerns only simple gifts of serfs to the church, beginning with manumission rites.)

[151] "*Licet omne genus hominum in terris ab ortu surgat consimili, et omnes qui christiano vocabulo censentur et secundum legam poli unum in Xristo sint, lege tamen fori hoc agitur ut alli liberi, alli servi sive coliberti esse dicantur.*" Bibl. Nat., nouv. acq. lat. 1930, fol. 136, vo. (Saint-Florent of Saumur, abbacy of Sion; 30 November 1035-12 June 1070).

[152] In March 1244, old style, the monks of Saint-Mesmin of Micy, enfranchising some of their serfs, declared they were doing so "*salvis tamen talliis nostris, justiciis, consuetudinibus, redibitionibus, quas habemus in terris nostris, et qua nobis debent homines liberi qui manent vel qui domos habent in terris et villis nostris, a quibus omnibus supradictis sese vel heredes eorum non poterunt excusare occasione eis corporalis a nobis prestite libertatis.*" Bibl. Nat., Baluze, ms. 78, fol. 145. A mediocre edition in E. Jarossay, *Histoire de l'abbaye de Micy-Saint-Mesmin*, p. justif., no. xxx.

[153] "*Homines autem, qui a seculari potestate et dominio as jus et dominium ecclesie transeunt, quasi liberi sunt, videlicet a scorpionibus quibus secularis dominatio illos prius cedebat.*" G. Robert, "Les serfs de Saint-Rémi de Reims," in *Travaux Acad. Nationale de Reims*, CXL, p. justif. no. xiv.

[154] Ch. Métais, *Cartulaire de l'abbaye cardinale de La Trinité de Vendôme*, I, no. ccii ("before 1070"): "*Licet homines apud Deum sola dicernantur qualitate meritorum, tamen apud homines quadam libertatis imagine discernuntur quilibet a servili jugo personarum. Sed mundana, sicut dixi, non est libertas, sed falla potius imago libertatis; vera siquidem nobilitas est hominis sui se sponte subdere Creatoris obsequiis.*"

[155] *Cartulaire de Saint-Vaast*, p. 178: "*Si vero homo sancti Vedasti uxorem extra legem suam ducit XVIII denarios dabit, quia nimirum heredes suos a libertate sancti Vedasti alienat.*" Undoubtedly one must similarly explain the decree of 1092 wherein a land given to Saint-Sernin of Toulouse is exempt of any "servile" tax, but each house on it is charged an annual rent of four deniers "*quod est signum libertatis.*" The tax would have been "servile" if paid to a lay person; paid to the church it becomes a "sign of liberty." *Musée des Archives départementales*, pl. XIX, and C. Douais, *Cartulaire de l'abbaye de Saint-Sernin*, p. 476, no. 18; see F. Lot, *L'impôt foncier et la capitation personnelle*, p. 12, n. 1, whose interpretation appears questionable.

[156] *Cartulaire de la Trinité de Vendôme*, I, no. cci ("before 1070"): "*quod multi hominum perpendentes, cum essent apud servilem mundi libertatem liberi, sponte se tradiderunt sui Creatoris libere servituti.*" This note and that cited above, note 154, are visibly written by the same hand. Here is another characteristic comparison: In 1150, Sainte-Waudru of Mons transferred the land of Braisne to the count of Hainaut, but kept possession of the servile subjects on it. Where the charter says of these serfs that they will remain "under their ancient law" (*in lege pristina*), they remain "under their ancient liberties" (*in pristina libertate*) according to the chronicler Gilbert de Mons, carefully softening the charter's language while

paraphrasing it. Devillers, *Charte de . . . Sainte-Waudru*, I, no. ix; *SS.*, XXI, 511.

[157] "The 'colliberti,' " p. 140.

[158] The obligation for a dependent to marry only within his own more or less narrowly conceived group was such a necessity of the seigneurial system that it continued in somewhat attenuated form in some localities even when other servile duties had disappeared; see E. Bonvalot, *Le Tiers-Etat d'après la charte de Beaumont*, pp. 336 ff.

[159] "The 'colliberti,' " p. 141, nn. 259-261. Also add the *capitula* of Hatto, bishop of Basle (*Cap.*, I, no. 177, c. 21, 807-823) where the exact meaning of the word *mancipia* is difficult to determine.

[160] "The 'colliberti,' " pp. 144 ff.

[161] See the texts gathered by M. Brunner, "Zur Geschichte der ältesten deutschen Erbschaftssteuer," in *Festschrift für F. von Martitz*; reprinted in *Abhandlungen zur Rechtgeschichte*, vol. II. Brunner's thesis regarding the origin of the tax justly emphasizes the relation of dependence. But his relating it to the pagan custom of "the dead man's share" does not appear to be necessary. The strength of the subjection is sufficient to explain the seigneur taking naturally his place among the family as an heir.

[162] At least this is the thesis I have argued in my article on the colliberti, and I still believe it to be correct. It has been criticized, in particular, in a very interesting and useful work titled "Colliberti ou culverts, réponse à diverses objections," by J. Petit, who had earlier proposed an interpretation differing from mine. See *Annales d'histoire économique*, III (1931), pp. 253 ff.

[163] *Lex Vis.*, V, 7, 13. Council of Toledo of 633, Mansi, Vol X, col. 636, c. 73.

[164] "The 'colliberti,' " p. 144, n. 280.

[165] J. Halkin and G. G. Roland, *Recueil des chartes de l'abbaye de Stavelot-Malmédy*, I, no. 56 (2 October 962). In the statutes of Alard de Corbie, in 822, *servitus* designates the duty tour of the monks, employed, in turn, in the kitchen. Levillain, ed., *Le Moyen Age*, (1900) II, c. 6.

[166] *Cap.*, I, no. 164, c. 8.

[167] *Formul. Turon.*, 43

[168] Letter from Zachary in *Bonifatii . . . epistolae*, Tangl, ed., no. 60, p. 163. Mentioning the tax that henceforth will be paid to the churches by each family of tenants living on the lands taken from the clergy by the Frankish princes, the pope says: "*ab unoquoque conjugio servorum XII denarii reddantur.*" He thus refers to the council of Estinnes, *Cap.*, I, no. 11, c. 2, where the same payment is prescribed in a much more general form: "*de unaquaque casata solidus, id est duodecim denarii . . . reddatur.*" It is this same word "*casata*" which he employs a little later in 751 (no. 87, p. 199). These comparisons clearly show that servus, in the first letter, was taken in the vague sense that probably was the common language one. But if the rent had been paid only by the servi, in the juridical sense of this word, the churches would not have received very much.

[169] "*Dono . . . cidlaros meos duos servos; unus est liber et alter est servus; uxores vero ejus ambo ancillas.*" Pez, *Thesaurus*, VI, 1, col. 18 (year 21 of the reign of Tassilon, therefore 768-769). See, much later, A. Bernard and A. Bruel, *Recueil des chartes . . . de Cluny*, IV, no. 3380, 19 January 1062: "*cum servis et ancillis qui ubicumque in ipsa hereditate degunt et habitant, sive sint liberi, sive sint servi.*"

[170] "*Et sicut enim alii liberi homines servilia opera nobis exhibent, ita et illi.*" M. Wartmann, *Urkundenbuch der abtei St. Gallen*, I, no. 271.

[171] Wartmann, *Urkundenbuch*, I, no. 42 (1 September 764). B. Guérard, *Polyptyque de Saint-Remi*, XVIII, 23.

[172] VIII, B, and LV.

[173] On all this see "The 'colliberti,' " p. 128 and for the enfranchisement of the colonus, p. 142, n. 265. Regarding texts on the beginning of the assimilation of coloni with servi in penal law (before Charles the Bald), see *Lex Burg.*, VII and *Lex*

Rom. Burg., XII, c. 2. I must note here the various studies by Fabien Thibault on the colonate during the Frankish era: "Les coloni dans le Polyptyque d'Irminon" and "Le colonus dans la loi des Alamans," in *Revue Historique du Droit*, 1928 and 1932. The few indications here and the more developed ones in my article on the *Colliberti*—which, it appears, M. Thibault did not notice—make it clear why I cannot agree with his thesis.

[174] *Cap.*, I, no. 58, c. 1.
[175] E. Stengel, *Die Immunität*, I, pp. 498-512.
[176] *Concilia aevi Karolini*, I, p. 283, c. 51 (Chalon-sur-Saône).
[177] "The 'colliberti,' " p. 136.
[178] *Ibid.*, pp. 132, 142.
[179] Edict of Clotaire II, 18 Oct. 614: *Cap.*, I, no. 9, c. 5, 15.
[180] Gufard, *Cartulaire de Saint-Père*, I, p. 48. It would be desirable to have a better edition of this important text.
[181] A. Lesort, *Chronique et chartes ... de Saint-Mihiel*, no. 333 (1024-1033).
[182] Good examples from the eleventh century in *Miracula ecclesie Constantiensis*, c. vi and ix; *Biblioth. de l'Ec. des Chartes* (1848) p. 346, and Pigeon, *Histoire de la Cathédrale de Coutances*.
[183] Examples (decrees cited without any other indication are those where the term serfdom does not appear): Decree of 987 cited by J. Warichez, *L'abbaye de Lobes*, p. 205; notices inserted in Longnon, ed., *Polyptyque de l'abbaye de Saint-Germain-des-Prés*, VII, 85 and XII, 49 (end of the tenth century); A. Lesort, *Chronique et chartes ... de Saint-Mihiel*, no. 33 (1024-1033; the *matrona* in this document seems to have called herself noble because she owned alodial land); subjection dating from Baudoin III of Hainaut (1098-1120), recalled in a decree of 1193, cited below, note 184; see the voluntary subjection, for pious reasons, of a *vir militaris*, in favor of the abbey of Homblières in Mabillon, *Annales* (1739 edition) IV, p. 485 (1051); the gift of one self consented to by a *illustris femina*, Ch. Piot, *Cartulaire de l'abbaye de Saint-Trond*, I, no. lx; the text regarding Saint-Bavon cited below, note 185; a decree dated April 1221 shows the parental bond between a female serf of Saint-Sépulcre of Cambrai and a nobleman, Wauters, *Preuves*, p. 83. Of course, this list is not exhaustive, but it will suffice, I think, to prove that many persons of relatively high status were driven to pledge their posterity, as well as themselves, to hereditary bonds.
[184] One cannot consider as an explicit enslavement a decree such as the one from Saint-Mihiel, cited in the preceding note, where Lady *Gysa* gives herself "*in famulam*," for this last word does not necessarily imply the idea of nonfreedom. An odd decree of Count Baudoin V of Hainaut recalls the time of Beaudoin III (1098-1120) when a noble daughter gave to Sainte-Waudru of Mons "her body and her freedom"; the charter adds that although subject, together with her descendants, to the chevage and to a fixed tax on inheritance, she nevertheless had obtained exemption from all "servile exaction." But the context proves that in reality this exemption was only of the right claimed by the count; no mainmorte in particular could be claimed to his benefit. This person's descendants were in fact called "serfs" (*servis et ancillis*) of Sainte-Waudru. L. Devillers, *Chartes du chapitre de Sainte-Waudru*, I, no. xxi; see J. Flach, *Origines*, I, 463, n. 2.
[185] *Miracula S. Bavonis*, II, 16, in *SS.*, XV, 395: "*Matrona praeclarae nobilitatis, sed familiae sancti confessoris, capitalem censum persolvere erubuit, Gandavum adiit, ac substituto pro se mancipio, jam quasi libera recessit. Ipso autem in itinere inmanissimo corripitur languore ... Revehitur a suis et quod deliquit ingemiscendo penituit. Redonavit se sancto confessori et restituta est sanitati.*" See M. Pirenne in *Bullet. Acad. Royale Belgique, Cl. Lettres*, (1908) p. 228 n. 1. An episode with the same sense is related in the life of Garnier de Mailly, abbot of Saint-Etienne of Dijon, who died in 1050 or 1051: Bloch, "La ministérialité," p. 523.
[186] "La rénovation des titres d'asservissement en Belgique au XIIe siècle," in

Annales Soc. Emulation de Bruges (1924). It is to be wished that a similar work be undertaken for the archives of France proper.

[187] On the history of these *commendati*, see P. Petot, "La commendise personnelle," in *Mélanges Paul Fournier*, and my account in *Annales d'histoire économique*, III (1931), pp. 254 ff; see also "The 'colliberti,' " p. 148, n. 296

[188] *Formul. Turon.*, 43.

[189] J. Depoin, *Liber testamentorum Sancti Martini de Campis*, no. xv and *Recueil de chartes ... de Saint-Martin-des-Champs*, I, cxi (1106-1113).

[190] M. Quantin, *Cartulaire général de l'Yonne*, II, no. cii. Toward 1090, uses the term *"commendavit se"* for a free man who gives himself to a seigneur and thereby apparently ceases to live *in libera voce*.

[191] Similarly in the North, the *gentes de advocatia*, or *advocati*, peasant groups who had placed themselves under the protection of a grandee, are often compared to serfs. See a decree of 10 June 1227, regarding the region of Tongres, in G. G. Dept, *Les influences anglaise et française dans le comté de Flandre*, p. 195, and for Saint-Bertin, a decree of 1194 cited by G. W. Coopland, *The Abbey of St. Bertin*, p. 110. In fact the charges of Saint-Bertin—chevage, tax on marriages and inheritances—closely approximate servile charges.

[192] Lambert d'Ardres, c. cviii; see a slightly different tale, c. cxx.

[193] We do not today have the means to draw up, even approximately, maps showing the distribution of serfdom. Among those countries where this condition did not develop, Normandy, probably influenced by the Scandinavian population—as with the "Danelaw" of England—must be set apart. The term is rare in Brittany—and this should be explained—but the condition does exist. In the Roussillon the situation is similar, and it is easy to realize this; see p. 89. The case of other regions, such as the Forez, where there does not seem to have been many serfs (see F. Neufbourg in his preface to *Chartrier forézien*) is more disturbing.

[194] One also should study, more thoroughly than I can do here, the status of the foreigners, the *aubains*. Protected by the king in the Frankish period, subject, under him, to a kind of mainmorte, and soon probably also to the chevage, that essential mark of protection (see, for the beginning of the Capetian era, M. Prou, *Recueil des actes de Philippe Ier*, no. xxviii, p. 85, after 1 October 1066), their subjection under the king or under lords with regal rights slowly takes forms akin to serfdm. Thus in the fourteenth century, a customary will find in their condition a "flavor of servitude," *servitutis saporem*. See *Rois et Serfs*, pp. 80 ff., and the decree cited above in note 40. The same "flavor"—a clever formula worth remembering—following a similar evolution impregnates the somewhat uncertain status of two other protected classes: the bastards (see Henri Regnault, *De la condition du bâtard au Moyen Age*, pp. 86 ff particularly), and the Jews. A decree from Parliament in 1272 goes to great effort in trying to explain why one cannot consider Jews to be the king's serfs; L. Tanon, *Histoire des justices des anciennes églises et communautés de Paris*, p. 424. As can be seen, all hereditary dependence tended to evolve into serfdom.

[195] Enfranchisement of the borough of Saint-Germain-des-Prés: Arch. Nat., LL 1025, fol. 39 and 50 (May 1250). Enfranchisement of sixty-six persons of families living in Saint-Marcel, Saint-Médard, and the "Mont de Paris" (*Monte Parisiensis*, the "Montagne-Sainte-Geneviève") Bibl. Sainte-Geneviève, ms. 351, fol. 106 vo. and 119 vo. (June 1248) and for the obligation of payment see fol. 100 vo. (in this last case the relatively small number of enfranchised persons leads one to wonder if they were not immigrants; but this hypothesis, when faced with the enfranchisement of the borough of Saint-Germain loses much of its strength).

[196] *Rois et Serfs*, pp. 51 ff.

[197] I borrow these examples, if not always their interpretation, from the excellent works of Paul Rolland, "Les 'Hommes de Sainte-Marie' à Tournai," in *Revue Belge de Philologie* and *Les origines de la commune de Tournai*, pp. 80 ff.

[198] These conditions have been most interestingly detailed by J. Massiet du Biest in "Le chef-cens et la demi-liberté," in *Revue Historique du Droit* (1927), pp. 470 ff. My interpretation is quite different from his, but his article has consistently served me as a guide. In the same work Massiet du Biest has gathered a great number of texts regarding the chevage in various localities of the North of France or of neighboring regions. I do not wish to discuss them here in detail. The reader will easily see that the deas developed here would end by giving these facts a totally different significance. See, on Corbie, note 140 above. I will only say a few words about the "hommes de meiz de moyne" which the author (pp. 651 ff) has studied in Donchery-sur-Meuse. His editing is odd. Massiet du Biest must have realized—although he does not take note of it anywhere—that one must read "de meiz de moyne," *de manso dominico*. The neighborhood these people lived in, in the thirteenth century, was called by that name. We evidently are dealing with a group of serfs for which, in accordance with a practice often used from the tenth to the thirteenth centuries, the prior of Donchery had allotted an old seigneurial land. The relatively recent date of their establishment there allowed them to escape lay justice, and their mainmorte was paid to the prior only, rather than being split between him and the solicitor.

[199] These juridical details are known to us through a small customary in the French language published by V. de Beauvillé, *Recueil de documents inédits concernant la Picardie*, IV, p. 18, no. xv. It was part of a rather disparate collection destroyed during the First World War. About the dated pieces, the most recent is of 1292. The customary most probably was a reproduction of a Latin original before the decree of November 1226 (see below note 202), which lowered the chevage—called here *répit* (*respectus*)—to three deniers per household, since the customary still fixes it as four deniers.

[200] Precisely at Amiens, at least beginning with the granting of the communal charter of 1185, the full exemption to tonlieu was granted only to those persons who, being "of church," were also part of the commune. If they were strangers to the latter, only a half-exemption was given. On Tournai, see above note 197. On Arras, see *Cartulaire*, pp. 177 ff. On Corbie, see J. Massiet du Biest, in *Revue du Nord* (1923), p. 44.

[201] *Cartulaire*, pp. 182 ff. *Gallia christ.*, III, *instr.*, col. 44.

[202] A. Thierry, *Monuments du Tiers-Etats*, I, p. 200, no. xlix.

[203] In his very interesting work, *Le servage dans le comté de Hainaut* (Acad. Royale de Belgique, Cl. des Lettres, Mémoires, in-8o, 2e série, VI, 1910) L. Verriest has studied a class of men he calls *sainteurs*, although, he says, the term taken in this sense is rare and was late in adoption (p. 172). At least in the Hainaut, one must add, for this term is found frequently in the Champagne as early as the beginning of the thirteenth century (see Bibl. Nat., lat. 5993, fol. 171 vo., November 1211; Longnon, *Documents*, I, p. 127, no. 3748; p. 186, no. 5217), and in the Valois in 1273 (*Olim*, I, p. 936, no. xxx). In fact, these are church serfs, subject to chevage, to "meilleur catel" (or analogous taxes), and to a tax on marriages. The latter, in fact, at least since the thirteenth century, seems to have been collected in all cases, even when there was no formariage; but such was the rule for serfs in the same region at the same time according to Verriest himself (p. 66). Yet Verriest refuses to recognize in these *sainteurs* the servile condition. Wrongly, most certainly. The texts he cites to prove his thesis do not prove anything, for they are uniformly decrees by this or the other seigneur foregoing a claim that a sainteur was one of his serfs (see in particular *pièces justificatives*, nos. lvii and lviii); this naturally would not preclude the particular individual being the serf of a church that could then fully claim possession of him. On the contrary, a number of texts unambiguously demonstrate that the sainteur was not considered free: thus this decree of 1228 (*P. Justif.*, no. x) which Verriest entitles "Aloetrudi s'asseinteure à Saint-Ghislain" and where one reads: "*libertati mee originali in*

qua pacifice permanebam . . . solempniter [re]*nuntiavi meque ipsam Deo et beato Gylleno im perpetuam dedi servitutem.*" And Verriest also writes that "The Middle Ages often applied to 'sainteurs' the names of *servi* and *ancillae* and their romance equivalent. It confused under the same nomenclature totally different status, so that the historian is often incapable of finding out whether he is faced with real serfs or with 'sainteurs'." Must one recall once again that the "historian" should wisely try to understand the mental categories of the past rather than to state that they are, in view of his own categories, confused or absurd. It may be that toward the end of the Middle Ages the notion of the servile character attached to the condition of the sainteur became obscure because just like Verriest, one had become accustomed to understand something quite different in the term servitude. Still I note that an account of 1534 (p. 313 n. 4) calls the "best catel" foreign to persons "*de noble lignie et de francque origine, sans nulz quelzconques saincteurs avoir*" [sainteur here being used in its most frequent manner in the Hainaut; one did not say "so and so is the sainteur of this church" but rather "so and so has this church for sainteur" (see p. 174)]. This formula seems to indicate that to recognize a church as your sainteur equaled not being *franc.*

[204] See L. Verriest, *Le servage dans le comté de Hainaut*, p. 149; and for Flanders the enfranchisement of the comital serfs in 1252 cited above note 39. The count's selection among the catel was in any case limited to poultry (*pecus melius de domo*; the meaning is doubtful) and to furniture and clothing (*ornamentum*), excluding large livestock (*armentum*); the text even specifies that the count may not take the house itself: a curious testimony to the fact that constructions were long considered movables. The chevage is also maintained; the annual payment specified in the charter—three deniers for men, one denier for women—is too small to see in it, I believe, the payment for freedom itself.

[205] R. Debuisson, *Etude sur la condition des personnes . . . d'après les coutumes de Reims*, p. 120. For the Laons and Soisson regions, see above note 16. In the twelfth century, when the right of persons was still not well systematized, some seigneurs, it seems, wishing to enfranchise their serfs, were content to specifically abolish only the mainmorte; the disappearance of this characteristic duty generally carried with it the erasure of all other aspects of the servile status. Thus, the decree of Suger for the inhabitants of Saint-Denis on 15 March 1125 only formally ends the mainmorte, but bears, in the Cartulary of the thirteenth century, the heading *De servis libertati traditis* (Suger, *OEuvres*, p. 319). Such also, probably, is the charter by which, between 1182 and 1190, the monks of Saint-Martin-des-Champs replaced in Limoges and in Fourches the mainmorte by a *relief* duty (J. Depoin, *Recueil des chartes et documents de Saint-Martin-des-Champs*, III, no. 568). But in the thirteenth and fourteenth centuries the enfranchisement documents were too well fixed for anyone to understand such limited concessions as real manumissions.

[206] A. Longnon, *Documents relatifs au comté de Champagne*, III, p. 236.

[207] *Liber practicus de consuetudine Remensi*, XXXV, in Varin, *Archives législatives*, I, p. 55. This customary seems never to have been closely studied and the date, already very approximative, is conjectural.

[208] Beaumanoir, para. 1449-1450. Similarly, already around 1250, in Curzon, ed., *Règle du Temple*, c. 435: "*A chevalier ne demande t'on pas se il est sers ou esclaf de nul home, quar puis que il est chevalier devers pere, de loial matrimoine, se il est vers, il est frans par nature.*" On the serf-knights of the earlier epoch, see Bloch, "La ministérialité," pp. 523 ff.

[209] Bloch, "The Transformation of Serfdom," pp. 151 ff.

[210] Decree of Philippe III abolishing the obligation for the *homines seu hospites* of the abbey to escort to Paris, upon summons of the royal provost, thieves and other criminals; August 1275; Arch. Nat., LL 1026, fol. 19.

[211] The millers escorted condemned men to the gallows and apparently assisted

with the execution. A. Dupré, in *Mém. Soc. Sciences ... Loir-et-Cher*, VII (1867), pp. 114, 116.

[212] H. Sée, *Les classes rurales en Bretagne du XVIe siècle à la Révolution*, p. 124, n. 1.

[213] Probably the same kind of evolution explains why the serfs of the count of Neufchâtel had to assist with capital punishment: P. Darmstädter, *Die Befreiung der Leibeigenen*, p. 107 (no date given).

[214] In this last section I will deliberately refrain from any bibliographic references; the facts, if not always their interpretation, are well known. If I do support a few statements with references to documents, it is only as examples that could easily be multiplied.

[215] *Landrecht*, III, 45, 6.

[216] There are also in Germany examples of seizure of the whole inheritance. See K. Weimann, *Die Misnisterialität im späteren Mittelalter*, p. 24. B. Poll, *Das Heimfallsrecht auf den Grundherrschaften Oesterreichs*, p. 28; and for a specific case (in the absence of direct heirs), *Codex Laureshamensis*, Glöckner, ed., p. 385, no. 119.

[217] Ortlieb de Zwiefalten, *Chronicon*, I, c. 9 in *SS.*, X, p. 78. Although the monastery's *tributarii*—who appear not to pay the chevage—as well as the subjects, of all ranks, of the priory of Tigerfeld are judged by the avoué in the presence of the mons' provost, in courts held on fixed dates, the heirs, no doubt, of those Carolingian comital courts, "*illi autem qui ex toto lure proprietatis ad monasterium pertinent, tametsi certis temporibus ab advocatis sicut tributarii non iudicentur, tamen si quid vel in nos, vel in quemquam aliquid deliquerint aut iustae querelae commiserint, tam acriter a preposito vel advocato coercendi sunt, ut caeteri metum habeant....*"

[218] See Conrad II's diploma determining the condition of the men of a variety of lands given to the abbey of Limbourg, 17 January 1035. *Dipl. Conradi II*, no. 216, c. 11. The dispensation covered here, it seems, the rights over inheritance which, had they been collected, would not have amounted to much.

[219] The "law" of Bishop Burchard (1023-1025), c. 16 and c. 9, illuminates both this inferiority of the *dagewardus* vis-à-vis the *fiscalin* (serf of the church's land, separated rom the royal "fisc") and the clearly servile character of the latter's status: note the text in Altmann and Bernheim, *Ausgewählte Urkunden*, no. 74.

[220] On the servi's inferiority when compared to the *censuales*, see in particular a treaty between the chapter of Constance and the monastery of Petershausen, 22 October 1207, in *Zeitschrift für die Geschichte des Oberrheins*, VII (1856), p. 153. The chronicle of Ebersheim, c. 3 (*SS.*, xxiii, p. 433) around 1160 distinguishes between the censuales and the servi who, however, also pay a chevage. See A. Dopsch in *Mitteil. des Instit. für österr. Geschichtsforschung*, XIX, (1898), p. 605.

[221] On slavery in Roussillon and Catalonia, see A. Brutails in *Nouv. Rev. Historique du Droit* (1886). J. Miret y Sans, in *Revue Hispanique* (1917). M. Kowalewsky, *Die ökonomische Entwicklung Europas*, VI, pp. 477 ff. J. M. Ramos y Loscertales, *El cautiverio en la corona de Aragón*. On the forms of hereditary subjection, see J. A. Brutails, *Etude sur la condition des populations rurales du Roussillon*. E. de Hinojosa, *El regimen señorial y la cuestión agraria en Cataluña*.

[222] It is probable that the rule binding the serf to the soil was established in England earlier than in France, since the royal jurisdiction had the whole country under its control as early as the Plantagenets. There is nothing more significant than that summons of 1158 by Henry II to "*justiciis, vicecomitibus et ministris suis Anglie*": "*Precipio quod sine dilacione et juste faciatis habare abbati et monachis de Gemmetico omnes fugitivos et nativos suos, cum catallis suis, qui fugerunt post mortem regis Henrici ari mei, ubicunque inventi fuerint. Et prohibeo quod nullus eos injuste retineat super x libris forifacture.*" (L. Delisle and E. Berger, *Recueil des actes de Henri II*, no. xcii.) One cannot conceive of Louis VII, at the

same time, proceeding to such a pursuit throughout the kingdom.

²²³ C. 70, 2 and 4.

²²⁴ It is interesting to note that as early as the end of the eleventh century, the canon of Hereford, who was writing *Le Roman de Philosophie*, opposed villein to freeman. See Ch. Langlois, *La vie en France au Moyen Age . . . La vie spirituelle*, p. 295.

²²⁵ It is curious to see that a theory, quite similar to the one that was to appear in English law, was sketched in France under Saint Louis by Pierre de Fontaines. Generally, this author's whole description of the social classifications of his time is warped by constant borrowings from texts quoting Roman law regarding the servi, then all too frequent in the literature of customs. See what was said above regarding the *Livre de Justice et de Plet*. However, the following passage is worthy of being quoted. After observing that the villein is not a serf, Pierre de Fontaines adds: "*mes par nostre usage n'a-t-il, entre toi et ton vilein, juge fors Deu, tant com il est tes couchans es tes levans, s'il n'a autre lois vers toi que la commune.*" (Marnier, ed., *Le Conseil de Pierre de Fontaines*, chapter xix, VIII, p. 225.) The differences between the various national and regional laws of medieval Europe are indeed the result of the uneven development of tendencies that, in existence everywhere at first, found in some regions conditions favorable to their flourishing, while elsewhere, on the contrary, rapidly disappeared.

Chapter 3

¹ Originally published in French in *Revue Historique*, 1928, CLVII, pp. 1-48, 225-263.

² One must add to the examples cited in my "Collibertus or Culibertus," *Mélanges Historiques*, Paris, pp. 379-384; the term *culverta* in the *Premier cartulaire de l'aumônerie de Saint-Martial* (A. Leroux, *Documents historiques . . . concernant principalement la Marche et le Limousin*, II, no. 7).

³ "Collibertus or Culibertus." Refer to this article for all that concerns the history of this word. However, I now do not dare to use as evidence the Spanish form; I now believe that it was borrowed from the French; see page 123.

⁴ See the remarks by Viollet, *Histoire du droit civil français*, p. 306. But I do not believe at all that the "scholars'" error, so justly denounced by Viollet, "obliges" us to employ the "useless word" they forged.

⁵ I know of four studies specifically concerned with the "colliberts": V. de Rochas, "Note sur les colliberts," in *Bulletin de la Société des sciences, lettres et arts de Pau*, 2e série, IV (1874-1875), pp. 8-17; A. Richard, "Les colliberts," in *Mémoires de la Société des Antiquaires de l'Ouest*, XXXIX (1875), pp. 3-35; Guillouard, "Recherches sur les colliberts," in *Bulletin de la Société des Antiquaires de Normandie*, IX (1878-1880), pp. 332-380; A. Petit, *Coliberti ou Culverts, essai d'interpretation des textes qui les concernent (Xe-XIIe siècles)*, Limoges (1926). This last work (whose conclusions are different from mine) is quite extraordinary by the breadth of its documentation and the ingenuity of its opinions. In addition, the "colliberts" have been the object of more or less ample treatments, some of great interest, in a rather large number of works of a more general character. To cite only a few: P. Bernard, *Etude sur les esclaves et les serfs d'Eglise en France*

(1919), pp. 116-119; Du Cange, *Glossarium*, under the words *Colliberti, Culverta, Culvertagium, Cuvertus*; G. d'Espinay, *Les cartulaires angevins, étude sur le droit de l'Anjou au Moyen Age* (1864), pp. 111-114; H. Lafond, *Etude sur le servage en Poitou* (1923); K. Lamprecht, *Etudes sur l'état économique de la France pendant la première partie du Moyen Age*, pp. 213-216, and also *Zeitschrift für Rechtsgeschichte*, 1878, pp. 507-514; A. Luchaire, *Manuel des institutions françaises*, pp. 313-317; E. Mayer, *Deutsche und französische Verfassungsgeschichte*, II, p. 15, n. 48.; Francisque Michel, *Histoire des races maudites de la France et de l'Espagne* (1847), II, pp. 1-32; H. Sée, *Les classes rurales et le régime domanial*, pp. 190-199. (The observations in this last work, however brief, are particularly pertinent.)

[6] The oldest document in which culverts appear as a truly distinct class dates, as far as I know, from 973 or 975: see below note 19. It is true that the "Cartulaire de Vierzon," Bibl. Nat., lat. 9865, fol. 6, and, after it, the *Gallia Christiana*, II, col. 135, mention a charter dated from the reign of Charles the Bald and from the episcopate of the archbishop of Bourges Raoul (840 or 841-866), in which lands are occupied by serfs and by culverts, or uniquely by culverts; but this charter must be considered extremely suspect.

[7] *Historiens de France*, XI, p. 572 (H. Soehnée, "Catalogue des actes d'Henri Ier," no. 45: 1035)–A. Luchaire, *Louis VI le Gros*, no. 28 (1104)–"Cartulaire de Saint-Quentin de Beauvais", Bibl. Nat., nouv. acq. lat. 1656, fol. 1 (29 January 1103). A notice from the eleventh century published by Guérard in *Polyptyque d'Irminon*, II, App. no. xxviii, and V. Leblond, in *Mémoires de la Société Académique de l'Oise*, XXIV (1), p. 11. M. Béreux, archivist of the Oise has kindly collated this piece for me and insured that the writing, at least in the first part which contains the note regarding a culvertile family (up to "Odo major de Senentis": Leblond, p. 13), dates incontestably from the eleventh century.

[8] Decree of the bishop of Meaux, Bernier (attested in 1028 and 1029; his predecessor was still living in 1017; his successor was bishop in 1045) granting to the canons of his cathedral, in Changis (Seine-et-Marne, La Ferté-sous-Jouarre canton), "culibertos quos mihi calumpniabant"; Bibliothèque de la ville de Meaux, ms. 65, p. 11. (There is only a fragment, without the passage that concerns us, in Toussaint-Duplessis, *Histoire de l'église de Meaux*, II, p. justif. no. ix.) Another cartulary from the chapter in the same library, ms. 63, p. 18, says "cum libertos."

[9] *Recueil des actes de Philippe Ier*, no. 147 (Grandchamp, Yonne, Charny canton): 1103.

[10] Guérard, *Cartulaire de l'abbaye de Saint-Père de Chartres*, I, p. 187, no. lxi (Juziers, Seine-et-Oise, Limay canton); M. Prou, *Receuil des actes de Philippe Ier*, no. 63 (Saint-Germain-en-Laye region); *ibid.*, no. 70 (Mantes region); A. Salmon and Ch.-L. de Grandmaison, *Liber de servis Majoris Monasterii*, App. no. xxxvii (Chateaufort, Seine-et-Oise, Palaiseau canton); *Cartulaire du prieuré de Notre-Dame de Longpont*, no. clxxv (Morsang-sur-Orge). All these texts date from the eleventh century, except perhaps for the last one that could in any case not date from very much after 1100.

[11] Barret, *Cartulaire de Marmoutier pour le Perche*, no. I (toward 997-1038). See below note 17.

[12] In order not to add inordinately to the number of references, I shall direct the reader to Ch. Métais, *Cartulaire de l'abbaye ... de la Trinité de Vendôme*, and to A. de Trémault, *Cartulaire de Marmoutier pour le Vendômois*. All the eleventh century decrees.

[13] G. Busson and A. Ledru, *Acta pontificum Cenomanensium*, p. 358; A. Cauvin, *Chartularium insignis ecclesie Cenomannensis*, no. cxvi; R. Charles and S. Menjot d'Elbenne, *Cartulaire de Saint-Vincent du Mans*, nos. 87 (same decree as the one from the previous reference), 303 (cf. 306), 392; *Cartulaire des abbayes de Saint-Pierre-de-la-Couture et de Saint-Pierre de Solesmes*, no. v; Menjot d'Elbenne, *Cartulaire du chapitre ... de Saint-Pierre-de-la-Cour*, nos. I (same decree as the

preceding one) and IV; P. Marchegay, *Chartes mancelles de l'abbaye de Saint-Florent près Saumur*, no. iii; Decree of Joël II de Mayenne, in Martène, "Preuves de l'Histoire de Marmoutier," II (Bibl. Nat., lat. 12880), fol. 257, edited from another source, ("Titres de Géhard") but with errors, by J.-B. Guyard de la Fosse, *Histoire des seigneurs de Mayenne*, p. vii. All from the eleventh or the first years of the twelfth centuries. The most recent decree is that of Joël de Mayenne. Joël's predecessor, Gautier, was most certainly still alive in 1118 (Halphen and Poupardin, eds., *Chroniques des comtes d'Anjou*, p. 158); according to Ménage, *Histoire de Sablé*, p. 184, he died in 1124. On the other hand, the decree is anterior to the elevation of Hildebert de Lavardin at the seat of Tours (1125) and to the death of the abbot of Marmoutier, Guillaume (probably 23 May 1124). A decree attributed to the count of le Mans, Hugue II (died before 992), in *Cartul. de Saint-Pierre-de-la-Couture*, no. v, and in *Cartul. de Saint-Pierre-de-la-Cour*, no. i, is a counterfeit written no doubt between 1134 and 1136, as shown by R. Latouche, *Histoire du comté du Maine*, pp. 107-109.

¹⁴ A. Salmon and Ch.-L. de Grandmaison, *Liber de servis*, no. lxii: a mention of two culverts born approximately two miles from Dol "in villa Funals" (an unidentified site); but these two "culverts" went to live in Touraine: perhaps it is there that they were called by this name.

¹⁵ For the Bourbonnais and the Berry: *Recueil des actes de Phillipe Ier*, no. 145; M.-A. Chazaud, *Fragments du cartulaire de la Chapelle-Aude*, no. xvi; L. de Kersers, *Essai de reconstitution du Cartulaire A de Saint-Sulpice de Bourges*, nos. iii, lxxii, cxxv, cxxviii; "Cartulaire de Saint-Pierre de Vierzon," Bibl. Nat., lat. 9865, fols. 6 vo., 11 (Toulgoët-Tréanna, ed., *Histoire de Vierzon*, p. justif. no. vii), 15 vo., 16, 17 (*Ibid.*, no. xii), 20 vo. (no. ix), 22, 22 vo., 24 vo., 25 vo., 27 vo.; Decrees of the council of Bourges, below, note 82. All from the eleventh century or at least anterior to the death of Philippe I (1108); on a suposedly older decree, see above note 6.

¹⁶ R. de Lespinasse, *Cartulaire de Saint-Cyr de Nevers*, nos. 65, 81, 83 (all, without doubt, from the eleventh century).

¹⁷ *Recueil des actes de Philippe Ier*, no. 156 (1106): the possessions of the abbey of Morigny; Guérard, *Cartulaire de l'abbaye de Saint-Père de Chartres*, I, p. 180, no. liv; II, p. 295, no. xl, and p. 297, no. xlii (the last from Beauce or from Perche?), eleventh century.

¹⁸ In the Blésois, the Touraine, and the Anjou the decrees are so numerous that I can only indicate the collections where they can be found: A. Salmon and Ch.-L. de Grandmaison, *Liber de Servis Majoris Monasterii*; Ch. Métais, *Marmoutier, cartulaire blésois*; J.-L. Denis, "Chartes de Saint-Julien de Tours", in *Arch. hist. du Maine*, XII, 1; J. Bourassé, *Cartulaire de Cormery*; C. Chevalier, *Cartulaire de l'abbaye de Noyers*; A. Salmon, "Recueil de titres relatifs à l'abbaye de Bourgueil," Bibl. de la ville de Tours, ms. 1338; *Gallia Christiana*, XIV, instr. p. 71, no. lii; Mabillon, *Annales ord. S. Benedicti*, LI, c. xi; L. Lex, *Eudes, comte de Blois*, p. 143, no. xiii; Urseau, *Cartulaire noir de la cathédrale d'Angers*; B. de Broussillon, *Cartulaire de l'abbaye de Saint-Aubin d'Angers*; P. Marchegay, *Archives d'Anjou*, I (Glanfeuil) and III (Notre-Dame du Ronceray); "Livre noir de Saint-Florent de Saumur", Bibl. Nat., nouv. acq. lat. 1930; Marchegay, "Essai de reconstitution du premier cartulaire de Saint-Serge d'Angers", Arch. de Maine-et-Loire, H non coté; Th. Grasilier, *Cartulaire ... de l'abbaye de Notre-Dame de Saintes*, no. I; d'Espinay, *Les cartulaires angevins*; L. Halphen, *Le comté d'Anjou*. The oldest reliably dated document is from August 20, 985 (*Liber de servis*, no. I); the most recent is from 1163 (*ibid.*, App. no. lv). Most are from the eleventh century or from the first twenty years of the twelfth. The author of the *Chronique de Nantes*, writing between 1050 and 1059, recounts that Alain Barbe-Torte obtained from Louis d'Outre-Mer "*ut quicumque servus vel collibertus Britanniam, causa manendi ibi, petierit, liber ab omni servitute ... permaneret.*" (R. Merlet, ed., c. xxxiv).

The tradition is of little value but the passage shows that chroniclers knew of two categories of nonfree persons, serfs and culverts, in the region of Brittany.

[19] L. Rédet, *Documents pour l'histoire de l'église de Saint-Hilaire de Poitiers*, no. XC; *Cartulaire du prieuré de Saint-Nicolas de Poitiers*, nos. I, XXX, XXXIX, and *Cartulaire de l'abbaye de Saint-Cyprien de Poitiers*, nos. 200, 329; L. Marchegay, *Chartes poitevines de l'abbaye Saint-Florent de Saumur*, nos. viii, xxxii; Th. Grasilier, *Cartulaire de l'abbaye ... de Notre-Dame de Saintes*, no. liii; A. Richard, *Chartes et documents pour servir a l'histoire de l'abbaye de Saint-Maixent*, nos. cxiii, cxv; A. Salmon, Bourgeuil, bibl. de Tours, ms. 1338, fol 274; L. Halphen and F. Lot, *Recueil des actes de Lothaire et de Louis V*, no. lxii; *Recueil des actes de Philippe Ier*, no. 83; J. Besly, *Histoire des comtes de Poictou*, p. 407; Arcère, *Histoire de La Rochelle*, II, p. 663; bibl. de la ville de Poitiers, ms. Fonteneau 26, p. 143, cited in A. Petit, *Coliberti ou Culverts*, ns. 203, 204. All from the eleventh century or from the first years of the twelfth (*Saint-Nicolas de Poitiers*, no. xxxiv, "toward 1106"), with the exception of the diploma from Lothaire of 973 or 975, probably authentic despite a few oddities in the writing.

[20] J. de Font-Réaulx, "S. Stephani Lemovicensis Chartularium," in *Bull. Soc. hist. Limousin*, LXIX, 1919, nos. xxxi, xxxii, li, clxxviii; J.-B. Champeval, *Cartulaire des abbayes de Tulle*, nos. 370, 391, 649; J.-B. Champeval, *Cartulaire de l'abbaye d'Uzerche*, nos. 465, 481, 1007, 1154; H. de Montégut, *Cartulaire du monastère de Saint-Pierre de Vigeois*, nos. xii, xv, cxiii, cxxiv, cxlvi, cccxxxii; "Premier cartulaire de l'aumônerie de Saint-Martial," in A. Leroux, *Documents historiques concernant principalement la Marche et le Limousin*, II, no. 7; "Cartulaire de Solignac," Bibl. Nat., lat. 18363, fol. 17; Decrees of the council of Limoges, see below note 82. All from the eleventh century or from the beginning of the twelfth. (*Uzerche*, no. 1154, "toward 1120" might be the most recent piece, but on what does the dating rest?)

[21] I have wondered if those *colvekerli*, subject to servile duties, mentioned between 1194 and 1198 by Lambert d'Ardres (*SS.*, XXVI, c. xxvi), who dates their enfranchisement from Count Manassé (1091-1137) were not culverts with a Germanized name. Lambert derives their names from the mace (middle netherlandish *colve*) these people were allowed to arm themselves with; all other weapons were forbidden to them; this is probably only one of those false etymologies common to writers of that period. But I would be hard put to prove my hypothesis, since objections of a phonetic order can be placed against it.

[22] A decree from the *Cartulaire de la Sainte-Trinité-du-Mont de Rouen*, no. lxviii, gives the form *Culvertvilla* to the name of a village called Cuverville (there are four villages by this name in Normandy). This writing is probably nothing more than an attempt at etymology.

[23] M.-A. Chazaud, *Fragments du cartulaire de la Chapelle-Aude*, no. xvi, p. 35: "*Emendabit tantum catallum et talem legem qua vixerit, sive sit liber, sive servus, sive colibertus.*"

[24] Decree published in part in Ménage, *Histoire de Sablé*, p. 157. I have used the text established by Marchegay in his manuscript attempt at the reconstitution of the first cartulary of Saint-Serge d'Angers (Arch. de Maine-et-Loire, H, fol. 142). The date is drawn from the presence among the witnesses of Count Geoffroi Martel and of Countess Audearde (cf. L. Halphen *Le comté d'Anjou*, p. 11, n. 1). "*Praeter haec quicumque de hominibus meis dederit aliquid Sancto Marcello, sive miles, sive servus, sive colibertus, sine ulla emptione vel malivolentia omnium talium donationem auctoritate et favore mea concessi sancto loco.*"

[25] Note in an eleventh-century hand on the covering sheet at the end of ms. 24 of the Angers library: "*Rainaldus Monterius emit dimidium arpennum vinoee Morani, tali conventu ut illam non vendat ulli homini consuetudinario comitis nec servo nec coliberto, nec ulli sancto dimittat nec vendat nisi sancto Sergio.*" See also in Toulgoët-Tréanna, *Histoire de Vierzon*, p. justif, no. xii, a note from 1052:

Abbot Béranger agrees to grant an aid of 500 sous to the seigneur of Vierzon, Arnoul, only the condition that the latter sanctions in advance all gifts to the monastery by "*omnes qui ejus erant in potestate constituti, sive milites, sive burgenses rusticique et colliberti pariter et servi.*"

[26] Here are a few examples highlighting this distinction: Ch. Métais, *Cartulaire de l'abbaye ... de la Trinité de Vendôme*, I, no. clxi (23 August 1062): "*Donavit Sanctae Trinitati collibertum et unum servum*"; *ibid.*, no. ccxcix (2 March 1080): Robert de Montcontour gives his land in Coulommiers "*cum servis et ancillis et utriusque sexus collibertis*"; Toulgoët-Tréanna, *Histoire de Vierzon*, p. justif. no. vii (abbatiate of Martin, toward 1030), decree of the seigneur Evrard: "*Servi et coliberti ad monachos pertinentes similiter habebunt silvas ad omnia facienda preter porcorum consuetudinem*"; A. Richard, *Chartes ... pour servir à l'histoire de ... Saint-Maixent*, no. cxiii (1051): "*Quidam vir nobilis, nomine Petrus ... qui quandiu vixit tam in servis quam in colibertis possessor extitit*"; J.-B. Champeval, *Cartul. des abbayes de Tulle et de Roc-Amadour*, no. 391 (1100) (Also Baluze, *Historiae Tutelensis*, col. 445): Alaiz de Magnac gives "*duos mansos in villa de Castanet cum servis et ancillis et colibertis.*" See also the documents relating to the rights to justice, notes 57-60 below.

[27] Court proceedings to discover whether a man is a serf or a culvert. See p. 97 and note 35. Whether culvert or free, see pp. 97, 106; *Cartulaire de Saint-Aubin d'Angers*, no. cxciv (judicial duel).

[28] Bibl. Nat., nouv. acq. lat. 1930, fol. 136 vo. (Abbatiate of Sion, 30 November 1055-12 June 1070). Enfranchisement of the culvert Lambert Fantin by Hugue Mange-Breton: "*Licet omne genus hominum in terris ab ortu surgat consimili et omnes qui christiano vocabulo censentur et secundum legem poli unum in Xristo sint, lege tamen fori hoc agitur ut ali liberti, alii servi sive coliberti esse dicantur.*" On the full significance of this decree, see pp. 109-110. One can recognize in this passage the classical medieval theory that serfdom is contrary to the natural state or—and this is all the same—to the state of innocence, but that it is the fruit of man's laws and of sin. The same theme can be found in decree of donation of a culvertile family, *ibid.*, fol. 134, vo.: "*Quod sorte hominum accidit ut homo homini serviat conditione legali ....*"

[29] Notice published in fragments in Du Cange, *Glossarium* under "Collibertus." Perreciot, *De l'état civil des personnes*, 2e ed., II, p. 415, n. 1; Sammarthani, *Gallia Christiana*, IV, fol. 205. I have used the transcription made from several ancient copies by A. Salmon, bibl. de Tours, ms. 1338, fol. 420.

[30] "*Cum jurisjurandi finem fecisset, adjecit quod non debuit, dicens: 'in libera voce dico, sicut paulo ante dixi.'*"

[31] Enfranchisement of the culvert Robert by the count of Anjou Geoffroi Martel: Marchegay, *Archives d'Anjou*, III ("Cartulaire de Notre-Dame du Ronceray), no. xxxv (Halphen, *Le comté d'Anjou*, Catal. no. 89): "*Et liberum eum facio a lege conditionis ab hoc die in evum ... ac si ab ingenuis parentibus fuisset progenitus.*"

[32] A note from the time of Jean, abbot of Bourgueil (between 1040 and 1047 approximately), published in *Liber de servis Majoris Monasterii*, App. no. xi, calls a culvert and an *ancilla*: *servulis*. Between 1053 and 1064 a culvert sold to Marmoutier is said to become the monks's *servum* (see below note 94); I do not believe this implies a very improbable change in condition; this is just a manner of saying that this culvert is entering into the monastery's servitude. The *ancilla* of the text cited below, end of note 36, is probably a female culvert. For examples posterior to 1060, see pp. 116-117.

[33] A note published on several occasions, notably by B. Guérard, *Polyptyque d'Irminon*, II, p. 361: *Liber de servis Majoris Monasterii*, App. no. xxix. A. de Trémault, *Cartulaire de Marmoutier pour le Vendômois*, no. clxi. The lawsuit occured in the seventh year of tenure of Abbot Barthélemi: 1070, June or a little earlier; 1071, June, or a little earlier.

³⁴ *Liber de servis Majoris Monasterii*, no. lxvi (1062); cf. *ibid.*, no. lxxvi (1061 January 22).

³⁵ The rule that the children were to be divided equally in case of marriage between culverts belonging to two different seigneurs is highlighted by several documents: B. de Broussillon, *Cartulaire de l'abbaye de Saint-Aubin d'Angers*, nos. lxvii, ccccxxx; Urseau, *Cartulaire noir de la cathédrale d'Angers*, nos. lxxxii, cxi. A notice published in the *Liber de servis Majoris Monasterii*, App. no. lv, illustrates a delicate point: three sons issued from such a marriage; the monks received two of them, but only after paying a fee.

³⁶ Another similar affair is shown in two notices from the *Liber de servis Majoris Monasterii*. A serf named Guérin had been given to Marmoutier. He married a culvert of Foubert de Vendôme, Hélène. The children, of whom only one, Engerri le Tailleur, is named, reverted as was normal, to Marmoutier, not without some difficulties that are shown in notice no. cii. The expressed renunciation had to be obtained from Foubert's son, Geoffroi, probably for a price. Then this Geoffroi claimed that he had excepted Engerri in his renunciation; this was incorrect but the monks still had to pay him a second time. This necessity for the monks to pay in order to receive what they judged to be theirs by right perhaps proves that, like many other juridical rulings of the time, particularly rulings applying to culvertage, the principle established by the judges in Montoire was not universally recognized (see p. 000 and note 76). But above all, this incident, similar to many others, illustrates that in a society where judicial power is extremely ill organized, the best way to get rid of an inopportune adversary, even were he a thousand times in the wrong, was to compromise. Guérin's case was the subject of still another suit, recounted in notice ci; this time it was brought against the monks by one Gautier de Vendôme. This person claimed in turn that Guérin had been given to Marmoutier as a culvert and not as a serf, then that Guérin's wife, Hélène, had been a serf, and not a culvert. One can easily see the object of either claim: once the spouses had been recognized as equal—either as serfs or as culverts—then the monks would have had to divide the children with the mother's seigneur. One does not know what was Gautier de Vendôme's interest in this whole affair. Perhaps he had claims on Foubert's succession, perhaps he acted as a front-man for Foubert's heirs. In any case he failed. At the time of the abbatiate of Hubert in Saint-Aubin d'Angers (3 September 999-1027), the monks of Saint-Aubin divided with the monks of Saint-Florent the children of a culvert of Saint-Aubin and of an *ancilla* of Saint-Florent (*Cartul. de Saint-Aubin*, no. ccxxix). This could be another instance of the uncertainty of the rules, but this ancilla could have been a culvert in reality.

³⁷ P. Vinogradoff, *The Growth of the Manor*, p. 338.

³⁸ *D. B.*, I, 38 and 38b., cf. on this subject, F. W. Maitland, *Domesday Book and Beyond*, pp. 36 ff.

³⁹ For example, in P. Marchegay, *Chartes poitevines de Saint-Florent*, no. viii, abbatiate of Ferri (1 September 1022-28 September 1055); the knight *Gerorius* gives his culvert Freauld "*ita ut ... tam ipse collibertus, Fredaldus scilicet, quam omnis fructus ex eo genitus vel adhuc generandus ipsius Sancti Florenti atque monachorum ejus ditioni sese subjectos esse recognoscant.*"

⁴⁰ "Cartulaire de l'abbaye du Ronceray," in P. Marchegay, *Archives d'Anjou*, III, no. xxxviii: "*Dicebat vero idem Fulco Normannus avum suum Rogerium Vetulum eorumdem collibertorum patres, hoc est Frogerium et Actardum, duos scilicet fratres, ex domo Fulconis Antiqui comitis tenuisse et ideo sobolem eorum sibi jure pertinere*" (1062 or 1063; the evidence for the date is contradictory).

⁴¹ Text in Martène, "Preuves de l'Histoire de Marmoutier," Bibl. Nat., lat. 12880, fol. 257, and a faulty edition in Guyard de La Fosse. *Histoire des seigneurs de Mayenne*, Pr., p. vii. For the date, see above note 13. The phrase, "*Iratus graviter contra eum, dixi quod meus colibertus era et poteram eum vendere vel ardere et terram suam cuicumque vellem dare tanquam terram coliberti mei,*" has been

reproduced in Du Cange under the word *Colliberti*. The enfranchisement was the result of complicated negotiations. A *vir prudens*, Chotard de Mayenne, who offered his services to obtain the enfranchisement, gave Joel a white palfrey originally given to him at Dijon by the duke of Burgundy; in addition Chotard returned a cup to Joel who originally had received it from King Henry I of England, and who had given it to Chotard as a security against a loan. Guérin paid Chotard with a field that he in turn had received as security against a loan of 300 sous (perhaps to Joel himself). Obviously Joel, as a good knight, preferred horses and plate to land; and furthermore he was in debt. The Latin transcription of the culvert is Garinus Probus; I render this by "Prudhomme."

⁴² Examples: L. de Kersers, *Essai de reconstitution du Cartulaire A de Saint-Sulpice de Bourges*, no. xciv (1017); Berna gives one alod "*et servos et ancillas, ingenuos et ingenuas*"; ibid., no. xcvi: Isitia gives half the same alod "*et liberos ingenuasque servos et ancillas huc illucque diffusos*"; R. de Lespinasse, *Cartulaire du prieuré de La Charité-sur-Loire*, no. xxix (1089-1108; cf. no. xxxii): sale of two lands "*et servos et ancillas et liberos.*" Similar examples for the Frankish period are well known. Cf. for Italy P. Vaccari, *Ricerche di storia giuridica*, I: *Il colonato Romano et l'invasione longobarda*, pp. 5-6.

⁴³ J. Petot, "L'hommage servile," in *Revue historique du droit*, 1927, p. 68, n. 1.

⁴⁴ Example, for a culvert, "Livre noir de Saint-Florent de Saumur," Bibl. Nat., nouv. acq. lat. 1930, fol. 134: the knight Geoffroi le Fort sells "*collibertam quamdam nomine Richildem et omnes res ejus totamque substantiam.*"

⁴⁵ Ch. Métais, *Cartulaire de l'abbaye ... de la Trinité de Vendôme*, I, no. clxxiii (1060-1064): "*Aliorum collibertos, quos de terra nostra effugavimus, ne nobis de eorum aedificiis malum aut poena contra ipsorum dominos surgat, ille, nolentibus nobis, ibi esse et aedificare compellit, nec ob aliud aliquod nisi ut nobis semper adversetur in omnibus.*"

⁴⁶ A notice in *Liber de servis Majoris Monasterii*, no. lxv, shows a fugitive culvert who became the monks's shepherd; the monks finally purchased him from his seigneur; the complaint was more that he had attempted to escape servitude than that he had left.

⁴⁷ J.-B. Champeval, *Cartulaire de l'abbaye d'Uzerche*, no. 1007 (1097-1108); cf. no. 481.

⁴⁸ I have discussed this question concerning serfs, and gathered together a few examples in *Revue historique du droit*, 1928, pp. 60-63.

⁴⁹ For this definition of fief, see the article on ministeriality. In addition to the example of the fief of provost Geoffroi cited below in the text, one finds in Mayenne Guérin le Prudhomme, in possession of a *casamentum* (*chasement*), a word that is in general taken as the synonym for fief (see below note 100).

⁵⁰ This incident is based on a notice published by B. de Broussillon, *Cartulaire de l'abbaye de Saint-Aubin d'Angers*, II, no. ccccxxx (30 November 1113).

⁵¹ The argument based on the lateness of the request is expressly given in the notice as having served as the basis for the judgment of the monks's court against Maurice's request. The other argument is based on the manner in which the enfranchisement of the two daughters of the provost is presented in the same text (p. 38): "*Libere facte ac per hoc a rebus patris sui Godefredi funditus separate.*"

⁵² E. Mabille, *Cartulaire de Marmoutier pour le Dunois*, no. XVII; *Liber de servis*, no. lxxvi.

⁵³ P. 38: "*Quia non poterat esse ingenuus quamdiu fiscum coliberti possideret.*" *Fiscus* is a translation or a pedantic transcription of fief; there are numerous examples of this in contemporary texts. At the head of Marchegay's edition of this notice in *Bibl. de l'Ecole des Chartes*, 1856, p. 424, are the following two phrases: "*Non potest quis esse ingenuus quamdiu fiscum colliberti possideret. Si quis fiscum colliberti possedisset, etiam servitutis dedecus indueret.*" I first believed these to

be a contemporary rubric, and I believe others thought so too. But Mr. Saché, archivist of the Maine-et-Loire, has been kind enough to let me know that the original (H 51, fol. 3) does not carry the two phrases. These words were apparently added as a kind of title by Marchegay himself. In any case they are not found in B. de Broussillon's edition.

[54] The passage from this practice to a notion of servile land is shown with particular clarity in two texts regarding lands called "Eighths" (*Octave*), located near Etampes, in the king's seigneurie. The first—a diploma from Louis VII, dating from 1158 (E. Menault, *Morigny*, p. justif. p. 157)—recounts that these lands, customarily reserved to the king's serfs, having been occupied by several persons who were not of servile status (in particular by the monks of Morigny) were seized by royal officers. The second text, a customary charter from Etampes dated 1179, 1 April to the beginning of August (*Ordonn.* XI, p. 211; cf. Cartellieri, *Philipp-August*, I, p. 60, no. 45), declaring henceforth licit to anyone the purchase of these same lands, adds "*nec ob hoc emptor servus noste efficiatur.*" In fact in 1158 the freedom of the occupiers had not been menaced; they simply were evicted. It is by error that Olivier Martin, *Histoire de la coutume de Paris*, I, p. 144, n. 1, cites, next to texts regarding the *Octave*, the text no. 167 in J. Depoin, *Chartes de l'abbaye de Saint-Martin-des-Champs*; this document does not mention serfdom.

[55] As is the case in the two decrees cited above, note 52. For the first, cf. *Cartulaire pour le Dunois*, nos. xiii and xv. Notice no. lxxvi of the *Liber de servis* contains a particularly clear declaration: "*Otbertus . . . tenuit quamdam terram . . . propter quam etiam ipse erat servus Sancti Martini*"; but this declaration has for sole object to explain the necessity of the daughter of the mayor Aubert to divest herself of this land if she wants to be enfranchised. Also compare the following incident recounted in a notice published by L. Halphen in *Le comté d'Anjou*, p. justif. no. 6 (8 August 1011 to 8 April 1013): Ferri, abbot of Saint-Florent of Saumur marries his niece, a serf of Saint-Maurice of Angers, to a serf of Saint-Florent who, charged with the administration of the village of [Saint-Martin de] la Place, held a fief (*casamentum*) from the monks; the two communities divided the children in such a way that the mayor's fief remained in the hands of those of his sons who belonged to Saint-Florent.

[56] A notice from the Cartulary of Saint-Pierre of Vierzon, Bibl. Nat., lat. 9865, fol. 24 ro., relates how under Abbot Humbauld (ca. 1082-ca. 1095) Eude des Champs gave to Saint-Pierre three culverts with their born and unborn posterity: "*Cum terra colibertina, casa, casualibus videlicet duobus et nemusculis circumpositis et pratis et terra culta et inculta que omnia ipsi possident*" (emphasis added). (Cf. also the reference to this gift in another notice, fol. 2 vo.) I do not think we need to give any precise juridical meaning to the adjective *colibertina*; it simply means the culverts's land.

[57] Cf. Marc Bloch, *Rois et Serfs*, p. 22, n. 2.

[58] Bertrand de Broussillon, *Cartulaire de l'abbaye de Saint-Aubin d'Angers*, no. ccxxi (1080-1082), p. 265: "*Sanguinem de hominibus familie Sancti Albini et de colibertis ejus nunquam habebit dominus castelli Mosterioli.*" I do not know whether here *familia* designates the whole of the serfs of just the group of sergeants. The word is used in this second sense, clearly explained, in a judgment by Eude de Blois, cited below, note 59, regarding a rule of similar nature.

[59] "Livre noir de Saint-Florent," Bibl. Nat., nouv. acq. lat. 1930, fol. 97 (1062, reign of Philippe I): "*Excipiuntur vero servi et colliberti eorum qui tantum a priore monasterii sive abbate de quacunque re justificabuntur.*" The agreement concluded, under Eude [de Blois] and Abbot Robert (995 or 998 to August 1011), between the same monastery and one Gédouin (*ibid.*, fol. 27 vo.) is somewhat different. Gédouin and the monks will hold common courts for cases of theft, kidnapping, arson, murder, assault when the crime is committed (1) by (free?) men of the seigneurie of Saint-Florent upon men of other seigneuries; (2) by culverts of

Saint-Florent either on men of other condition on the same seigneurie or on all men, whatever their condition, from other seigneurie; however if the crime is committed within either of the two groups, then Gédouin cannot participate in the judgment. The same spirit is found in a decision of the court of Eude de Blois as count of Tours rendered between 1015 and 1023 (L. Lex, *Eudes, comte de Blois*, p. 143, no. xiii.) In case of kidnapping, arson, unauthorized departure, and theft, the *voyer* Tiais who as a general rule held jurisdiction over such acts on one of the lands of Marmoutier, does not, as an exception, judge over the monks's culverts if the crime is committed between men of this condition, but does hold jurisdiction if one of the parties is a free man. Only the *familia*, made up of the free men and culverts who are charged with the *ministeria* of the religious and receive from them goods and clothing, completely escapes the voyer's jurisdiction.

[60] L. de Kersers, *Essai de reconstitution du Cartulaire A de Saint-Sulpice de Bourges*, no. lxxii (July 1064).

[61] Ch. Métais, *Cartulaire de l'abbaye ... de la Trinité de Vendôme*, I, no. ccii ("before 1070"): "*Martinus idem superposuit altari hanc cartam, oblatis in testimonio IVor denariis, quod servilis est conditionis.*" There were other forms for the servile testimonial: a ceremony recalling the symbolism of the rope; perhaps also in some exceptional cases a true homage from the hand and from the mouth; cf. Petot, "L'hommage servile," in *Revue historique du droit*, 1927.

[62] I am borrowing this expression from four notices regarding culverts from the "Livre noir de Saint-Florent de Saumur," Bibl. Nat., nouv. acq. lat. 1930, fol. 22, 127 vo, 130 vo, 132 vo. Cf. P. Marchegay, *Chartes poitevines de Saint-Florent*, no. viii.

[63] Urseau, *Cartulaire noir de la cathédrale d'Angers*, no. lxxxiii (1103-1110): "*In conspectu Rainaldi episcopi junioris se colibertum sancti Mauricii esse professus est et quatuor denarios in signum professionis in manu episcopi posuit.*" Cf. also, as particularly characteristic, a notice from the eleventh century regarding the family of Gibert, mayor of Saint-Michel-de-Beauvais in Marisel: Guérard, *Polyptyque d'Irminon*, App. no. xxxviii, and V. Leblond, in *Mem. Soc. Acad. de l'Oise*, XXIV (1), p. 11.

[64] R. de Lespinasse, *Cartulaire de Saint-Cyr de Nevers*, no. 83.

[65] *Homo de capite* is used as a synonym for *collibertus* in several documents: see in particular B. de Broussillon, *Cartulaire de ... Saint-Aubin d'Angers*, II, no. ccccxx; the decree regarding the knight Alon, above, note 29; the Beauvais notice, below, note 66. An Orléans formula, preserved in six mss. (cf. above, note 7) concerns the enfranchisement of a man (at times called *servum*) from all *debito collibertatis servicii* or *colibertilis servicii*; one of the mss.—written between 1251 and 1270—gives the formula the title: *De quitatione cavagii* (L. Wahrmund, *Quellen zur Geschichte des römisch-kanonischen Processes*, I, 3, p. 62, . ccviii).

[66] Guérard, *Polyptyque d'Irminon*, App. no. xxxviii, and V. Leblond, in *Mém. Soc. Acad. de l'Oise*, XXIV (1), p. 11. The word *coliberta* is only uttered regarding one of the women of this family; only the charges weighing on the others are mentioned: *chevage, formariage, mainmorte*. No doubt they were all of the same condition.

[67] Ch. Métais, *Cartulaire de l'abbaye ... de la Trinité de Vendôme*, II, no. cccxxii (1066-1085); the monks secured "*quatinus loco isto concederet ancillam et servo indulgeret culpam.*"

[68] Urseau, *Cartulaire noir de la cathédrale d'Angers*, no. lxxxiii (1103-1110). If one is to believe a decree from Philippe I, apparently inspired by the monks of Saint-Benoît-sur-Loire (*Recueil*, no. 147), this monastery enjoyed, according to the Gâtinais custom, a singular privilege: when one of its "women" married a man—in this case a culvert—belonging to another seigneur, the latter lost all claims on the children issuing from this union. However, since, as in the case considered by the decree, the consent of the concerned seigneur had to be purchased for forty sous,

one can believe that this custom was not universally recognized. The monks of Saint-Florent of Saumur, also arguing this was the "custom of the country," had similar pretensions regarding their serfs, and they seemed not to have had any more success than the other monastery. (L. Halphen, *Le comté d'Anjou*, p. justif. no. 6, 8 August 1011 through 8 April 1013). Between 1032 and 1060 Archembaud II de Bourbon and the priory of Saint-Léopoldin came to an agreement regulating intermariages between their serfs and their culverts: L. de Kersers, *Essai de reconstitution du Cartulaire A de Saint-Sulpice de Bourges*, no. cxxv (cf. M. Fazy, *Catalogue des actes concernant l'histoire du Bourbonnais*, no. 114).

[69] There are numerous definitions in the jurisprudence and the charters beginning in the thirteenth century: cf. *Rois et serfs*, pp. 30 ff; "The Transformation of Serfdom," p. 156; F. Autorde, "Le servage dans la Marche," in *Mémoires de la Société des sciences naturelles de la Creuse*, 2e série, II (1891-1892). Among the customaries, one of the most characteristic is *Ancien coutumier de Champagne*, c., lx; among the unpublished diplomatic texts, see two charters from Saint-Germain-des-Prés of June 1225 (Arch. Nat., L. 806, no. 48) and of June 1251 (L. 809, no. 50). In the documents from the Paris region in the thirteenth century one sometimes witnesses enfranchised serfs forego the inheritance from their "consanguins" (half-brothers or sisters on the father's side) who remained in servitude (for example, the general manumission of Orly, May 1263, Guérard, *Cartulaire de Notre-Dame de Paris*, II, p. 5). Is this the renunciation of one share in a family community, a precaution born from uncertainty about the law or from the notaries's taste for even the most useless renunciations? I do not know.

[70] There are good examples of this in K. Weimann, *Die Ministerialität im späteren Mittelalter*, p. 24.

[71] Guiman, *Cartulaire de Saint-Vaast d'Arras*, ed. by Van Drival, pp. 178, 258, 362 (under the word mainmorte).

[72] Here and there in Germanic countries, one can come across the outline of rules similar to that of French mainmorte; see for example, B. Poll, *Das Heimfallsrecht auf den Grundherrschaften Oesterreichs*, p. 28. But the institution never achieved full development there.

[73] Guérard, *Polyptyque*, App. no. xxxviii, and V. Leblond, in *Mém. Soc. Acad. de l'Oise*, XXIV (1), p. 11; cf. above, note 7. It is incredible to read in Boissonnade's *Le travail dans l'Europe chrétienne au Moyen Age*, p. 170: "The *colliberts* . . . whose families could not be split up and who probably were exempted from the rights of formariage and of mainmorte."

[74] B. de Broussillon, *Cartulaire de l'abbaye de Saint-Aubin d'Angers*, I, no. clxxxiii (1000-1027): a lady called Alsent gives to Saint-Aubin a culvert; this latter will, however, have to abandon to her donor "*omnia quae ei pater suus de ipsa hereditate dederat, id est terram, aquas, medietatem domui suae*" (note the use of the dowry, correlative to the rights to the inheritance); L. Rédet, *Cartulaire . . . de Saint-Nicolas de Poitiers*, no. I (ca. 1050), p. 6: "*Unum colibertum cum ipsa sua hereditate*"; "Livre noir de Saint-Florent de Saumur," Bibl. Nat., nouv. acq. lat. 1930, fol. 38 vo (abbatiate of Ferri, 1 September 1022 to 28 September 1055): "*hereditatem duorum colibertorum*"; C. Chevalier, *Cartulaire . . . de Noyers*, no. cccxi: gift of three culverts, each with their *hereditas*.

[75] No. cciii. The meaning of the words *frerage*, *freresche*, and the like, is well-known; see in particular the *Diss*. III of Du Cange.

[76] A notice of 29 November 1096 published in Urseau, *Cartulaire noir de la cathédrale d'Angers*, no. lxviii, concerning the inheritance of two culverts of the bishop of Angers who had ceded their succession to the canons; unfortunately, except for the Latin rubric, this text is known only through a bad translation dating from the eighteenth century. The inheritance was claimed by two collaterals ("parents" according to the translator); the chapter kept it, but, following the usages of the time, was obligated to purchase their adversaries' disinterest. The absence

of any regular justice robbed the law of any permanence; rules were recognized in principle, but the absence of any authority capable of enforcement made them rarely applicable in practice.

[77] Here are the rules of servile inheritance in the eleventh century, taken from documents from Marmoutier or from neighboring abbeys. (a) The children receive the inheritance (notably *Liber de Servis*, App. no. xxiv, and a curious notice in the *Cartulaire de Noyers*, no. cccl, where a serf, first provided for by the monks as a stableman, then, once adult, given for life a small land as a salary for his office, receives, on the occasion of his marriage, his tenure *in perpetuam hereditatem*; cf. also, in texts from the Berri dating from the same period, on the use of the word *heres* to designate the free or serf tenant, the wise remarks of E. Chénon, *Histoire et coutumes du prieuré de La Chapelle-Aude*, p. 16). (b) The brother is excluded from the inheritance, but the monks readily give him a right of preemption if they sell the inheritance (*Liber de servis*, App. no. xl). (c) The serf, even if he has children, can dispose, in favor of his seigneur the monastery, as a pious gift, of an undetermined portion of his estate (*ibid.*, App. no. xxi). This last rule seems to have been applied to the culvert also; this is no doubt how one can explain a notice from the "Livre noir de Saint-Florent" (Bibl. Nat., nouv. acq. lat. 1930, fol. 137 vo.) in which the culvert Létard, who has sons and daughters, promises to give to Saint-Florent "*quicquid in fine suo possessurus esset.*" Cf. also Kersers, *Essai de reconstitution du cartulaire A de Saint-Sulpice de Bourges*, no. lxxii, p. 153.

[78] The case in which the brother receives a right of preemption (see note 179, *Liber de Servis*, App. no. xl, 1095), does not concern a rural exploitation or peasants, but a house, probably in Tours, and a fisherman's family.

[79] *Rois et serfs*, p. 33 and the chapter on the collectors of mainmortes.

[80] And by other characteristics also: cf. Olivier-Martin, *Histoire de la coutume de Paris*, I, p. 152.

[81] In the second charter from Saint-Germain-des-Prés cited above in note 69, the presence of a compromise with the *foris familiata* daughter of a serf shows at least that the definition of *foris familiatio* was not without some difficulties.

[82] Hardouin, *Coll. Conciliorum*, VI, col. 850, c. ix, and col. 879, D: "*Similiter nullus servorum vel collibertum amodo clericus fiat, nisi prius libertatem de dominis suis habuerit ab idoneis testibus.*"

[83] *Decretum Gratiani*, Dist. LIV, c. xii.

[84] C. Chevalier, *Cartulaire de l'abbaye de Noyers*, no. xv.

[85] A. Cauvin, *Chartularium insignis ecclesie Cenomanensis*, no. cxvi, and R. Charles and S. Menjot d'Elbenne, *Cartulaire de Saint-Vincent du Mans*, no. 87. The decree, which includes the general account of the differences between the chapter and the abbey, registers the canons's waver of this indemnity. Cf. a very similar incident concerning a serf, Guérard, *Cartulaire de Notre-Dame de Paris*, III, p. 356, no. ix.

[86] See, for example, L. Rédet, *Documents pour l'histoire de ... Saint-Hilaire de Poitiers*, nos. lxxxiii, xc: two enfranchisement decrees almost literally identical, the first for a serf, the second for a culvert.

[87] Enfranchisement of Lambert Fantin by Hugue Mange-Breton; the first phrase of the preamble has been cited above, note 28. It continues as follows: "*Qui autem servus seu colibertus est, si sibi libertatem a domino suo vindicare potest ut ea magis uti velit apostolus monet. Qui vero libertate seculari ab ipso genio fulget et servuum aut colibertum sibi subditum habet, magnum pietatis opus et elemosine exercet, si hunc a deprimente conditione liberum reddendo erigat, quatinus in filiorum Dei vera et perpetua libertate connumerari valeat.*" See another preamble with two endings: Ch. Métais, *Cartulaire de l'abbaye ... de la Trinité de Vendôme*, I, no. clxix.

[88] Bibl. Nat., lat. 1093, fol. 72 vo.; 8653, fol. 25 vo.; 15170, fol. 20; University

of Leipzig, 350, fol. 132 vo. Cf. L. Delisle in *Annuaire-Bulletin de la Soc. de l'hist. de France*, 1869, p. 142; B. Stehle, *Ueber ein Hildesheimer Formelbuch*, Diss. Strasbourg, 1878.

[89] Donaueschinger Fürstliche Bibliothek, ms. 910, fol. 10 vo. Cf. A. Cartellieri, *Ein Donaueschinger Briefsteller*.

[90] "Cartulaire de Solignac," Bibl. Nat., lat. 18363, fol. 17 ro. (abbatiate of Robert: 1090 at the earliest to 1100 at the latest).

[91] Cf. note 41: "*Pater meus franchisaverat eum et ob hoc fecit sibi carcerem lapideum juxta portam castri mei situm.*"

[92] I already have noted the existence of this practice in *Rois et Serfs*, pp. 41-42. M. Petit, *Colliberti ou Culverts*, pp. 41 ff. has since independently confirmed this, supporting his observation with some valuable citations. Cf. also Vanderkindere, "Les tributaires ou serfs d'église," in *Académie de Belgique. Bull. de la classe des Lettres*, 1897, pp. 413-414.

[93] The preamble was cited above, notes 32 and 87. Here is what follows: "*Ego igitur Hugo nomine, Manduca Britonem dictus cognomine, hujus vere salutis ac libertatis amore, hominem quendam vocabulo Lambertum, cognomento Fantinum, pro salute anime proprie parentumque meorum et uxoris mee Hersendis ab omni colibertatis jugo, quo huc usque ligatum tenui, absolutum facio et a propria potestate et dominio in servorum Dei potestatem et dominium abbatis scilicet cenobii Sancti Florentii et monachorum jure perpetuo trado, et non hunc solum, verum etiam sobolem omnem per consanguinitatis lineam ab eo processuram similiter habendam concedo.*" The mention of the price paid follows, in the cartulary, the validating marks; apparently it was not part of the original decree. An enfranchising decree granted by two seigneurs to their culvert Hailde is kept in the archives of the priory of Lavardin (to be found now in the Archives of the Loir-et-Cher) and has been published in the *Liber de servis*, App. no. xlix, and by Ch. Métais, *Cartulaire blésois de Marmoutier*, no. cxxviii (29 July 1108-1125). The latter editor notes an endorsement on the back of the document as follows: "*Hec littera facit mentionem de quadam colliberta nobis donata.*" However, this endorsement, as the archivist of the Loir-et-Cher kindly let me know, is, according to the paleographic evidence, anterior to the fourteenth century; it has, therefore, little authority.

[94] *Liber de servis*, no. xliii (1053-1061): "*Qui colibertus, ut a Deo vera mereretur libertate donari, semetipsum pro ejus amore Sancto Martino in servum tali pacto tradidit, ut non solum ipse verum etiam omnis ejus posteritas per succedentia secula abbatibus hujus loci et caeteris fratribus servili conditione subjaceat et famuletur. Et ut haec ejus spontanea traditio certior et ab ipso facta appareret, IIIor denarios, ut est consuetudinis, super caput proprium posuit, et sic se Deo Sanctoque Martino perpetuo serviendum obtulit.*" On the word servus used in this notice, see above, note 56.

[95] Cf. L. Halphen, "L'histoire de Maillezais du moine Pierre," in *Revue Historique*, XCIX (1908).

[96] Arcère, *Histoire de La Rochelle*, II, p. 663.

[97] It is very unwise to conclude from this "intractability" that these people were "surely of free condition," as does Petit, *Colliberti ou Culverts*, p. 11. There were many servile revolts in the Middle Ages.

[98] "*Qualiter fuit constructum Malleacense monasterium*," I, 1 (Migne, *Patrol. lat.*, CXLVI, col. 1249-1250; I have collated it with the unique ms., Bibl. Nat., lat. 4892, fol. 246): "*In extremis quoque insule unde agitur, supra Separis alveum, quoddam genus hominum piscando queritans victum, nonnulla tuguria confecerat, quod a majoribus collibertorum vocabulum contraxerat. Quod nomen quanquam quedam servorum portio sortita sit, videtur tamen quod in istis conditione aliqua derivatum sit. Unde quoniam adest occasio, ipsius vocabuli perscrutetur interpretatio. Etenim* collibertus *a cultu imbrium descendere putatur ab aliquibus. Progenies autem istorum collibertorum hinc forte istud ore vulgi, multa interdum ex usibus*

rerum vera dicentis, contraxit vocabulum quoniam, ubi inundantia pluviarum Separis excrescere fecisset fluvium, relictis quibus incolebant locis, hinc enim procul habitabant nonnulli, properabant illo causa piscium. Sive ergo sit hoc aut aliud aliquid, hoc unum de illis fertur quod sint et ira leves, et pene implacabiles, inmites, crudeles, increduli, et indociles et omnis prope modum humanitatis expertes. Aquilonalis certe gens, Normanni videlicet... prephatum flumen quam sepe solita erat introire ac quoscunque poterat bonis omnibus nudatos neci dabat. Horum gladio collibertorum post non minimam suorum stragem deleta cantatur maxima multitudo." For *cultu imbrium,* I follow the interpretation (slightly different in form) given by A. Petit, *Coliberti ou Culverts,* p. 5; the standard translation ("the cult of rains") introduces a religious connotation that I do not believe can be found in the text.

[99] *Etudes sur l'état économique,* p. 215.

[100] Above, note 41. He may also have been at the same time seignorial officer: the land he possessed in Mayenne between the church and the river and which he ceded to the monks of Marmoutier was called a *casamentum* ("chasement" or fief).

[101] C. Chevalier, *Cartulaire de l'abbaye de Noyers,* no. clxviii (a clear case of hereditary profession: a blacksmith son of a blacksmith); also, no doubt, Marchegay, *Cartulaire de Saint-Maur-sur-Loire,* no. xlvii.

[102] *Liber de servis,* no. lx; Ch. Métais, *Cartulaire de l'abbaye ... de la Trinité de Vendôme,* I, no. ccliii.

[103] Ch. Métais, *Cartulaire de l'abbaye ... de la Trinité de Vendôme,* no. ccxix.

[104] *Liber de servis,* no. xcvii; Montégut, *Cartulaire de Viegeois,* no. cxlvi.

[105] "Livre noir de Saint-Florent de Saumur," Bibl. Nat., nouv. acqu. lat. 1930, fol. 137 vo. (L. Halphen, *Le comté d'Anjou,* Catal., no. 213).

[106] *Liber de servis,* no. lv; C. Chevalier, *Cartulaire de l'abbaye de Noyers,* no. cccxxix; cf. no. xv; P. Marchegay, "Cartulaire de Notre-Dame du Ronceray," in *Arch. d'Anjou,* III, no. ccxix; J. de Font-Réaulx, "Sancti Stephani Lemovicensis cartularium," (*Bull. soc. hist. Limousin,* LXIX), nos. xxxi, xxxii, li.

[107] *Gallia Christiana,* XIV, Inst., p. 71, no. lii.

[108] *Liber de servis,* App. no. iii; Th. Grasilier, *Cartulaire de l'abbaye ... de Notre-Dame de Saintes,* no. liii.

[109] B. de Broussillon, *Cartulaire ... de Saint-Aubin d'Angers,* I, no. cclxxi; Urseau, *Cartulaire noir de la cathédrale d'Angers,* no. lxxx (L. Halphen, *Le comté d'Anjou,* catal., no. 54). The existence of the seigneurial duty of laundryman is attested to by other documents: see, for example, H. Pirenne, *Le livre de l'abbé Guillaume de Ryckel,* in the table under the ord *lautor,* and E. Lodge, "Serfdom in the Pyrenees," in *Viertelj. für Soz. und Wirtschaftgesch.,* III (1905), p. 29, n. 6.

[110] *Liber de servis,* no. lxv and no doubt no. vii. The fisherman (*arte piscatorem*) of the *Liber de servis,* no. xvi (L. Halphen, *Le comté d'Anjou,* Catal., no. 160) and the one in the appendix to the same collection, no. lx, to whom is given a house formerly owned by a cook of the monk, were both in the monks's service. It is always difficult to distinguish artisans from true sergeants.

[111] *Liber de servis,* no. xxviii.

[112] *Liber de servis,* no. xliii: "*Quendam ... colibertum ... filium Gausberti, vicarii de Monte Laudiaco.*"

[113] *Liber de servis,* App. no. xxxiii; the same decree in J. Bourassé, *Cartulaire de Cormery,* no. xlviii, and the texts cited above, note 50, (Saint-Aubin of Angers); below, note 117 (Saint-Vincent of Le Mans).

[114] Notice regarding Saint-Michel of Beauvais in Guérard, *Polyptyque d'Irminon,* App. no. xxxviii; also *Mém. Soc. Acad. de l'Oise,* XXIV (1); it concerns Gibert, mayor of Marisel.

[115] See p. 102.

[116] See p. 96 and n. 29.

[117] R. Charles and S. Menjot d'Elbenne, *Cartulaire de Saint-Vincent du Mans*, no. 309.

[118] *Ibid.*, nos. 307, 308, 310.

[119] See the story of the provost Geoffroi, above p. 102. Decrees of exchanges of serfs in order to allow marriages between serfs of different seigneuries regard families of ministeriales for the most part, as late as the first half of the thirteenth century, at least in the Ile-de-France, a region where I believe I have seen all of them.

[120] "*Quid sit collibertus. Ille collibertus vocatur qui ante mancipium et servus fuit et postea causa devotionis a domino suo ad aliquem privatum locum, id est ad episcopatum vel ad monasterium sive ad aliquam consecratam ecclesiam pro redemptione peccaminum suorum libertati ecclesiastice donatur, non ut ex toto sit vel privatus sicut liberti, set sub jure ecclesiastice familie conditionaliter servitio divino sit mancipatus, quam conditionem nullo modo ausus sit transgredi. Verbi gratia: si habeo servum, servit mihi sicut proprius et non est libertus neque collibertus. At si ego ad sancti alicujus altare illum pro anima mea tradidero, ut aut singulis annis censum a me constitutum persolvat, aut cotidianum servitium per semetipsum reddat, jam postea non erit servus meus, set collibertus, id est ejusdem libertatis mecum est secundum spem, quoniam ego sum servus Dei et illius sancti, cui illum tradidi.*" This text, first published by B. J. Docen in *Archiv. für Geographie, Historie, Staats- und Kriegskunst*, 1822, p. 147, was then rediscovered by Lamprecht who thought it unpublished and published it on several occasions: *Zeitschrift für Rechtsgeschichte*, XIII (1878), p. 507; *Französische Wirtschaftsgeschichte*, p. 151; *Etudes sur l'état économique*, p. 215, n. 2; it has been reproduced in *Bibliothèque de l'Ecole des Chartes*, 1878, p. 584. The site of composition of the ms. (it belonged at one time to Saint-Emmeran of Ratisbonne) is unknown. The term *privatus*, repeated twice (*privatum locum*; *liber sit vel privatus*) presents a difficulty; must one read, as my colleague Le Bras suggests, *pium locum* in the first case?

[121] See the notice in *Liber de servis* of Marmoutier cited above, note 94 (avowal of culvertage "*qui* colibertus, *ut a Deo vera mereretur libertate donari* ... "). In 1178, Nivelon, bishop of Soissons, stated (G. Robert, "Les serfs de Saint-Remi de Reims," in *Travaux de l'Académie nationale de Reims*, CXL, no. xiv): "*Homines autem qui a seculari potestate et dominio ad jus et dominium ecclesie transeunt quasi liberi sunt, videlicet a scorpionibus quibus secularis dominatio illos prius cedebat.*" This is not the place to renew an old and idle controversy by wondering whether it was really "good" to "live under the cross"—a problem already given different answers by Abélard and Pierre le Vénérable in the twelfth century (Vacandard, *Vie de saint Bernard*, I, 4th ed., p. 432, n. 1); but it must be noted that, as evident in some decrees, culverts sometimes requested to be placed under the dependence of a religious establishment from that of a lay seigneur: Ch. Métais, *Cartulaire ... de la Trinité de Vendôme*, I, nos. civ, ccviii. Cf. for serfs, *Liber de servis*, no. lxiii; de Lépinois and Merlet, *Cartulaire de Notre-Dame de Chartres*, I, no. cxxiii.

[122] M. Prou, *Recueil des actes de Philippe Ier*, no. 63.

[123] Decrees of donation of culverts to churches by lay seigneurs, notices or charters telling of lay claims upon culverts, or in any way mentioning culverts dependent upon lay persons are too numerous to cite here. See, as an example, how clearly one Ferri expresses himself in a Chartres charter, as he is giving two culverts to the monks of Saint-Père: "*ut ab hac die sint colliberti sancti Petri sicut sunt mei*" (Guérard, *Cartulaire de Saint-Père de Chartres*, II, p. 296, no. xl).

[124] See below, note 135 regarding a text from the *Coutume de Touraine-Anjou* used by M. Petit to support his thesis.

[125] Above, notes 41 and 100.

[126] *Liber de servis*, App. no. lv. Charter no. cccxxxii of the *Cartulaire de Vigeois* dates from the abbatiate of Adémar, that is from 1124 to 1164.

[127] M. Prou, *Recueil des actes de Philippe Ier*, no. 156.

[128] A. Luchaire, *Louis VI le Gros*, no. 292; E. Menault, *Morigny*, p. justif. p. 26.

[129] For example, Marchegay, "Cartulaire de Notre-Dame du Ronceray," *Arch. d'Anjou*, III, no. cccxci (under count Foulque de Vendôme or Count Geoffroi Martel or Geoffroi le Barbu [of Anjou], i.e., 1050 to April 1068); "Livre noir de Saint-Florent," Bibl. Nat., nouv. acq. lat. 1930, fol. 137 vo. (Halphen, *Le comté d'Anjou*, Catal. no. 213) (1068); A. de Trémault, *Cartulaire de Marmoutier pour le Vendômois*, no. cxv (same as *Liber de servis*, App. no. ix) (1066-1075); L. Rédet, *Cartulaire ... de Saint-Cyprien de Poitiers*, no. 200 (1073-1100); Urseau, *Cartulaire noir de la cathédrale d'Angers*, no. cxi (31 May 1116); C. Chevalier, *Cartulaire de ... Noyers*, no. cdlxxxvi (?1132-?1149).

[130] Bibl. Nat., lat. 15170, fol. 20: "*Ego B. de tali loco servum meum B. nomine ... nunc et semper ab omni debito collibertatis servicii relaxavi.*" The same formula with a few variations of no interest here is given in Bibl. Nat., lat. 8653, fol. 25, and by four other mss. that do not include *servum meum*: Bibl. Nat., lat. 1093, fol. 72; Donaueschinger Fürstliche Bibl. 910, fol. 42 vo.; Leipzig Univ. Libr., 350, fol. 132 vo.; and Bibl. Nat., lat. 4604, edited by L. Wahrmund, *Quellen zur Geschichte des römisch-Kanonischen Processes*, I, 3, p. 62, c. ccviii. The Leipzig ms, although it does not include *servum* in the text, has for title *Testamentum de libertate cujusdam servi et sue progeniei*.

[131] Examples for the first type: *Codex argenteus* of Saint-Père of Chartres, (beginning of the twelfth century) in Guérard, *Cartulaire de l'abbaye de Saint-Père de Chartres*, II, p. 295, no. xl; Cartulary of the Trinité of Vendôme (end of the eleventh century) in Ch. Métais, *Cartulaire ... de Vendôme*, II, no. cccxx; *Liber de servis* (beginning of the twelfth century), no. lxv. Examples for the second type: Cartulary from Saint-Père of Chartres known as the *Aganon vetus* (around 1100) in Guérard, *Cartulaire ... de Saint-Père*, I, p. 158, no. xxxi; p. 159, no. xxxii (the rubric of the first of these two decrees in the *Codex argenteus*, Bibl. Nat., lat. 10101, fol. 12, is, on the contrary, exact); Métais, *Cartulaire ... de la Trinité de Vendôme*, I, no. ccxxii.

[132] C. Chevalier, *Cartulaire de ... Noyers*, no. ccxciv: "*Medietatem filiorum ejus habeat Rotbertus, si per judicium legalium virorum eos adquirere potuerit.*" The notice is not dated; it is part of a group of decrees regarding the abbatiate of Etienne (?1080-?1111). At the same time the monks acknowledged the right of their serf's wife to collect upon his death half of his estate (apparently in perpetuity, as a dowry); this they did in an absolute manner, without any necessity to have this universally recognized rule subjected to the scrutiny of the *legales viri*.

[133] Bloch, "Serfs de la glèbe," pp. 181 ff.

[134] *Rois et serfs*, pp. 80-82.

[135] Beautemps-Beaupré, *Coutumes et institutions de l'Anjou et du Maine*, 1ere partie, vol. I, p. 126, no. 105; cf. Viollet, *Etablissements de saint Louis*, III, p. 58, c. 89, and vol. IV, p. 68, n. 101. The passage must be compared with art. 96 (Viollet, art. 80); cf. R. Caillemer, *Confiscation et administration des successions par les pouvoirs publics au Moyen Age*, p. 149. Art. 96 states that the movables of the *aubain* who has not performed "seigneurage" go to the baron, unless the aubain had paid four deniers ("*n'aüst comandé a randre IIII. d.*") to the baron. Caillemer translates this as "if ... he does not bequeath four deniers to the baron." Such a small bequest seems hardly sufficient to stop the confiscation. Rather, it seems more natural to believe that custom gave the aubain, who had acknowledge his obligation to pay the chevage but died before he could carry this out, the benefit of the doubt. Petit (p. 7) has naturally tried to exploit art. 105 to support his thesis. I believe my interpretation to be simpler. The aubain is called "culvert" because he pays the servile chevage; he is culvert of the baron whose lands he inhabits, not, as Petit has it, of his original seigneur. On the chevage of aubains,

see a curious text, rewritten in the thirteenth century or later, in Prou, *Recueil des actes de Philippe Ier*, no. xxviii.

[136] I, 1, 4 (*Dig.*, I, 1, 4); I, 8, 2 (*Dig.*, I, 5, 5); III, 7 (*Dig.*, IV, 2, 4); X, 9, 2 (*Decret.*, IV, 9, 2); X, 9, 4 (*Decret.*, IV, 9, 10). Following a usage found elsewhere and for which I have tried to give some reasons ("Serf de la glèbe," p. 191, n. 49) it happens that the *Livre de Jostice et de Plet* translates *libertus* by *serf* (I, 19, 2, *Dig.*, I, 12, 1).

[137] X. 10. Another passage (II, 19, 7) that shows that the "couvert" (*sic*, probably a copyist's mistake) cannot be a lawyer without his seigneur's permission, does not appear to go back to a Latin model either.

[138] Archives of the Vienne, G. 1142: in 1260 the abbot and the chapter of Notre-Dame-la-Grande of Poitiers, against payment of sixty-eight sous and the increase of the taxes levied on the shelters and lands of the beneficiaries of the decree, remit to three men of Beaumont the "*consuetudinem seu prestacionem quatuor denariorum ad quos solvendos singulis annis nobis et ecclesie nostre tenebantur astricti sive illa consuetudo seu prestacio, costuma vel garda aut commenda et servitus aut cuvertisia seu quocunque alio nomine vel vocabulo censeretur sive de corpore seu quocunque modo aliter deberetur.*" *Ibid.*, C. 334: Recognition of the seigneur of Morthemer (Vienne, canton of Lussac-les-Châteaux), 13 January 1478. This seigneur levied a tax called *culvertistes* or *culvertisses* on both his own lands and on those of the bishop of Poitiers and of the abbess of the Trinité. I have been led to these two texts by a reference in Godefroy under the word *culvertise*.

[139] De Lépinois and Merlet, *Cartulaire de Notre-Dame de Chartres*, II, p. 281: "*Quod estis libere condicionis, nec estis colibertus nec filius coliberti.*" What indicates that the word is here taken in its general sense (= serf) and not as designating the culvertile condition as distinguished from serfdom is that the canon only swears that he is not a culvert; in the other case, he would have to say, as in the Council text cited above, note 82, culvert or serf. The word *collibertus* also appears in the vows of the canons of Le Mans known through a document dating from 1408 (Du Cange, *Glossarium*, at word *Colliberti*); but these are only pedantic enumeration of all kinds of real or fictitious conditions.

[140] "*Colliberti sui homines de corpore nuncupati.*" The bull is known only through an analysis—one that can surely be trusted—by dom Chazal: bibl. de la ville d'Orléans, ms. 490-491, p. 477. On the value of the works of dom Chazal, see Prou and Vidier, *Recueil des chartes de l'abbaye de Saint-Benoît-sur-Loire*, I, p. lxxxix; it is through a kind letter from MM. Prou and Vidier that I came to know of this document.

[141] Roger de Wendover, *Flores historiarum*, Hewlett, ed., II, p. 66; cf. *ibid.*, p. 65, where the same action in the same terms (but without any textual citation) is attributed to Philip-Augustus.

[142] J.-J. Hisely, "Monuments de l'histoire du comté de Gruyère" (*Mém. et doc. publiés par la Soc. d'histoire de la Suisse Romande*, XXII), no. 57: "nomine corporum ipsorum seu nomine obsequii coliberti"; and further: "coliberti servitii," "servitii coliberti." Culvertage as a condition is not documented for this region. J. J. Hisely, "Histoire du comté de Gruyère" (*ibid.*, IX), p. 202, does not know of any other example of the word colibertus in the documents he has consulted; this peculiarity of language would probably be explained if we knew who wrote the charter of 1264.

[143] Raimbert de Paris, *La chevalerie Ogier de Danemarche*, J. Barrois, ed., II, v. 1491-1492.

[144] F. Castets, ed., *La Chanson des quatre fils Aymon*, v. 8148-8149.

[145] Hélinant, *Les vers de la mort*, Fr. Wulff and Em. Walberg eds., st. XXXI, v. 8.

[146] Leroux de Lincy, *Recueil de chants historiques*, I, p. 218.

[147] I. Wrobel, *Corpus grammaticorum medii aevi*, I, cap. ix, v. 129 ff.: "*Libertate carens colibertus dicitur esse,—De servo factus liber libertus, at ille—Libertinus erit, quem libertus generabit.*" Evrard de Béthune appears to have lived in Anjou (cf. Wrobel, p. viii).

[148] V. 373, E. Höpffner and P. Alfaric eds.

[149] See the "Glossary" in the Bédier edition. Dom Carpentier in Du Cange, *Glossarium*, under the word *cuvertus*, points to the word used, apparently, in an insulting manner, in a judgment of the *Olim*, of 1269, that I have been unable to find.

[150] Queux de Saint-Hilaire edition, I, p. 241, no. cxx, v. 22.

[151] The key works are G. Salvioli, " 'Consortes e colliberti' secondo il diritto longobardo," in *Atti e Memorie della R. Deputazione di storia patria per le provincie Modenesi*, series III, vol. II (1883); Volpe, "Pisa e i lungobardi," in *Studi Storici*, X (1901), pp. 378, 392 ff.; N. Tamassia, "I colliberti nella storia di diritto italiano," in *Studi ... pubblicati in onore di V. Scialoja*, 1905; E. Besta, *La Sardegna medioevale*, II, pp. 59 ff.; A. Solmi, *Studi storici sulle istituzioni della Sardegna nel medio evo*, p. 68.

[152] U. Balzani, Ed., *Chronicon Farfense* (in the *Fonti per la storia d'Italia*), II, p. 272: "*In tantum Dei ecclesiam affligebant, ut* culvertas suas *mitterent que offertiones de manu presbyteri per vim distraherent, in quarum manibus qui offerebant osculum prebebant.*"

[153] Tola, *Codex diplomaticus Sardiniae*, p. 179, no. iv ("*de culvertis, scilicet de servis et ancillis*") and p. 199, no. xxvii.

[154] G. Bonazzi, *Il Condaghe di San Pietro di Silki*, no. 95: "*sa coliuerta mea, su servu.*"

[155] Yepes, *Cronica general de la Orden de San Benito*, III, Apendice, escritura xxviii (1125): "*Concedo ut ... nullus homo, potestas, seu miles, clericus vel rusticus, culibertus, vel burgensis sit ausus domos vestras ... violenter invadere*"; and later: "*Mando etiam ut quidquid hactenus a regibus, seu a militibus, rusticis, vel clericis seu etiam culibertis aliquo modo, sive mei juris sit vel cujuslibet alterius, ad quisistis vos ... a vivis vel a defunctis, omnia illa sint ingenua et libera ad servitium vestri monasterii.*" I owe this quotation to the good will of M. Ramos y Loscertales.

[156] "*E fó establido por fuero todo ome de oltra puertos qui viengua a cavayllo en Espayna é se asentáne en quoalquiere vila, é non toviere el aynno primero et hun dia cavayllo et armas que non sea ynfanzon, et est atal esdito* culbert: *el rey ò seynnor ha cada aynno sobre eyll dos sueldos; et si toviere el aynno é dia primero cavayllo et armas sia infanzon et non dará al seynnor nulla renta: é si non viniere à cavayllo si se asentaren en caso, co és palacio de cavayllero ó ynfanzon-hermunio que pende de seynnor, tal será villano é el rey ó seynnor habrá del vilano dreyto sobre quanto eyll enxamplara de aynno dia en adelant.*" Art. 5 of the *fuero*, cited by F. Michel, *Histoire des races maudites*, II, p. 15, n. 3, and analyzed by J. Yanguas, *Diccionario de antigüedades de Navarra*, I, p. 467. On the ms. see the latter work, p. 563, n. 3. On the document itself, often designated as the *fuero* of Sobrarbe, and still unpublished, see E. Mayer in *Zeitschrift der Savigny Stiftung, G. A.*, 1919, p. 247; the report by Ramos y Loscertales in *Anuario de Historia del Derecho Español*, 1924, p. 448, and the answer by E. Mayer, *ibid.*, 1926, p. 156. It is to be hoped that a Spanish historian will soon give us an edition of this curious text.

[157] Beside the fuero of Tudela itself, which concerns, as we have seen, foreigners from "beyond the harbors," see for example the fuero of Logrono, granted by Alphonso VII, "emperor" of Spain (1135-1157): "*Habitantes qui modo in presenti in supradictum locum populant, vel deincepts usque in finem mundi, Deo jubante, populaverint, tam ex Francigenis quam ex Hispanis, vel ex quibuscumque gentibus, vivere debeant ad foros francos*" (Llorente, *Noticias históricas de las tres provincias*, parte III, vol. III, p. 464).

[158] I have not found any mention of *culberti* in J. A. Llorente, *Noticias históricas de las tres provincias vascongadas*, parte III, vols. III, IV; *Collección de documentos para el estudio de la historia de Aragón*, I, III, IX; M. Arigita y Lasa, *Collección de documentos inéditos para la Historia de Navarra*, I.

[159] Hinojosa, *Documentos para la historia de las institutiones de Léon y de Castilla*, no. vi.

[160] H. de Gama-Barros, *Historia da administração publica em Portugal nos seculos XII a XV*, II, p. 82, n.; Hinojosa, *Documentos . . . de Léon y de Castilla*, no. xxxii. Both editors apparently believe that this is a second manumission giving full liberty to an enfranchised person who enjoyed only partial freedom before. But is it the beneficiary of this decree who had already been favored with a first enfranchisement, or was it one of his ancestors? As shall be seen, what we can guess of the history of French culverts would lead us to prefer the second hypothesis, particularly with regard to the most recent decree.

[161] *Poen.*, 910. Very complete information on ancient colliberti are given by Tamassia in the article cited in note 151; this excellent study allows me not to give detailed references; see also the *Thesaurus linguae latinae*, III, under collibertus, and Ch. Poisnel, "Recherches sur les sociétés universelles chez les Romains," in *Nouvelle Revue historique du droit*, 1879.

[162] *Dig.*, XXXVII, 15, 1.

[163] *Dig.*, XVII, 2, 71.

[164] C.I.L., VI, 3, no. 22355 A: "*Inter me et te, sanctissime mi conliberte, nullum unquam disjurgium fuisse conscius sum mihi . . . Testor . . . in venalicio una domo liberos esse factos neque ullus unquam nos diunxisset nisi hic tuus fatalis dies.*"

[165] *Dig.*, XXXII, 38, 5.

[166] *Ad Galat.*, V. 13, Cf. *ibid.* IV, 31.

[167] *Dialogi*, III, 24 (U. Moricca, ed., in *Fonti per la storia d'Italia*, 1924, p. 193): "*Conliberte, quare tam citius surrexisti.*" For the difficulties Greek, Anglo-Saxon, and French translators have had with this passage, see *Revue de linguistique romane*, II, p. 16, n. 2.

[168] Marini, *I Papiri diplomatici*, no. cxix, a. 551. The clerics of the gothic (arian) church of Saint Anastasia, giving some of the church goods to a creditor as payment, renounce these goods in their own name and in the name of *conlivertorum comministrorum nostrorum* (line 55); cf. below, after the *signum* of the subdeacon: *collivertis vel conministris meis* (line 100). The religious meaning of the word *conliverti* in this text has apparently not been noticed by commentators.

[169] *Formul. Bituricenses*, no. 15 a. On the other hand, in a phrase of the testament of Saint Bertrand (G. Busson and A. Ledru, *Acta episcoporum Cenomanensium*, p. 125), "tam ingenui quam liberi et servientes," *liberi* should perhaps be read as *liberti*.

[170] *Leges Baiwariorum*, II, 3; *Saxonum*, c. 17 (at variants); *Alamannorum*, Lehmann ed., p. 37, cod. 9, c. 2.

[171] *Lex Baiwariorum*, E. von Schwind, ed., IX, 4: "*Tunc ipse fur perdat libertatem suam pro eo, quod conlibertum suum servitio tradidit.*"

[172] C. 38.

[173] C. 131.

[174] C. 91.

[175] C. 8.

[176] C. 368.

[177] C. 3.

[178] C. 14. For an interpretation of the text, see H. Brunner, "Zeugen und Inquisitionsbeweis," in his *Forschungen zur Geschichte des deutschen und französischen Rechts*, p. 131 (47).

[179] That is the thesis of M. Salvioli, *loc. cit.*: see p. 199 in particular. M. Salvioli has made the error of joining in a common piece of research the colliberti of the

laws and those of the charters; the latter, as we shall see, are in all particulars in the same situation as the colliberti in classical Roman law.

[180] Guérard, *Polyptyque d'Irminon, Proleg.*, p. 249, n. 10. This interpretation is also favored by M. Volpe, *Studi Storici*, X (1901), p. 378, n. 2.

[181] E. Gattola, *Ad historiam Abbatiae Cassinensis Accessiones*, pars I, p. 20. Cf. also a Neapolitan testament dating from 932 (wherein the two coenfranchised are not called colliberti) cited by Tamassia, *loc. cit.*, p. 150.

[182] Troya, *Cod. Dipl. Longob.*, IV, no. 617 (748), p. 325; V, no. 912 (764-771). See also *ibid.*, III, no. 481 (730), a very obscure and often cited decree (due to the mention of the grazing rights, *fiuwaida*); corrected text in A. Dopsch, *Die Wirtschaftsentwicklung der Karolingerzeit*, 1st edition, I, p. 342; 2nd ed., p. 371. There is also mention of an enfranchised and of his culiberto in the testament of Docibile, *ypatos* of Gaëte, February 906: *Tabularium Casinense*, I, no. 19.

[183] See, for example, the decrees cited by F. Schneider, *Entstehung von Burg und Landgemeinde in Italien*, pp. 284-285, 295 n. 1.

[184] J. Nanglard, *Cartulaire de l'église d'Angoulême*, no. cxxxv. The authenticity of this decree, attacked by Esmein (*Bull. de la Soc. archéologique de la Charente*, 1905-06, pp. 31 ff.), appears to have been definitely established by M. de La Martinière (*ibid.*, 1906-07, pp. 31 ff.). The obligation to offer lights at the tomb of the manumissor is found elsewhere (cf. notably *Marculfi Formul.*, II, 17 and 34, and what is said below, p. 144, of dues in wax); I am only citing here examples of collective obligations, without any pretense of comprehensiveness.

[185] *Acta pontificum Cenomanensium*, G. Busson and A. Ledru, eds., pp. 135-136.

[186] Cf. in particular in M. Bonnet, *Le latin de Grégoire de Tours*, the paragraph on page 229 entitled "Echange de mots composés et de mots simples."

[187] A. d'Herbomez, *Cartulaire de l'abbaye de Gorze*, no. 5 (donation of Moivron by the bishop Chrodegang); *Codex principis olim Laureshamensis abbatiae diplomaticus*, I, p. 3, and "Chronicon Laureshamense," in *Mon. Germ., SS.*, XXI, p. 342 (donation of Hahnheim by Williswinda and his son the count Cancor).

[188] One sometimes finds in diplomatic language the term *conservi* (for example, P. Marchegay, "Cartulaire de Notre-Dame du Ronceray," in *Arch. d'Anjou*, III, p. 28, no. xxxiv: "*Unus ex conservis domini Castri Celsi*") meaning serfs belonging to the same master: this is in usage by notaries and has no influence on the common language.

[189] It is impossible to give here a bibliography on enfranchisement. The best overall survey remains H. Brunner, *Deutsche Rechtsgeschichte*, I, 2nd. ed., pp. 142 ff and 359 ff. For Italy, use F. Schupfer, *Il diritto privato dei popoli germanici*, I, 2nd. ed., pp. 243 ff.; and "Aldi, liti e romani," in *Enciclopedia giuridica italiana*, I, p. 2, 1121-1195; for the lites see Maurice Kroell, "Etude sur l'institution des lites en droit franc," in *Etudes d'histoire juridique offertes à P.-F. Girard.*

[190] Cf. "litus, laz," Steinmeyer and Sievers, *Die althochdeutschen Glossen*, II, p. 354. The old English form is *laet*, the Frisian form is *let*.

[191] Steinmeyer and Sievers, III, pp. 645, 652; II, pp. 95 (*hantlâzza* with long *a*), 139; Ulfilas, *I Cor.*, VII, 22.

[192] Another etymology, once proposed by J. Grimm, *Deutsche Rechtsaltertümer*, 308, proposed that the juridical term evolved from the OHG adjective *lāz* (old English *laet*, Gotthic *lats*), "lazy"; besides the obvious semantic objections to this, it is phonetically impossible since it does not take into account the agreement between the latinized and the German forms, an agreement that assumes an *ê* in the primitive German. All of the preceding development follows very closely the ideas put forward by my colleague, teacher, and friend E.-H. Lévy; it is his expertise that made me dare to venture into Germanic linguistics, where his competence is well known; naturally he is not responsible for any awkwardness I may be guilty of.

[193] Du Cange, *Glossarium*, under *aldius*: "Aldius est libertus cum impositione

operarum factus." M. Lafond, *Etudes sur le servage en Poitou*, p. 78, n. 2, points to the existence of aldions in Saintonge; I have not been able to verify the texts cited; if it is correct it may be explained by the settlement in this country of small Germanic groups belonging to peoples (such as the Lombards or the Bavarians) familiar with the aldionate.

[194] *Capitul.*, no. 98, c. 6. Cf. "aldo et leto," in Fantuzzi, *Monumenti Ravennati*, I, p. 45, no. 90.

[195] *Rothari*, c. 224, iii.

[196] M. F. Thibaut, "La question des Gemeinfreien," in *Rev. histor. du droit*, 1922, pp. 415 ff., denies the existence of the lidile class; in his view, lites are slaves in a slightly better economic position than their companions in servitude, and not enfranchised persons. Without entering into a long and perhaps useless discussion here, let me observe that the "Carta Senonica," no. 43 (*Formulae*, Zeumer, ed., p. 204), which likens the *litimonium* to the *libertaticum*; the "Formula Bituricensis," no. 9 (*ibid.*, p. 172), which likens the *litimunium* to the *libertinitatis . . . obsequium*, are sufficient in themselves to ruin this paradoxical thesis.

[197] In Italy royal privileges, one from Liutprand for Saint Anthony of Plaisance (lost, but known by its confirmation by Hildebrand—Troya, *Codice diplomatico*, IV, no. dlxvi, 31 March 744—and this latter confirmed in turn by Ratchis on 4 March 746, *ibid.*, no. dxci), the other by Adelchis for San Salvatore of Brescia (*ibid.*, V, no. dccclxxxv, p. 717, 11 November 772 or 773), rank among the aldionate children born of free women and *servi* of those monasteries. I do not know of official dispositions of this type in Gaul. But one reads in the *Polyptyque d'Irminon*, XIII, 65, regarding the sons of a servus: "*Sunt lidi quoniam de colona sunt nati.*" M. Kroell, *loc. cit.*, p. 158, failing to compare this with the Lombard texts, only sees in this passage the marks of a loose terminology; he is wrong in my opinion.

[198] In truth the fact, for lidism, is only attested to with the Frisians: *Lex Fris.*, XI, 2. For the aldionate, Porro, *Codex diplomaticus Langobardiae*, no. cxxvi (col. 225 C).

[199] *L. Salica*, XLI, 6. For the Wergeld of the lite, cf. Brunner, *Deutsche Rechtsgeschichte*, I, 2nd ed., p. 355. But Brunner's too clever explanation of the wergeld of the Roman (vol. II, p. 614, n. 7) cannot be accepted in my opinion: cf. Geffcken's observations in his edition of the *Loi salique*, p. 163, and Kroell, *loc. cit.*, pp. 198 ff. It is known that the wergeld of the Roman *tributarius*, lower than that of lite (to whom the Roman *possessor* alone was likened) according to Salic Law (XVI, 7) was raised to this level by the fourth additional capitulary to this law (c. 1).

[200] In the article cited in note 189.

[201] Edited by Warichez in *Bulletin de la Commission royale d'histoire*, 1909, p. 255 (existance of four lidile manses in Leernes, canton Fontaine-l'Evêque, arr. Charleroi).

[202] Edited by Busson and Ledru, pp. 160 (6 February 643) and 232 (December 712) (Cellier, *Catalogue des actes des évêques du Mans*, nos. 4, 7), Cf. a diploma from Charlemagne for Saint-Calais, *Diplomata Karolina*, no. 79. I have not systematically analyzed these texts in the belief, outlined in the text, that such an analysis would not give worth-while results. It is to be noted that M. Kroell, while noting that in the formulas of the Zeumer edition lites are only mentioned once, does not mention that the *lidimonium* (a dues proper to lites) is listed several times.

[203] As M. Kroell himself highlighted after other authors, pp. 128-129. Add to the examples cited by M. Kroell the synonymy *litimonium = libertinitatis obsequium* or *libertaticum* shown in "Formula Bituricensis," no. 9, and in "Carta Senonica," no. 43. Cf. also Steinmeyer and Sievers, *Die althochdeutschen Glossen*, III, p. 615.

[204] However, since an obscure history invites the full play of one's imagination, there is an author—M. Vormoor, "Soziale Gliederung im Frankreich," in *Leipziger Histor. Abh.*, H. 6, p. 24—who has the enfranchisement *cum obsequio* as it appears in the Frankish period derive from the Latin enfranchisement of Roman law; but

he has no proof to support this hypothesis, which is in any case belied by one of the texts he cites (p. 25, n. 1).

[205] *Formulae*, Zeumer, ed., p. 134, c. 35.

[206] *Liber Diurnus*, no. xxxix.

[207] In Italy these burdens on the enfranchised, particularly the enfranchised by German law (aldions), often took the form of an obligation to a duty as messenger: G. Luzzato, *I servi nelle grande proprietà ecclesiastiche nei secoli IX e X*, pp. 122, 147, n. 1, 177. German customs acknowledged certain rights of the master over the enfranchised's inheritance—but in what cases? The state of the sources does not allow a precise determination; cf. in particular, besides the manuals, Zeumer, "Ueber die Beerbung der Freigelassenen durch den Fiskus nach fränkischem Recht," in *Forsch. zur deutschen Geschichte*, XXIII (1883), and, for the relation between this law and the servile mainmorte, below, note 294.

[208] C. 73 (Mansi, X, col. 636): "*Quicumque libertatem a dominis suis percipiunt ut nullum sibimet obsequium patronus retentet, isti, si sine crimine sunt, ad clericatus ordinem libere suscipiantur; quia directa manumissione absoluti noscuntur: qui vero retento obsequio manumissi sunt, pro eo quod adhuc a patrone servitute tenentur obnoxii, nullatenus sunt ad ecclesiasticum ordinem promovendi: ne, quando voluerint eorum domini, fiant ex clericis servi.*" The canon, conveyed to France by the *Hispana*, figures in the great collections since the end of the ninth century, beginning with the *Anselmo dicata* and Reginon of Prüm, and was finally collected in Gratian's *Decretum*, dist. LIV, c. 5. Other solutions have earlier been proposed regarding the ordination of *liberti*: (a) in the interest of the patron, an obligation to obtain his consent before ordination: Council of Toledo of 400, c. 1 (*Decret Grat.*, dist. LIV, c. 7); Council of Orléans of 549, c. 6 (*Concil. aevi merov.*, I, p. 102 b) much earlier, at the Council of Elvire of 305 or 306, c. 80, in the interest of the Church, an interdiction to ordinate enfranchised whose patrons are "in the century" (meaning probably the laity; pagans are always designated *gentiles* in the council's texts).

[209] C. Troya, *Codice diplomatico longobardo*, IV, no. dclxxxiii, p. 530 (20 May 754): "*Ipse Vulpo et Mitilde et filii et filie sue cum agnitione sua diserunt quod non voluit quatuor vias et quod contenti sunt pro postera libertate sua ea condicione quod maneant in custodia, tutale et tuitione de jamdictis presbiteris et diaconis beate Marie Majoris istius civitatis Cremone.*"

[210] This distinction became somewhat obscured later in imperial legislation, but after the events that detached Gaul from the Empire; see particularly *C. J.*, XI, 48, 21, and the interpolations pointed out by A. Piganiol, *L'impôt de capitulation sous le Bas-Empire romain*, p. 85, n. 1.

[211] *C. J.*, XI, 51: "*Cum per alias provincias ... lex a maioribus constituta colonos quodam aeternitatis jure detineat....*"

[212] Cf. N.-A. Constantinescu, "Réforme sociale ou réforme fiscale? Une hypothèse pour expliquer la disparition du servage de la glèbe dans l'Empire byzantin," in *Académie roumaine, Bull. de la Section historique*, XI (1924).

[213] *Ed. Theod.*, c. 142. A controversy has arisen around this text, some scholars believing that it concerns only servi, others extending it to cover coloni: see the latest arguments for the first thesis in G. Luzzato, *I servi nelle grande proprietà ecclesiastiche italiane nei sec. IX e X*, pp. 136 ff; arguments in favor of the second: P. Vaccari, *L'affrancazione dei servi della gleba nell'Emilia e nella Toscana* (Preface to this volume published by the Acad. dei Lincei, Commissione per gli atti delle Assemblee), p. 24. I agree with the first theory. Cf. in a letter of Athalaric (Cassiodore, *Var.*, VIII, 33) the expression of the principle "*servos posse meliorari qui de labore agrorum ad urbana servitia transferuntur.*" The reestablishment of the old body of laws regarding slaves by the Byzantine reconquest is established by Greg., *Ep.*, IV, 21.

[214] For the relaxing in Italy, cf. M. Kowalewsky, *Die ökonomische Entwicklung*

Europas, I, particularly pp. 351, 421, 432, 466; G. Luzzato, *I servi nelle grande proprietà ecclesiastiche*, pp. 140 ff.

[215] Pardessus, *Diplomata*, II, no. dxiv: "*Volumus etiam ut ingenuos quos fecimus aut in antea fecerimus, quanticumque in ipsa loca manent quae ad Sanctam Andochium et ad Sanctam Reginam et Sanctum Ferreolum vel ad Sanctum Praejectum delegavimus, inspectas eorum libertatis, super ipsas terras pro ingenuis commaneant et aliubi commanendi nullam habeant potestatem.*" Cf. Zeumer, *Formulae*, p. 476, n. 8. The legislation of the later Empire had likened the fugitive liberti to the free coloni guilty of a similar crime: law of 371, *C. J.*, XI, 53, 3.

[216] One must put aside the nonhereditary, "censile" manses leased for a specific period. Cf. *Capitul.*, II, no. 275, c. 12, with Mgr Lesne's commentary, in *Revue d'histoire ecclésiastique*, XIV (1913), p. 492. See also a decree of precarium granted on 14 September 900 by Saint-Martin of Tours to Gui, "noble vassal" of the count-abbot, Robert (Bibl. Nat., Baluze 76, fols. 99 ff; cf. Mabille, *La pancarte noire*, no. xxii). The decree names in Martigny [-sur-Loire] (Indre-et-Loire, comm. Fondettes), besides colonile manses (thirteen and one-half) and servile manses (two), "*mansus unus et medius censilis ex quibus habet Ragambaldus quartam unam per manum firmam, et Blatherius presbyter habuit alteram et Rambertus clericus tenet tertiam, monetarius vero tenet quartam unam quae fuit semper ab initio censilis.*" The comparison between the censile manse and the "mainferme" was already accomplished in the text of the capitulary cited above. Contracts giving birth to censile manses were rare in Gaul; in Italy, on the other hand, a similar institution, called *livello*, has played a considerable role beginning with the Lombard era.

[217] B. Guérard, *Prolégomènes*, p. 583.

[218] C. 4 of the *Capitul*, no. 56, in which some authors have seen an effort made to maintain the "bond to the land," only establishes that lawsuits for recovery of property for *fiscalins*, whether colons or *servi*, must be held in the home site of the claimed individuals, so as to allow for the verification of family ties.

[219] *C. J.*, XI, 52: "*Licet [coloni] condicione videantur ingenui, servi tamen terrae ipsius cui nati sunt aestimentur.*"

[220] *Capitul.*, I, no. 40, c. 10: "*Ut nec colonus nec fiscalinus foras mitio possint aliubi tradiciones facere.*"

[222] *Capitul*, II, no. 278, c. 3.

[223] Bibl. Nat., Baluze 76, fol 321 (cf. Mabille, *La pancarte noire*, no. cx): "*Tunc judicatum est ibi a multis nobilibus viris et colonis qui subtus tenentur inserti....*"

[224] Guérard, *Polyptyque de Saint-Remi*, p. xiv. The terminology of the *capitulare de villis* appears to be similar, since there is no mention of coloni, but rather of "*ingenuis qui per fiscos aut villas nostras commanent.*" (c. 52; cf. c. 4). P. Allard in *Les origines du servage en France*, pp. 186-187, believes that the coloni are included under the name servi; but his hypothesis, based on the distinction made in this text between two classes of people, one subject to corporal punishment, the other exempt from it, does not take into account the fact that the coloni appear not to have been merged with the servi in penal law until the reign of Charles the Bald: cf. below, note 233.

[225] Indeed it appears that the very fixity of the charges, and in particular of the services, was considered a characteristic of the colonile condition. Despite the general tendency of seigneurial customs to remain stable, the servus continued to be sometimes considered as belonging in body and in his belongings to his master. It is thus that one must interpret, in my opinion, a decree in the *Cartulaire de Cormery*, no. xix (ca. 900): the cleric Gautier bequeaths to Saint-Paul of Cormery property in the *pagus* of Tours together with the servi and ancillae living there; and he adds: "*Hos veros servos vel ancillas superius nominatas sub conditione colonorum constitutos tributum amplius ut non requiratur quam unicuique mansum tenenti biduam in hebdomada ij, vinum aut frumentum sextarios viij, pullos ij cum*

ovis, cambortum (?) *inter duos, carum unum.*" What is the meaning of *sub conditione colonorum constitutos*? It does not concern enfranchisement; the enfranchised *servi* are mentioned elsewhere. The word *colonus* probably signifies nothing more than the protection against any arbitrary demands which is highlighted in more detail in the kind of charter of customs that follows. (Levillain suggests that this hypothesis is confirmed by the judgment of 828 regarding the *coloni* of Saint-Paul of Cormery.) In their letter to Louis the German (*Capitul.*, II, no. 297, c. 14), the bishops of the synod of Quiersy, urging him to avoid any oppression of the peasants of the royal *villae* by the *judices*, are visibly attempting to distinguish between the abuses against *servi* and those against *coloni*. Unfortunately, the distinction is not perfectly clear. For the *servi* the danger is in demands contrary to custom, and, concerning the corvées that probably were not completely determined by customary law, in convocations at "inopportune" moments (*in tempore incongruo*). For the *coloni* the bishops appear to foresee that the *judices* will proceed along circuitous routes (*per dolos aut per mala ingenia*); illegitimate or intemperate corvées will be extracted through pressure rather than through violence; at least I assume the meaning of the word selected here to indicate the *coloni*: *precationes*. But in the same paragraph, a little later (p. 438, 1. 12) the word *colonos* is applied to all the inhabitants of the royal *villae*, without class distinction.

[226] Tardif, *Cartons des rois*, no. 180 (1 July 861). Also on 14 September 900, a decree of precarium granted by Saint-Martin of Tours to the "noble vassal" Gui (Bibl. Nat., Baluze 76, fol. 96; cf. Mabille, *La pancarte noire*, no. xxii) takes notice in Martigny [-sur-Loire] (Indre-et-Loire, comm. Fondettes) not only of colonile or servile manses (incidentally these were practically not farmed due to Norman invasions) but also of *homines coloninas lege viventes* and of *servi*.

[227] Guérard, *Polyptyque de Saint-Remi*, xxviii, 65. The *coloni "qui se addonaverunt"* owe a chevage, but one smaller than the one owed by the *coloni ex nativitate*.

[228] J. Garnier, *Chartes bourguignonnes inédites (Mém. présentés . . . à l'Académie des Inscriptions*, 2e série, *Antiquités de la France*, vol. II), p. 113, no. lxxvi: "*Sic ut sit ingenuus colonus et absolutus.*"

[229] "Livre noir de Saint-Florent de Saumur," Bibl. Nat., nouv. acq. lat. 1930, fol. 129 vo. Gibert was a monk in Saint-Benoît [-sur-Loire] under Abbot Wlfadus (951-962). The charter simply states: "*Quosdam servos quos in seculo habui, ut Deus propicietur michi et sanctus Florentius pro me intercedat, trado ad locum ipsius sancti, id est Mainfredum et filios eius Geraldum et Ansbertum et duas filias ejus; eo tenore ut ab hodie non sint servi, sed coloni, nec alio servitio deprimantur quam quod legitimi coloni ex solvere consuerunt.*" The notice that precedes the charter (*Kartalem*) in the cartulary adds the following two informations: (1) The matter concerned fugitive *mancipia* owed by Gibert through inheritance from his parents; he had been unable to find them for many years; he happened upon them at Saint-Florent one day when he was visiting the monastery; (2) The new *coloni* shall pay four *deniers* "*se id facturum promisit ut ... servitutis nexibus absolutos in colinicio eos et IIIIor denariorum redditione faceret transire.*" The contrast between this condition and that of serfdom is well highlighted by this clause in the charter: "*Mainardum vero fratrem Mainfredi qui adhuc in confugio permanet in perpetua servitute prefato loco relinquo.*"

[230] Ripuarian law already stated, LXII, 1: "*Si quis servum suum tributarium aut lidum fecerat. ...*"

[231] *Capitul.*, I, no. 25, c. 4.

[232] For the fugitive *colonus* law of 371 (*C. J.*, XI, 53, 1); a law of Constantine (*C. Th.*, V, 17, 1), prescribing the placing in irons of *coloni "qui fugam meditantur,"* took care to indicate that they thus suffered a servile punishment. For donatist *coloni*, laws of 412 and 414 (*C. Th.*, XVI, 5, 52, 4, and 54, 8). For the *colonus* who violated tombs, law of 447 (*Nov. Val.*, XXIII, 3). Justinian's legislation prescribing corporal punishments for *coloni* guilty of marrying free women (*C. J.*,

VII, 24, 1; XI, 48, 24, 1; *Nov.*, XXII, 17), does not apply to Gaul. In the *Vie* of Saint Césaire (I, 25; *SS. rer. merov.*, III, p. 466), one can note that in the sixth century the great landowners exercised in practice the right of corporal punishment not only on their slaves (servis) but also on their *ingenuis obsequentibus sibi*; this probably indicates free domestics.

[233] This is brought out by consultation with the following texts. (1) Complicity in counterfeiting money: *Capitul. legibus addenda*, 818 or 819 (I, no. 139, c. 19), "*Si liber est, sexaginta solidos componat; si servus est, sexaginta ictus accipiat*"; Edict of Pitres, 25 June 864 (II, no. 273), c. 16 (with specific reference to the preceding text, cited after Anséis), "*Si liber est, LX solidos componat; si servus vel colonus nudus cum virgis vapulet*"; analogous formulas, c. 17 and c. 23; cf. also c. 22. (2) Refusal of good money: corporal punishment for the servus according to capitularies of 794 (I, no. 28, c. 5), of 809 (no. 63, c. 7), of 818-819 (no. 139, c. 18); the Edict of Pitres, c. 15, reproduces (after Anséis) this last text but adds a precision regarding the mode of punishment and states, "*ut quorumcumque coloni et servi pro hoc convicti fuerint, non cum grosso fuste sed nudi cum virgis vapulent*"; already a little earlier, a caputulary of July 861 (II, no. 271) prescribes the beating with the rod the "colonis ... *et servis*" who committed this crime at the market. (3) Theft of harvest during the ost: capitulary dating probably from Emperor Charlemagne, and preserved by Anséis (I, no. 70, c. 4), the free man pays triple damages and royal ban; the servus triple damages and, instead of the ban, is subject to a corporal punishment; the Edict of Ver of March 884 (II, no. 287, c. 4), broadening this rule to theft in general, applies its second part to "colonus *aut servus*." Finally, concerning the crime of false measure (c. 20) and that consisting in selling the pound of pure gold for more than twelve pounds of silver (c. 24), the Edict of Pitres shows the same assimilation; the Edict of Servais of November 853 (II, no. 260, c. 5) reproduced by the Edict of Quierzy (no. 278, c. 2) orders the beating with sixty blows the colonus who refuses to lend aid in the apprehension of a thief; a circular sent to the *missi* in April 853 (no. 259, c. 9) prescribes corporal punishment for coloni guilty of crimes against ecclesiastical discipline. Note that in Frankish Italy judgments assume that corporal punishment inflicted by the master is a mark of servitude: Muratori, *Antiquitates*, III, col. 1015 (796) and *Scriptores*, I, 2, p. 398 (854); cf. Luzzato, *I servi nelle grande proprietà ecclesiastiche*, pp. 128, 130.

[234] *Prolégomènes*, p. 391.

[235] *Capitul.*, I, no. 58, c. 1: "*Continebatur namque in primo capitulo utrum, ubi colonam servus cuiuslibet uxorem acceperit, infantes illorum petinere deberent ad illam colonam an ad illum. Considera enim, si proprius servus tuus alterius propriam ancillam sibi sociaverit aut alterius servus proprius tuam propriam ancillam uxorem acceperit ad quem ex vobis eorum procreatio petinere debeat, et taliter de istis fac; quia non est amplius nisi liber et servus.*" It is totally impossible to date the text.

[236] *Lex Rom. Vis.: Liber Gaii*, I: "*Gaius Institutionum libro primo dicit omnes homines aut liberos esse aut servos.*" Cf. *Dig.*, V, 3 (*Gaii Institut.*, I, 9). A famous law of Justinian (*C. J.*, XI, 48, 21) applies to children born of a marriage between adscripts and servi the principle, until then only applied to servi, that the child follows the condition of the mother, and insists that there is little difference between the adscript and the servus. It is not probable that this law influenced the decision of the Carolingian palace, where, on the contrary, "Alaric's Breviary" was certainly well known; cf. Max Conrat, *Geschichte der Quellen und Literatur des römischen Rechts im früheren Mittelalter*, pp. 33 ff.

[237] As early as 764, a rough copy of a decree preserved in the archives of Saint Gall (Wartmann, *Urkundenbuch der Abtei St. Gallen*, I, no. 42) ranks among the *mancipia*, together with servi, some ingenui who live on a land. An article wrongly inserted in a capitulary of Louis the Pious in a manuscript of the tenth century (*Capitul.*, I, p. 286) states that the enfranchised woman who marries a servus or

a colonus must once again fall under the rule of her former master. Germanic law applied this rule only in case of marriage with a servus (*L. Alamann*, c. xviii).

[238] Cf. besides the dictionaries, H. Hauser, *Ouvriers du temps passé*, 4th ed., p. 43.

[239] For example, *Capitul.*, II, no. 297, c. 14 (p. 438, 1. 12; cf. above, note 225).

[240] "Livre noir de Saint-Florent," Bibl. Nat., nouv. acq. lat. 1930, fol. 97: "*Notum facere volumus ... quod avunculus noster Gausfredus ... monachilem habitum suscipiens remisit omnes malas exactiones quae vulgo dicuntur consuetudines quas imposuerat colonis ecclesiarum sive quibuslibet dominationis suae diversi oficii hominibus.*"

[241] A. Bernard and A. Bruel, *Recueil des chartes de l'abbaye de Cluny*, V, no. 3660: "*Unam etiam cavannariam cum servo ipsius terre colono.*"

[242] This general usage is very frequent in Italy in the High Middle Ages; cf. Calisse in *Archivio della r. Società Romana di storia patria*, VIII (1885), p. 67; P. Vaccari, *Il colonato romano e l'invasione lombarda*, p. 7; Luzzato, *I servi nelle grande proprietà ecclesiastiche*, p. 124.

[243] Cf. G. Jeanton, *Le servage en Bourgogne*, p. 22, and Guy de Valous, *Le domaine de l'abbaye de Cluny*, p. 107.

[244] A. Luchaire, *Histoire des institutions monarchiques*, II, p. 343; 1179 (probably April; cf. A. Cartellieri, *Philipp II August*; Vol. I: *Regesta Philipp August von der Geburt*, no. 41): "*Cum in nostra presentia Stephanus, abbas Sancte Genovofe, et canonici ejusdem ecclesie assererent homines de Rodoniaco servos esse ecclesie sue, homines id penitus negaverunt, et sese tantum hospites ecclesie et colonos esse confessi sunt.*"

[245] *Serf de la glèbe*, pp. 179-195 and particularly p. 185. In any case it concerns relatively late usages (XIIIth century).

[246] J. Thillier and E. Jarry, *Cartulaire de l'église cathédrale de Sainte-Croix d'Orléans*, no. xxxiv (Böhmer-Mühlbacher, no. 541): "*Praecepimus ... ut nullus judex publicus ... in ecclesias aut loca vel agros seu reliquas possessiones quas ... tenet ... ecclesia ... ad causas audiendas ... aut homines ipsius ecclesiae tam ingenuos quam servos super terram ipsius commanentes ditringendos ... ingredi audeat.*"

[247] L. Halphen and F. Lot, *Recueil des actes de Lothaire et Louis V*, no. xxxiii: "*Homines ipsius ecclesie tam ingenuos quam servos.*" From that time on, the two formulas are used almost interchangeably: that of Louis the Pious reappears in a diploma of Louis V (*ibid.*, no. lxix, 979, 9 June); that of Lothaire in a diploma of Hugues Capet (*Cartulaire de Sainte-Croix*, no. xxxix, November 990).

[248] Halphen and Lot, *loc. cit.*, nos. 27, 34, 56. Perhaps the presence of this characteristic expression in the last diploma should convince the editors' hypothesis (p. ix) that it was written outside the royal chancelry. The word coloni already appears where one would expect to see servi in a diploma of Carloman for Sainte-Cécile of Urgel: Marca, *Marca hispanica*, col. 812, no. xlii: "*Ut nullus judex publicus audeat a famulis tam liberis quam colonis ipsius loci hospitaticum ... aut inferenda aliqua exigere praesumat.*"

[249] One can find a few texts conveniently gathered in the notes to P. Bernard, *Etude sur les esclaves et les serfs d'Eglise en France*, p. 113; see also G. d'Espinay, *Les cartulaires angevins*, pp. 104-105.

[250] This traditional usage is maintained for centuries. One of the oldest judicial treatises on serfdom to be printed—perhaps the oldest—is that of Anthoine Colombet which appeared in 1578 in Lyon, entitled *Colonia celtica lucrosa. Traicté rare des personnes de mainmorte censites et taillables.*

[251] This uncertainty in the use of colonus, a scholarly word arbitrarily applied to all kinds of social conditions, is naturally generalized in all countries where diplomatic Latin was written; cf. for England the observations of C. M. Andrews, *The Old-English Manor*, p. 150.

[252] "Livre noir de Saint-Florent," Bibl. Nat., nouv. acq. lat. 1930, fol. 134: "*Unum mancipium nomine Hildricum colonii michi servitute obnoxium*"; further: "*predictum collibertum.*"

[253] *Ibid.*, fol. 21 vo.: "*Trado quoque sancto Florentio colibertum quendam nomine Adelelmum . . . ut ab hac die et deinceps tam ipsi sancto Florentio quam monachis colonili jure subiciatur et eis debitae servitutis pensum reddere cogatur.*"

[254] As the decrees of manumissions themselves would suffice to prove, even in the absence of other testimony.

[255] Seine-et-Marne, cant. Montereau-Fault-Yonne.

[256] As is shown in an inquiry dating from around 1250 published by Guilhiermoz, *Enquêtes et procès*, Appendix, p. 293 (the villagers, like many others at that time, had admitted their servile condition only reluctantly; but the inquiry is decisive on this subject) and the decree of enfranchisement of 1289 noted by dom Bouilliard, *Histoire de Saint-Germain-des-Prés*, p. 142.

[257] Seine-et-Oise, cant. Boissy-Saint-Léger.

[258] Seine, cant. Ivry-sur-Seine. My figures for the two villages differ from Guérard's; I do not understand how he arrived at his figures.

[259] Guérard, *Polyptyque d'Irminon*, App. nos. xl and xli.

[260] *Prolégomènes*, p. 498: "This slow and silent revolution which destroyed the classes of *coloni*, *lides*, and serfs to make of them one single estate of people, that is serfdom. . . ."

[261] *Essai sur les origines de la noblesse*, particularly pp. 322 ff. For Anglo-Saxon England, cf. F. M. Maitland, *Domesday Book and Beyond*, p. 325.

[262] J. Halkin and C.-G. Roland, *Recueil des chartes de l'abbaye de Stavelot-Malmédy*, no. 56 (2 October 926). A *miles* received a manse in precarium for the duration of his life, that of his wife, and of his two sons, "*et post finem illorum si aliquis de heredibus in ipsa se servitute contra limina predictorum patrum preparare cupit, nemo aliorum virorum ipsam precariam fieri valeat nisi ipse qui de ipsa stirpe processerit.*"

[263] In England a passage in the *Lois de Cnut* (II, 20, 1) shows that in order to best protect their men powerful lords had best to have them thought as free at times, and at other times as servi (*theow*), in the latter case undoubtedly in order to shield them from public justice: cf. Maitland, *Domesday Book and Beyond*. Similar influences may have played a part in France.

[264] Cf. J. Petot, "L'hommage servile," in *Revue historique du droit*, 1927.

[265] Council of Orleans of 538, cited below, note 267. Testament of Saint Remi, in *SS. rer. merov.*, III, p. 338, l. 24 and p. 339, l. 9 (probably a counterfeit written by Hincmar, but useful for the latter's era). Letter of Hincmar summarized by Flodoard, *Histor. Remensis eccles.*, III, c. 20 (*SS.*, XIII, p. 513, l. 38). Testament of the canons Haganon and Adjutor (28 January 818-28 January 819), in Martène, *Thesaurus*, I, col. 20 (they bequeath to Saint-Martin lands with their *liberi coloni*—these are farmers who cultivate the land in return for half the harvest—*excepto qui a nobis ingenuitates promeruerunt*; the text is difficult to interpret; the canons apparently indicate that they had earlier made this men into coloni: *quos colonarios fecimus*; are these former servi whose originally more or less arbitrary dues were then fixed as in the text cited above, note 225?). The practice of enfranchisement of the colonus appears to go back, according to a letter from Sidoine Apollonaire—V, 19—as far as the end of the Roman epoch: cf. A. Esmein, *Mélanges d'histoire du droit et de critique. Droit romain*, pp. 370 ff.

[266] Above, p. 133.

[267] Council of Orléans of 538, c. 29 (*Conc. aevi merov.*, p. 81): "*ut nullus servilibus colonariisque conditionibus obligatus iuxtu statuta sedis apostolicae ad honores ecclesiasticus admittatur, nisi prius aut testamento aut per tabolas eum legeteme consteterit absolutum.*" Cf. also the text from the collection of Albi cited in Loening, *Geschichte des deutschen Kirchenrechts*, II, p. 282, n. 3. However, the councilar

texts cited below, note 287 regarding the *ascripti censibus*, are less strict: they only make the ordination dependent upon the consent of the king or of his representative. Similarly, Leon the Great (*Decret. Grat.*, dist. LIV, c. 21) did not forbid entrance into orders for *originarii* so long as they had their seigneur's authorization. In Roman law the condition of *adscriptitius* never constituted an impediment to ordination: see in particular, *Nov. Just.*, 123, 17, 1, and cf. 0. Seeck, in *Pauly-Wissowa*, IV, col. 505. Naturally these prohibitions were far from universally observed in practice. A capitulary regarding the churches of Poitiers, dating from 817-825 (vol. I, no. 149, c. 7) shows that one expected to find coloni and servi among the canons of Sainte-Radegonde.

[268] *Nov.*, CLVII.

[269] By a letter of Gregory the Great: *Ep.*, IX, 128. The marriage of peasants (*rustici*) from the domains was an occasion for dues, even when there was no formariage (*ibid.*, I, 42, p. 65). On the other hand, there was nothing in law resembling a mainmorte since the parents of coloni could inherit from them, on the condition that they also live on the lands of the Church (I, 42, p. 65; the text concerns *conductores*, who are colons in normal circumstances); however, the pontifical prescription itself proves that the administrators of domains did not always recognize this hereditary right. The prohibition of formariage for slaves, something that was almost a matter of course, is shown in the Roman era in almost the same terms as in the Middle Ages ("*foras nubere*") in a text of Tertullian, *Ad uxorem*, II, 8; cf. Luzzato, *I servi*, p. 168, n. 2.

[270] *Capitul.*, II, no. 273, c. 31 (with explicit references to the letter of Gregory the Great cited in the preceding note and to a letter I do not identify from Leon the Great).

[271] If one is to believe the monk Guiman who compiled, between 1170 and 1192, the "cartulary" of Saint-Vaast of Arras, serfs, careful to hide themselves and neglecting to pay their chevage during peaceful periods, "*in tempore vero tribulationis et oppressionis divitum ad patrocinium sancti Vedasti et advocaturam abbatis recurrunt*" (Van Drival ed., p. 177). Naturally, Guiman was perhaps somewhat biased; it is up to the historian to redress the balance.

[272] *L'alleu et le domaine rural*, p. 463. Cf. *Les transformations de la royauté*, p. 587, n. 1: "Serfdom had no relation with feudalism." This is Cujas's old theory: "*Servi et census et alia innumera praediorum hominumque onera e jure romano originem sumpsisse testor*," and also Gui Coquille's (cited in *Serf de la glèbe*, p. 191).

[273] *Prolégomènes*, p. 422.

[274] This is the expression in the famous formula of recommendation. *Formul. Tur.*, 43.

[275] Cipolla, *Monumenta Novalicensia*, I, no. xxviii (8 May 827).

[276] See pp. 130, 136.

[277] The texts are too numerous and too well known to be cited here. For the Merovingian period, the most ancient text is no doubt Greg. Tur., *Hist. Franc.*, VII, 45: "*Subdebant pauperis servitio, ut quantulumcumque de alimento porregerent.*"

[278] J. Flach, "Le droit romain dans les chartes," in *Mélanges Fitting*, I, pp. 414-415.

[279] H. Wartmann, *Urkundenbuch der Abtei St. Gallen*, I, no. 240 (16 January 819), no. 281 (20 June 824), no. 287 (11 December 824).

[280] *Capitul.*, no. 98, c. 6; *Lex Frisionum*, XI, 2. Nithard, IV, 2, uses the word serviles (no doubt it is on purpose that he does not say servi; serviles indicates a condition comparable to servitude rather than servitude itself) as the equivalent to *lazzi*, rendered by the *Ann. Fuldenses* (842) as liberti, and included by the *Ann. Xantenses* (841) under the general term servi.

[281] Since the writing of the present work the problem of chevage has been taken up by J. Massiet du Biest, "Le chef-cens et la demi-liberté dans les villes du Nord

avant le développement des institutions urbaines (Xe-XIIe siécles)," in *Revue historique du droit*, 1927. It is impossible to discuss here in detail the results of this important article. One finds in it several items that confirm my conception of the chevage as an expression of seigneurial protection. However, may I once again protest against this word "demi-liberté?" Where are the medieval texts that ever make use of it?

[282] B. Guérard, *Polyptyque d'Irminon, Prolég.*, p. 692; *Polyptyque de Saint-Rémi*, p. xviii. Three formulae from a Senonian collection approximately contemporary with the *Polyptyque d'Irminon* (*Form. Senon. recentiores*, nos. 2, 4, 5) mention under the name of *colonitium* the tax paid by the colonus *de capud suum* and consider it as normal for his condition. It is remarkable that more ancient texts (for example, *Cartae Senon.*, no. 20), concerning, as the formulae just cited, a seigneur's claim for his rights over a colonus do not mention this tax.

[283] A. d'Herbomez, *Cartulaire de l'abbaye de Gorze*, no. 116 (17 August 984). These *mundiales* were probably not considered free for it is said of them that each owes the six deniers "*etiam si libere sit filius.*" Compare this text with a notice published by Van Lokeren, *Chartes et documents de l'abbaye de Saint-Pierre au Mont-Blandin*, no. 4: at the time of King Louis (II or III: 8 December 977-5 August 882), a free woman "*tributariam se esse constituit ut ibi annis singulis* propter mundeburdem *in censum solveret denarios II*"; at the same time she submits to a tax on marriage and to a successorial tax. Cf. p. 147.

[284] *Polypt.*, XII, 27; cf. XII, 9, and IX, 268 (in the last case the *munboratus* pays a tax in silver, but it is meant for candles). A curious survival of the practice of a tax in wax paid "*de garde*" and "*commandise*" in a decree from Franche-Comté of 7 May 1288: Perreciot, *De l'état civil des personnes*, 2nd ed., III, pr. no. 89.

[285] J. Garnier, *Chartes bourguignonnes inédites*, p. 141, no. vii: "*Duos denarics in cera*"; p. 113, no. lxxvi: "*Denarios II vel dies II.*" Still in 1261, *Histor. de France*, XXIV, p. 326, no. 179: "*Unam denariatam cere.*" Cf. the examples cited for Germany in A. Meister, "Studien zur Geschichte der Wachszinsigkeit," in *Münstersche Beiträge zur Geschichtsforschung*, N. F., H. 32-33, p. 16. Following the tendency proper to German law, which has been to develop to an extreme the division of society into distinct classes, the *cerocensuales* in Germany finally constituted a separate juridical group: cf. A. Meister, *loc. cit.* for a bibliography, and the account of Minnigerode, *Vierteljahrschr. für Sozial- und Wirtschaftsgeschichte*, 1916. In France the wax chevage is simply, like the ordinary chevage, a mark of serfdom proving the obligation to formariage and to mainmorte; cf. *Histor. de France, loc. cit.*

[286] For the bibliography, see A. Piganiol, *L'impôt de capitation sous le Bas-Empire romain*.

[287] It has sometimes been believed that there existed a state, personal head tax during the Merovingian era, as shown in a formula of Marculfe (I, 19), where the permission to have oneself ordained is granted to the postulant only when "*se memoratus ille* de caput suum *bene ingenuus esse videtur et in poleptico publico censitus non est.*" However caput, as F. Thibaut in *Nouv. Rev. histor. du droit*, 1907, p. 68, has well shown, has here only its figurative sense that is so frequent both in classical Latin (for example, Plautus, *Merc.*, 153: "*Liberum caput tibi faciam*") and in Merovingian Latin (*Formul. Andecav.*, 59: "*Ingenuitatem capitis eorum*"). The ordination is forbidden either to the slave or to the man *ascriptus censibus*, enrolled on the cadastres of land taxes. Cf. c. 8 of the council of Clichy and c. 6 of the council of Reims (*Consilia aevi mer.*, pp. 198, 203). One of the rare texts to explicitly mention a public head tax, the Edict of Pitres (*Cap.*, II, no. 273, c. 34), specifies that it applies to freemen. The *Capitul.*, no. 44, c. 20 is less precise.

[288] The texts regarding the *litimonium* in the *Polyptyque de Saint-Germain-des-Prés* are rather obscure. Kroell, *loc. cit.*, pp. 187-188, believed he could conclude

that on the lands of the abbey only women of lidile condition, excluding men, paid this tax. The explanation provided by Guérard, *Prolégomènes*, p. 696, seems more natural, and I believe it stands up to Kroell's arguments.

[289] In Italy the word, applied to aldions and to enfranchised men in general, sometimes indicates an annual tax (in the sense given here), as for the litimonium, sometimes a sum fixed in the manumission itself, that once paid allowed the enfranchised, if he so wished, to rid himself of the patronal mundium by purchasing it. French decrees appear not to offer anything similar to this latter case. Cf. on these two meanings, G. Luzzato, *I servi nelle grandi proprietà ecclesiastiche nei secoli IX e X*, p. 115.

[290] E. Pérard, *Recueil de pièces curieuses servant à l'histoire de Bourgogne*, p. 57, n.d. (IXth century).

[291] I cite, without attempting to be comprehensive, a few characteristic examples: Guérard, *Cartulaire de Saint-Bertin*, p. 160, no. lxxxvii (November 838); Pérard, *Recueil de pièces curieuses*, p. 57 (n.d.) and 58 (888; reproduced in Thévenin, *Textes*, no. 112); J. Garnier, *Chartes bourguignonnes inédites*, p. 113, no. lxxvi (January 876); enfranchisement by the monk Gibert, cited above, note 229. The tax in the second case is of one denier for women, two for men; in the third case of two deniers; in the first, fourth, and fifth cases, four deniers.

[292] The words litimonium and *cavaticum* are compared, and it appears, are considered as almost synonymous by a formula of the eighth century (*Form. Salic. Merkel*, no. 28). A man affirms, in front of the *mallus*, that he is "*bene ingenuus sive Salicus.*" He is asked if he has ever rendered the services of a slave or paid the litimonium to the man who claims him as his servus; he answers "*quod nec servilio nec litimonium nec nullun cavaticum nec ullum obsequium ei reddebat.*"

[293] For the first case, Pérard, *Recueil*, pp. 57, 58. For the second case, J. Garnier, *Chartes bourguignonnes inédites*, p. 141, no. vii (April 928); p. 143, no. x (953); p. 149, no. xviii (1012).

[294] Compare in particular (considering only the most ancient decrees) in Van Lokeren, *Chartes et documents* ..., on the one hand, nos. 23, 66, 72, 79, 81, and on the other, nos. 4, 68, 77, 80, 82 to 86 (ninth and tenth centuries). Cf. Vanderkindere, "Les tributaires ou serfs d'Eglises," in *Académie de Belgique, Bulletin de la classe des Lettres*, 1897. It is to be noted that one of the oldest examples of successorial tax known in the Frankish kingdom regards enfranchised (Lacomblet, *Niederrheinisches Urkundenbuch*, I, no. 73: 13 August 882; cf. no. 84: 907). The mention in no. 4 of Van Lokeren's collection, regarding a free woman who gave herself to a monastery, is from approximately the same date (reign of King Louis—II or III—8 December 877-5 August 882). Cf. von Below, article entitled "Sterbfall," in Hoops, *Reallexikon der germanischen Altertumskunde*, IV. The obligation for enfranchised to obtain the consent of their patron before marriage—equivalent no doubt, in the majority of these cases, to the obligation of purchasing this authorization—is mentioned as early as 555 in Saint Cybard's testament: cf. La Martinière in *Bull. Soc. Archéol. de la Charente*, 1906-1907, p. 23.

[295] The formula preserving one's freedom is still found in decrees of self-donation of 959 (no. 27) and of 1050 (no. 128); but the expressions *ancillam, ancillatum, servituti,* can be found increasingly frequently beginning in 1034 (nos. 108, 155, 157, 158, 161, 172, 174, 195, 221, 234, 265, and so on). No. 249 (1155) where a woman gives herself "*pro indesinenti libertate optinenda,*" cannot be considered, despite Van Lokeren (p. 23, n. 1); it concerns eternal freedom, salvation (cf. no. 111).

[296] Some documents from the eleventh and twelfth centuries, particularly in the region of the Loire, mention men called *commendaticii*, who appear to be in a condition similar to serfdom, but may be thought of as superior since one witnesses, in the time of the abbot of Vierzon Humbauld (ca. 1082-ca. 1095), a lady allowing the marriage of one of her *commanda* to a culvert of the monks, and prescribing that the division of the children will be done on an equal basis (Bibl. Nat., lat.

9865, fol. 22 vo.). Are these descendants of *"recommandés"* whose bond had become hereditary? I have begun to gather texts on this subject without coming to a clear solution so far.

[297] P. Vaccari, *L'affrancazione dei servi della gleba*, pp. 32, 39 n. 1; F. Schupfer, *Il diritto privato*, I, 2nd. ed., p. 79; Fedor Schneider, *Die Reichsverwaltung in Toscana (Bibliothek des kgl. Preuss. Histor. Instituts in Rom*, XI), p. 203 n. 2.

[298] On the other hand, the Bavarian *barschalken*, placed in a situation similar to that of the *laten*, but much fewer in number, disappeared, like the French culvert—but about a century later than the latter: cf. A. Janda, *Die Barschalken*, p. 10.

[299] On the German *laten, lazzen*, one can consult, among others, Waitz, *Deutsche Verfassungsgeschichte*, V, 2nd. ed., p. 220; H. A. Lüntzel, *Die bauerlichen Lasten im Fürstenthume Hildesheim*, p. 54; W. Wittich, *Die Grundherrschaft im Nordwestdeutschland*, p. 282. On the Flemish *laeten*: Warnkönig, *Flandrische Rechts- und Staatsgeschichte*, III, 1, p. 46; Wauters, *Histoire des environs de Bruxelles*, III, p. 616; Des Marez, *Etude sur la propriété foncière dans les villes du Moyen Age*, p. 190. For northern Netherlands: S. J. Fockema Andreae, *Bijdragen tot de nederlandsche Rechtsgeschiedenis*, III, pp. 26 ff. (p. 27 and note 5, text of 1475, where *laeten* is synonymous to *horige en eigen luiden*); Th. Ilgen, in *Westdeutsche Zeitschrift*, XXXII (1913), p. 82 n. 24 (a definition, in a customary of 1277, of *lati* as *qui pleno jure et proprietate corporis debent*). The *summa dictaminum* of Ludolf (*Quellen und Erörterungen zur bayerischen und deutschen Geschichte*, IX), written toward 1250 in Hildesheim gives, page 396, two manumissions of *litones*, which can be compared to the enfranchisements of culverts in the French formulae of the preceding century. H. Aubin, *Die Entstehung der Landeshoheit nach niederrheinisschen Quellen (Histor. Studien*, H. 143), p. 92, n. 306, observes that toward the end of the Middle Ages, in the lower Rhine, the servile class, unified elsewhere, here carries different names according to the region.

Chapter 4

[1] *Mélanges d'histoire du Moyen Age offerts à Ferdinand Lot*, pp. 55-74.
[2] Seine-et-Oise, *arrondissement* of Pontoise.
[3] Since the copier omitted the final protocol, the only item that allows us to determine the approximate date of the decree is the presence of Jean des Vignes as provost of Paris. He appears for the first time in this function in 1223 or 1224 and for the last in 1227 (*Rec. des Historiens de France*, 24, p. 20). Another personage appears in the decree, as investigator: Hugue d'Athis. He is well known (cf. *ibid.*), but the mention of his name here does not allow us to be more precise chronologically. It is to be noticed that this document was not included in Petit-Dutaillis's *Catalogue des actes de Louis VIII*. It is not alluded to either in L. Delisle's monograph *Fragments de l'histoire de Gonnesse*, in - *Bibliothèque de l'Ecole des Chartes*, 1859.
[4] See in particular the enfranchisement of Pierrefonds by Philip Augustus. (Delisle, *Catalogue*, no. 2012; discussed in Bloch, *Rois et Serfs*, p. 58 n. 2). Compare with a decree edited by Guérard, *Cartulaire de Notre-Dame de Paris*, II, p. 51, no. 9.
[5] Cf. *Rois et Serfs*, p. 35.

[6] It is to be noted that this rubric is most inaccurate. A few details regarding the charter-box of Saint-Pierre of Lagny (Seine-et-Marne, arrondissement of Meaux) will be useful here. I extract them from the preface to the cartulary (fols. D and E; mutilated text which, thanks to the copy in ms. Latin 12690 of the Bibl. Nat., fol. 170, can be reconstructed), and to the history of the monastery written in the seventeenth century by dom Michel Germain (ms. Latin 12690, fols. 82-102 vo; 105-142 vo; 143-160 vo). Lagny suffered much from the Hundred Years War. At the beginning of the sixteenth century only remnants of the old archives were left. A notary, Nicolas Wincelot, gathered these together and wrote an authentic cartulary which is today ms. Latin 9902. The collection is dedicated to Cardinal François de Clermont who was head abbot from 1512 at the latest to 1540 at least. The *Gallia Christiana* (v. VII, col. 305) claims it was written in 1530, but this information is based on a reading error for which Michel Germain (fol. 96 vo) must be held responsible. An indication in the preface (fol. F) was misread. It states simply that the most recent piece reproduced in the cartulary (fol. 136 vo) dates exactly from October 5, 1503 (and not 1530). Once the cartulary was completed the monks, as so often happened, did not take great care of the original documents. The oldest decree found in the Lagny collection in the departmental archives of Seine-et-Marne dates from 1535 (H 178); see *Inventaire Sommaire, série H*, pp. 45-50, and *Supplément à la série H*, p. 12. One must add that the abbey was cruelly pillaged during the wars of religion (dom Germain, fol. 88 vo). It is clear the loss of the original is neither astonishing nor suspect. In addition to dom Germain's history, the Bibl. Nat. possesses also (coll. de Champagne, 18, fols. 1-13 vo) the "Extrait de l'Histoire de l'abbaye royale de S. Pierre de Lagny, faite par dom Chaugy." This work is of no interest to us here.

[7] Questionable reading.

[8] Conjectural reading.

[9] Example of the deduction of the dowry: decree of Philip Augustus, August 1220 (Arch. Nat., S 1337, no. 9; Delisle, *Catalogue*, no. 1988). Example of the deduction of half the estate: Guérard, *Cartulaire de Notre-Dame de Paris*, I, p. 435, no. xxiv (July 1234).

[10] One of the points on which the various local customs differ the most is the serf's will. It is remarkable that the rule given on this subject in this bull is found again, near Lagny, and around the same period, in Meaux, on the bishop's land; there is only one difference: in Meaux, in principle, legacies can be made only for pious works: "Potest etiam decedens [*homo de corpore*] de mobilibus legare terciam partem pro anima sua" (Bibl. de Meaux, ms. 64, pp. 200-201, the bishop's census).

[11] In earlier times a serf could not dispose of his tenure with the same ease as a free tenant. In fact, he had to obtain not only the consent of the seigneur owning the land, as had the free tenant, but also the consent of the seigneur from which he depended "from his body," as a serf. Most often this was the same individual exercising his seigneurial right on two different levels. But sometimes—and this very early on—the serf possessed fields on seigneurial lands other than that of his personal seigneur. In that case he truly needed a double authorization. See, for example, a decree of the counts Geoffroy Martel and Foulque l'Oison (Halphen, *Le comté d'Anjou*, p. 288, no. 152; 1050-14 November 1060) in A. de Trémault, *Cartulaire de Marmoutier pour le Vendômois*, no. XX (also *Liber de Servis Majoris Monasterii*, App. no. xiv). In the thirteenth century, however, it appears that in such cases the assent of the serf's personal seigneur was only rarely required. As for the land's seigneur in the same period, his role in general is limited to collecting the duties on the exchange of tenants, and placing in seisin the new occupants. In regard to this latter seigneur, the serf, as well as the free man, enjoyed in fact, if not in law, an almost unlimited freedom of alienation of his property (see on this last point, O. Martin, *Histoire de la coutume de la prévôté et vicomté de Paris*, I, p. 369). The decree recognizing the serfdom of the men of Rosny, cited below, note

16, states: "Possunt enim sicut homines de corpore emere, vendere, dare de rebus suis, salvo jure ecclesie antedicte." Elsewhere, between 1244 and 1256, a peasant from Esmans (Seine-et-Marne, Montereau canton) already attempted to use the freedom of alienation as well as the matrimonial freedom (which, along with the author of the bull of Lagny, he most probably exaggerated) to prove that the people of his village were not subject to the mainmorte. In all probability, he was wrong. Traditionally, the men of Esmans were mainmortables: "Requisitus de manu mortua, dixit quod non debent manum mortuam. Requisitus quomodo scit, dixit quod scit ad hoc quod ipsi possunt vendere terram suam et ire quocumque loco volunt, et possunt contrahere matrimonium ad voluntatem suam, et sic dicit quod sunt liberi homines, requisitus super hoc" (Guilhiermoz, *Enquêtes et procès*, p. 307).

[12] I limit myself to a few very brief indications: Infringements to the rule, examples in Jeanton, *Le servage en Bourgogne*, p. 45 (but there is no argument to be drawn from Innocent II's bull, cited by this author. The seigneurial consent asked for by the Pope for the ordination of the serfs of the monks of Saint-Michel de Tonnerre was probably, in the author's mind, an enfranchisement). In the eleventh and twelfth centuries, the rule, no doubt, was bent in favor of serfs who were seigneurial functionaries, the *ministeriales*, who then sought everywhere to penetrate the seigneurial society. But the *conditionarii* of the countess of Chartres, which this town's chapter, in Bishop Yves' era, reluctantly had to accept within its bosom (see P. Fournier, *Yves de Chartres et le droit canonique*, in *Revue des questions historiques*, LXIII, 1898, pp. 80-82, and B. Monod, *Essai sur les rapports de Pascal II avec Philippe Ier*, pp. 38-39) were, I believe in reality not serfs proper, but former serfs who had been enfranchised. The proud chapter of Chartres pretended to exclude even enfranchised and the sons of enfranchised (see Ives de Chartres, ep. 133 and see the text of the sermon whose formula must be very ancient, *Cartulaire de Notre-Dame de Chartres*, II, p. 281). Example of a suit against tonsured serfs in the region of Paris: L. Tanon, *Histoire des justices des anciennes églises et communautés de Paris*, pp. 342-344 (1277-1280). On the more tolerant attitude of the late Middle Ages, see p. 148. It must be said here, that, contrary to some recent theories, I continue to see in the mainmorte an essentially servile charge.

[13] I must admit that this obscurity misled me at first. I have in the past presented the bull as recognizing freedom only to these persons subject to arbitrary taille (see *Rois et Serfs*, p. 26 n. 3). A closer examination of the text has convinced me that this interpretation could not be supported. Indeed, let us suppose that this was the author's purpose. He had the choice between two modes of exposition: either to speak only of men subject to the arbitrary taille and simply keep silent about *mainmortables* who did not belong here (and this would have been the simplest manner), or mention the mainmortables, but only to say as follows: those are of servile condition, as opposed to those who pay the arbitrary taille, who are free. Since our notary, devoting a long development to the men on whom weighed the mainmorte, did not oppose them to those who only had to pay the arbitrary taille, one must believe that it was his intention to merge the two categories within one declaration of freedom.

[14] Cartulaire, fol 7 and vo; 8 and vo; 9; 17.

[15] Of course, there is one other way to explain the juridical oddness of the bull: it could be the work of a forger. But this forger would have had to be extremely clever for nothing in the document, except for the very foundation of it, is open to suspicion. To proclaim a document to be a forgery, although it is perfectly correct in its formulation and in its language, because its dispositions are surprising is a far-reaching critical principle. This is why, in my opinion, it is better to hold the apostolic chancellery responsible for this assimilation of mainmortables with free men. Pope Lucius III in his bull also relating to a problem of serfdom (the case of the men of Rosny-sous-Bois against the Abbey Sainte-Geneviève) let this candid avowal slip by: "cum autem, pro negociorum multitudine que ad sedem apostolicam

referuntur, non possint scriptorum nostrorum tenor et alia que facimus memoriter retineri, quorumdam circumvenimus quandoque versutis et *ad scribendum ignoranter inducimur contra ea que antea scripseramus*" (Bibl. Sainte-Geneviève, ms. 356, p. 87, Verona, 7 Kal. October; the Pope's itinerary makes it uncertain whether it was in 1184 or 1185).

[16] See, toward the end of the twelfth century (1168-1185, probably after 1179), a decree of Henri Bishop of Senlis, noting that the men of Rosny-sous-Bois (Seine, Noisy-le-Sec canton) had acknowledged their status as serfs of Sainte-Geneviève (*Mémoires de la Société de l'Histoire de Paris*, 1903, p. 98); a decree of the Parliament of the winter St. Martin 1263 (*Olim*, I, p. 181, no. xiii); another decree of Parliament, in 1272, explaining the reasons why a Jew cannot be compared to a royal serf (L. Tanon, *Histoire des justices des anciennes églises et communautés de Paris*, p. 424).

[17] *Polyptyque de l'abbé Irminon, Prolégomènes*, p. 422: "Dans le Moyen Age, la ligne qui séparait le vassal du serf était souvent bien peu marquée, le serf n'étant qu'un vassal du degré inférieur, et le vassal pouvant être considéré comme un serf de l'ordre le plus élevé."

[18] See Jeanton, *Le servage en Bourgogne*, p. 100, and Léon Girard, *De la condition des mainmortables dans la coutume de Franche-Comté*, p. 68. One can complete the information given by Jeanton, p. 45, on Bishop Jean Germain by consulting M. L. Poussereau's speech given to the 57th Congress of the *Sociétés Savantes* analyzed in the *Journal Officiel*, 25 April 1924, p. 3761.

Chapter 5

[1] *Mémoires de la Société de l'Histoire de Paris et de l'Ile-de France*, t. XXXVIII, 1911, pp. 224-272.

[2] *Chronique anonyme finissant en 1380, Hist. de Fr.*, t. XXI, p. 141; Du Cange, *Glossariium, Ve Manumissio.*, ed. Henschel, t. IV, p. 455, col. 2. The text of Du Cange differs slightly from that of the *Historiens de France* which we give here.

[3] *Homme de corps* is the word commonly employed, in the Parisian region in the thirteenth century, to designate "serf."

[4] They speak of the "men of the town of Oli and of Chastenai and of other neighboring villages," when it appears from the documents that only the men of Orly made the acquaintance of the cells of the chapter. They represent the role of the queen in the little scuffle in the cloister in a completely false light. Finally, mixing up the dates, they ascribe the honor of the enfranchisement of the serfs of Orly to royal intervention (see pp. 165, 177).

[5] *Hist. de Fr.*, t. XXI, p. 117; ed. Paulin Paris, t. IV, p. 331. The *Grandes Chroniques* have no known source here. Cf. Du Cange, *loc. cit.*; Du Bois, *Historia Ecclesiae Parisiensis*, t. II (Paris, 1710), p. 380; Lenain de Tillemont, *Vie de Saint Louis* (*éd. de la Sec. de l'Hist. de France*), t. III, p. 450-452; E. Berger, *Histoire de Blanche de Castille*, pp. 410-411.

[6] Principally by the parts of an inquiry conducted under circumstances we will examine below; we publish these texts as an appendix [not included in the present translation—*Trans*].

[7] Seine, canton of Villejuif.

[8] We also do not know if the tax was levied on all the lands of the chapter,

or on Orly alone. On the question of the date, see note 20.

⁹ Sixteen guarantors, as many as the detained.

¹⁰ Besides the act itself, drawn up by the officials of the three archdeacons of the diocese, we have the draft that served for its compilation. *Arch. Nat.* S346A (*anc.* L 466, nos. 35 and 36). Release with guarantees was the procedure normally followed by the ecclesiastical authorities of Paris, v. Tanon, *Histoire des justices des anciennes églises de Paris*, pp. 50 ff.

¹¹ See p. 175.

¹² See *Pièces Justificatives* (hereafter referred to as *P. Justif.*), part III, para. 17, in Bloch, *Mélanges Historiques*, t. I, Paris, 1963, p. 487.

¹³ Or Garnier de Verberie. Cf. *Hist. de Fr.*, t. XXIV, I, pp. 21, 22, 127.

¹⁴ *P. Justif.* III, para. 14, in Bloch, op. cit., p. 486.

¹⁵ It is impossible not to note where the information provided by the provost of Paris agrees with the statistical data that we can obtain through our own means. We will see below the seven "towns" of Orly, Bagneux, Chatenay, L'Hay, Chevilly, Sucy, and Creteil acting in concert in serious circumstances. Now, by the acts of manumission, which extended from 1243 to 1323, we can calculate that 2,033 serfs were freed on these seven land holdings by the chapter of Paris. We must add to that the 47 free peasants (whose names are not found in any act of manumission) who subscribed to the tax, at L'Hay and at Chevilly, in December 1267 and January 1269 (Guérard, *Cartul. de N.-D.*, t. 11, p. 36, III, and p. 48, XXVII).

¹⁶ "All" the men of Orly, according to the *Grandes Chroniques*, but they must have exaggerated.

¹⁷ What follows, up to the incidents in the cloister, is according to the *Grandes Chroniques*.

¹⁸ *P. Justif.* III, para. 14, in Bloch, op. cit., p. 486.

¹⁹ The account of the incidents in the cloister is provided for us by the depositions published in the supporting documents. P. Justif. III, para. 1, pp. 14-24 and 55-57, in Bloch, op. cit. pp. 479-480.

²⁰ The two extreme dates between which this incident must have taken place are August 28, 1251, the date on which the sixteen men of Orly were supposed to give themselves up at the prison of the chapter, and March 8, 1252, when the mayor of Corbreuse was questioned by a delegate of the arbiters who had already been recognized by the chapter (v. *infra*, p. 000). We must, therefore, add to the catalogue of the provosts of Paris drawn up by Léopold DeLisle (*Hist. de. Fr.* t. XXIV, i. pp. 15 ff.), on August 28, 1251-March 8, 1252, the two names of Garnier de Verberie and Gautier le Maître, who already appear in it elsewhere. Moreover, it seems to us that the expression *tunc prepositi*, which is used in depositions that cannot have been made after December 1, 1252 (*P. Justif.* III, para. 14, pp. 17, 22, in Bloch, op. cit., pp. 486, 487, 488), indicates that Garnier and Gautier were no longer provosts when these depositions were collected. We should remark, in addition, that the same expression (para. 50) was used concerning Eudes Popin, who was definitely no longer provost in 1252. We must, therefore, suppose that two other provosts administered Paris after Garnier and Gautier, and before Garnier de Verberie took up the provostship again, at the latest in February of 1253, jointly with Etienne Tastesaveur (DeLisle, *loc. cit.*, p. 22).

²¹ Eudes de Machault, knight, castellan of the Louvre since May of 1249 at the earliest (*Cartulaire de Saint Lazare de Paris*, Arch. Nat. MM 210, fol. 131 V to 133), died before January 22, 1257 (Guérard, t. 1, p. 165, CCIV). *Cf. Hist. de Fr.*, t. XXI, pp. 248c, k, 345h, 359e, 360a, 372h, 274j; t. XXII, 587j. The name of the castellan is found with different spellings: "de Machel," "de Machouel," de Macheul," "de Machol," "de Macholio," "de Machou." It is evidently the same person whom we find under the name "Eudes de Machault" in the analysis of an obituary of the abbey of Barbeaux (Melinier and Legnon, *Obituaires de la prov. de Sens*, t. 1, p. 34, n. 1. *Cf. ibid.*, t. 1, p. 657). The spelling of the name of the

village of Machault (Seine-et-Marne, canton of Châtelet-en-Brie) was poorly established in the thirteenth century.

[22] *P. Justif.* III, para. 24, in Bloch, *op. cit.*, p. 488.

[23] Cf. *Livre des Serments*, Arch Nat. LL 79, p. 150, "*in celario, in carcere capituli*" (April 18, 1271).

[24] See, especially *P. Justif.* III, para. 16 and 24, in Bloch, *op. cit.*, pp. 487, 488.

[25] There were actually two saints named Léonard: Saint Léonard de Noblat and Saint Léonard de Corbigny; both were considered to have the gift of freeing prisoners. Cf. Paul Meyer in *Notices et extr. des manusc. de la Bibl. Nat.*, t. XXVI, ii, p. 61.

[26] The tablets of Jean Sarrazin, *Hist. de. Fr.*, t. XXI, pp. 360k, 363d. Cf. *ibid.*, pp. 291, 326h, 357f, 376eg, 381k, 389b.d., 392c. *Olim.* I, p. 30, xii.

[27] "*Servientes excubie*" ("sentinel servants"), *P. Justif.* III, para. 16, in Bloch, *op. cit.*, p. 487. Concerning the royal guard, *cf.* Borelli de Serres, *Recherches sur divers services publics*, I, p. 46, n. 2.

[28] *P. Justif.* III, para. 16, in Bloch, *op. cit.*, p. 487. Eudes de Roux—like all the townspeople called to testify by the investigators—belonged to the aristocracy of the Parisian bourgeoisie. He was provost of Paris for four terms, for the first time in 1250 (*Hist. de Fr.*, t. XXIV, i, pp. 22-23).

[29] Pierre, lord of an estate at Châtres (it is Arpajon today, *Olim.* I, p. 228, xix), definitely belonged to the staff of the Curia Regis; we find him conducting an inquiry concerning the fair of Lendit, in 1245. *Hist. de Fr.*, t. XXIV, i, p. 21.

[30] S 345A, 90.

[31] S 345A, 88; reproduced as the preceding in the arbiters' decision published by Guérard, t. II, p. 7, ii.

[32] That of the chapter on November 24.

[33] Seine-et-Oise, canton of Dourdan.

[34] *P. Justif.* I, in Bloch, *op. cit.*, pp. 477-479.

[35] *P. Justif.* II in *ibid*, p. 479.

[36] *P. Justif.* III in *ibid.*, pp. 479-490. The peasants definitely lied when they asserted that the people of Orly had never paid anything but the royal tax. See pp. 168 ff.

[37] Which would seem to prove that these two documents came later than the third of the depositions that form our supporting documents.

[38] Compare with our inquiry the one whose subject, in October of 1270, was the rights of the chapter of Saint-Aignan d'Orléans; as in this case, it concerned the collection of the tax. Beugnot, *Olim.* I, pp. 1010-1012.

[39] *P. Justif.* III, para. 2, in Bloch, *op. cit.*, pp. 480-481.

[40] It dates from June of 829; perhaps in 1252 the canons already knew it more as we do, only through copies (Lasteyrie, *Cartul. de Paris*, no. 35); *P. Justif.* III, c. 8, in Bloch, *op. cit.*, pp. 483-484.

[41] Still, in one of the two cases, we cannot properly speak of confirmation. Cf. p. 172, n. 73.

[42] The investigators seem to have been equally preoccupied with making sure that the men of Orly were serfs; what is more, the fact was obvious, and the peasants did not intend to deny it. Obviously the investigators were laboring under the impression that the tax—or at least the so-called "arbitrary" tax that this is—was in some way a servile duty; this was an impression that was certainly false (for examples of free men paying the arbitrary tax: Guérard, t. II, p. 36, iii; p. 64, xliii; p. 48, xxvii; of serfs paying the regularly collected levy, S 1128^2; for a definition of the characteristics of the servile condition, see *Olim.* I, p. 181, xiii), but that was widespread already in the thirteenth century (Guérard, t. II, p. 65) and especially after that time. Also, the investigators do not seem to have remembered this argument. However, the depositions of the witnesses are found to provide a certain amount of valuable information on the indicators of the servile condition. We

willingly pass over them here in silence; they will gain by being used in a comprehensive study.

[43] For the royal tax, see *P. Justif.* III, para. 28, in Bloch, *op. cit.*, p. 488.

[44] Each was taxed in proportion to his wealth in land (for example Guérard, t. II, p. 33). When a seigneurial tax and perhaps even the royal tax was concerned, the sergents, functionaries or servants of the Chapter—mayors, doyens, cooks, and the like—were exempted from any duty (Guérard, II, p. 9; S 163B: enfranchisement of Jean de Bagneux).

[45] The chapter seems to have wanted to make the impost that the king levied upon his men, by its intervention, pass for a complimentary gift. Aubert, the priest of Saint-Pierre-des-Arcis, who had kept the writings of the chapter for a long time, informs us of the final formula used in the accounts of the royal tax: "*Capitulum in fine dicebat quod dominus rex haberet de gratia ab ipso capitulo trecentas libras Parisiensum.*" *P. Justif.* III, para. 2, in Bloch, *op. cit.*, p. 480.

[46] *P. Justif.* III, para. 44, 45, 47, in Bloch, *op. cit.*, pp. 489-490.

[47] According to *P. Justif.* III, para. 25-54, in *ibid.*, pp. 488-490.

[48] *Recherches sur divers services publics*, t. i, pp. 517 ff.

[49] *P. Justif.* III, para. 50, in *ibid.*, p. 490. Eudes Popin was still provost in June 1241. *Hist. de Fr.*, t. XXIV, i, p. 20.

[50] This date can be established with some certainty. On the one hand, the actual placing of the interdict upon Notre Dame after "*captione hominum nostrorum et redemptione seu talliatum eorum*" was necessarily prior to March 24, 1238, the day when the interdict was lifted for the first time (see p. 169). On the other hand, in the letter that Pope Gregory IX sent on January 6, 1238, to Saint Louis to complain about the offenses of the royal policy towards the chapter of Paris, it was not concerned with the facts that concern us here, but only with two other grievances (Teulet, Layettes du Trésor, t. II, p. 361; Auvray, Régistres de Grégoire IX, no. 4018; cf. Auvray, nos. 4016, 4017, 4019).

[51] Which follows from *P. Justif.* III, para. 47-52, in Bloch, *op. cit.*, p. 490.

[52] It is interesting, for the history of the *bailli*, to note the expression used by the chapter in the thirteen charters of the lifting of the interdict: "*Interdictum positum in ecclesia nostra propter injurias ecclesie ipsi illatas a domino nostro rege et baillivis ejus.*" See also the sentence of arbitration referred to below.

[53] See the enumeration of these complaints, Guérard, t. II, p. 395, xvii. Two of these—which dealt with the levies demanded by the king from the townspeople of Paris whose responsibility was to negotiate the goods of the chapter and with the jurisdiction of the land of Garlande—were already pointed out in the letter of Gregory IX, of January 6, 1238 (see p. 235, n. 3).

[54] And during this last period by twelve charters, followed by two in three months. Arch Nat. L 463[34]-[46]. The charter of September 25, 1238 (L 463[34]) informs us that Queen Blanche and the king were ill at the time; that of April 6, 1242, says that at the time Louis was far from Paris and that his return was expected at the end of June at the latest (L 463[35]). On this matter, see Haureau, in *Notices et extr. des manusc. de la Bibl. Nat.*, t. XXI, ii, pp. 210 ff. and especially N. Valois, *Guillaume d'Auvergne*, pp. 73 ff. M. Valois did not know of the acts of suspension of the interdict that we have just cited. On March 10, 1239, the Pope recommended to the canons that they suspend the interdict (Valois, *loc. cit.*, p. 80). We do not know if they complied.

[55] Lenain de Tillemont, t. III, p. 58. The sentence of arbitration is cited.

[56] Guérard, t. II, p. 395, xvii. *Annuaire de la Soc. de l'Hist. de Fr.*, 1838, p. 273.

[57] Guérard, t. II, p. 398, n. 1

[58] It follows that the levy could also be paid over time (cf. *P. Justif.* III, para 4, in Bloch, *op. cit.*, pp. 481-482); we do not concern ourselves here with this way of collecting the levy. Besides, a levy paid over time always implies an arbitrary levy that preceded it.

[59] *P. Justif.* I, para. 3, in *ibid.*, p. 477.

[60] *P. Justif.* II, in *ibid.*, p. 479.

[61] The information on the collection of the levy is given primarily according to *P. Justif.* III, para. 1, 6, 8, 10, 12, in *ibid.*, pp. 479-486. Guérard, t. II, p. 443, liii. On all that concerns the administrative practices of the chapter, see the introduction of Guérard, in t. I, pp. cxxxvii-clxii, and on the levy in particular, see *ibid.*, pp. cxc-cxcvii.

[62] Guérard, t. II, p. 46, xxii. S 1128² (purchase of the town hall of Créteil).

[63] *P. Justif.* III, para. 10, in Bloch, *op. cit.*, pp. 484-485. Arch. Nat. LL 79[135].

[64] "*In pluribus pellibus que sunt registra capituli,*" *P. Justif.* III, c. 8, in Bloch, *op. cit.*, pp. 483-484.

[65] *P. Justif.* III, para. 1, in *ibid.*, pp. 479-480. It was a question, in the *Livre des Serments*, of "*pelle compoti cammere.*" Guérard, t. III, p. 433. None of these precious scrolls has come down to us.

[66] Guérard, t. I, p. 389, xxiii. Its collection only appears to us to occur upon the land of Rozoy-en-Brie.

[67] Old style date; this is the date of the charter of Louis VII cited in note 83 below. The collection of this levy only appears to us as occurring on the land of Epone.

[68] *P. Justif.* III, para. 1, in Bloch, *op. cit.*, pp. 479-490; cf. *P. Justif.* I, in *ibid.*, p. 478: "*Ita usitatum est a tempore a quo non exstat memoria.*"

[69] Only one of them, Raoul de Chevry (*P. Justif.* III, para. 8, in Bloch, *op. cit.*, pp. 483-484) knew of the levy of 1178, and he could not even date it approximately.

[70] This is the date indicated by the mayor of Corbreuse, who states: in the summer, around the Nativity of Saint Jean (June 24), *P. Justif.* I, in *ibid.*, p. 478. Two other depositions (which also confuse several levies between them) say 1222. But nearly all the depositions are in agreement in recognizing that the construction of the cloister preceded that of the houses in the rue du Fumier. Thus the levy of the tax designed to subsidize the expenses of these projects could not have been after 1220 (see below, note 74). A witness (in Bloch, *op. cit.*, pp. 483-484) says that Saint Denis-du-Pas was, at the same time, the object of architectural work; cf. *ibid.*, pp. 484-485.

[71] It was a question of these granaries of the chapter "*que sunt in claustro Parisiensi*" in a text of July 1225. Guérard, t. I, p. 419. iv.

[72] This sum was collected at Orly: 50 livres. *P. Justif.* I, in Bloch, *op. cit.*, p. 478.

[73] *P. Justif.* I and III, para. 7, in *ibid.*, pp. 478 and 483.

[74] In 1223 according to master Aubert de Nemours (*P. Justif.* III, para. 18, in *ibid.*, p. 487); but the same witness informs us that the Doyen Etienne de Reims, who was certainly dead in 1220 (Guérard, t. IV, p. 215) was still alive at the time when this tax was raised. Moreover, we know that in 1219 the chapter acquired from the Templars all that they possessed in the rue du Fumier (Guérard, t. I, p. 416, ii). Finally the date of 1219 agrees more or less with those indicated by the priest of Fontenay (*P. Justif.* III, para. 12, in Bloch, *op. cit.*, pp. 485-486) and by the mayor of Corbreuse (*P. Justif.* I, in *ibid.*, p. 478). The sum demanded of Corbreuse was 50 livres, and the tax was collected in the winter after the festival of Saint-Rémy (October 1).

[75] The purchase took place in March of 1221 and cost a thousand livres (S 385[10]). Orly paid 65 livres (*P. Justif.* III, para. 12, in Bloch, *op. cit.*, pp. 485-486).

[76] Seine-et-Marne, *canton* of Brie-Comte-Robert.

[77] *P. Justif.* I, in *ibid.*, p. 478. It is not certain that it was levied anywhere besides at L'Hay.

[78] *Ibid.* From Corbreuse only; actually, all the accounts are unanimous is telling us that those of the canons who did not want taxes (see below) succeeded in preventing the collections during a number of years, which we cannot truly

enumerate precisely, but which was definitely greater than four years.

⁷⁹ Cf. *P. Justif.* II, para. 11, in *ibid.*, p. 485. "*Audivit tamen multotiens laicos murmurantes quod non deberent talliari, nisi pro domino rege.*"

⁸⁰ Seine-et-Marne, *arrondissement* of Coulommiers.

⁸¹ Guérard, t. I, p. 389, xxiii. This was a levy "over time" (*abonnement*).

⁸² Seine-et-Oise, *canton* of Mantes.

⁸³ *P. Justif.* III, para. 8, in Bloch, *op. cit.*, pp. 483-484. The patent "letter" of Louis VII, providing us with the same expression as used by Raoul de Chevry, still exists in the *Archives Nationales*, under the call number S 260A11: even though it was transcribed in the *Grand Pastoral* (p. 489) it was left out by Guérard, and consequently escaped M. Luchaire. It is only dated with the year of the Incarnation (1178), and from Paris, showing the royal monogram and the signatures of the Comte Thibault (de Blois), seneschal of the butler Guy (de Senlis) of the chamberlain Renaud and of the constable Raoul (de Clermont), the chancellery being vacant. The king stated the judgment of the chapter, handed down in the presence of royal envoys (*nuntiis*); whatever Raoul de Chevry said of it, he did not *confirm* it, as testified by the insertion into the act of the formula, "*salvo tamen predictorum hominum jure, si aliquo tempore agere contra voluerunt.*"

⁸⁴ Seine-et-Marne, *canton* of Moret.

⁸⁵ *P. Justif.* III, para. 8, in Bloch, *op. cit.*, pp. 483-484. Henri de Chancelier (*P. Justif.* III, para. 2, in *ibid.*, pp. 480-481) relates the same affair while "toning it down": "*Et tunc precepit quod redderent, vel ponentur in loco dishonesto.*" The canon Pierre le Jeune (*ibid.*, pp. 481-482) thought that the delegates had returned with a charter of the king, but could not say for sure. We have not been able to find any trace of an act of this kind. Probably the canons thought it was useless to pay chancellery fees, and trusted the record of the court. As for the date, it is impossible to state it precisely. Philip-Augustus' visits to Melun were very frequent from March of 1193 to June of 1223 (see De Lisle, *Cat. des ates de Phil. Aug.*, p. cv to cx). Cf. *P. Justif.* II-III, para. 1, 2, 4, 6, 8, in Bloch, *op. cit.*, pp. 479-484.

⁸⁶ Which follows especially from *P. Justif.* III, para. 1, 2, 5, 7, 9, in *ibid.*, pp. 479-484.

⁸⁷ *P. Justif.*, in *ibid.*, pp. 484-485.

⁸⁸ "De Columpna." Cf. Lognon, *Pouillés de la Prov. de Sens*, p. 181 E.

⁸⁹ Etienne de Reims has also been cited as a preacher (Lecoy de la Marche, *La chaire française*, p. 72); but he was much less well known.

⁹⁰ Concerning Guiard de Laon, see Haureau, *Notices et extr. de qq. manuscrits latins*, t. VI, pp. 220-228, and *Journal des Savants*, 1893, p. 365.

⁹¹ Concerning Eudes de Chateauroux, see Haureau, in *Notices et extr. des manusc. de la Bib. Nat.*, t. XXIV, ii, pp. 204-285, and *Notics et extr. des quelques manusc. lat.*, t. VI, pp. 200-220.

⁹² Sucy-en-Brie, Seine-et-Oise, *canton* of Boissy-Saint-Leger.

⁹³ Seine, *canton* of Charenton.

⁹⁴ Seine, *canton* of Villejuif.

⁹⁵ Seine, *canton* of Villejuif.

⁹⁶ Seine, *canton* of Sceaux.

⁹⁷ Seine, *canton* of Sceaux.

⁹⁸ *P. Justif.* III, para. 1-10, 17-18, in Bloch, *op. cit.*, pp. 479-485, 487.

⁹⁹ *P. Justif.* III, para. 1, 4, 8, 9, 10, in *ibid.*, pp. 479-485.

¹⁰⁰ Gerbout de Villeneuve was enfranchised by the chapter, with his wife and his two children, in April of 1255 a.s.: S 163B; cf. Guérard, t. II, p. 385, iv.

¹⁰¹ Arch. Nat. L 259¹ (October 1248) for Philippe Boucel; L 529² (January 1249) for Thomas "Tyboud." On Philippe Boucel, cf. Guérard, t. II, p. 449, lxiii. *Hist. de Fr.* t. XXIV, i, pp. 20-21. Borrelli de Serres, *Recherches sur divers services publics*, t. 1, p. 240, n. 1.

¹⁰² "*Evroinus de Valencinis, prepositus mercatorum*," in an act of 1263 published

by Leroux de Lincy, *Recherches sur la Grande Confrérie Notre Dame. Mem. de la Soc. des Antiqu.*, t. XVII, p. 273. He was definitely not still provost of the merchants in 1252.

[103] *P. Justif.*, III, para. 1, 4, 9, 10, in Bloch, *op. cit.*, pp. 479, 481-482, 484-485.

[104] There are two copies of it: S 345^{85} and S 345^{86}. Guérard, t. II, p. 7, ii.

[105] In spite of this decision, which could have been a test case, the chapter of Paris, in 1264, encountered difficulties in making the serfs of Bagneux accept the levy; the serfs ended by giving in (Guérard, t. II, p. 123, xxiv). There were the same difficulties several years later at Itteville, (Seine-et-Oise, *canton* of La Ferté Alais) where there was a veritable riot. The affair resulted in an arbitration; the arbiters—Robert de Sorgon, the Archdeacon of Laon, Clement, and a canon, Milon de Corbeil—whose judgment was rendered on March 17, 1268, made the two parties accept the subscription of the tax over time (Guérard, t. II, p. 364, 1, and 366, ii); their inquiry has left no trace. Evidently, the arbitrary levy was always a disputed duty on the lands of Notre Dame.

[106] For the evidence of these acts of enfranchisement (which are very numerous) I must refer to a study under preparation on the rural population of Ile-de France during the time of serfdom.

[107] S 344^1; Guérard, t. II, p. 3.

[108] Guérard, t. II, p. 3.

Chapter 6

[1] *Revue Historique*, 1921, pp. 220-242.

[2] Ed. Salmon *Collection de textes pour servir à l'étude et à l'enseignement de l'histoire*, t. II, chap. xlv, c. 1451 and 1452, pp. 233-234.

[3] German historians ordinarily say *Leibeigene* and the English say "villain." In spite of notable differences, which continued to be stressed, the fundamental similarity of Leibeigenen, villains, and serfs is evident.

[4] In 1837. Here is the text of the two questions asked in the competition: "1. By what causes was ancient slavery abolished? 2. After this slavery had entirely ceased in Western Europe, when did servitude de la glèbe alone remain?" The prize was bestowed upon a memoire composed jointly by H. Wallon and J. Yanoski. From this the first of the two authors extracted his *Histoire de l'esclavage dans l'antiquité*, and the second a work that is much less well known (and that scarcely deserves it), entitled *De l'abolition de l'esclavage en Occident*, in 8°, Paris, 1842. One can find the account of the competition in volume II (1842) of the *Mémoires de l'Académie des sciences morales*.

[5] The feminine is sometimes *ancele*, and sometimes—more often, it seems—*serve*. Ancele (from ancilla) seems to have been rather specialized in the sense of "serving girl."

[6] Besides, serf was, as it were, a legally recognized insult; certain customs punished a person who called a free man by this name with a fine: Coutumes de Clune (1161-1172), in Bernard and Bruel, *Recueil des chartes de l'abbaye de Cluny* (*Documents inédits*), t. V, n. 4205, c. vii; *Charte d'Amiens* (1185) in Beauville, *Receuil des documents inédits concernant la Picardie*, t. IV, in-8°, 1882, p. 19, c. 42. In literary language, *cuvert*, *cuivert* and *culvert* were used perhaps even more frequently (aside from *vilain*, which means "peasant" without any precise juridical meaning).

The cuverts—the *colliberti* in Latin—formed a class of men whose condition was very similar to serfdom; historians of law normally call them colliberts; but this term (invented by contemporaries) is only a clumsy tracing of the Latin, and is a pure barbarism, frankly; the old French term must be used [Marc Bloch subsequently dealt with this question in *Collibertus ou Colibertus?* in Marc Bloch, *Mélanges Historiques*, Paris, 1963, pp. 379-384; and in "The Colliberti," in the present volume, pp. 93-149].

[7] *L'alleu et le domaine rural*, p. 463. Cf. *Les Transformations de la royauté pendant l'époque carolingienne*, p. 587, n. 1.

[8] Cf. G. Jeanton, *Le Servage en Bourgogne* (thesis in law, Paris), in 8°, Paris, 1906, p. 80; L. Verriest, *Le Servage dans le comté de Hainaut*, in *Acad. royale de Belgique. Classe des lettres.* Mem., 2e série, t. IV, fasc 3, 1900, p. 57. I myself have confirmed the fact for the Ile-de-France (including the area of Chartres and of Orléans); it appears in this region with great clarity. It also seems to me to have been very general, but there were probably local variations. I have scarcely studied the language of the notaries around the end of the Middle Ages. Perhaps the word serf came back into fashion in acts written in French, if only in the form "*de serve condicion.*"

[9] *Omnes servos et ancillas quos homines de corpore appellamus*. Enfranchisement of the serfs living in Orléans and neighboring villages. *Ordonnances*, t. IX, p. 214 (Luchaire, Louis VII, no. 774, and A. Cartelleri, Phillipp II, August, *Beilagen*, no. 75). Cf. the confirmation in the *Actes de Philippe Auguste*, published by H. F. Delaborde, t. I, no. 3. Note the parallel of homme de corps and *Leibeigene* (in Latin, *propius de corpore*).

[10] Finally, see a note by J. Bruch, *Zeitschrift für roman. Philologie*. t. XXXVIII, 1917, p. 701 (whose conclusions, to me at least, seem arguable).

[11] I have provided a short bibliography of the usage of *homme lige* in the sense of "serf" in a note of my work. *Rois et serfs*, p. 23, n. 2, and *Additions et rectifications* (where an error slipped in: that of joining the two paragraphs into one).

[12] Beaumanoir, for example. But Beaumanoir also thought of serf in the Latin meaning of "slave." When he talks of these "sers" who "*sont sougiet a leur seigneur que leurs sires puet prendre quanQu'il ont et a mort et a vie. ...*" para. 1452, cf. para. 1457—a type of human being which he had never seen in Beauvaisis—he simply conformed to what he had read in Roman law concerning the servi. Besides serf had been the translation of servus for a long time; the word *esclave* took a long time to appear and even longer to be accepted by all. In 1694, the *Dictionnaire de l'Académie*, which knew very well about *hommes de mainmorte* (see the article *Glèbe*), still wrote, in the article *Serf*, this astonishing sentence: "There are no serfs at all in France." This is because academic usage still saw the word servus behind that of serf.

[13] Mandate of Charles VI to the *bailli* of Vermandois, Paris, September 22, 1404, cited and partially published by A. A. Monteil, *Histoire des Français des divers états*, 4th ed., t. I, im-12, Paris, 1853, notes, p. 81, according to the original, which is in his possession.

[14] Paul Fournier, *Les Officialités au Moyen Age*, pp. 8 and 9.

[15] In the Ile-de-France, the acts of enfranchisement that were passed under the seal of ecclesiastical communities or of lay lords still kept the words servus and ancilla, whereas the acts that were passed under the seal of officiality and compiled by it strictly excluded these words. Here are some examples: *les affranchissements de Rosny-sous-Bois (aout 1246) et de Nanterre (mars 1248) par les chanoines de Sainte-Geneviève de Paris:* Arch Nat. S1574, no. 1. and 1567, no. 1 (in which the words servi and homines de corpore alternate as if they were two synonyms); *l'affranchissement de trente-six personnes de condition servile par le chevalier Simon de Corbeil (1-27 mars 1255):* Arch. Nat. JJ26, fol. 369 v°, and Bibl. Nat. ms. lat. 9778, fol. 255 v° (where we find the curious expression *homines meos et*

ancillas de corpore, in which the uncertainty over terminology is clearly indicated). To illuminate the disappearance of servus and the new fashion of *homo de corpore*, it would be interesting to put some statistical data together, but that is impossible; nearly all the cartularies or collections of charters that have been published are incomplete after the thirteenth century; they only give the more recent items in analytical form, in most cases.

[16] See note 45.

[17] See note 21.

[18] Here are some examples: Bulls of Innocent IV for Notre-Dame de Paris (B. Guerard, *Cartul. de Notre-Dame de Paris*, t. II, p. 393, no. XIII) and for Saint-Denis (Doublet, *Histoire de l'Abbaye de Saint-Denys en France*, in-4°, Paris, 1625, p. 579).

[19] May 29, 1239 (4 kal. June, year 13 of the pontificat), Latran: *Livre Noir de Saint-Maur-des-Fosses*, Arch. Nat., LL46, fol 5v°.

[20] R. de Lasteyrie, *Cartul. général de Paris* no. 150 (Luchaire, *Louis VI*, no. 63): 1108, the first year of the reign.

[21] W. Ganzenmumler, in *Die flandrische Ministerialität Westdeutsche Zeitschrift*, 1906, pp. 374 and 384, sees only *ministeriales* in this phrase and not serfs in general—completely without reason: "*Ipsius ecclesie famuli qui apud vos servi vulgo improprie nuncupantur*," January 24, 1113. B. Guérard, *Cartul. de Notre Dame de Paris*, t. 1, p. 223, no. VIII; cf. Lasteyrie, *Cartul. général de Paris*, no. 162 (where the date is corrected). The word servus is rejected as improper for designating the unfree English of its time by an English book of customs from the thirteenth century, the *Mirror of Justices*, edited by Whittaker, (Selden Society) in-4°, London, 1895, p. 79.

[22] "*Cum habeatis plures servos qui homines de corpore vulgariter nuncupantur*," February 3, 1245 (3 nones February, year 2 of the pontificat), Lyon: *Arch. Nat.* L 244, no. 6; there is a copy, without any indication of location, in the *Livre des Privilèges*, Arch. Nat. LL 1027, fol. 16.

[23] "*In homines ipsorum de corpore qui servi vulgariter appellantur*," March 19, 1289: Bull addressed to the archbishop of Sens and to the bishop of Auxerre, in E. Langlois, *Registres de Nicolas IV*, t. 1, no. 736, p. 163; bull addressed to the king of France, which is analyzed in *ibid.*, no. 738, p. 167, and whose complete text is in the *Livre Rouge du Chapitre de Chartres*, in the library of the City of Chartres, ms. 1162, fol. 34, and the cartulary of the same chapter preserved in the library of the city of Toulouse, ms. 590, fol. 18. These bulls were compiled by a clerk who was a particular purist; cf. Langlois, p. 164, "*ab omni consuetudine vel costuma, ut utamur vocabulo regionis*," p. 165, "*alique placita, ut patrie verbis utamur*."

[24] We find homme de condition after the thirteenth century. It is curious that this term, which was to serve as a synonym for "gentleman" in the seventeenth and eighteenth centuries, would have designated primarily men "of servile condition" in the Middle Ages.

[25] I know of one example of servus glebe in Italy, in an inquiry of 1258 on the rights of the bishop of Trente, *Archiv fur österreichische Geschichte*, 94 (1907), p. 403, n. 1 (cf. *Gotting. Gelehrte Anzeigen*, 1909, II, p. 699). Is it an isolated case? I know too little about Italian juridical history to dare to say anything for certain. As we will see below, the creators of this association of words were professors of Bologna; perhaps Italian clerks borrowed it from them sometimes. As for Germany, the fourth edition of the *Reichsaltertümer* of Grimm, t. 1, Leipzig, 1899, p. 454, gives (without any date) an example with reference to Heider, *Grundlich Ausführung der Reichsstadt Lindau*, in-fol. Nüremburg, 1643, p. 293; but on the page indicated, I found nothing of the sort, and I could not get hold of the act cited in the entire volume. At any rate, the expression would be completely anomalous. The German historians of the nineteenth century sometimes used "*an der Scholie gebunden*":

a simple imitation, it would seem, of the French *"attaché a la glèbe"* (or of the Latin *glebis inhaerere*).

[26] *"Ascripticia enim condicio non est ea qua quis alieno subicitur dominio, sed glebe servus intelligitur, non principaliter persone"* (E. Besta, *L'Opere d'Irenerio II*, in-8°, Turin, 1896, p. 9). My attention was drawn to this gloss by a note by R. W. and A. J. Carlyle, *A History of Medieval Political Theory in the West*, v. II, in-8°, London, 1909, p. 39, n. 3. Servus glebe (in the sense of ascriptitius) also can be found in section v, c. 7 of *Questiones de juris subtilitatibus* which are perhaps by Irnerius, edited by H. Fitting, in-4°, Berlin, 1894, p. 60.

[27] *Placentini jurisconsulti vetustissimi*, in *Summam Institutionum*, libri III in-fol., Mayence, 1535, pp. 4 and 6.

[28] Cf. Jaffe-Wattenbach, *Regesta pontificum romanorum*, I, no. 658.

[29] *Die Summa des Paucapalea über das Decretum Gratiani*, edited by J. F. v. Schulte, in-8°, Giessen, 1891, p. 36, c. 11.

[30] Edited by J. S. v. Schulte, in-8°, Giessen, 1892, p. 122, c. 11; edited by Singer, in-8°, Paderborn, 1902, p. 141, c. 11.

[31] *Die Summa des Stephanus Tornacensis über das Decretum Gratiani*, edited by J. F. v. Schulte, in-8°, Giessen, 1891, p. 81, c. 20, *"Ascripticios, qui se ascriptserunt certa conditione fundo, hique servi glebe dicuntur."*

[32] Irnerius did not find the expression servus glebe in the text of the *Corpus Juris*, such as we know it today. One could, it is true, presume that he had a different text in his hands where, for example, in the Justinian Code, XI, 52, 1, servi glebae could have been read instead of *servi terrae*. But this hypothesis would be in contradiction with what we believe we know today about the history of the manuscripts of the Justinian compilation. A last conjecture remains: Irnerius could have come across servus glebe in the juridical literature of the first centuries of the Middle Ages. We cannot absolutely reject this, because we certainly do not possess the material prior to Irnerius in its entirety. What we have preserved has in part remained in manuscript form and, after all, I do not pretend to have read everything that has been printed. I would note, though, that I did not find servus glebe in the *Exceptiones Petri*. To be absolutely precise, Irnerius can only be considered the creator of this expression on condition of future discoveries.

[33] Cf. O. Seeck, *Geschichte des Untergangs der antiken Welt*, II in-8°, Berlin, 1901, book II, ch. vii: *Die Erblichkeit der Stande*.

[34] *"... licet condicione videantur ingenui, servi tamen terrae ipsius cui nati sunt aestimentur."* Justinian Code, XI, 52, 1. M. A. Piganiol, *L'Impôt de capitation sous le Bas-Empire romain*, Chambéry, 1916 (thesis at Paris), p. 67, proposes the correction of nati to dati; but what interests us here is the text that Irnerius had in hand. Cf. Justinian Code, XI, 53, 1, *"Inservient terris."*

[35] Law of Valentinian and Valens of July 31, 365: Theodosian Code, XI, 1, 12; Justinian Code XI, 48, 3.

[36] *"... quos ita glebis inhaerere praecipimus, ut ne puncto quidem temporis debeant amoveri"* (Justinian Code, XI, 48, 15).

[37] We might include the text of Iavolenus, *Dig.* VIII, 3, 13, 1, *"omnes glebae serviant"*, where *glebae* is the subject of the sentence, and where praedial (and not personal) servitude is discussed, but which, if read a little hastily and especially with a rather mixed-up memory, could have contributed to the suggestion of the verbal association of servi and glebae.

[38] In everything that is said above, I presume that Irnerius knew sections 48 and 52 of Book XI of the Justinian Code. I am aware that this could be contested. In general, the first glossarists are considered not to have used the last three books of the code. Nonetheless, the following remarks should be made: (1) that precisely section 48 never ceased to be accepted in the juridical literature (Max Conrat, *Geschichte der Quellen und Literatur des Romischen Rechts in früheren Mittelalter*, I, in-8°, Leipzig, 1889, p. 55, n. 3); (2) that these three books were entirely left aside

rather than exactly being unknown (*ibid.*, p. 355). In sum, Irnerius could certainly have read section 48, and he probably could have read section 52. And I do not see where else he could have gotten the idea of servus glebe.

³⁹ Edited by Desilve, Valenciennes, and Paris, 1893.

⁴⁰ Archives that are for the most part unedited; I have had the chance to go through them.

⁴¹ As was seen by A. Lecoy de la Marche, *La Chaire Française au Moyen Age*, in-8°, Paris, 1886, pp. 57 and 421.

⁴² Also sometimes *garsons*, it seems, but more rarely. For the serving women, the terminology seems not very well established; we find *ancele* (see above, note 5), *chambrière, meschine*. See the texts—which are insufficient, besides—collected by H. Doercks, *Haus und Hof in den Epen des Crestien von Troies*, Greifswald, 1885, p. 42, and Fritz Meyer, *Die Stände, ihr Leben und Treiben dargestellt nach den altfr. Artus und Abenteuerromanen (Ausg. u. Abh aus dem Gebiete der romanischen Philologie,* 89) Marburg, 1892, pp. 98 and 104.

⁴³ For example, from the moralists, Thomas de Cantimpré, *Bonum universale de apibus*, II, i, c. 10. and c. 23; XXVIII, c. 11 (edition of Douai, in-8°, 1627); from the lexicographers, Jean de Garlande, edited by Scheler, *Jahrb. für romanische und englische Literatur*, VI (1865), p. 149, edited by J. Depoin *(publ. Soc. histor. Pontoise)* in-8°, Pontoise, 1900, p. 198 and the archives of the *département* of Seine-et-Oise, série H, ms. non coté, fol. 13 (where *servi de cellario* is translated in French as *les vendeurs dudit cellier*). Brunetto Latino, for whom French is a second language, treats serf as a synonym for *sergeant*: Livres dou Tresor, edited by Chabaille (unedited documents), II, 2, chap. xciv, pp. 442 ff. This use of servus in the sense of "servant" was to persist in juridical language, to the extent that in the sixteenth century, Hippolyte Bonacossa could begin a treatise "De servis et famulis" with this surprising definition: *"Et servus (de quo noster sit sermo) est homo liber ... quem oportet alii famulari." Tractatus illustrium jurisconsultorum*, V. 1 in-fol., Venice, 1584, fol. 121 v°. Medieval Latin is sometimes a particularly odd jargon!

⁴⁴ See his *Exempla*, edited by Crane (Folk Lore Society), in 8°, London, 1890, nos. XLII, LXXXII (p. 37), CXX and CXCV; edited by Frenken (*Quellen und Unters. zur lateinischen Philologie des Mittelalters*, V, H. 1), in-8°, Munich, 1914, nos. XXIII, XXV (p. 112), and LIV. Much has been written about Jacques de Vitry; it suffices to refer to the introduction to the Frenken edition, since it is the most recent work to appear.

⁴⁵ The sermons *ad servos et ancillas* are still unedited. They do not appear among the extracts of the "Sermones vulgares" that Dom Petra presented in his *Analecta Novissima*, II, in-4°, Tivoli, 1888, pp. 344 ff. I cite, according to Latin manuscript 17509 of the *Bibliothèque Nationale*, fol. *133*: "*Homo servus dicitur qui servilis est conditionis; nec habet potestatem sui corporis.... Servi etiam hominis sunt qui vocantur ascripticii, seu serve glebe qui astricti solo. Servi vero originarii dicuntur qui nati sunt ascripticiis in ipso solo. Sunt insuper servi qui dicuntur conducticii famuli, scilicet quos ad tempus conducimus, et post terminum possunt recedere liberi,*" Cf. Latin manuscript 3284, fol. 174 v°.

⁴⁶ Edited by H. F. Delaborde (*Société de l'Histoire de France*), I, c. 97, p. 204.

⁴⁷ Edited by H. F. Delaborde, II, chap. iv, v. 561 and 566: "*Sed ascripti quibus dabatur ... qui sint vel glebe servi vel conditionis.*"

⁴⁸ *Les Coustumes du pays et comté de Nivernois*, chap. viii art. VI (*Oeuvres*, Bordeaux edition, in-fol., 1703, II, p.130).

⁴⁹ Serfdom in the south has scarcely been studied. I have sought to give some indications, which are necessarily very vague, in *Rois et serfs*, p. 100. After the beginning of the thirteenth century, in Languedoc the serf ceased to be a serf if he abandoned all his possessions. Later on, in the north, as soon as this juridical rule appeared there, this person was called the *désaveu*: see the customary laws

promulgated by Simon de Montfort at Pamiers on December 1, 1212, *Histoire de Languedoc, nouvelle édition*, t. VIII, col. 631, art. XXVII.

[50] This was an ordinance abolishing (or pretending to abolish) servitude in the sénéchaussée of Toulouse and Albi, in April of 1290, *Histoire de Languedoc*, t. X, Preuves, col. 348: "*Nos ... omnes universitates et singulas personas ... in quibus aliquod jus habemus vel habere seu pretendere possumus ratione vel occasione servitutis, que de corpore tantum vel de casalagio tantum dicitur, aut etiam de utroque, vel rerum casalagii conjunctim vel separatim, aut ascripticiatus vel quasi, seu libertinitatis vel cujuslibet alterius generis servitutis premissorum natalibus et plene libertati ac ingenuitati restituimus ...*" Note the effort to liken serfdom to the two conditions that in Roman law could pass as intermediaries between slavery and full liberty—the status of the coloni and of the freed man.

[51] See note 55.

[52] See note 58.

[53] *Institution au droit des François* (*Oeuvres*, Bordeaux edition, II) in the paragraph entitled *Des servitudes personnelles et des mainmortes*, p. 46. Cf. above, p. 190.

[54] In the paragraph cited in the preceding note, p. 45 of t. II of the edition of 1703. The *Institution* appeared for the first time in 1607; Guy Coquille died in 1603. Among later authors, where the similarity can be found, we can cite Desiderius Heraldus, *De Rerum judicatorum auctoritate*, book II, chap. xvii, para X, in the *Thesaurus* by Otto, t. 11, col. 1247.

[55] The two texts, French and Latin, can be found in article 9 of the ordinance concerning the bourgeoisies in César Chabrun, *Les bourgeois du roi*, law thesis at Paris, 1908, p. 142. The two editions of this ordinance (that of 1287 and that of 1303) were also published many times, notably in the *Recueil des Ordonnances*, t. I, pp. 314 and 367. The Latin edition was promulgated anew in 1351 (cf. Chabrun, *loc. cit.*, p. 73), which could have contributed to the popularization of the expression "*glebe affixos.*"

[56] We might note that in England, Bracton, who composed a famous book of customs between 1250 and 1258, was already using glebae ascripticii: Bracton, *De legibus et consuetudinibus Angliae*, book I, chap. xi, para. 1, edited by Twiss (Rolls series), t. I, p. 52; edited by F. W. Maitland, *Selected Passages from the Works of Bracton and Azo* (Selden Society), in-4°, London, 1895, pp. 81 and 83.

[57] Olivier-Martin, *Textes inédits de droit champenois* (extracted from the *Travaux juridiques et économiques de la Faculté de droit de l'Université de Rennes*, 1913), in-8°, Rennes, 1914, p. 35.

[58] *Decisiones Gratianopolitanae*, Qu. 314, 315, Lyon edition, in-8°, 1550, fol. 183: "*Et tales homines talliabiles possunt aequiparari hominibus adscriptis glebae seu oneri talliarum solvendarum sicut ascriptitii se adstringunt.*" And above, the title of the Justinian Code relating to coloni is cited. It is true that Gui Pape is speaking of the *taillables*, but his word seems likely to be a synonym for "serf" for him. M. Esmein cited this passage in his *Cours élémentaire d'histoire du droit français*, 11th ed., p. 272, no. 4. At the moment of correcting the proofs, I again found the expression *astrictos glebe* in a legal plea of June 14, 1435, published by A. Thomas, *Le Comté de la Marche et le Parlement de Poitiers, Bibl. Ecole Hautes Etudes*, fasc. 174. p. 237, no. CCLXXIX, c. 3; cf. *ibid.*, the response of the same lawyer, p. 239, c. 15.

[59] See, in the *Oeuvres*, Bordeaux edition, *Les Coustumes du pays et comté de Nivernois*, chap. viii (p. 127), and ix (p. 142).

[60] *Les Recherches de la France*, book IV, chap. v, where there is a long discussion of *serfs fonciers et ascripices* (p. 437 of the 1617 edition, Paris, in-4°).

[61] Voltaire, *Coutume de Franche-Comté: sur l'esclavage imposé à des citoyens par une vieille coutume*, edited by Garnier, t. XXVIII, p. 373.

[62] Francois Ragneau, *Indice des droicts roiaux et seigneuriaux*; the firt first edition

is from 1583; I have only managed to see the third (in-4°, Paris, 1609). In 1704, E. de Laurière put out a new edition of the old work of Ragneau, entitled, *Glossaire du droit français*: the *Glossaire* of de Laurière was reprinted in 1882 by L. Fabre, in 4°, Niort.

⁶³ On the other hand, the orator Jérôme Vignier, who had read the canonists knew it well and thought he was working wonders when he introduced *servus glebatica* into the pseudo-testament of the bishop of Saint Perpetus, and from there is passed into Du Cange. Cf. Julien Havet, *Les Découvertes de Jérôme Vignier* (*Oeuvres*, I) p. 31.

⁶⁴ XXX, 5 and 10.
⁶⁵ XIII, 3.
⁶⁶ Fourth edition, that of 1762.
⁶⁷ *Les Institutions du droit français suivant l'ordre de celles de Justinien*, in-4°, Paris, 1753, p. 12 (on serfdom).
⁶⁸ *Les Vrais principes des fiefs*, t. II, in-4°, Paris, 1769, p. 20 (under the word mainmorte).
⁶⁹ See his *Traité des personnes et des choses*, t. I, sec. iv. where the omission of serf de la glèbe is all the more striking, since Pothier discourses on the "*serfs d'héritage.*"
⁷⁰ *Dictionnaire Philosophique*, under the word *Esclaves*, edited by Garnier, t. XVIII, p. 603, 604; *Commentaires sur l'Esprit des lois*, t. XXX, p. 445; *Au Roi en son Conseil pour les sujets du roi qui réclament la liberté en France, t. XXVIII*, p. 354, n. 1.
⁷¹ Article, "Serf" (in t. XV which appeared in 1765).
⁷² *Archives Parlementaires*, t. II, p. 316, art. 9; cf. *ibid.*, t. III, p. 540, art. 16; p. 543, art. 17; p. 662, chap. i, art. 7; t. V, p. 357, see section, art. 18, t. VI, p. 503, art. 32; and the *Cahier du Tiers de Paris hors des murs*, in Ch. L. Chassin, *Les Elections et les cahiers de Paris en 1789 (Collection de documents relatifs à l'histoire de Paris pendant la Révolution française)*, t. IV, sec. II, art. XV, p. 434.
⁷³ *Revue des Etudes anciennes*, t. XXVIII, no. 4, 1926, pp. 352-358.
⁷⁴ See p. 179.
⁷⁵ *Bull. de la Soc. des Antiquaires en France*, 1923, pp. 238-243.
⁷⁶ E. Besta, *L'Opera d'Irnerio*, t. II, p. 9.
⁷⁷ As far as Italy is concerned, I can now contribute a text to the debate, which I had omitted in my previous article; it illuminates the synonym established by the jurists of the eleventh century between ascriptitius and servus glebae, and at the same time makes us grasp the penetration of the language of learned law into the vocabulary of practice. It is an assize of King Roger II of Sicily, refusing the right of asylum to the *servus aut colonus aut servus glebe* (F. Brandileone, *Il diritto romano nelle leggi normanne e sueve del regno di Sicilia*, p. 98, VI; cf. p. 120, IV, 2); it takes its inspiration from Emperor Leo (Justinian Code, I, 12, 6), where it reads: *servus aut colonus vel adscripticius*; in addition, the influence of the Romanists of northern Italy on Sicilian legislation is well known (cf. Brandileone, *loc. cit.*, pp. 84-85, and H. Niese, *Die Gesetzgebung der normanischen Dynastie*, p. 90). The association *adscriptitii et servi glebae* can be found in the *Constitutiones* of Frederic II, III, 3 (on the history of this title, see Niese, *loc. cit.*, pp. 108 and 140).
⁷⁸ Justinian Code, XI, 52. Cf. above, on this same page, M. Piganiol (*L'Impôt de capitation sous le Bas-Empire romain*, p. 67) proposes a correction that does not concern us; Irnerius definitely read the same text as we.
⁷⁹ Justinian Code, XI, 48, 15, "*quos ita glebis in haerere praecipimus, ut ne puncto quidem temporis debeant amoveri.*"
⁸⁰ In the two texts, one of Cicero, *Leges*, II, 22, 57 and the other of Varro, *De lingua latina*, V, 23, both relating funeral practices, gleba seems to designate a

certain quantity of earth, rather than, strictly speaking, a clod. The text of Jean Lydus, cited by M. Martroye, p. 238, n. 1, *De magistratibus*, I, 37, according to which gleba is supposed to mean "fertile ground," hardly needs to be discussed, in light of this later author's poor authority as far as lexicographic and historical material is concerned.

[81] Cf., around the same time, gleba used in the sense of "country" by the poet Avienus, *Orbis terrae*, v. 482. It is well to note that in the law of Honorius and of Theodosius II cited above (Justinian Code, XI, 48, 15), *"quos ita glebis inhaerere praecipimus,"* the plural glebae retains its original and concrete meaning that, again, creates an image.

[82] Theodosian Code, X, 10, 19 (M. Martroye, who asserts, on p. 241 that *"Terra* only appears three times in the Theodosian Code," ignored this passage). Cf. a law of 400 A.D., *ibid.*, XI, 1, 28: *"terras censibus obligatas."*

[83] Cf. notably, P. Kruger, *Geschichte der Quellen und Literatur des Romischen Rechts*, 2nd ed., p. 390.

Glossary

The explanations given in this glossary are only the most basic. For the terms in modern French, German, or Spanish, any dictionary will do for further elucidation. For Medieval French, the *Dictionnaire de l'Ancienne Langue Francaise* by Frederic Godefroy (Paris, 1881-1902) is an exhaustive lexicon. For Medieval Latin, J. F. Niermayer's *Mediae Latinitatis Lexicon Minus* (Leiden, 1954-1964) provides translations into French and English. For the Catalan term, A. Alcover's *Diccionari Catala-Valencia-Balear* (Palma, 1950) was used, and the reader can use it for reference as well. Finally, for the Classical Latin terms, *A Latin Dictionary* by E. A. Andrews, edited by Lewis and Short (Oxford, 1969) can be used. (Abbreviations: CL—Classical Latin, ML—Medieval Latin, MF—Medieval French)

Adscriptitius, ascriptitius, ascripticius: A serf who is attached to the land, who is part of a domaine's property.
Affranchissement: Enfranchisement, manumission, emancipation.
Aide: Tax, duty, rent.
Aldion: Synonym for lidis, see below.
Alduin: Synonym for lidis, see below.
Allodial: A term characterizing land that is not subject to rent or service, the opposite of feudal.
Ancilla: In CL, a female slave; in ML, a female slave, a female servant or serf.
Arare: To plough, to till, to farm.
Articuli: Article, paragraph; artifice, trick.
Ascriptitius: Var. of adscriptitius, see above.
Aubain: A person who has no right to transmit his inheritance to his heirs.
Avoué: Var. of voué, see below.
Banalités: Dues paid for the use of property belonging to the seigneur.
Besthaupt: Heriot, see below.
Bordarius: Boarder, tenant.
Bourgeoisie: In MF, a town or city over which a king or a seigneur had special rights.
Capitatio: A capitation tax, a land tax, from the Theodosian Code.
Carta: Var. of charta, see below.

Cartularius: Var. of chartularius, see below.
Casalage: A kind of feudal privilege (droit de casalage).
Castrum: Fortress, castle.
Catel, chatel, cateil: Possession, good, movable property.
Cautivo: Captive.
Cavaticum: Var. of capaticum, chevage, see below.
Censier: A person to whom a land-rent, cens, is due.
Censif, censive: Subject to land-rent, cens.
Censualis: Subject to rent; a man who owes rent.
Champart: A special duty based on assessment of a tenant's land holding.
Chanson de geste: A Medieval French epic poem.
Charta: Writing, document, charter.
Chartularius: Archivist, one who keeps public documents.
Chasé: Vassal, liege man, tenant; as an adjective, it refers to a serf provided with a house and settled on the lord's land.
Chatelain: Owner of a castle; local agent of a lord's or king's administration.
Chevage: A tax on people and goods, particularly yearly levy owed to a seigneur by each of his serfs.
Cliens: In CL, a dependent, follower, subordinate; in ML, a vassal, esquire, man-at-arms.
Collibertus: Culvert, see below.
Colonus: In CL, a tiller of the soil or a farmer, especially one who tills land belonging to another; the coloni were an originally free group of dependent farmers who for the most part were absorbed into serfdom.
Columbarium: A sepulchre, a depository for the ashes of the cremated.
Commandé: Vassal.
Commendise, commandise: Order, command; the payment to a lord for the protection he provided.
Corvée: A field cultivated by a serf; a duty in work paid to a lord.
Cugucia: The right of a seigneur to take all or part of the property of a woman declared guilty of adultery.
Culbert: Culvert, see below.
Culvert, culbert, collibert, culibertus, collibertus: A serf who is between freedom and slavery, but closer to slavery.
Culvertage: Servitude, subjection.
Culvertagium: Culvertage, see above.
Culvertise: The rent of culverts.
Decurio: The commander of a decuria of cavalry.
Demesne: Lands held by oneself, as opposed to those held by permission of a superior; a manor house and the lands attached to it.
Deneree: Denier, see below.
Denier: A quantity of money in silver.
Dienstmann: Liege man, retainer.
Domini Eundorum: Lords of the estate.
Echoite, eschoite, escheoite: Collateral inheritance, particularly inheritance of property or rent that is not noble.
Epistolarius: Royal secretary, messenger; a former serf who has been manumitted by charter.

Famulus: In CL, a servant; in ML, a vassal, squire, or serf.
Forain: Foreign.
Foris Familiatus: Freed from patriarchal dependence.
Formariage: Marriage between two people from different seigneuries or between a free person and one attached to a seigneurie; the duty paid to the lord for marriages of this kind.
Freresche: An undivided inheritance, or one that is divided between brothers.
Fuero: Statute, law; exemption, privilege.
Gasindus: Armed retainer in the household of a seigneur.
Gast: Tenant, from hôte, see below.
Heres: Tenant possessing land by tenure that he has inherited; a minor who is to succeed to a fief.
Heriot: Heriot, a fee paid to the seigneur by an heir upon receiving his inheritance.
Hommage: Homage.
Homme de corps: A man who is born into servitude, a serf by birth.
Host: Military call-up of vassals.
Hôte, hoste: Tenants who were taxable and who owed duties but who were not inescapably servile.
Infanzon: A noble who had limited rights.
Ingenu: Free.
Ingenuus: In CL, free-born, born of free parents; in ML, noble or freed.
Knecht: Serf, menial.
Laborare: To labor, to be oppressed.
Landsasse: Peasant, freeholder.
Langue d'Oc: Southern France; the language of Southern France.
Langue d'Oïl: Northern France; the language of Northern France.
Latifundium: Estate, large landed property.
Lex Fori: Secular law.
Liber: Free man.
Libertas Ecclesiastica: The freedom of the Church.
Libertus: Freed man; an emancipated serf or slave.
Lidilis: Lidile, referring to litis, see below.
Litis, lidis, lidus: A person between freedom and serfdom.
Mainmortable: Subject to mainmorte, see below.
Mainmorte: The right of a lord to take possession of the property of a dead serf; the denial of serfs' heirs to take possession of their property.
Mallus: Judicial assembly.
Manant: Tenant, servant.
Mancipium: In CL, a possession, a slave; in ML, the term includes various kinds of dependents.
Manse: The residence of a seigneur or landowner, manor.
Mansus: Manor.
Manumissio: Manumission, enfranchisement, emancipation.
Massip: Var. of mancipium, see above.
Mesnie: Household.
Ministerium: Office, household post.
Mise en saisine: See saisine.

Mithium, mithio: The liability of a lord for the actions of his dependents; the area in which this liability holds.
Mortaille: The right of a lord to appropriate the possessions of a dependent who dies without confession or without relations; the possessions themselves.
Mouvance: Dependence of a fief on another domaine of which it is part.
Munboratus: One who enjoys protection, subject to mundium, see below.
Mundium: Protection; the price paid for protection; the price paid for release from this condition.
Nativus; Native; serf.
Nief, naif: Natural; serf.
Obsequium: Obedience.
Octave: Tax of one eighth of property.
Originarius: Colonus, see above.
Pensum Servitutis: Burden of servitude.
Polyptiques: Seigneurial estate records listing serfs, property units, dues, and workdays.
Precarium: Precarial tenure, a tenure subject to the wish of the grantor.
Razzia: Razzia, slave-raid.
Sainteur: A free person who makes himself the serf of a sanctuary.
Saisine, seisin: Possession; mettre en saisine—take possession of.
Schalk: Knave, servant.
Seigneur: Lord.
Seigneurie: Domain, manor.
Semons, semonce: Summons, appointment.
Serf: An unfree (usually agricultural) worker: the degree of freedom of the serf varied widely according to time and place; the unfreedom of the serf was hereditary.
Sergeant, sergant: Servant; man-at-arms, officer of the judiciary.
Servaille: The servile class, a group of serfs.
Servitium: Servitude.
Servitus: Servitude; a lord's dominion.
Servus: In CL, a slave; in ML, it came to designate a serf as well.
Tageschalk: Day-laborer; serf owing day-labor.
Taille: Duty, tax, fee, levy.
Taillable: Subject to the taille, see above.
Theow: Servant.
Tonlieu: Duty collector, toll-collector.
Tributarius: Subject to tribute.
Vassus, vassalus: Vassal.
Vilain: Villein, see below.
Villein: In the early Middle Ages, villeins were free agricultural workers, while in later times they were free with respect to everyone except their lord.
Vollschuldig: Subject to dues or obligations.
Voué: One who defends the rights of the Church.
Wergeld: Money paid to atone for homicide by the kin of the offender to the relatives of the slain or injured party.

www.ingramcontent.com/pod-product-compliance
Lightning Source LLC
Chambersburg PA
CBHW021657230426
43668CB00008B/647